PREFACE

I have no apology to offer for placing before the reading public this commentary more than I would have in preaching on a subject that had been discussed by others. In the preparation of the contents of this volume, free use has been made of all help in my possession. Space was limited by the publisher, and for this reason I was forced to cut out many comments I wished to insert. If the reader discovers some things that he thinks the author should have discussed but did not, probably the reason he did not was for the lack of space.

David Lipscomb, who edited and published the Gospel Advocate, beginning January 1, 1866, became the most outstanding man in the church of Christ in the South. In my research of the writings of the scholarship of other churches in connection with my work on this volume, I have been convinced that David Lipscomb had a keener and deeper insight to the meaning of the Holy Scriptures and of God's dealings with the race than any other one man in all Christendom. In this he stands alone. I wish all his editorials in the Gospel Advocate together with his other writings were in permanent form.

David Lipscomb prepared notes on the book of John and on all the epistles, expecting to enlarge upon them and publish the same in book form, but the infirmities of age slipped upon him, and when he saw that he would be unable to finish the task mapped out, he selected another, J. W. Shepherd, a close associate for a long period of years, to complete the work for him and turned over to him all of his notes and all his writings. But Brother Shepherd, after spending much time for many years in arranging these notes for publication, discovered that age was rapidly slipping upon him (being born August 18, 1861) and probably would be unable to complete the work, and desiring to execute his promise made to Lipscomb, on consulting with other brethren, it was deemed wise to associate with him H. Leo Boles, John T. Hinds, and C. E. W. Dorris to aid him in completing the work. It was decided to include the books of Matthew, Mark, and Luke in the series of volumes mapped out by Lipscomb, gleaning from his editorials in the Gospel Advocate as well as from his other writings and embody as much of them as possible in the commentaries. The editing of Mark and John fell to my lot. Most of the extracts in this volume from the pen of Lipscomb are taken from the quarterlies written by him for class study on Lord's day. They are enclosed in [] brackets. I acknowledge the valuable help rendered me by Brethren J. W. Shepherd and H. Leo Boles and especially Brother Shepherd, who has been my faithful counselor and advisor. I have considered him the editor in chief of the whole works and shall give to him the credit of pushing the work begun by Lipscomb to completion when it shall have been finished.

I would be ungrateful should I close this preface without mentioning sister Sarah Deen, who was so interested in learning more of the truths revealed in the writings of Mark and of getting the commentary before the reading public as to take time from her other duties to type the manuscript. She has done her work well.

American Revised Version has been used throughout this volume including quotations from different parts of the Bible in the comments. The main design has been to give a just explanation of the scriptures. Of the imperfections of the comments no one can be more sensible than the author. Of the time and patience indispensable in preparing such a work no one can realize who has never made such an effort. If this work can only serve to get a better knowledge and understanding among the people among whom it may be circulated, the prayer of the author during this work will be answered. He sends it out, therefore, with the prayer that it may be instrumental under the guidance of God in forming correct views of the Bible and promoting a practical love and appreciation for the Word of God in the hearts of men.

More than two years ago this work was begun, and on this my sixty-sixth anniversary I write the last word and lay my pen down to pick it up again to start on the laborious task of preparing the commentary on the Book of John.

C. E. W. DORRIS.

Nashville, Tennessee, April 7, 1937.

A COMMENTARY

ON

The Gospel
According to Mark

BY

C. E. W. DORRIS

GOSPEL ADVOCATE COMPANY
Nashville, Tennessee
1992

ISBN 0-89225-002-X
Paperback ISBN 0-89225-434-3

CONTENTS

PART FIRST
The Ministry of Jesus in Galilee (1: 1 to 9: 50)

SECTION ONE
The Baptism and Temptation of Jesus (1: 1-13)

SECTION TWO
The Beginning of the Ministry of Jesus in Galilee (1: 14-45)

SECTION THREE
Discussions with Scribes and Pharisees (2: 1 to 3: 35)

SECTION FOUR
A Series of Parables (4: 1-34)

PART SECOND
From the Departure Out of Galilee to the Ascension (10: 1 to 16: 20)

SECTION ONE
Events in Perea (10: 1-52)

SECTION TWO
Incidents and Discussions in Jerusalem (11: 1 to 12: 44)

SECTION THREE
The Destruction of the Temple Foretold (13: 1-37)

SECTION FOUR
Preparations for the Death of Jesus (14: 1-52)

Page

SECTION FIVE
(14: 53 to 15: 15)

SECTION SIX
The Death, Burial, and Resurrection of Jesus (15: 16 to 16: 20)

APPENDIX

INTRODUCTION

I. THE WRITER

Mark was not an apostle but an evangelist. He is mentioned in Acts 12: 12, 25 as "John whose surname was Mark." John was the Jewish name, and Mark, a name frequently used by the Romans, was adopted afterwards, and gradually superseded the other. The passages in the New Testament where the names are mentioned enable us to trace the process of the change. The John Mark of Acts 12: 12, 25 and the John of Acts 13: 5, 13 becomes Mark only in Acts 15: 39; Col. 4: 10; 2 Tim. 4: 11; and Phile. 24. The change from John to Mark is analogous to that of Saul to Paul. We doubt not that the disuse of the Jewish name in favor of the other was intentional, and that it was overruled by the providence of God.

The mother of John Mark was named Mary. She lived at Jerusalem, and was probably born in that city. (Acts 12: 12.) She was a well-known disciple of our Lord in Jerusalem and her home was a well-known resort for the brethren. (Acts 12: 12-17.) Her home was so well known among the brethren as a resort for the disciples of Christ, that when Peter was released from prison by an angel, though it was midnight, he immediately went to her home to make known his release, and to send word to James and the brethren. (Acts 12: 12-17.) There he found "many were gathered together and were praying," doubtless for his release from prison. Mark and Barnabas were cousins. (Col. 4: 10.) Barnabas early became one of the most noted men in the church at Jerusalem. (Acts 4: 36, 47; 19: 26, 27; 11: 22-24.) Probably Mark was converted by Peter by associating with him in his mother's home, for he speaks of him as "Marcus my son." (1 Pet. 5: 13.)

Mary, the mother of Mark, seems to have been a woman of some financial means and influence. Her home being a rallying place and center for the representatives of Christ in those dangerous days seems to indicate this to be a fact. The indications are that she was a widow, owning other property besides her home in Jerusalem and that she was in easy financial circumstances, very hospitable, and well acquainted with the apostles and other leading brethren in the church at Jerusalem.

Some think that the "young man," who followed Jesus on the night of his betrayal, and who, on being caught by men of the mob, fled naked leaving his night robe in their hands, and which is related by Mark (14: 51, 52), was Mark himself—that he suppressed his own name while relating the story which he had the best means of knowing.

II. SOURCES OF INFORMATION

It seems that from the beginning of the mother congregation in Jerusalem, if not during the personal ministry of Jesus, John Mark associated with the apostles in his mother's home where, doubtless, he acquired much knowledge of Jesus from them. In addition to these opportunities of learning about the life and works of Jesus from these inspired men, Mark for some years was intimately associated with Paul and Barnabas, laboring as their "minister," or assistant (Acts 12: 25; 13: 5; 15: 37-39) ; later associated with Peter in a similar way (1 Pet. 5: 13) ; and then again with Paul (Col. 4: 10; 2 Tim. 4: 11).

During Mark's associations with the apostles he must have heard them repeat many times the events in the life of our Lord. It must have been impossible for Mark to have had better natural advantages to know of the facts of which he wrote unless it had been an opportunity to have been an eyewitness of the sayings and doings of Jesus.

We consider the position of some that Mark was an uninspired man to be false. True we have no direct statement in the New Testament that he was inspired, yet we have ample testimony from inspired writers to warrant us in saying that he was inspired and that he was guided by inspiration in the things he wrote. The apostles had the power to impart miraculous gifts to others through laying on of their hands. It was a custom of the apostles to impart spiritual gifts to prominent men in the churches where they went, and especially to their travelling companions and fellow laborers. It was in this way that Philip, Barnabas, Simeon, Lucius, Manaen, Silas, Judas, Timothy and Titus received their miraculous gifts (Acts 8: 6; 13:1; 15: 32; 2 Tim. 1: 6); and individuals in the churches in Samaria, Ephesus, Corinth, Rome, Galatia—in fact all churches in apostolic days received similar gifts (Acts 8: 14-17; 19: 6; 1 Cor. 1: 4-7; Rom. 15: 14; Gal. 3: 5). Now for one to assume that Mark, who was, at different times, and for many years, a companion and fellow laborer of two apostles, was overlooked in the distribution of these gifts, would not only be unwarrantable but absurd. Not only is this true but Mark was regarded by inspired men as especially fitted for work which was usually performed by men possessed of miraculous gifts. He was selected by Paul and Barnabas to assist them in their work while on their first tour among the Gentiles (Acts 12: 25; 13: 5); and although, on their second tour, Paul declined his company, Barnabas preferred him and separated from Paul rather than separate from Mark (Acts 15: 36-39). Later he was sent for by Paul during the last imprisonment of the latter, for the reason he was profitable to him for the ministry. (2 Tim. 4: 11.) We therefore conclude that Mark was well prepared both in knowledge and spiritual gifts to write the book that bears his name. Its right to a place among inspired books has never been questioned.

In the early ages of the church the gospel by Mark was called Peter's gospel for the reason it was thought Mark wrote as a scribe for Peter but we doubt that he did. We see no reason for concluding that he wrote as Peter dictated, nor for calling it Peter's gospel. Mark writes more briefly than Matthew or Luke. He was a Jew.

III. FOR WHOM WRITTEN?

It is thought by some authors that Mark wrote specially for Gentile Christians. They reach this conclusion for the reasons that he omits the genealogy and all the accounts of the early years of both John and Jesus—that he quotes but little from the Old Testament, and makes but few references to the prophets—that he makes no effort, like Matthew in the sermon on the mount, to show the relation of Jesus to the old dispensation and does not use the word "law" a single time, to all of which Gentiles would attach less importance than would the Jew. But this position has but little if any bedrock for a foundation to rest upon, since the New Testament is silent on the question.

IV. WHEN WRITTEN?

Irenaeus tells us that Mark wrote his book after the death of Peter and Paul; but Papias and Clement of Alexandria, who were also early writers, tell us it was written during Peter's lifetime. Since the early writers do not agree and since the New Testament is silent on the question, the time when Mark wrote the book that bears his name cannot be positively ascertained. It must have been written some time before the destruction of Jerusalem, A.D. 70, otherwise so remarkable a fulfillment of Christ's prediction in the thirteenth chapter would have been mentioned.

V. PLACE WRITTEN

Clement of Alexandria, Eusebius, and Jerome mention Rome as the place of the writing; but Papias and Irenaeus, who wrote earlier, do not speak of it. Some think because Mark was with Peter at Babylon (1 Pet. 5: 13) that Babylon was the place of composition. Alexandria is mentioned as the place by Chrysostom, but this is not confirmed by any of the other early writers. As the New Testament does not locate the place and since the early writers are not agreed, we conclude that the place of writing is as uncertain as the time.

VI. EVIDENCES OF ITS TRUTHFULNESS

The four writers of the New Testament of the life of Jesus give brief and clear statements of some things Jesus said without comment—without praise or blame. This is peculiar to all the writers of the Bible. All other biographers praise or blame their heroes; try to prove they are good or bad. The Bible writers state facts with more than human impartiality and fairness, and leave the facts for the readers to draw their own conclusions. This, of itself, indicates a quality in the writers that is above human. It indicates God directed in the writings, as perfect fairness and impartiality are characteristics of God. The simple, clear, pure style of the Bible has been recognized as the perfect model for all nations into whose language it has been translated. The words used are the simplest, are those of the common people. The illustrations are from the common everyday affairs of the life of the common people. This shows it was intended for the common people—especially, and it was intended that the common people should understand it. While all admire the style of the Bible writers, even with them as models none have ever been able to equal or even approximate them in simplicity of style or in the impartial and unprejudiced style in which they write. While inspiration secures this perfect impartiality and fairness of narration, it does not destroy the peculiar and personal characteristics of each writer. Matthew, Mark, Luke, John, Paul, Peter, James, each has his own peculiar style, uses the phrases and words peculiar to himself, as do uninspired writers; so that while the divine spirit secures to them infallible faithfulness and truthfulness, it does not destroy their human tastes and peculiarities. The records of the sayings and doing of Jesus, like himself, combine the divine and the human. These writers, as do all the writers of the Bible, tell exactly what was done. They set down the evil deeds of the best men, and of their best friends, without favor or affection. They record the good deeds of the evil and of their worst enemies without partiality or prejudice. The writers of the gospel never say that Jesus was a good man. They never praise or blame him, his teachings, or his actions. They tell what he did, what he said. They tell this one said he was a good man, that one said he was a bad man, one said he hath a devil, another he is of God, but no shadow of opinion do they give. They tell their own sins and shortcomings without excuse or palliation. The testimony they bear concerning Jesus and all is the perfect model of the testimony which human courts and judiciaries have in vain sought to attain through all the ages of man's existence. It is only found in its perfection in the Bible. This simple, pure, impartial style in the Bible declares its divine origin. In this it is in perfect harmony with the claims and the works of Jesus.

Some raise objection to the characters of the men of the Bible because the best of men are recorded as doing evil—frequently guilty of gross crimes. They do not consider that the knowledge of these sins comes through the more than human fairness and truthfulness of the witnesses, which stamp more indelibly the truthfulness of the story that is told. That they are willing to tell the sins of their friends gives the stronger assurance that the good things they tell are true. The best of men commit great sins. Only Jesus, though tempted in all things as we are, was without sin. He gave to the world the only spotless character it has ever seen. He fulfilled the law with faultless obedience, and gave to man the perfect model of the character that God desires him to strive to attain.

COMMENTARY ON THE GOSPEL
ACCORDING TO MARK

PART FIRST
THE MINISTRY OF JESUS IN GALILEE
1: 1 to 9: 50

SECTION ONE

THE BAPTISM AND TEMPTATION OF JESUS
1: 1-13

1. THE BEGINNING OF THE GOSPEL
1: 1-8
(Matt. 3: 1-12; Luke 3: 1-18; John 1: 6-34)

1 The beginning of the [1]gospel of Jesus Christ, [2]the Son of God.

[1]Or, *good tidings:* and so elsewhere.
[2]Some ancient authorities omit *the Son of God.*

1 **The beginning**—[Mark begins the account of the gospel of Jesus Christ by quoting the prophecy concerning the messenger that was to prepare for the coming of Jesus. John came as his herald to announce his coming, and to make ready the people whom God had been preparing from the days of Abraham to receive Jesus.]

of Jesus Christ,—The promised Messiah. [Jesus means Savior. He came to save people from their sins. To save from sin is to save from all evil—from all suffering. Sin is the cause of all sorrow—all suffering. Jesus was given as the human name of him who came to save people from sin. "Christ" means anointed—sent of God. Christ and Messiah mean the same. He was sent and anointed of God to save man from sin. Jesus was divine—begotten of God, born of woman. He was the God-man, both divine and human.]

the Son of God.—Matthew and Luke introduce Jesus first as "son of David, the son of Abraham." (Matt. 1: 1.) Mark introduces him as "the Son of God." He emphasizes the relation of Jesus to God rather than to Abraham and the Jewish people. Mark points out his divine origin and Matthew his human.

Not only is the ministry of John the beginning of the unfolding of a new dispensation of mercy and love; but it is the *beginning* of the *end* of the old dispensation. The old cove-

2 Even as it is written ³in Isaiah the prophet,
  ⁴Behold, I send my messenger before thy face,
  Who shall prepare thy way;
3 ⁵The voice of one crying in the wilderness,

³Some ancient authorities read *in the prophets*.
⁴Mal. iii. 1.
⁵Is. xl. 3.

nant was having its death knell tolled by John in the wilderness and the work was completed by Christ "nailing it to the cross." (Col. 2: 14.)

2 **Even as it is written in Isaiah the prophet,**—[He quotes here the prophecy first of Malachi (3: 1) to show that the coming of John as the forerunner of Christ had been foretold by the prophets, and that the gospel had begun in accordance with the prophecy.] "The gospel of Jesus Christ" began to be unfolded, not according to uninspired men, but according to the prediction of inspired prophets, with the preaching and practices of John the Baptist.

Behold, I send my messenger before thy face, who shall prepare thy way;—[It was customary with princes and kings and the great ones of earth, when going on a journey or visiting a new place, to send messengers, or herald, before to make ready for the reception. Jesus adopted this order, but the preparation differed from that of the kings of earth. Malachi says (4: 5, 6): "Behold, I will send you Elijah the prophet before the great and terrible day of Jehovah come. And he shall turn the heart of the fathers to the children, and the heart of the children to their fathers; lest I come and smite the earth with a curse." Jesus has told us that John was the Elijah that was to come. Jesus as the Son of God was coming, and if he should come and find the people unprepared to receive him, he would smite the earth with a curse. When God meets man, it is to bless, if he is worthy. If he is not worthy, then he will smite with a curse. John says he is not the very Elijah. Jesus says he came in the power and spirit of Elijah.]

3 **The voice of one crying in the wilderness,**—[A thinly populated country. John grew up in this country south of Jerusalem, and began his preaching preparatory to the coming of Jesus.] This was the wilderness of Judea. (Verse 1.)

Make ye ready the way of the Lord,
Make his paths straight;
4 John came, who baptized in the wilderness and preached the baptism of

---

Make ye ready the way of the Lord,—Luke records him as more fully quoting the prophecy of Isa. 40: 3-5.

All of which means that John should turn the people from their sins and make them willing to receive the message that Christ should bring. He preached Christ as the coming Savior. The people too were to prepare "the way of the Lord." That is, make ready themselves—prepare your own hearts, to entertain the glad tidings of the gospel. The preparation was to be made in their hearts. *The way of the Lord is through* the heart. They prepared "the way of the Lord" by preparing and making the heart fit for receiving the Lord. John prepared the way by telling the people what the Lord required of them and they by removing everything from the heart that might obstruct or hinder the Lord from entering.

Make his paths straight;—Highways that have not been properly surveyed at the beginning are straightened later. So are the ways of men when no preparation of heart has been made by them to receive Christ. The burden of John's work was to induce men to stop their crooked ways and prepare themselves to receive their coming guest—Christ. He admonished them to remove all obstructions out of the way, so that the Savior and King might have a ready passage, and free access to their hearts, and there erect his spiritual kingdom of righteousness, peace, and joy, and rule their lives and conduct by his holy laws. "His paths" which he travels is the heart of man. Every human heart is a path.

4 **John came,**—[John the Baptist was six months older than Jesus. He had grown to manhood in the wilderness of Judea; was stern, unbending, courageous, and faithful in denouncing sin and warning the people to repent and flee from the wrath to come. He began his ministry at about thirty years of age, as he seems to have been preaching only a few months when Jesus, about thirty years of age, came to him to be baptized of him. At thirty years of age the Levites were required to enter on their service in the temple. It is said in Numbers (8: 24) that they began at twenty-five. It is supposed at twenty-

repentance unto remission of sins. 5 And there went out unto him all the

five they entered the service as pupils under the old Levites to fit them for the full service at thirty. David (1 Chron. 23 : 27) reduced the age of entering on the service to twenty. "For by the last words of David the sons of Levi were numbered, from twenty years old and upward." David greatly extended the service. It is thought this made need of greater numbers in the service. Whether this addition to the service and change of the age by David was acceptable to God has always been a question of doubt with many. When the added service is referred to in subsequent history, it is spoken of "as ordained by David." John and Jesus entered upon their missions at the age of thirty years.]

who baptized in the wilderness and preached—[This does not mean that he baptized before he preached, but that he preached repentance that led them to baptism. He preached baptism of repentance. This means the baptism connected with repentance. John preached that they should repent of their sins—turn to God—and to show their repentance they must be baptized. Baptism was commanded by God as the act of the person which declared his repentance. Their sins arose from disobedience to God. Baptism was an act of submission that declared to the world their willingness to obey God. Baptism is what is called a positive ordinance—a command of God—humiliating in itself, is unpleasant to be submitted to, in which human reason can see no good, resting on the authority of God, and given to test man's willingness to obey God. It is claimed by some that baptism had been an ordinance of admission of proselytes to the Jewish faith, but there is no intimation of such ordinance in the Bible, nor in any authentic history before John preached it. Bathings and ablutions had been connected with the purifications of the Jewish law, but John introduced the ordinance, and by preeminence he is called the "Baptist"—one who baptizes.]

unto remission of sins.—Baptism connected with the repentance as preached by John was for, or unto, the remission of sins. This means God had appointed this act as the expression and embodiment of repentance which brought the state

country of Judaea, and all they of Jerusalem; and they were baptized of him in the river Jordan, confessing their sins. 6 And John was clothed with camel's hair, and *had* a leathern girdle about his loins, and did eat locusts

and place in which God would forgive sins. There was no virtue or efficacy in the act to bring pardon. God forgives sin.

5 And there went out unto him all the country of Judaea, and all they of Jerusalem;—This is a figurative expression, as the land itself could not go to him. The place, or country, where the people lived is placed for the people themselves. It means the people, not all the people, but the people generally from all the land of Judea and they of Jerusalem.

and they were baptized of him—Whether John in person baptized all that were baptized we know not. Jesus is said to have baptized, and yet it is stated that he in person did not baptize but his disciples. (John 3: 22; 4: 1, 2.)

in the river Jordan,—The baptism did not take place *at,* or *near,* but *in* the river Jordan.

confessing their sins.—They, in coming to baptism, confessed their sins as preparatory to God forgiving their sins when they were baptized. Confession of sins—owning their sins—is in order to the forgiveness of sins. The sins were forgiven in baptism, the confession preceded the baptism. Pardon takes place in heaven where the pardoning power is. Baptism is nothing, if it does not carry with it the confession and abandonment of sin.

6 And John was clothed with camel's hair,—[The camel's hair cloth was the sackcloth that the poorer classes wore, and that was worn in affliction and humiliation. It was made of coarse hair of the goat, or camel. John lived an abstemious life. He was of the priestly order, and lived the life of a Nazarite. Jesus says to the people: "John the Baptist is come eating no bread nor drinking wine; and ye say, He hath a demon. The Son of man is come eating and drinking; and ye say, Behold, a gluttonous man, and a winebibber, a friend of publicans and sinners!" (Luke 7: 33, 34.)]

and had a leathern girdle about his loins,—[He had a girdle of untanned skins about his loins.]

and did eat locusts—Living in the wilderness, his food was

and wild honey. 7 And he preached, saying, There cometh after me he that
is mightier than I, the latchet of whose shoes I am not ⁶worthy to stoop

⁶Gr. *sufficient.*

that of the wilderness. Several varieties of locusts, after
being denuded of the legs and wings, are boiled, roasted or
fried, sprinkled with salt, and eaten by the poorer classes to
this day. This probably was the Egyptian locust. It was a
large, voracious insect which the Jews were permitted to eat.
"Even these of them ye may eat: the locust after its kind, and
the bald locust after its kind." (Lev. 11: 22.)

and wild honey.—[The wild honey was the honey of the
wild bees that abounded in the land of Judea. This dress and
food showed that he lived an austere life of self-denial. There
is but little doubt that this life lends zeal and fervor to the religious and devotional spirit. He denounced sin in great and
small, and proclaimed repentance with such earnestness and
fervor that he struck terror to the multitudes and they came
to him to be baptized. Luke and Matthew both tell us that he
saw many of the Pharisees and Sadducees coming to his baptism, and said unto them: "Ye offspring of vipers, who
warned you to flee from the wrath to come? Bring forth
therefore fruit worthy of repentance: and think not to say
within yourselves, We have Abraham to our father: for I say
unto you, that God is able of these stones to raise up children
unto Abraham." (Matt. 3: 7-9.) Many think he refused to
baptize these persons until they had first brought forth fruit
worthy of repentance. I do not believe this is true. He baptized them, and told them, now bring forth fruit worthy of the
repentance into which he had baptized them. The meaning of
the language as reported by Luke is, the Jewish family, as the
people of God, will be rejected, and every man must depend
on what fruit he bears in his life for favor of God. He cannot
depend on fleshly relation to Abraham.]

7 **And he preached, saying, There cometh after me he that
is mightier than I, the latchet of whose shoes I am not worthy
to stoop down and unloose.**—An expression of intense humility. Matthew says: "Whose shoes I am not worthy to bear."
Luke and John omit the expression "stoop down."

[John came to make ready a people for the Lord, Christ; so

down and unloose. 8 I baptized you ⁷in water; but he shall baptize you ⁷in the Holy Spirit.

⁷Or, *with*

he preached the coming of Christ—his majesty, and power. Those who heard John thought highly of him as a prophet of God and a preacher of righteousness; but he exalts Jesus by saying, "I am not worthy to stoop down and unloose" his shoes. Loosing the shoes was a menial service. Jesus was so much greater than he, he was not worthy to do this for him.]

8 **I baptized you in water;**—[John shows here the contrast between himself and Jesus. John used water, Jesus the Spirit of the living God, with which to overwhelm man. The Spirit is in reality at the command of Jesus to be used by him, as water was at the command of John. The Authorized Version puts it "with water." From the expression "with" many contend the water was applied to the individual, not the person baptized in the water. The first meaning of the word translated "with" is "in," but "with" does not carry the idea of applying the substance to the person. A woman colors her cloth with dye; the smith cools his iron with water; but neither does it by sprinkling or pouring water on the substance. The woman colors her cloth and the smith cools his iron by dipping—immersing them in water, and "baptized with water" shows the substance used in baptism and not the manner of applying it.]

but he shall baptize you in the Holy Spirit.—[Some would ask, were they baptized in the Spirit? They were overwhelmed with it. It does not mean a little of the Holy Spirit was poured out, or sprinkled, on one spot of the person. The expressions, the baptism of the Spirit, the pouring out of the Spirit, the shedding forth of the Spirit, are figurative expressions. The Spirit is a person of the Godhead, and we cannot pour out the person of the Godhead as a liquid from one vessel to another. It indicates the person is brought completely under the influence and control of the Spirit of God, or that the Spirit is sent from heaven to control and guide man. So were they baptized—overwhelmed in suffering.] Matthew (3: 11) adds "and in fire," which shows that John's audience was mixed—

some good and some bad. Some to be baptized in the Holy Spirit, and others in fire.

2. THE BAPTISM OF JESUS
1: 9-11
(Matt. 3: 13-17; Luke 3: 21-23)

9 And it came to pass in those days, that Jesus came from Nazareth of Galilee, and was baptized of John [8]in the Jordan. 10 And straightway com-

[8]Gr. *into*

---

9 **And it came to pass in those days, that Jesus came from Nazareth of Galilee,**—[John was baptizing in Jordan; Nazareth was sixty miles or more from where John was baptizing. Jesus doubtless walked the distance, that he might be baptized of John. This was his emergence into history from the obscurity of his village life in Nazareth since his visit to Jerusalem at twelve years of age. He could go to John by way of the plain of the Jordan without passing through Jerusalem, and probably did so. During this interval of about eighteen years he seems to have been working at the carpenter's bench (Mark 6: 3; Matt. 13: 55) with Joseph. He *came,* therefore, from obscurity to publicity, from manual labor to spiritual teaching.]

and was baptized of John in the Jordan.—Immersed. [Matthew and Luke give more of the incidents connected with the baptism of Jesus than Mark. Matthew (3: 13-17) says: "Then cometh Jesus from Galilee to the Jordan unto John, to be baptized of him. But John would have hindered him, saying, I have need to be baptized of thee, and comest thou to me? But Jesus answering said unto him, Suffer it now: for thus it becometh us to fulfil all righteousness. Then he suffereth him. And Jesus, when he was baptized, went up straightway from the water: and lo, the heavens were opened unto him, and he saw the Spirit of God descending as a dove, and coming upon him; and lo, a voice out of the heavens, saying, This is my beloved Son, in whom I am well pleased." Luke (3: 21, 22) gives this account of it: "Now it came to pass, when all the people were baptized, that, Jesus also having been baptized, and praying, the heaven was opened, and the Holy Spirit descended in a bodily form, as a dove, upon him, and a voice came out of heaven, Thou art my beloved

ing up out of the water, he saw the heavens rent asunder, and the Spirit as a dove descending upon him: 11 and a voice came out of the heavens, Thou art my beloved Son, in thee I am well pleased.

Son; in thee I am well pleased." John (1: 31-34) says: "And I knew him not; but that he should be made manifest to Israel, for this cause came I baptizing in water. And John bare witness, saying, I have beheld the Spirit descending as a dove out of heaven; and it abode upon him. And I knew him not: but he that sent me to baptize in water, he said unto me, Upon whomsoever thou shalt see the Spirit descending, and abiding upon him, the same is he that baptizeth in the Holy Spirit. And I have seen, and have borne witness that this is the Son of God."] From obscurity Jesus went to widespread fame, through duty performed. Do your duty; the rest will take care of itself.

10 **And straightway coming up out of the water,**—How needless, if baptism was sprinkling or pouring! (See verse 9.)

he saw the heavens rent asunder,—The sky seemed to have parted to allow the emergence of the beautiful vision: the heavens were opened to show that which had been closed against us on account of our sins. The first Adam shut us out of heaven, but the second Adam opened, and will now let us into it.

and the Spirit as a dove descending upon him:—The Spirit's connection with Jesus was made unmistakable. This was necessary for the reason it was the sign given by God to John, by which he was to recognize the Son of God. (John 1: 33.)

11 **and a voice came out of the heavens, Thou art my beloved Son,**—God spake from heaven and sanctioned the acts of both John and Jesus. Expressing the relationship between the two. Son, not by adoption, but by eternal existence.

in thee I am well pleased.—The Father was pleased when at twelve years of age he manifested anxiety to be about his life-work; he was pleased when he quietly submitted in hard-working obscurity to wait his time; he was pleased by his daily life; and he was pleased when he came to John to be baptized by him. [From Luke (3: 23) we learn he was thirty years old. From Matthew (3: 14), that when he came to

John to be baptized of him, John objected. As the weaker he felt he had need to be baptized of Jesus. He was preaching that they should repent, and baptizing for the remission of sins. Jesus had no sin to repent of or to be remitted. Why should he baptize him then? Jesus said: "Suffer it now: for thus it becometh us to fulfil all righteousness." Righteousness means the provisions of God for making men righteous. It becomes us to, or we ought to, fulfill all the will of God for making men righteous. He then baptized him, and as he came up out of the water, he prayed (Luke 3: 21), and the heavens were opened, and the Holy Spirit in the likeness of the dove descended, lighted upon him, and abode with him, and a voice out of the heavens said, "This is my beloved Son, in whom I am well pleased." Both Jesus and John saw the Spirit descending, and heard the voice. We are not told that others saw or heard these.]

3. TEMPTATION OF JESUS
1: 12, 13
(Matt. 4: 1-11; Luke 4: 1-13)

12 And straightway the Spirit driveth him forth into the wilderness. 13

12 **And straightway the Spirit driveth him forth into the wilderness.**—Mark uses a stronger term than any of the other writers. Matthew says he was "led up of the Spirit." (Matt. 4: 1.) Mark shows more clearly that it was not at the volition of Jesus that he entered into the temptation. That he was led by the Spirit to be tempted shows that he was subjected to temptation in accordance with a deliberate purpose, but a purpose not his own. It was not of voluntary entrance into temptation, but of being divinely led into it for a special divine purpose. God desires the faith and loyalty of all his children and servants to be tried and approved before he can commit high trust to them. Jesus was entering on the highest work that pertained to earth—that of rescuing the world from the rule of the devil and of bringing it back to its loyalty to God, and to its proper and harmonious relations to the universe, and of adjusting all the forces and operations of the world to the workings of the divine order. They had all been disturbed and broken by the rule of the devil on earth. Christ

And he was in the wilderness forty days tempted of Satan; and he was with the wild beasts; and the angels ministered unto him.

---

had come to rescue the world from the devil. The devil naturally sought to induce him to turn from his purpose and to enter his service.

13 **And he was in the wilderness forty days tempted of Satan;**—[Whether this fast was entered upon voluntarily to bring him into a state of close and holy communion with God, and to give him spiritual strength for the temptation, or whether it was the devil's work to weaken him bodily to make him an easy prey to the tempter, we have no means of determining. He fasted forty days, so had Moses done twice (Ex. 34: 28; Deut. 9: 9), and once Elijah (1 Kings 19: 8). Possibly this was the limit of human endurance, that it was selected by or for each of them. Some have thought they were miraculously sustained. If so, the effect of the fast would have been counteracted. But at the close of the forty days he hungered—the pangs of hunger were intense, the bodily powers were exhausted, and all fleshly strength of will, he was at the mercy of the tempter. But his spirit by the fast had been probably drawn into closer union with God, and had grown the stronger. Spiritual power was and is gained by fasting and prayer. "This kind goeth not out save by prayer and fasting," explained Jesus when his disciples could not cast out a demon. (Matt. 17: 19.)]

and he was with the wild beasts;—He had no comfort from and no association with man. His only earthly companions were wild beasts, which were more likely to annoy and hurt him than in any way to help and comfort him.

and the angels ministered unto him.—The angelic world is represented. No human being was with him, yet he was not alone. Angels were present. Angels communed with Christ in his glory of transfiguration, sustained him in the anguish of the garden, watched over him at the tomb; they thronged the earth at his coming, and hovered in the air at the hour of his ascension. We could not imagine our Lord in the wilderness without angelic love. Twice has the destiny of the world been suspended on the action of a single person, and each of these was made an object of especial temptation by our cunning adversary. The first Adam fell and the race fell with him. The second Adam defeated the tempter and redeemed the race from the fall. He won his victory by familiarity with the word of God, coupled with his loyalty to the will of the Father.

[It is a part of the order of God that every servant of God shall be tried and tested. This means that only what is worthy and well-approved shall enter into the eternal home of God. The testing, the proving of persons, is temptation in the better sense of that word. All suffering, all self-denial for right is temptation. "My son, regard not lightly the chastening of the Lord, nor faint when thou art reproved of him; for whom the Lord loveth he chasteneth, and scourgeth every son whom he receiveth. It is for chastening that ye endure; God dealeth with you as with sons; for what son is there whom his father chasteneth not?" (Heb. 12: 5-7.) Jesus was tried and tempted that he might prove himself worthy to be the Son of God, and that he might fully sympathize with man whom he came to rescue and redeem. "For we have not a high priest that cannot be touched with the feeling of our infirmities; but one that hath been in all points tempted like as we are, yet without sin." (Heb. 4: 15.)]

It seems to our wisdom needful that man should be tempted and his weakness shaken to call out the character of God. If we had no trials, temptations, and weaknesses we would never know good from evil. If our fellow men never sinned against us, were never weak, helpless, and in distress, our own better natures would never be brought out and strengthened. If man had not sinned there would have been no occasion to call out the mercy, love, wisdom, and to prove the excellencies and glory of God; and we would be in ignorance of the qualities of the divine character that are most helpful to us and that draw us to God and call out the best elements of man. The mistakes, errors, misfortunes, weaknesses, and wants of the child call out the love and tenderness of the parent. So man, a weak, erring sinner, calls out the love of God, shows who and what he is, and excites man's love to him. "We love, because he first loved us."

SECTION TWO

THE BEGINNING OF THE MINISTRY OF JESUS IN GALILEE
1: 14-45

1. TIME AND THEME OF HIS PREACHING
1: 14, 15
(Matt. 4: 12-17; Luke 4: 14, 15; John 4: 1-3)

14 Now after John was delivered up, Jesus came into Galilee, preaching the ¹gospel of God, 15 and saying, The time is fulfilled, and the kingdom of God is at hand: repent ye, and believe in the ¹gospel.

---

14 Now after John was delivered up, Jesus came into Galilee, preaching the gospel of God,—He "returned in the power of the Spirit into Galilee." (Luke 4: 14.) The same Spirit that had impelled him into the wilderness to be tempted. Having presented the preliminaries of our Savior's ministry, Mark now proceeds to the ministry itself.

15 and saying,—The mouth and organ of speech are very necessary in proclaiming the gospel. Christ used both and authorized his disciples to do likewise which thing they did. Paul requested the brethren to pray in his behalf; "that utterance may be given unto me in opening my mouth, to make known with boldness the mystery of the gospel, for which I am an ambassador in chains; that in it I may speak boldly, as I ought to speak." (Eph. 6: 19, 20.) However, we are not to understand from this that the Lord forbids teaching through the medium of the pen and printing press. The apostles taught through the medium of the pen when they wrote the gospel on scrolls and sent it out. The art of printing had not been invented at that time. If it had doubtless they would have taken advantage of it. Whether we teach by word of mouth, pen, or the printed sheet, in either case, we do no more nor no less than what the Lord commanded—we *teach*.

The time is fulfilled,—The time foretold by the prophets for the appearance of Christ is accomplished. "When the fulness of the time came, God sent forth his Son, born of a woman, born under the law." (Gal. 4: 4; Dan. 9: 24-27.)

and the kingdom of God is at hand: repent ye, and believe in the gospel.—The kingdom of God, so long promised by the prophets and expected by the people, has drawn near. (Luke 10:9.) The doctrine of faith and repentance is taught at the threshold of the kingdom of Christ, and accordingly ought, in a special manner, to be preached and insisted upon by all proclaimers of the gospel.

2. CALL OF THE FOUR FISHERMEN
1: 16-20
(Matt. 4: 18-22; Luke 1: 11)

16 And passing along by the sea of Galilee, he saw Simon and Andrew the brother of Simon casting a net in the sea; for they were fishers. 17 And Jesus said unto them, Come ye after me, and I will make you to become fishers of men. 18 And straightway they left the nets, and followed him. 19

16 **And passing along by the sea of Galilee,**—This sea was formed by a depression in the ground where the river Jordan spread out, for it ran into the northern end of the sea and out at the southern end. At Capernaum and around this lake Jesus did the most of his marvelous works and spent the most of his public life.

he saw Simon and Andrew the brother of Simon casting a net in the sea: for they were fishers.—It was a *casting net*— one that could be thrown in different directions in order to enclose the fish. Fishing was their occupation. Moses and David were called from keeping sheep; Gideon from threshing wheat; Elisha from the plow. God has honored humble, yet honest labor, from the beginning.

17 **And Jesus said unto them, Come ye after me, and I will make you to become fishers of men.**—Passing over the extraordinary draught of fishes recorded by Luke (5: 4-7), Mark records the call of these two brothers. The last clause is a beautiful allusion to their former occupation as a figure of the one which they were now to undertake. They are now to be fishers of men, winners of souls to Christ. They were to catch men in the gospel net and lead them into the kingdom of God. Note that Jesus did not at this time call them to be fishers of men, but promised to train them to be such on their becoming his followers. He said: "I will *make* you to *become* fishers of men."

18 **And straightway they left the nets, and followed him.**— Leaving their nets, not only for the present but forever, as their permanent employment and the means of their

And going on a little further, he saw ⁹James the *son* of Zebedee, and John his brother, who also were in the boat mending the nets. 20 And straightway he called them: and they left their father Zebedee in the boat with the hired servants, and went after him.

⁹Or, *Jacob*

subsistence.

19 **And going on a little further, he saw James the son of Zebedee, and John his brother, who also were in the boat mending the nets.**—Counting the "hired servants" of the next verse, there were not less than five in this fishing crew. Jesus saw only two of this number with enough material in them to suit his purpose at this particular time.

20 **And straightway he called them: and they left their father Zebedee in the boat with the hired servants, and went after him.**—The fact that they left their father with the *hired servants* shows that they did not leave him without help or company. Doubtless he was just as able to continue his business as when his sons were with him.

3. A DEMON CAST OUT
1: 21-28
(Luke 4: 21-28)

21 And they go into Capernaum; and straightway on the sabbath day he entered into the synagogue and taught. 22 And they were astonished at his

21 **And they go into Capernaum; and straightway on the sabbath day**—Our Saturday. The seventh day was used by our Creator as a rest from his six days' work of creation (Gen. 2: 3), and enacted as a Jewish law at the exodus from Egypt (Ex. 20: 8-11) to commemorate the day Israel was delivered from Egyptian bondage.

he entered into the synagogue and taught.—[After his baptism Jesus made Capernaum his home. It is called "his own city." (Matt. 9: 1.) It was on the shore of the Sea of Galilee. It was more accessible as a center of travel that suited his work. Peter and Andrew, James and John, were with him here, and also made the city their home. On the Sabbath he went into the synagogue. It was the custom of the Jews to meet in the synagogue on the Sabbath to read the law and to worship God. The synagogue grew up after the Babylonian captivity, and brought the worship of God to the homes of the Jews, secured the reading and expounding of the law on every

teaching: for he taught them as having authority, and not as the scribes. 23 And straightway there was in their synagogue a man with an unclean spirit;

Sabbath, and from this time there was much less tendency to idolatry and to rebellion against God. Their responsibility to God and their knowledge of the law was kept before them more constantly by these more frequent meetings and reading of the law. In the synagogue the reading and expounding of the law were not confined to the priests, but every Jew could do this. Jesus did it here, as did the apostles afterwards. (Acts 13: 15-17.)]

22 And they were astonished at his teaching: for he taught them as having authority, and not as the scribes.—This is a broad contrast, most accurately drawn, between the manner in which Jesus taught and that of the scribes.

[They were accustomed to the reasonings of the scribes dealing in forms and traditions and observances. The teaching of Jesus was peculiar. First, the matter of it differed from that of the scribes and Pharisees. He taught not traditions or ceremonials or observances, but he taught great, practical truths embodying man's duty to God and to his fellow men. He demanded right, justice, mercy, and love to man. He demanded reverence and love for God shown by obedience to his laws. He announced these duties in plain and simple terms that the simplest could understand. He did not reason and philosophize about them, nor undertake to show their reasonableness, but he announced the truth as without doubt and as one speaking by authority, knowing whereof he spoke, and he presented these truths in simple, axiomatic forms and addressed them to the hearts of his hearers. He spoke as one who knew the truth without doubt and spoke it by the authority of God. You are not to listen to Jesus as an expounder, but as an authoritative lawgiver.]

23 And straightway there was in their synagogue a man with an unclean spirit; and he cried out,—[The unclean spirits were demons. They were evil spirits that took possession of men and afflicted them in various ways. It is often a trouble to know why they should have existed then and not now. This seems to be true that when God exercised miraculous power or sent forth angels, or good spirits to minister good

and he cried out, 24 saying, What have we to do with thee, Jesus thou Nazarene? art thou come to destroy us? I know thee who thou art, the Holy
One of God. 25 And Jesus rebuked [10]him, saying, Hold thy peace, and come

[10]Or, *it*

---

under his direction, he permitted the devil to exercise miraculous power and to send forth evil spirits to do his bidding.
The difference between them was in the quality of their **work**.
God wrought miracles, and sent forth his Spirit to bless, help,
benefit man. The devil could not do this kind of work. He
did evil. "Can a demon open the eyes of the blind?" the Jews
asked. (John 10: 21.) The devil and his spirits always
wrought to injure, afflict, degrade man. When God ceased to
work miracles or to use these evil spirits as his messengers,
he curtailed the power of the devil so that he could not work
miracles. These demons, or unclean spirits, all seemed to
know Jesus and his true work and character, and would cry
out at his approach. We think it true that none save immoral
and bad persons were possessed of demons. As God's Spirit
dwells with, and his angels watch over, only the holy and upright, so the demons, or spirits of the Evil One, dwell only in
the hearts of the wicked. The devil seeks to ruin both soul
and body.]

**24 saying, What have we to do with thee, Jesus thou Naza-
rene? art thou come to destroy us? I know thee who thou
art,**—"The demons also believe, and shudder." (James 2: 19.)
The invisible world of evil had a clear recognition of the character and mission of Jesus.

the Holy One of God.—King James Version adds: "Let us
alone," which is a common cry today among those in error.
They do not want their error exposed, so they preach the doctrine, "Let us alone." [The demons and evil spirits seemed to
understand that Jesus came into the world to overthrow and
destroy them and to consign them to torment. He came to
overthrow the devil, to "destroy the works of the devil." (1
John 3: 8.) He came to overthrow and consign to ruin all his
servants and subjects, so they begged Jesus to let them alone,
and asked what they had to do with him. "Art thou come to
destroy us" or "to torment us before the time?" (Matt. 8:
29); and then he declared, "I know thee who thou art, the

out of him. 26 And the unclean spirit, [11]tearing him and crying with a loud voice, came out of him. 27 And they were all amazed, insomuch that they

[11]Or, *convulsing*

Holy One of God." What prompted the demons to testify that Jesus was the Son of God, or the Holy One of God, we do not understand. They always were ready to bear this testimony, possibly with the view to appease his wrath and to cause him to deal kindly with them.]

25 **And Jesus rebuked him,**—From the beginning of his encounters with these evil spirits he rebuked them for speaking favorably of him, and commanded them to hold their peace and depart from their victims. It was important that he do this for at least two reasons: (1) That the faith of those who believed in him should not rest *even in part* on the testimony of evil spirits. (2) That he should not appear to sustain friendly relations with these evil beings and with the devil who ruled over them. In spite of all his precautions the charge was made that he cast out demons by the power of Satan (Matt. 3: 22-26); and it was perhaps for this very purpose of giving apparent grounds for this charge that the devil prompted the demons to testify as they did.

saying, Hold thy peace,—Be muzzled, restrain thyself. Cease from complaints. He would accept no testimony from such a source.

and come out of him.—This was proof of the power of Jesus and that he had no hesitancy in using it. Instead of accepting the testimony of the demon that he was "the Holy One of God," Jesus rebuked his impious audacity, forbade him to speak further, and commanded him to leave his victim. The most brilliant proclamation of the claims of Christ does not authorize an unholy proclaimer. The church should reject an unholy preacher.

26 **And the unclean spirit, tearing him and crying with a loud voice, came out of him.**—The demon yields because he was obliged to, not because he chose to do so. He exerted his last power, tried to inflict all the pain he could, and then unwillingly bowed to the Son of God and came out of the man.

questioned among themselves, saying, What is this? a new teaching! with authority he commandeth even the unclean spirits, and they obey him. 28 And the report of him went out straightway everywhere into all the region of Galilee round about.

27 **And they were all amazed, insomuch that they questioned among themselves, saying, What is this? a new teaching!**—They did not know whether to rejoice or to be alarmed. What might not such a being as Jesus do to those around him? How powerful is this man's word or command? His calm assumption of original authority as a teacher had already excited their wonder.

with authority he commandeth even the unclean spirits, and they obey him.—The climax is reached, the teaching is vindicated, the authority is proved and acknowledged, and the result is what might be expected.

28 **And the report of him went out straightway everywhere into all the region of Galilee round about.**—[It was natural that a report of these wonderful manifestations of power and this deliverance from afflictions so terrible, this power over the demons that were subject to no human power, should spread abroad among these people of Galilee. The evil spirits, or those possessed of them, entered the synagogue. Such could not enter the temple.]

[They were amazed to see one who could command these demons so they would obey him, and they questioned one another, and said: What thing is this? What does it mean? What new teacher and power is this? It was unheard of that these unclean spirits should be subjected to the authority of man. But Jesus was ruler over the spiritual as over the material world, and when he commanded they obeyed.]

The miraculous cure, which led them to make earnest inquiry of the doctrine of this new teacher in the synagogue, to whom the demons even were obedient, had great effect on the people. The evil spirits could exert miraculous power, but it was always for evil to those possessed of them. We must sometimes suffer greatly to get rid of our sins, but had better suffer than sin. They are never idle, working night and day seeing whom they can devour.

4. PETER'S MOTHER-IN-LAW HEALED
1: 29-31
(Matt. 8: 14, 15; Luke 4: 38, 39)

29 And straightway, [1]when they were come out of the synagogue, they came into the house of Simon and Andrew, with [2]James and John. 30 Now Simon's wife's mother lay sick of a fever; and straightway they tell him of her: 31 and he came and took her by the hand, and raised her up; and the fever left her, and she ministered unto them.

[1]Some ancient authorities read *when he was come out of the synagogue, he came &c.*
[2]Or, *Jacob*

29 **And straightway, when they were come out of the synagogue, they came into the house of Simon and Andrew, with James and John.**—These are specially mentioned as guests. Simon, together with Andrew his brother, had lived at Bethsaida, and had also removed to Capernaum with Jesus.

30 **Now Simon's wife's mother**—A conclusive proof that Peter was a married man. Roman Catholics claim Peter is the head of the church, and the vicegerent of Christ. The Pope, according to their views, is the successor of Peter. On what pretense do they claim that it is wrong for *priests* to marry? Why did Christ not at once reject Peter from being an apostle for having a wife?

lay sick of a fever; and straightway they tell him of her:— Luke (4: 38) says: "Holden with a great fever," indicating length and severity. How long she had been confined to her bed we have no means of knowing.

31 **and he came and took her by the hand, and raised her up; and the fever left her, and she ministered unto them.**— Matthew interjects "and she arose," which Luke intensified with "immediately."

The completeness of the restoration is seen by her returning to her ordinary household duties, so that she, who a moment before, lay helpless in their presence, was now serving them. The fever did not leave her weak and exhausted; she was raised to her full strength and to perfect health.

5. MANY OTHERS WERE HEALED
1 : 32-34
(Matt. 8: 16, 17; Luke 4: 40, 41)

32 And at even, when the sun did set, they brought unto him all that were sick, and them that were [3]possessed with demons. 33 And all the city was gathered together at the door. 34 And he healed many that were sick with divers diseases, and cast out many demons; and he suffered not the demons to speak, because they knew him[4].

[3]Or, *demoniacs*
[4]Many ancient authorities add *to be Christ* See Lk. 4. 41.

---

32 And at even, when the sun did set, they brought unto him all that were sick, and them that were possessed with demons.—[These miracles occurred on the Sabbath day. There was a feeling against even the healing of the sick on the Sabbath. Jesus, from the beginning, healed as occasion offered on the Sabbath, and spoke not a word during his ministry urging the observance of the Sabbath. Many of the Jews, especially the scribes and Pharisees about Jerusalem, insisted rigidly on the observance, and as the Sabbath ended at six o'clock in the evening, it is generally thought that those sick were not brought until this hour to avoid breaking the Sabbath, or to avoid the condemnation of the scribes and Pharisees. But it is certain that those living in Galilee did not so sacredly observe the day as did the Jews. In Galilee they had failed to retain the strong religious feelings of the Jews. So while this feeling may have influenced them it is probable that the sun was hot, and they waited until the setting of the sun and the cool evening shadows made it more favorable to bring them out. Whatever the cause, all that were sick in Capernaum and many possessed of evil spirits at even were brought unto him.]

33 And all the city was gathered together at the door.—[All the well were gathered at the door, curious and interested to see what they could of his wonderful deeds in healing the diseased and casting out the evil spirits. Many followed him from curiosity and to see and hear something wonderful.]

34 And he healed many that were sick with divers diseases, and cast out many demons; and he suffered not the demons to speak, because they knew him.—They knew him as the Holy One of God (Luke 4: 41), but he adhered to his steady purpose to accept no testimony from them. Mark 3: 22 and its parallels show how ready the scribes, etc., were to ascribe these miracles to a compact with Beelzebub. To such a charge Jesus will furnish no help. [Luke (4: 40) says, "He laid his hands on every one of them, and healed them." The persons were many, the diseases were manifold. He laid his hands on everyone suffering and healed them. He cast out the demons from all that were possessed with them, and suffered not the devils to speak because they knew him. If they spoke they would declare who he was, and he would not permit this.]

6. RETIREMENT AND PRAYER OF JESUS
1: 35-39
(Luke 4: 42-44)

35 And in the morning, a great while before day, he rose up and went out, and departed into a desert place, and there prayed. 36 And Simon and they that were with him followed after him; 37 and they found him, and say

---

35 **And in the morning, a great while before day, he rose up and went out, and departed into a desert place, and there prayed.**—Luke (4: 42) says: "When it was day." The writers do not contradict each other, since both are proper expressions for a point of time not certainly defined, to wit, the dawn or break of day, when light and darkness are in conflict, and although the day is breaking, it is really still night. One of the notable things in the life of Jesus is the record of his habits of prayer. Divine as he was, there was a constant appeal to and communion with his Father. The vision at his baptism was given while he prayed. (Luke 3: 21.) The night before he selected the twelve, he continued the whole night in prayer on a mountain. (Luke 6: 12.) The conversation about his Messiahship in Cesarea was preceded by prayer. It was during prayer in a mountain that the transfiguration took place. (Luke 9: 28, 29.) It was at the close of a season of prayer that he taught his disciples how to pray. (Luke 11: 1.) Also we may recall the prayer of John 17, and the agonizing prayer of Gethsemane.

36 **And Simon and they that were with him followed after him;**—On rising, they missed him, and, perhaps in some alarm, went to seek him.

unto him, All are seeking thee. 38 And he saith unto them, Let us go elsewhere into the next towns, that I may preach there also; for to this end
came I forth. 39 And he went into their synagogues throughout all Galilee,
preaching and casting out demons.

**37 and they found him, and say unto him, All are seeking
thee.**—The town was already astir to see and hear the wonderful stranger, and finding him not at Peter's house, were seeking him in all directions.

**38 And he saith unto them, Let us go elsewhere into the
next towns,**—There was much ground to cover, and a short
time in which to do it. Capernaum had received a great benefit. It must not engross too much of his time.

that I may preach there also; for to this end came I forth.—
He came, not from the house of Peter, as some claim, but
from his Father, as explained by Luke (4: 43). Christianity
is for all the world. As soon as one town receives the gospel,
the motto should be, "Let us go elsewhere into the next
towns."

**39 And he went into their synagogues throughout all Gali-
lee,**—The plan of going into the "next towns" so he could
preach to the people there was carried into execution. Not
only did he preach in "the next towns" as first proposed but
throughout all Galilee.

preaching and casting out demons.—He doubtless wrought
other healings, but this is put for the whole, as the most striking, up to his time, of his wonderful works. Jesus confirmed
and attested his teaching by the miracles he performed wherever he went, the chief among which was casting out demons.
This showed his great opposition to the kingdom of Satan.

He did not become a "pastor" devoting his time and talent
at one place. He made Capernaum his headquarters and from
there he carried the gospel of the kingdom into *all Galilee.* It
was his purpose to preach this gospel everywhere, and for this
reason he never located and confined his ministry to any particular place, but went to the smallest towns and villages. The
place never got too small and the people too poor for Jesus to
visit and break unto them the bread of life. He was no sala-
ried preacher, seeking the largest towns and the greatest pay.
Herein is an example of wisdom that ought to be followed by
preachers now.

7. JESUS HEALS A LEPER
1: 40-45
(Matt. 8: 2-4; Luke 5: 12-16)

40 And there cometh to him a leper, beseeching him, [5]and kneeling down to him, and saying unto him, If thou wilt, thou canst make me clean. 41 And being moved with compassion, he stretched forth his hand, and touched him, and saith unto him, I will; be thou made clean. 42 And straightway

[5]Some ancient authorities omit *and kneeling down to him.*

---

40 And there cometh to him a leper,—"A man full of leprosy." (Luke 5: 12.) One of the greatest unfortunates the world contains physically. This awful disease demands special notice, for a description of which consult Lev. 13: 1-46, where a variety of symptoms and manifestations are described. God selected this disease as a type of sin.

beseeching him, and kneeling down to him, and saying unto him, If thou wilt, thou canst make me clean.—That is, "Thou canst completely heal my leprosy." According to Matthew he called him "Lord," but the term was used with much latitude. The clearness of faith shown by his words we must notice. His only doubt is as to Christ's willingness, but the words do not imply strong doubt even of this.

41 And being moved with compassion,—This expresses the Savior's feelings of pity. We may be assured that he looks on no scene of suffering without deep sympathy. If thus tenderly compassionate to the type of the sinner, how much more to the more wretched antitype?

he stretched forth his hand, and touched him, and saith unto him, I will; be thou made clean.—Jesus is just as compassionate now as ever. He will be as sympathizing with us as with the poor leper. If you are not saved through him it will not be because he is not willing, but because you are not.

42 And straightway the leprosy departed from him, and he was made clean.—The offensive appearance was all gone on the instant, and his flesh was like the flesh of those about him. The certainty and suddenness of the cure without means was a proof of his Messiahship. Jesus not only showed a willingness but power and authority. The instruction which this miracle gives us is that our soul is overspread with the leprosy of sin, and that we must apply for help to the healing power and recovering grace of this same Jesus. His blood is

the leprosy departed from him, and he was made clean. 43 and he [6]strictly charged him, and straightway sent him out, 44 and saith unto him, See thou say nothing to any man: but go show thyself to the priest, and offer for thy cleansing the things which Moses [7]commanded, for a testimony unto them.

[6]Or, *sternly*
[7]Lev. viii. 49; xiv. 2 ff.

our remedy. We appropriate its cleansing power to ourselves by complying with all conditions upon which salvation is promised in the gospel.

43 **And he strictly charged him, and straightway sent him out,**—It was characteristic of the miracles of Christ that they were neither preceded nor followed by unnecessary words or acts, but as soon as the desired change was wrought, the subject was dismissed to make way for another. Peter's mother-in-law instantly returned to her household duties (verse 31) without any interval of convalescence. So the leper is no sooner healed than he is sent away.

44 **and saith unto him, See thou say nothing to any man:**— He was not to talk about being healed to any one except the priest. Our Lord frequently gave such prohibition. (5: 43; 7: 36.) His reasons for doing so varied according to circumstances.

but go show thyself to the priest, and offer for thy cleansing the things which Moses commanded,—That is, for his ceremonial cleansing, in order that he might be officially declared free of the disease. This was the duty of subjecting himself to the inspection of a priest and making the offering Moses commanded. While Christ was Lord also of the law, yet he required the man to make the offerings prescribed in the Mosaic law for such occasions. (Lev. 14: 1-12.)

for a testimony unto them.—Unto whom? Meyer says: "Unto the people that thou art healed." Crysostom says: "For a testimony that I do not destroy the law." We do not think either the true meaning. If the man shall go to the priest, be pronounced clean, offer the sacrifices and be restored to his family, whenever the question of the claims of Jesus shall arise, all this will be a "testimony unto them," which will also be a testimony *against* them if they reject him. Prior to this the priest had pronounced him unclean, and had

45 But he went out, and began to publish it much, and to spread abroad the
[8]matter, insomuch that [9]Jesus could no more openly enter into [10]a city, but
was without in desert places: and they came to him from every quarter.

[8]Gr. *word.*
[9]Gr. *he.*
[10]Or, *the city*

---

cast him out of the congregation, and now the priest must
pronounce him clean and restore him to society.

45 **But he went out, and began to publish it much, and to
spread abroad the matter,**—He gives vent to his joy not real-
izing the importance of obeying his Lord in the matter. He
was so deeply affected and overjoyed with the cure that he
followed the dictates of his own feelings rather than the command of his Lord.

Probably his intentions were good, but his disobedience to
Christ's command was a fault and shows the weakness in
human nature in following the dictates of human feelings
rather than obeying exactly what the Lord commands. He
might have felt that he was honoring Christ, but it is a sin to
do anything against the command of Christ, though with ever
so good a meaning, purpose, and intention to exalt and honor
him. Christ can never be exalted and honored save through
his own appointments. He can never be honored and exalted
through the appointments and institutions of men. These are
only parasites sucking the life's blood out of the appointments
and institutions ordained of God and sealed by the blood of
his Son. Whether the healed man went to the priest at all is
no record.

**insomuch that Jesus could no more openly enter into a city,
but was without in desert places:**—Any city. Perhaps on account of a false report of a legal defilement contracted by his
contact with the leper, which had made scandal, or perhaps
on account of the disturbance made by the crowds which
thronged around him.

and they came to him from every quarter.—Every quarter of
Galilee. Out in the wilderness the great throngs could incom-
mode no one but themselves. So the fame of Jesus is spreading in ever-widening circles.

SECTION THREE

DISCUSSIONS WITH SCRIBES AND PHARISEES
2: 1 to 3: 35

1. ABOUT POWER TO FORGIVE SINS
2: 1-12
(Matt. 9: 1-8; Luke 5: 17-26)

1 And when he entered again into Capernaum after some days, it was noised that he was [11]in the house. 2 And many were gathered together, so

[11]Or, *at home*

---

1 And when he entered again into Capernaum—Matthew says "his own city." [After traveling around the cities of Galilee for some time, preaching and healing in their synagogues, Jesus returned to Capernaum—his home. Time is told in very indefinite language in the scriptures, and frequently a few verses include a considerable time. All we can tell is it was yet in the first year of his ministry. We measure the years of his ministry by the Passover feasts at Jerusalem noted only by John. Jesus, after journeying from city to city on foot until worn and wearied with his journey, his labors, the constant crowds that thronged him, would naturally, at his home, seek quiet and rest preparatory to starting again upon his lifework. He returned to Capernaum, as the narrative would indicate, quietly, and entered his home.]

after some days,—How many days elapsed after "Jesus could no more openly enter into a city" (1: 45) is not stated. The fact that he goes again into the city is evidence that a sufficient time had passed, for the cause that hindered his entering into the cities had, in some way, been removed; and therefore, there is no inconsistency between the two statements.

it was noised that he was in the house.—[It was told from one to another, until the news spread through the city that he was in the house.] Jesus had no house of his own (Matt. 8: 20); but he dwelt in Capernaum (Matt. 4: 13) in a house occupied by some friend, probably Peter (Mark 1: 29), as at Bethany his home was with Lazarus and his sisters.

2 And many were gathered together,—Eager to hear from the lips of him who had so recently shown the possession of

that there was no longer room *for them,* no, not even about the door : and he

---

unparalleled power. [So soon as the people heard he was at his home many were gathered together to see him.]

so that there was no longer room for them, no, not even about the door:—[They crowded into the house until there was no room in the house to receive them, and they pressed around the door, so that it became impossible to approach it even.] Jesus was so far from seeking praise and commendation of people that he came into the city without observation, and betook himself to his home there; but the more he sought seclusion, the more he was taken notice of. Honor flees from those that pursue it, and pursues those that run from it. The way to be honored is to be humble. God seldom honors a proud man by making him either eminently serviceable or successful.

and he spake the word unto them.—[The chief mission of Jesus was to preach to the people the word of God. The healing of the sick and the casting out of the devils was a matter of secondary importance, but helpful, to his preaching the word. Jesus moved with kindness to men, would heal their bodily infirmities. But the great thing with him was to teach them the word, and to heal their spiritual afflictions. The healing of the body showed the presence of God with him. They were separated from God, they were as sheep without a shepherd, and he came to call them back to God. The miracles were wrought to prove he was from God, God was with him, and that his words were the words of God. The good that words do depends much on who speaks them and how received. The words spoken by Jesus were comparatively without effect to those who received them as the words of men. They were full of power and grace to those who received them as the words of God. The word preached here was the specific words that the kingdom of heaven was at hand. Luke 4: 18-20 is an example of his preaching. He quoted a prophecy foretelling his coming and his mission, and then showed it was fulfilled in his person and work. The word "preach" is not used in the New Testament as we use it. In the scriptures there is a distinction between the preaching

spake the word unto them. 3 And they come, bringing unto him a man sick of the palsy, borne of four. 4 And when they could not [12]come nigh unto him for the crowd, they uncovered the roof where he was: and when they had broken it up, they let down the [13]bed whereon the sick of the palsy lay. 5 And Jesus seeing their faith saith unto the sick of the palsy, [14]Son, thy sins

[12]Many ancient authorities read *bring him unto him.*
[13]Or, *pallet*
[14]Gr. *Child.*

and teaching. Preaching is the original proclamation of a message or a truth. The teaching was showing the duties and obligations that belief of the truth required. Here Christ himself proclaimed or first made known his mission in a clear, concise statement of the work he came to do, or the mission he came to fulfill.]

3 And they come, bringing unto him a man sick of the palsy, borne of four.—His case was an extreme one. The bed must have been of a very portable character, from the manner in which it was later handled. Being light, Jesus might with propriety command him to take it up and walk. (Matt. 9: 6.) As a demonstration of Christ's divine power, he was pleased to single out the extreme cases, to work a cure upon such as were afflicted.

4 And when they could not come nigh unto him for the crowd, they uncovered the roof where he was:—The regular entrance to the house had been blocked by the multitude, so they could not have access to Jesus. Many of ordinary faith and perseverance would have given up the enterprise for that time. At all events, "they went up to the housetop." (Luke.) The roof was made of rafters, and over these were laid branches, twigs, matting and earth, and trodden down. The uncovering of such a roof would not be a very dangerous or difficult proceeding.

and when they had broken it up, they let down the bed whereon the sick of the palsy lay.—Luke says he was let down "into the midst before Jesus." Their part of the work was done. Their faith had been shown, for very doubtful men would never have taken all this trouble. The sufferer was before the healer. It is not difficult to imagine the suppressed excitement which such an occurrence would produce in this crowded audience.

5 And Jesus seeing their faith—[Their faith doubtless in-

are forgiven. 6 But there were certain of the scribes sitting there, and rea-

cluded the faith of the paralytic as well as of those who bore him—his friends. Their faith showed itself in their outward action in bringing him to Jesus, and in overcoming the difficulties that lay in the way. It was a faith made perfect by works. God blesses those who believe, but only when the faith expresses itself in outward action. Faith never affects a person's character until it so controls the heart as to direct the actions. When Jesus was here in person he had no fixed act in which faith was to be expressed. Before he left the earth he ordained a specific act in which man must express his faith, and in expressing it come to Christ. A burial in baptism with Christ into death is the act ordained by Jesus and sealed by his blood in which man must express his faith in Christ. Every man who truly believes in Christ and desires to come to him must do it in the way Jesus directs it to be done. Faith leads the believer to do what Jesus commands to be done, and to come to him in his appointed way. We have no example in the Bible of God blessing a man for his faith before that faith had showed itself in a bodily act. There being no specific act in force during the life of Jesus, these people showed their faith in him by their earnest efforts to reach him.]

saith unto the sick of the palsy, Son, thy sins are forgiven. —Jesus speaks to him; he does not disdain him. He turns from all the great rabbis gathered there, he even interrupts his teaching, that he may speak to him. Such is the condescending love of Jesus. The word "son" among the Jews had a great variety of significations. It means literally a son; then a grandson; a descendant; an adopted son; a disciple, or one who is an object of tender affection—one who is to us as a son. In this place, it denotes affection, or kindness. [The Jews regarded all afflictions as the result of sins. Jesus saw the faith of these men, was willing to forgive his sins, so he kindly said, "Son, thy sins are forgiven." The paralytic doubtless believed himself, but the faith of those bearing him was taken into account in the healing. Jesus is our model in all things. His tenderness and love for the unfortunate and erring are examples we should follow.] Luke says, "Man, thy sins are forgiven thee"; Matthew (9: 2, 6) says: "Son, be of

soning in their hearts, 7 Why doth this man thus speak? he blasphemeth:

good cheer; thy sins are forgiven." "But that ye may know that the Son of man hath authority on earth to forgive sins (then saith he to the sick of the palsy), Arise, and take up thy bed, and go unto thy house." Thus he demonstrates his power to forgive sins. Jesus healed the man by removing the cause that produced the affliction. He had been brought there on his bed, helpless; he returns home carrying his bed in his arms.

6 **But there were certain of the scribes**—[These scribes were the Pharisees and doctors of the law which Luke 5: 7 tells came out of every village of Galilee and Judea and Jerusalem. These scribes originally were those who kept the records, copied the law, studied it, became skilled in its explanation, so were called doctors of the law. Smith's Bible Dictionary says: "The special training for the office of scribe began, probably, about the age of thirteen. The boy who was destined by his parents for the calling of a scribe went to Jerusalem and applied for admission into the school of some learned doctor." This shows the office had come to embrace doctors of the law, or those who explained its teachings and taught the traditions. Scribes were Levites. The classes here mentioned were the leaders in religious teaching among the Jews, and had come to Capernaum attracted by the reports concerning the works of Jesus to examine into and report on them. They were those naturally most unfavorable to him and his claims, as the religious are more jealous than the common people of new theories and leaders. They were reasoning in their hearts, watching to catch him.]

sitting there, and reasoning in their hearts,—These scribes, acting as spies, were probably occupying prominent seats near Jesus where they could catch every word. Matthew (9: 3) adds: "Said within themselves." They were secretly and deliberately considering and debating in their own hearts how to trap Jesus, unconscious that he perceived their own wicked thoughts and designs.

7 **Why doth this man thus speak? he blasphemeth:**—A very pertinent question, if he was only a man. [It would have been blasphemy for a mere man to claim to forgive sins. This

who can forgive sins but one, *even* God? 8 And straightway Jesus, perceiving in his spirit that they so reasoned within themselves, saith unto them,

was claiming a power that belongs only to God. So they, in their minds, decide it is blasphemy in Jesus to claim to forgive sins, and ask, "Who can forgive sins but one, even God?" This was all done in their minds, no one speaking it openly. Jesus told them what they were thinking of to show his divine power, and thus introduce the more direct evidence to convince them of its truth.]

who can forgive sins but one, even God?—The answer is negative, none. They were correct in holding that it was God's prerogative to forgive sins; but they failed to see in his teaching and wonderful works the manifestations of divinity in Christ. Their doctrine was true, but their application false. Their denying Christ of this power was blasphemy in them, none in him. They were the guilty parties, he the innocent one. In forgiving sins Jesus drew the issue squarely; he either blasphemed, or he was divine. On this issue Jesus purposed to stand or fall. By forgiving sins, he affirms he is divine. None can forgive sins but God, but he has his appointed means of forgiveness.

8 And straightway Jesus, perceiving in his spirit—By his own omniscient and divine spirit. He perceived it at once. Their hearts lay bare before his spiritual gaze.

that they so reasoned within themselves, saith unto them, Why reason ye these things in your hearts?—That is, in their hearts, but not expressing their thoughts in words. Matt. 9: 4 says, "Wherefore think ye evil in your hearts?" Their reasoning was evil because there had already been enough done by Jesus, of which they were doubtless cognizant, to show that God was with him and that, consequently, he could not be a sinner. [Jesus had continually shown his power to read the thoughts of men without their expressing them, so he asked them, "Why reason ye these things in your hearts?" Showing he discerned their secret thoughts was a step in proving he had more than human power that enabled him to read the secrets of men's hearts. This was the evidence he brought to bear on Nathanael and the woman at the well of Samaria.]

Here Jesus gives some insight as to what the *heart is and where it is located*. Man is of a twofold nature—flesh and spirit—the inward man and the outward man. He is composed of body and spirit and is possessed with two hearts— the fleshly heart and the spiritual heart. The fleshly heart is a fleshly lobe located in the breast. It pumps to all the extremities of the human body the life-giving principle, the blood. This is its function. The spiritual heart is located in the spiritual man, and from it flows the life-giving principles to the inner man, the spirit and principles of Christ. This is the heart that undergoes a change in conversion. The fleshly heart located in the breast undergoes no change in man's conversion or turning to God. It is the same heart after that it was before conversion. It has undergone no change whatsoever. Not so with the spiritual heart. It has undergone a change. It has been changed from an impure to a pure heart. We may learn what the spiritual heart is from what it does. (1) It understands. "Apply thy heart to understanding." (Prov. 2: 2.) Should "understand with their heart." (Matt. 13: 15.) (2) It reasons. "Why reason ye these things in your hearts?" (Mark 2: 8.) (3) It thinks. "Wherefore think ye evil in your hearts?" (Matt. 9: 4.) (4) It desires. "Brethren, my heart's desire." (Rom. 10: 1.) (5) It believes. "With the heart man believeth unto righteousness." (Rom. 10: 10.) (6) It purposes. "And he exhorted them all, that with purpose of heart they would cleave unto the Lord." (Acts 11: 23.) (7) It condemns. For "if our heart condemn us." (1 John 3: 20.) (8) It obeys. "Ye became obedient from the heart to that form of teaching." (Rom. 6: 17.) It is clear that the physical heart located in the human breast cannot do the things here ascribed to the heart in the Bible, and therefore it is not the heart to be changed in turning to God.

[In opposing one extreme there is always danger of running into the other. The religious people around us hold that the emotions and the fleshly feelings constitute the heart to the exclusion of the mental, moral, and willing powers. In opposing these, many run to the other extreme and claim that the intellect is the heart. This is as erroneous and as hurtful as to make the emotions the heart. The fleshly heart is the center and active force in stirring and using all the faculties of the fleshly body. Without the activity of the heart the eyes could not see, nor the ears hear, nor the brain think. The eye is not the body or the fleshly heart, yet it is a faculty of both; so are all the senses and organs of the body. Within the fleshly body dwells the spiritual body. That body has faculties, members, and organs, just as the fleshly body has; only they are spiritual faculties and organs. The mind, the emotions, the volitions are all members or organs of the spiritual body, but no one of them is the body. The spiritual heart is the center and life of this spiritual body and directs and uses these faculties. The heart is frequently used to represent the whole inner or spiritual man. It thinks through the mind; loves or hates through its emotions; sees, wills, and purposes through the volition; and believes and trusts, decides and acts, through the harmonious action of all its faculties. Common experience ought to show that the mind alone is not the spiritual heart. Many things are memorized and retained in the mind that the heart does not take hold of at all; they do not arouse the emotions or volutions, consequently do not affect the heart. The mind perceives, discriminates, and decides what is true or false; carries this decision to the heart; and the heart believes or disbelieves. The Bible nowhere says the mind believes; the heart believes, and the scriptures require that the gospel shall be believed with the whole heart. This means the intellect approves, the emotions lay hold of the truth, and the volition, or will, acts on it. Needless prejudice has been excited and great harm has been done by saying that to believe with the heart is a mere mental perception or acknowledgment of the truth. The heart, properly speaking, embraces the mind, the emotions, and the will. Sometimes, to make sure the things spoken were understood, or to give emphasis, the heart and the parts of which the heart is composed are all mentioned. We sometimes say: "A man is buried head and ears." The ears constitute a part of the head. We sometimes say: "The man, soul, mind, and body." Each of these constitutes a part or member of the body to show the office of each is recognized; but to especially impress that all are spoken of the specific use or office of each part or member is meant, all the parts are mentioned. A man that really thinks the heart, spoken of as affected by our faith

Why reason ye these things in your hearts? 9 Which is easier, to say to the sick of the palsy, Thy sins are forgiven; or to say, Arise, and take up thy

and our relations to God, is the lobe of flesh in our body is hardly accountable. "Thy word have I laid up in my heart, that I might not sin against thee" (Ps. 119: 11) is an allusion of the puzzling declaration in 1 John 3: 9: "Whosoever is begotten of God doeth no sin, . . . because he is begotten of God." Connect with this the declaration of the Savior (Luke 8: 11): "The seed is the word of God." This manifests that the word of God is the seed of the kingdom which is implanted in the heart. While that seed is hid, covered up in the heart, the man cannot intentionally engage in sin. The heart means something more than the mind in this connection. The heart in the physical man is the common receptacle of the blood distilled from the food, received by the continual action of all the organs for receiving and assimilating food for invigorating the body. It not only receives this blood from the divers organs, but it is the distributing center by and from which the blood is distributed to the different members of the body, supplying life, warmth and strength to enable each member to perform its proper work. So in the spiritual man, the spiritual heart is that faculty that receives the impression, thoughts, affects, desires of the human soul and molds them into one supreme controlling purpose and end through which it strengthens all the faculties of soul, mind, and spirit to courageous activity in the attainment of that end. The word of God enfolded in this heart, in this receptacle, this distributing center of spiritual life, guides the soul so that it sins not. It cannot sin while the word of God enveloped in this heart is the guiding and controlling principle. Of the same purport, precisely, is the declaration concerning the righteous; "the law of his God is in his heart, none of his steps shall slide." (Ps. 37: 31.) When God's law is in the heart of a man, it makes him wise and though he walk through slippery places, his steps shall not slide. "And Jehovah helpeth them, and rescueth them: he rescueth them from the wicked, and saveth them, because they have taken refuge in him." (Ps. 37: 40.)]

9 Which is easier, to say to the sick of the palsy, Thy sins are forgiven; or to say, Arise, and take up thy bed, and walk?

bed, and walk?   10 But that ye may know that the Son of man hath authority on earth to forgive sins (he saith to the sick of the palsy), 11 I say unto

—[He intimates that one who could heal by his word the sick
of the palsy could forgive sins. This is true not because the
healing was necessarily equal to forgiving sins. The power to
heal by his word showed God was with him. (John 3: 2.)
He was divine, and if he was divine he could not lie about his
power to forgive sins. Then he asked, is it easier to say to
the sick of the palsy, "Thy sins are forgiven thee," or to say,
"Arise, and take up thy bed, and walk?" The power to do
this showed the power to do that. One could be manifested
to the eyes of those present, the other could not be.] Here
are two perplexing questions which the scribes made no attempt to answer. They could not without condemning themselves, so they preferred to keep silent.

10 **But that ye may know**—And thus never be excusable
again in such accusations, mental or spoken. [He proposed
by working a miracle they could all see, and about which
there could be no doubt, to show that he possessed divine
power. God was with him, and hence he had power to forgive
sins.]

that the Son of man hath authority—This is the first mention by Mark of that phrase which Jesus applied to himself as
a name oftener than any other. [He called himself the "Son
of man" alluding to the fact that he took on himself the nature
of a man. He called himself "the Son of man," owned that he
was human, and depended on his works to prove he was divine, the Son of God. "The works that I do in my Father's
name, these bear witness of me." (John 10: 25.) "If I do not
the works of my Father, believe me not. But if I do them,
though ye believe not me, believe the works: that ye may
know and understand that the Father is in me, and I in the
Father." (John 10: 37, 38.) The works he did were such as
only God could do, so for him to do the works that God only
could do showed God was in him.]

on earth to forgive sins (he saith to the sick of the palsy),
—He not only has power in heaven to forgive sins, but he had
it on earth where sins are committed. Pardon takes place
where the pardoning power is. He had this power while on

thee, Arise, take up thy [18]bed, and go unto thy house. 12 And he arose, and straightway took up the [18]bed, and went forth before them all; insomuch

---

earth, and had the right to exercise it, and did so. He carried this authority and power with him to heaven. All pardoning power is now in heaven. Men pardoned are on earth, but pardon takes place in heaven—in the mind of God.

11 I say unto thee, Arise, take up thy bed, and go unto thy house.—[The command was that he who could not walk, who was so helpless he had to be borne upon the bed by the four persons, should before their eyes arise, take up the bed on which he had been borne, and go his way to his home. To do this would show a wonderful change in his condition, and to do it at the word of Jesus would show he had power to work miracles, which no one save God could do. The works would prove God was in him and he in God.]

12 And he arose, and straightway took up the bed, and went forth before them all;—[In doing what was commanded the power of God helped him. The work he did proved God was with Jesus. All the fullness of the Godhead dwelled bodily in him (Col. 2: 9)—that is, the fullness of the power and majesty of the Godhead dwelled in Jesus Christ. In his bodily form all of its majesty and power dwelled. Hebrews (1: 3) says of Jesus: "Who being the effulgence of his glory, and the very image of his substance, and upholding all things by the word of his power, when he had made purification of sins, sat down on the right hand of the Majesty on high." These works of Jesus declared to the world the power he possessed from God. He gave these testimonies that God was in him and he in God to show he had power to forgive sins. Miracles showed God was with and in him.] The last minute for the final test of the claim of Jesus having authority to forgive sins on earth has arrived. Doubtless all eyes were centered on the paralytic. It is not easy to imagine the suspense with which both the enemies and friends of Jesus must have awaited the result. Had the paralytic failed to obey the command, the claims of the new religious teacher were refuted by the test of his own choosing. But "he arose," not by slow degrees, but "straightway," without delay, and "took up the bed, and went forth before them all." Thus a victory for the claims of "the Son of

that they were all amazed, and glorified God, saying, We never saw it on
this fashion.

man" was won. Luke (5: 25) tells us that the man went
forth, "glorifying God." It needs this to make the picture
complete.

insomuch that they were all amazed,—Matthew and Luke
say that they were "afraid." The presence of a being of such
power in their midst filled them with dread. What might he
not do next? They probably felt like Peter, when he said:
"Depart from me; for I am a sinful man, O Lord."

and glorified God,—Whether the scribes participated is not
certain, though the "all" may be literal, and take them in.
Matthew specifies "the multitudes," which may leave them
out. At all events, they did not long continue in this frame of
mind for they soon gave their voice against Jesus and he was
led to the cross and crucified.

saying, We never saw it on this fashion.—[When the people saw how he healed the palsied man and gave him health
and strength, they were amazed greatly. It was new and
wonderful. They glorified God, gave him the honor and
credit of the healing done by saying, "We never saw it on this
fashion." Hence he was not of man. It was above man.
Matthew (9: 8) says: "But when the multitudes saw it, they
were afraid, and glorified God, who had given such authority
unto men." Luke (5: 26) says: "And amazement took hold
on all, and they glorified God; and they were filled with fear,
saying, We have seen strange things today." This shows that
people may love to see the works of God, wonder and admire,
and yet not be benefited. It proves that great works and
wonders before people will not help them unless they wish to
serve God. Notwithstanding this fear and amazement and
this ascribing glory to Jesus as having God with him, they did
not become disciples of Jesus, and all these works and wonders in their presence became the ground of their deeper condemnation.]

The true end of the miracle was reached when God was glorified by the man and the people, and not till then. See that
you give God the glory of all work done, all results achieved.
They knew not that, in glorifying God, they glorified Jesus.

2. JESUS EATS WITH PUBLICANS AND SINNERS
2: 13-17
(Matt. 9: 9-13; Luke 5: 27-32)

13 And he went forth again by the sea side; and all the multitude resorted unto him, and he taught them. 14 And as he passed by, he saw Levi

13 **And he went forth**—Jesus goes from Capernaum. Capernaum means "Village of Comfort." It was one of the chief cities of Galilee. It had a custom station where Matthew collected the taxes (Matt. 9: 9), a Roman garrison, and a synagogue, built by the Roman centurion. The ruins of a synagogue at Tul Hum, said by McGarvey and other travelers to be the site of Capernaum, show it to have been finer than any other in all Galilee. No city could have enjoyed more exalted privileges. There Jesus not only resided, but taught in the synagogue, in homes, and on the seashore; did many miracles, and there five of his apostles lived. To it, in its wasted opportunities and despised privileges, Jesus said: "I say unto you that it shall be more tolerable for the land of Sodom in the day of judgment, than for thee." (Matt. 11: 23, 24.)

again by the sea side; and all the multitude resorted unto him, and he taught them.—The Lake of Galilee. The shore of this lake was a favorite resort of Jesus when surrounded by great multitudes. Jesus often taught by the seaside. (4: 1; Luke 5: 1.) By taking a position at the water's edge, or on a boat fastened at the shore, he could prevent the people from surrounding him. As they stood or sat on the shore, he could easily make his voice reach all the multitude. He never lost any time in teaching people. He demonstrates that his followers ought not to wait for an opportunity to speak in fashionable church houses before teaching the people, but that they ought to teach wherever and whenever they can get hearers.

14 **And as he passed by, he saw Levi the son of Alphaeus**— Luke (5: 27) speaks of him as Levi. But in Matthew (9: 9) we have the name of Matthew instead of Levi. The three narratives clearly relate the same circumstances, and point to Levi as identical with Matthew. He probably had two names as Peter and Paul.

the son of Alphaeus sitting at the place of toll, and he saith unto him, Follow me. And he arose and followed him.

15 And it came to pass, that he was sitting at meat in his house, and many [1]publicans and sinners sat down with Jesus and his disciples: for there

[1]That is, *collectors or renters of Roman taxes.*

---

sitting at the place of toll,—He was a tax collector and was sitting at his place of business in the customhouse. The revenues which the Roman government derived from conquered countries consisted chiefly of tolls, tithes, and harbor duties, taxes on public pasture lands, and duties on mines and saltworks. Customs were the taxes imposed by the government on both imported and exported goods. The Romans taxed almost everything—fish, trees, houses, doors, columns, and all property, real and personal. All human governments take this course and the burden of taxation grows heavier and heavier. This is the history of all human governments and the cause of their overthrow. Increased taxes become so burdensome, people rebel, rise up and overthrow the government. Christians cannot participate in such rebellions against civil government.

and he saith unto him, Follow me. And he arose and followed him.—Like Peter and Andrew (1: 16-20; John 1: 40-42), he did not delay his obedience but arose immediately and followed Jesus. He was not here called to be an apostle, though later he was made one. He was called as a disciple (learner) and a constant associate of Jesus. He, like those previously called, had to be schooled and trained before becoming an apostle. The apostles were chosen later. (Mark 3: 13, 14; Luke 6: 13.) Luke (5: 28) says: "He *forsook* all," which shows the great interest he had in Jesus from the start. He was called to a higher life, a nobler work—to gather no longer perishable money for the Roman treasury, but to gather souls for heaven.

15 **And it came to pass, that he was sitting at meat in his house**—Jesus and the guests were eating in the house of Matthew. Matthew made Jesus a great feast in his own house. "A great multitude" was present. (Luke 5: 29.) The guests consisted of Jesus and his disciples, publicans and sinners.

and many publicans and sinners sat down with Jesus and his

were many, and they followed him. 16 And the scribes ²of the Pharisees,
when they saw that he was eating with the sinners and ¹publicans, said unto

²Some ancient authorities read *and the Pharisees.*

disciples:—Levi, being a publican or tax collector, had been
excommunicated by loyal Jews, and hence forced to associate
with the outcast, such as publicans and sinners. In making
this feast in honor of Jesus, he invited his old associates, publicans and sinners, to enjoy his hospitality.

for there were many, and they followed him.—Probably it
was a farewell feast, preparatory to leaving all and following
Jesus.

16 And the scribes of the Pharisees,—These were learned
men who copied, preserved, and explained the law of Moses
and the traditions of the elders. (Ezra 7: 6, 12; Neh. 8: 1;
Matt. 15: 1-6.) They were called doctors of the law (Luke 5:
17, 21) and lawyers (Matt. 12: 35). Mark (1: 22) suggests
that the scribes were teachers as well as copyists and conservators of the law. They occupied the seat of Moses, but their
teaching was very defective. (Matt. 23: 2, 13, 23.) They
taught with authority, but it was of tradition. They enforced
the letter of the law. The Pharisees sprang up about one
hundred and fifty years before the birth of Christ. They were
a religious sect. The name "Pharisee" means *separatist.*
They separated from Levitical and traditional purity, and
were doubtless the most numerous sect among the Jews.
They would neither eat nor associate with publicans and
sinners, for as excommunicated persons they regarded them
as heathen. (Matt. 18: 17.) They held closely to the traditions
of the elders (7: 3) and attached more importance to them
than even to the written law of Moses (Matt. 15: 1-6).

when they saw that he was eating with the sinners and publicans,—Since Pharisees would hardly be found in the house
of a publican, we are not to conclude that they were in the
house where the feast was spread. They may have seen Jesus
eating through an open hall, window or some other opening.

said unto his disciples,—Doubtless the conversation here
mentioned took place with the disciples while they were going
in and out from the feast, or probably when they were leaving
for home.

his disciples, [3]*How is it* that he eateth [4]and drinketh with [1]publicans and sinners? 17 And when Jesus heard it, he saith unto them, They that are [5]whole have no need of a physician, but they that are sick: I came not to call the righteous, but sinners.

[3]Or, *He eateth . . . sinners.*
[4]Some ancient authorities omit *and drinketh.*
[5]Gr. *strong.*

How is it that he eateth and drinketh with publicans and sinners?—The complaint of the scribes is here put in the form of a question. To *eat* in the first clause and to *eat and drink* in the second are equivalent expressions, both conveying the same general ideas of food and participation in it. The scribes and Pharisees were on the watch to trap Jesus, and felt confident that they had succeeded.

17 And when Jesus heard it, he saith unto them, They that are whole have no need of a physician,—He either overheard the scribes and Pharisees when they asked the question, or through the disciples who went to him with it. The very idea of a healer or physician presupposes sickness—they that are whole—in good health—need no such help as rendered by physicians.

but they that are sick:—The sick man, not the well one, is in need of the doctor and is the party who sends for him. The physician attends the sick, not the well. Jesus was a spiritual physician and his great mission in the world was to heal the diseases of sin. If any were really righteous as the scribes and Pharisees imagined they were, then they did not need the healing power of Jesus. The fact that these publicans and sinners were notoriously depraved and wicked showed how sick they were, and how much they were in need of the best physician. The more complicated the disease, the more need there is for a skilled physician. Jesus was that physician.

I came not to call the righteous, but sinners.—Luke (5: 32) says: "I am not come to call the righteous but sinners to repentance." While Jesus made the application to the scribes and Pharisees, as to their own self-righteousness, yet he included all mankind for the reason "there is none righteous, no, not one." (Rom. 3: 10.) He came not to *call righteous men,* for there were really none. His mission was to sinners, and therefore no one should criticize him for trying to save them. The man who is sound physically does not need the physician; the spiritually whole, the righteous, do not need to repent. If these scribes and Pharisees were all they claimed for themselves—spiritually whole, strong and healthy morally—then they needed not the physician; but, from their own viewpoint, these publicans and sinners were in great need of relief and of repentance. These souls were sick. Jesus was the great soul physician. Hence, he went to the sin-sick—to those who felt their need of healing. The self-righteous Pharisees did not realize their own sinful condition, and, therefore, felt no need of Christ. There is but little hope for the self-righteous. Before one can be spiritually healed he must first realize his lost and ruined condition and feel the need of a Savior. There is more hope for sinners, however deep in sin and depravity they may be, who realize their unworthiness of Jesus and their lost condition without him, than for the self-righteous. There is none for them until they humble themselves and desire mercy. The objection was addressed to the disciples, but replied to by Jesus, and as usual in an unexpected way. His reply put them in their own snare. He presented the true question at issue, and stated the true principle or method of solution. Their reproach implied a false view of Christ's whole work and mission which was that of a spiritual physician.

Jesus is a wonderful physician. He makes no charges for his service. Salvation is without money and without price. His invitation is universal. (Matt 11: 28.) Our spiritual physician increases the happiness of the patient by giving unto him, instead of enriching his estate by charging for his services. Physicians of the human body bleed the patient, but Jesus bled and died to heal the patient.

3. ABOUT FASTING
2: 18-22
(Matt. 9: 14-17; Luke 5: 33-39)

18 And John's disciples and the Pharisees were fasting: and they come

---

18 **And John's disciples**—His converts. They (some, not all) were still holding John as their captain. A part of his disciples did not accept the leadership of Jesus as readily as did John. John recognized Jesus immediately as the Son of

and say unto him, Why do John's disciples and the disciples of the Pharisees

God and captain of the new movement and received him as such. He said: "He must increase, but I must decrease." (John 3: 30.) Had John's disciples possessed the spirit he himself had and followed his precepts, they too would have accepted Jesus as their great leader without delay. (John 1: 29-36; 3: 27-34.) But while John was baptizing some of them manifested a spirit of rivalry (John 3: 26) and much more now since his imprisonment. Those who held aloof from Christ really sympathized with the Pharisees. (Luke 5: 33.)

and the Pharisees were fasting: and they come and say unto him, Why do John's disciples and the disciples of the Pharisees fast, but thy disciples fast not?—A statement of what John's disciples and the Pharisees were doing. Both the foundation for and the question asked are plainly stated. They left no room for quibbling. A third ground of opposition to Jesus is now introduced. The opposition to Jesus about him eating with publicans and sinners had no sooner been disposed of than the question about his disciples not fasting was introduced. This question probably came up the day Matthew spread his feast, however, some think it is doubtful. Whether this charge was made upon the same or a different day is unimportant. John's disciples and the Pharisees fasted, the disciples of Jesus did not, so they ask for the reason why they did not. The question was fair and legitimate. The Pharisees fasted twice a week (Luke 18: 12), and John's disciples imitated them, and did not understand why Jesus did not require his disciples to do likewise. There was a great difference between John's disciples and Christ's in the matter of fasting. John's disciples imitated him, who "came neither eating nor drinking." On the other side, Christ's disciples followed him, who "came eating and drinking" as other men did. (Matt. 11: 18.) Thus did John's disciples and Christ's—the one fasted often, the other fasted not. The Pharisees fasted as well as John's disciples.

From this we learn that wicked men may be, and sometimes are, as strict and forward in the outward duties of religion as the holiest and best of Christians. They pray, they fast, they

fast, but thy disciples fast not? 19 And Jesus said unto them, Can the °sons of the bridechamber fast, while the bridegroom is with them? as long as they have the bridegroom with them, they cannot fast. 20 But the days will

°That is, *companions of the bridegroom.*

hear the word, they partake in the Lord's Supper; they do, yea, it may be, they outdo and go beyond the sincerest Christian in external duties and outward performances. Fasting was always connected with sorrow and humiliation. When the Jew sinned God forsook him or punished him. Under a sense of sin and sorrow he humbled himself, fasted and prayed that he might be freed from sin, might draw near to God, so that God would draw near to him. So fasting and mourning for sin are connected. Fasting rather grows out of a sense of sinfulness and a desire to humble the flesh before God than out of any command to fast. Fasting, like prayer, grows out of our sense of need of help from God, and leads us to draw close to him in spirit. The Pharisees fasted often as a display of piety. This was hypocrisy.

19 **And Jesus said unto them,**—In the question about eating with publicans and sinners, the complaint was made to the disciples about Jesus; but this time the complaint is placed before Jesus about his disciples. In both instances, Jesus makes the reply. The reply to this question is as unexpected and as logical as was the former, and made still more striking by its being borrowed from a well-known custom of that country, namely, from its marriage ceremonies, and especially from the practice of the bridegroom bringing home his bride accompanied by select friends, rejoicing over them and for them.

Can the sons of the bridechamber fast, while the bridegroom is with them? as long as they have the bridegroom with them, they cannot fast.—The form of the question here asked by Jesus is idiomatic, being that used when a negative answer is expected. The nearest approach to it in English is a negative followed by a question—they cannot—can they? The incapacity implied is not a physical but a moral one. They cannot be expected or required to fast; there is no reason why they should fast. The general principle involved or presupposed is that fasting is not a periodical or stated, but a special and occasional, observance, growing out of a particular emer-

come, when the bridegroom shall be taken away from them, and then will

gency. This doctrine underlies the whole defense of his disciples, which proceeds upon the supposition that a fast, to be acceptable and useful, must have a reason and occasion of its own, beyond a general propriety or usage. It is also assumed that fasting is not a mere *opus operatum,* but the cause and the effect of a particular condition, that of spiritual grief or sorrow. (Matt. 9: 15.) "Sons of the bridechamber" were the male attendants of the bridegroom, who, on the day of marriage, accompanied him to the home of the bride, to bring her home. This would remind John's disciples that he taught them Christ is the bridegroom (John 3: 29); and the Pharisees that their prophets, in speaking of Christ, used the same figure to illustrate the relation between God and Israel (Ps. 45; Isa. 54: 5; 62: 5). Jesus compared himself to the bridegroom, his disciples to the children of the bridechamber, or friends who were eating at the bridal feast; and that he, as the bridegroom, was with his friends.

The guests at the wedding cannot mourn. Mourning or fasting on such occasions would be out of order. It is a time of rejoicing and feasting, instead of mourning and fasting. While Jesus, the bridegroom, was with his disciples, they were enjoying a wedding feast, and it would be out of order to fast as if they were mourning. But when he left them they would fast, because that would be a time of sorrow. Real fasting takes place when there is real occasion for it. (Acts 13: 2; 14: 23; 2 Cor. 6: 5; 11: 27.) Probably John's disciples were mourning and fasting, because John, their friend, had been taken from them and placed in prison. If so, it was a time of fasting with them. But with the disciples of Jesus, it was a time of festivity and rejoicing. Their sorrow had not as yet come upon them. There must be a reason, something that calls for fasting and makes it appropriate. The arbitrary appointment of fast days, such as has been made by the Romish and other churches, is out of harmony with the teaching of Jesus.

20 **But the days will come,**—The time will come when Jesus, the bridegroom, will be put to death—when the circumstances will be changed, and fasting with his disciples will be

they fast in that day. 21 No man seweth a piece of undressed cloth on an

---

becoming and very appropriate. When he is taken away, then their festivity will be ended, *then* will be the proper time of sorrow and fasting.

when the bridegroom shall be taken away from them,—A prediction of the death of Christ.

and then will they fast in that day.—The day or time of Christ's death and removal. That will be a special time of sorrow and of fasting for his disciples. That will be the time to use the tokens of sorrow and grief. The duty of fasting, being thus dependent upon circumstances, may and will become incumbent when those circumstances change, as they are certainly to change hereafter. The bridegroom is not always to be visibly present, and when he departs, the time of fasting will be come. To express this more strongly, he is said to be removed or taken away, as if by violence. *Then,* at the time of this removal, as an immediate temporary cause of sorrow, not forever afterwards, which would be inconsistent with the principle already laid down, that the value of religious fasting is dependent on its being an occasional and not a stated duty. There is no foundation therefore for the doctrine of some Romish writers, who evade this argument against their stated fasts, by alleging that, according to our Lord's own declaration, the church after his departure was to be a fasting church. But this would be equivalent to saying that the Savior's exaltation would consign his people to perpetual sorrow. For he evidently speaks of grief and fasting as inseparable, and in Matthew's narrative of his reply, the former term is substituted for the latter. (Matt. 9: 15.) Even the plural form, *in those days,* has respect to the precise time of his departure, much more the singular, *in that day,* which the latest critics have adopted as the true text.

21 No man seweth a piece of undressed cloth on an old garment:—Jesus in reply to his interrogators used three illustrations, all of them going to establish the same thing, namely, that we should observe a fitness and propriety in things. The first is taken from a marriage. Having fully stated the facts and made the applications of this illustration, Jesus here in-

old garment: else that which should fill it up taketh from it, the new from the old, and a worse rent is made. 22 And no man putteth new wine into old 'wine-skins; else the wine will burst the skins, and the wine perisheth, and the skins: but *they put* new wine into fresh wine-skins.

'That is, *skins used as bottles*.

---

troduces a second which was familiar to all his auditors— namely, putting new cloth as patches on old garments. This, like the first illustration, shows that there is *a propriety or fitness of things*. Mark states how the patch is put on by the word "seweth." He points out to his hearers what no one of them would think of doing.

else that which should fill it up taketh from it, the new from the old, and a worse rent is made.—Jesus here gives the reason why an old garment should not be patched with new cloth. A patch from new cloth would shrink and tear the old cloth and make the slit in the old garment larger. Such patching would be folly. But it would be just as unbecoming and foolish to unite fasting, which is a sign of sorrow and grief, with the joyous work of the disciples of Jesus, while he, the bridegroom, is with them. "What is meant is not simply new cloth, but cloth which has not been completely dressed. A part of the process of preparing woolen cloth for use consists in shrinking it, and a patch of unfulled cloth not duly shrunk would contract the first time it became wet; and, as the older and weaker cloth around it must give way, the result would be a worse rent. We must remember that Jewish garments at that day were all wool; and if unfulled, would shrink like our flannel." (Broadus.)

22 And no man putteth new wine into old wine-skins; else the wine will burst the skins, and the wine perisheth, and the skins: but they put new wine into fresh wine-skins.—This is the third illustration to demonstrate that we should observe a fitness and propriety in things. It, like the other two, was familiar and well understood by his hearers. [He presents the incongruity of applying the rules and practices that had grown up under the Jewish law, or even the preaching of John the Baptist to the disciples of Jesus, by another comparison: putting unfermented wines into old, dried skins, that had been stretched and dried until they had lost all their elasticity.

Under the fermentation of the wine in the new skin, the skin
would yield and stretch so there would be no danger of the
skin bursting and losing both it and the wine. In the dried
skin the fermentation of the wine would cause the skin to
burst, and the wine would be spilled, the skin worthless.]
The argument drawn from these two examples is not, as some
have supposed, that it would be absurd to patch the old Jewish garment with the unfulled cloth of the gospel, or to put
the new wine of the gospel into the old Jewish bottles; for the
question at issue was not one concerning the proper relation
of the gospel dispensation to the old Jewish law, but one concerning the propriety of fasting on a certain occasion.
Moreover, in Luke's report of this answer we find the additional argument, "No man having drunk old wine desireth
new; for he saith, The old is good." (Luke 5: 39.) To carry
out the interpretation just named would make Jesus here
argue that the old dispensation was better than the new. But
the argument is the same as in the first example. It shows
that it would have been absurdly inappropriate to the occasion
for his disciples to fast, as much so as to mourn at a wedding,
to patch an old garment with unfulled cloth, or to put new
wine into old bottles. The arguments not only vindicated his
disciples, but taught John's disciples that fasting has value
only when it is demanded by a suitable occasion.

4. PLUCKING CORN ON THE SABBATH
2: 23-28
(Matt. 12: 1-8; Luke 6: 1-5)

23 And it came to pass, that he was going on the sabbath day through the

---

23 **And it came to pass, that he was going on the sabbath
day through the grainfields;**—Sabbath was the seventh day or
our Saturday. A day of rest for both man and beast of burden. The name is derived from a Hebrew verb, meaning to
rest from labor, to *cease* from action. In Judea, grain begins
to ripen around the first of May. It was at this time Jesus
and his disciples were going through the grainfields.
Matthew says: "They walked." They were fields sown with
wheat or barley.

grainfields; and his disciples [8]began, as they went, to pluck the ears. 24 And
the Pharisees said unto him, Behold, why do they on the sabbath day that
which is not lawful? 25 And he said unto them, [9]Did ye never read what

[8]Gr. *began to make* their *way plucking.*
[9]1 S. xxi. 6.

and his disciples began, as they went, to pluck the ears.—
[Several months have been passed over and we are now in the
early summer of the second year of the public ministry of
Jesus. The corn mentioned here is wheat or barley. Wheat
can be rubbed out in the hand and eaten, and will satisfy hunger, while it is fairly palatable. This must have been when
the wheat was ripe, yet in the fields, either before it was cut
or while in the shock. This is too late for the harvest of the
first year, so must be in the summer of the second year of the
public ministry of Jesus. They began to gather the wheat
heads and rub out the wheat in their hands (Luke 6: 1) and
eat. It was not wrong, according to the Jewish law, for men
to take enough of the fruits or the grain to satisfy hunger.
They could take nothing away. (Deut. 23: 24.) The disciples did not violate this law, but the point raised by the Pharisees, was it a violation of the Sabbath law to gather and eat
the grain on the Sabbath day?]

24 **And the Pharisees**—The Pharisees were a kind of Jewish
Puritans, but had in our Savior's time degenerated into a sect
of formalists, who paid more attention to outward forms than
to inner life. They were very scrupulous in observing ceremonies, very orthodox, but were filled with spiritual pride
and thought themselves wise. They soon became strong opposers of Christ.

**said unto him, Behold, why do they on the sabbath day that
which is not lawful?**—An exclamation of surprise expressed to
Jesus by the Pharisees. They desired to direct his attention
to something strange and unexpected. Here a fourth charge
or ground of opposition, on the part of the more scrupulous
and rigid Jews, was brought against Jesus, namely, suffering
his disciples to do what was unlawful. They demand with
what right, or by what authority, he allowed them to do this.
The question implies censure. They considered plucking the
heads was a kind of reaping, and rubbing out the grain, a kind
of threshing, and this they considered unlawful. It was doing

David did, when he had need, and was hungry, he, and they that were with him? 26 How he entered into the house of God [10]when Abiathar was high priest, and ate the showbread, which it is not lawful to eat save for the priests, and gave also to them that were with him? 27 And he said unto

[10]Some ancient authorities read *in the days of Abiathar the high priest.*

work, namely, harvesting on the Sabbath. The disciples really transgressed, not the divine law of the Sabbath, but the Pharisaical interpretation of that law. [All the Jews, in theory at least, held the law of Moses in reverence. The Pharisees were especial sticklers for the observance of all the forms of the law to the neglect of the spirit. The Sabbath had been very sacred by the enactment of Moses and the teaching of succeeding prophets. The Pharisees were shocked that the disciples of Christ should violate the law concerning the Sabbath and made complaints to Jesus. It was done in a fault-finding spirit with Jesus.]

25 **And he said unto them, Did ye never read what David did, when he had need, and was hungry, he, and they that were with him?**—Note the emphasis on *need* and *hungry*. His followers, too, were hungry; but it is on the act of David, as one of the most eminent of the Jews, that our Lord concentrates attention. [David (1 Sam. 21 : 1-6) had come to the priest at Nob hungry and wearied; had asked for bread. The priest said: "There is no common bread." So the priest gave him hallowed bread, "for there was no bread there but the showbread, that was taken from before Jehovah, to put hot bread in the day when it was taken away." The showbread was replaced with fresh bread every Sabbath. The priest then ate the old.] David and his followers under necessity took and ate the showbread which was lawful for priests only to eat. *Necessity* rose higher than ceremonials.

26 **How he entered into the house of God when Abiathar was high priest, and ate the showbread,**—The tabernacle was at Nob, an eminence near Jerusalem; on the north probably within sight of the city. The showbread was the bread that was kept on the golden table in the Holy Place.

which it is not lawful to eat save for the priests, and gave also to them that were with him?—David and those that were with him entered into the tabernacle and ate the showbread.

them, The sabbath was made for man, and not man for the sabbath: 28 so
that the Son of man is lord even of the sabbath.

David took, ate, and gave to his companions. Whatever may
have been the meaning of this singular observance, it was certainly a necessary and divinely instituted part of the tabernacle service, resting on the same authority, though not on the
equal moment with the Sabbath. [The tabernacle was movable
as long as the children of Israel were wandering and unset-
tled; but as soon as they had taken full possession of the
promised land, which was not till the reign of David, and in
the reign of Solomon, the portable tent was exchanged for a
permanent substantial dwelling.] To do good was made lawful by Moses without distinction of days but the Pharisees
had denied its lawfulness on the Sabbath day. Christ shows
them from their own law, and by the example of David, that it
was not unlawful to do good on the Sabbath day. [This
showbread was kept before the Lord seven days; it was then
replaced with fresh bread, and the old was eaten by the
priests. David, being hungry, ate of it and gave it to his companions. The meaning of it was that David, a servant of God,
was permitted, in case of necessity, to eat of this bread that
was lawful only for the priests.]

27 And he said unto them, The sabbath was made for man,
—For man's whole body, for body and soul, for physical rest,
for mental and social improvement, for his spiritual and moral
growth, and for his eternal salvation. They treat man as
nothing but an animal who advocate the use of the Sabbath
for mere physical recreation and pleasure. The Sabbath was
not made for man's *physical body* only, but for *man*, his whole
nature. And it was made for man as man, that is, *all men;*
and it was to be so kept so as not to take it away from others. Christ's principles carried out would have brought a perfect keeping of the Sabbath. It was made for man's benefit
and happiness. It was created for his use and intended for his
highest spiritual good. To keep it holy—that is, the manner
of keeping it, must be in accordance with its design. It was
for his rest from toil, the cares and anxieties of the world, to
give an opportunity to call off his attention from earthly con-
cerns, and to direct it to the affairs of eternity. It was a kind

provision for man that he might refresh his body by relaxing his labors; that he might have undisturbed time to seek the consolation of religion to cheer him in the anxieties and sorrows of a troubled world; and that he might render to God that homage which is most justly due to him as the Creator, Preserver, and Benefactor. The Sabbath here mentioned is the seventh day Sabbath and the Jews were to keep it in remembrance of their deliverance from bondage in Egypt. The Sabbath day and the first day of the week are two separate and distinct days and we ought not to confound the two. The Lord came from the grave on the first day of the week, making it possible for us to be delivered from the bondage of sin through his blood. For this cause the early Christians observed this day—they assembled around the Lord's table and partook of the Lord's Supper and carried out all the Lord's directions concerning that day. It was never called the Sabbath day in the New Testament and the name ought not to be applied to it now. The first day of the week is called the Lord's day (Rev. 1: 10), but never the Sabbath day. No day has been more blessed to man's welfare than the first day of the week—the Lord's day. To that day we owe more than to any other day, the peace and order of civilization. Where there is no Lord's day, there is ignorance, vice, disorder, and crime. On that day, man may offer his praises to the Giver of all good, and around the Lord's table seek the blessings of him whose favor is life. When that day is observed as it should be, order prevails, morals are promoted, the poor are elevated in their condition, vice flies away, and the community puts on the appearance of neatness, industry, morality, and religion.

and not man for the sabbath:—Man is not to be injured and his true interests destroyed for the sake of any law or any day. [It was made to bless and benefit man, and when the good of man demanded it the stringency of its law might be relaxed, or itself might be taken out of the way, as those concerning the eating the showbread had been for David. Matthew (12: 5, 6) adds: "Or have ye not read in the law, that on the sabbath day the priests in the temple profane the sabbath, and are guiltless? But I say unto you, that one greater than the temple is here." The law of God was, "Ye shall kindle no fire throughout your habitations upon the sabbath day" (Ex. 35: 3), and they were to do no cooking, yet in the temple service they cooked the showbread on the Sabbath. This was done by the order of God, and the point Jesus makes is that God, for the sake of the temple service, set aside the Sabbath law, and here is one greater than the temple, and who has the authority to repeal or supersede the Sabbath law. He acted by the authority of God, and being divine could set the law of the Sabbath aside. But he did not deny they broke the Sabbath law.] The argument here is the law of the Sabbath is to bend to the highest interest and happiness of man, and not the highest interest and happiness of man to the Sabbath. The Sabbath laws must not, by a superstitious observance, be perverted to the exclusion of mercy and necessity. The Sabbath was not first made, and then man made to fit the Sabbath. Man was made first, and then the Sabbath was made to fit the man. Since it was intended for his good, therefore, the law respecting it must not be interpreted so as to oppose his real welfare. It must be interpreted in consistency with a proper attention to the duties of mercy to the poor and the sick, and to those in peril.

28 so that the Son of man is lord even of the sabbath.—He ordained the Sabbath; he instituted the law; he knew its full meaning and object and value, and therefore had a right to interpret the meaning of the Sabbath law. [If they could set aside the law for David, in reference to the showbread, because he was hungry, or if God would change the Sabbath law to have the bread cooked on the Sabbath, he was Lord of the Sabbath to modify its laws for his disciples. The whole argument is an assertion of his power to supersede or set aside the law of the Sabbath. Necessity freed David from fault and blame in eating the showbread, for in cases of necessity a ceremonial precept must give way to a moral duty. Works of mercy and necessity for preserving life, and for better fitting men for Sabbath services, were certainly lawful on the Sabbath day. The passage teaches, then, not that men might violate the law of the Sabbath when their welfare *seemed* to them to demand it, but that Jesus could set it aside, as he afterward did, when his own judgment of man's welfare required him to do so. He made it clear on this occasion that said law was not to be so construed as to prevent men from providing necessary food on the Sabbath day.]

5. JESUS HEALING ON THE SABBATH
3: 1-6
(Matt. 12: 9-14; Luke 6: 6-11)

1 And he entered again into the synagogue; and there was a man there who had his hand withered. 2 And they watched him, whether he would heal him on the sabbath day; that they might accuse him. 3 And he saith unto the man that had his hand withered, [11]Stand forth. 4 And he saith unto

[11]Gr. *Arise into the midst.*

1 **And he entered again into the synagogue; and there was a man there who had his hand withered.**—Luke 6: 6 says: "His right hand," making it a more serious affliction than if it had been the left unless the man was left-handed. [Telling of what he did and said on one Sabbath seems to call up his action on another, and it is here given without regard to time. He entered into the synagogue on the Sabbath and found a man with a withered hand. His known readiness to relieve the afflicted, and the knowledge that he had not observed the Sabbath as strictly as they thought the law required, made them watch to see what he would do to the withered hand.]

2 **And they watched him, whether he would heal him on the sabbath day; that they might accuse him.**—Of Sabbath breaking, and thus be able to stop his preaching. They were watching his every move to get some ground of accusation, that they might accuse Jesus to both the people and the civil authorities. They asked him, "Is it lawful to heal on the, sabbath day?" (Matt. 12: 9.) They were anxious to lead him into a trap. [Seeing him, he determined to heal him, and so commanded him to stand forth in the midst so all could see what was done.] The law of Moses did not forbid works of healing on the Sabbath day, but the traditions and the interpretations of the Pharisees did; and they cared more for their conceited and perverted religious rules and ceremonies than they did for the welfare of any man.

3 **And he saith unto the man that had his hand withered, Stand forth.**—Luke 6: 8 says: "He knew their thoughts; and

them, Is it lawful on the sabbath day to do good, or to do harm? to save a
life, or to kill? But they held their peace. 5 And when he had looked

he said to the man that had his hand withered, Rise up, and
stand forth in the midst. And he arose and stood forth."
Jesus saw that a crisis was at hand and an issue must be
made, and he determined to make it bold and plain—as conspicuous as possible. [He was rooting out their ideas concerning the Sabbath, and brought the point before their
minds: it is to do good or evil on the Sabbath; to heal a man
or let him remain suffering; carried out to save life, or in failing to save to let it perish, or destroy it. To fail to save life
when we can is to be guilty of destroying it. These were the
questions involved. He laid them before them and asked,
What is right?]

4 **And he saith unto them, Is it lawful on the sabbath day to
do good, or to do harm? to save a life, or to kill?**—He puts it
squarely up to them. He answers not only their evil thoughts
which he knew (Luke 6: 8), but their question (Matt. 12: 10)
as well. The *principle* of *doing good* on the Sabbath is being
clearly drawn. He makes a center thrust at his opposers.

But they held their peace.—Refused to answer, for they
could not without condemning themselves. Jesus made a
home thrust and drove them to the wall. The question put
them in a dilemma. They were the ones that were breaking
the Sabbath law, and the whole sum of the commandments,
which is love. [Luke (6: 7) says: "And the scribes and the
Pharisees watched him." Matt. (12: 10-12) says: "And behold, a man having a withered hand. And they asked him,
saying, Is it lawful to heal on the sabbath day? that they
might accuse him. And he said unto them, What man shall
there be of you, that shall have one sheep, and if this fall into
a pit on the sabbath day, will he not lay hold on it, and lift it
out? How much then is a man of more value than a sheep!
Wherefore it is lawful to do good on the sabbath day." If
this was the same conversation, Matthew states it more fully,
and shows they were trying to excite the Jewish prejudices
against him for healing on the Sabbath. But he placed before
them their inconsistency in taking a sheep out of the pit,
which they did not condemn, while refusing to heal a man of

round about on them with anger, being grieved at the hardening of their heart, he saith unto the man, Stretch forth thy hand. And he stretched it

his afflictions, and placed before them the issue, it was to do good by healing, or evil by leaving him unhealed; carried out, to save life by healing, or to destroy it by leaving him to perish? Seeing their own inconsistency and determined to condemn him, they held their peace. This was an unfair and unmanly way of meeting a question they had raised. Saving the ox or the ass from the pit was doing good on the Sabbath day; to heal the man or to save his life was a greater good. To fail to save life when it is in our power is to destroy it.]

5 And when he had looked round about on them with anger, —Anger, when applied to God and to Jesus, is not passion, but a deep, moral resentment against wrong. It is perfectly consistent with love for the sinner; indeed it is a fruit of love. It would be base and sinful not to be kindled to indignation by baseness, treachery, cruelty, and hypocrisy. This indignation is one of the motive powers of all reformatory movements.

being grieved at the hardening of their heart,—He was as sorry as he was indignant. He was grieved at their spiritual dullness. The words translated "being grieved" imply sympathy and pity for those in such a miserable and hardhearted state. They were so blind to the truth that they mistook prejudice for religion. The heart, which is the seat of feeling, or affection, is tender when it is easily affected by the sufferings and pains of others; by our own sins and anger; by the love and commands of God. It is hard when nothing touches or moves it; when a man is alike insensible to the sufferings of others, the dangers of his own condition, and the commands, the love, and the threatenings of God. It is most tender in youth,   or   when   we   have   committed   the   fewest   sins. Doubtless the wise man had this in view, when he said: "Remember also thy Creator in the days of thy youth." (Eccl. 12: 1-3.) The heart is made hard by indulgence in sin; by resisting the offers of life; or by opposing appeals which God makes through the gospel.

he saith unto the man, Stretch forth thy hand. And he stretched it forth; and his hand was restored.—[He was grieved at the hardening of their hearts in refusing to see the

forth; and his hand was restored. 6 And the Pharisees went out, and straightway with the Herodians took counsel against him, how they might destroy him.

---

truth. He was angry with such a sinful course, but determined to pursue the right, he commanded the man to stretch forth his hand, and on stretching it out, it was restored whole. Here the man showed his faith by doing what Jesus commanded, and in trying to obey, Jesus gave the hand strength. He blessed when faith showed itself in stretching out the hand. Faith was made perfect by doing the thing commanded. In all the examples of healing through faith, this order is observed. Faith proves itself by obeying God, or, in the absence of a command, in doing something that expresses the faith in God. Faith never molds character until it moves to action. Let it be noted that God gives the needed help when we make an effort to do his commands.]

6 And the Pharisees went out, and straightway with the Herodians took counsel against him,—A political rather than a religious body. They were such Jews as favored Herod Antipas, especially in his attempts to be made king over the whole kingdom of his father, Herod the Great, which had been divided into several portions under governors appointed by Rome. "They joined the Sadducees in skepticism, the Greeks in licentiousness, pandered to the Herods in vice and cruelty, and truckled to the Romans." The union of these two opposite parties shows how intense was their feeling against Jesus. The Pharisees and Herodians were fierce political enemies, yet they unite in plotting against Jesus. Opposition to Jesus had been aroused some weeks before this at the Passover at Jerusalem (John 5: 16), and the flame was fanned by the memory of his driving out the cattle and money-changers from the temple the year before. It was increased also by his teaching and miracles, and still more so by his rising popularity and his wonderful works.

how they might destroy him.—They advised among themselves not whether they *would* destroy him, but *how* they might destroy him. They had already determined to do it, but *how* was the question to settle.

6. JESUS HEALS MANY
3: 7-12
(Matt. 12: 15-21)

7 And Jesus with his disciples withdrew to the sea: and a great multitude from Galilee followed; and from Judaea, 8 and from Jerusalem, and from

---

7 And Jesus with his disciples withdrew to the sea:—From Capernaum, and from the plots which ripened most easily in cities, the hotbeds of intrigue. He had been victorious in the conflict with the Pharisees, he now retires from the scene and pursues his own course, and in other places continues his work. His retreat before his enemies was prompted, not by fear, but by that wise discretion which he constantly employed in the selection and the use of the necessary means for the promotion of the great end which he came to accomplish. The prudent means which Jesus uses to preserve himself from the rage of his enemies ought to teach us our duty in time of danger, to flee from our enemies, and endeavor to preserve our lives. We ought not to remain in, nor press into danger. God has endowed us with wisdom, if rightly used, to avoid such dangers. He had one great purpose in view, and he faced his enemies or withdrew from them, according as he could best accomplish his work. He was not afraid to go away, nor afraid to remain if need be. In many cases it is better quietly to withdraw from a hostile crowd, and do one's work elsewhere.

and a great multitude from Galilee followed; and from Judaea,—[While the Pharisees and Herodians were consulting how they might destroy him, he quietly, with his disciples, withdrew from the city (they were yet in Capernaum) to the seaside. This was a favorite resort with them, and a great multitude of people from Galilee followed him (he was in Galilee) and from Judea. Judea was the territory and home of the Jews, the children of Judah, the son of Jacob, whose family remained faithful to the house of David and continued to meet at Jerusalem when the ten tribes of Israel withdrew and followed Jeroboam. But in the wars, captivities, and desolations of the people when they sinned, they were scattered, and these Jews seemed to have the ascendancy in Galilee.]

Idumaea, and beyond the Jordan, and about Tyre and Sidon, a great multitude, hearing [12]what great things he did, came unto him. 9 And he spake to his disciples, that a little boat should wait on him because of the crowd, lest they should throng him: 10 for he had healed many; insomuch that as many

[12]Or, *all the things that he did*

---

8 **and from Jerusalem, and from Idumaea, and beyond the Jordan, and about Tyre and Sidon, a great multitude, hearing what great things he did, came unto him.**—[The people from these different countries were Jews who had, in their dispersion, settled in these different countries. They, in common with the Jews in Judea, looked for a deliverer to come and gather the scattered tribes, the lost sheep of the house of Israel, back to their land and country. Hearing of the miracles and works of Jesus, they came from all these lands to Capernaum to see and hear him, and to judge of his claim. They followed him out to the seaside with his disciples on this occasion. The places named show how widely his influence had already reached. There must have been great power in him to attract the inhabitants of Jerusalem, the capital, to the province of Galilee, sixty or seventy miles away. Idumea, the Greek name for Edom, the territory that lay south of Palestine, stretched toward the southeast and included the mountainous region east of the Dead Sea. The Edomites were descendants of Esau, but had been conquered and made Jews by violence about 125 B.C. The Herod family came from Idumea. So from every quarter, and far out, many came seeking him. The Pharisees, the mighty, the noble, and the wise men after the flesh, despised his person, slighted his ministry, and sought his life. The ordinary sort of people have always been more zealous and forward in embracing the gospel than the rich, the great, and the honorable part of the world has been. It is a sad but a certain truth, heaven is a place where few, comparatively, of the great men of the world are likely to be.] Not because they *cannot,* but because they *will not.*

9 **And he spake to his disciples, that a little boat should wait on him because of the crowd, lest they should throng him:**—[When the multitudes pressed upon and crowded him on the shore, he sometimes got in the boat (the ships were but boats), and they pushed out a little from the shore. He sat in

as had ¹plagues ²pressed upon him that they might touch him. 11 And the
unclean spirits, whensoever they beheld him, fell down before him, and cried,

¹Gr. *scourges.*
²Gr. *fell.*

the boat and taught the people upon the shore. This was spoken for lest they should throng or crowd him uncomfortably.]
He who loves the Savior will not be surprised to find how
many things there are that he can consecrate, and that Christ
can use. Some persons cannot preach unless they have a proper pulpit, their priestly robe, organ, choir, and other things:
but Christ is at home anywhere, and can preach afloat as well
as in the synagogue.

**10 for he had healed many; insomuch that as many as had
plagues pressed upon him that they might touch him.**—Those
who merely touched him in faith were healed. (5: 28-30.)
Jesus required some sensible connection with himself in his
cures, to show that the healing came from him, and to teach
them the lessons of faith, that their spiritual healing came
from spiritual union with Christ. [His healing many without
fee or reward caused all who were afflicted, real and imaginary, to press upon him that they might touch him, as the
touch caused virtue to go out of him to heal. With those who
desired to be healed was the crowd that always is attracted by
wonderful works or strange performances.]

**11 And the unclean spirits, whensoever they beheld him, fell
down before him, and cried, saying, Thou art the Son of God**
—They fell down at his feet, doing homage as it were. As
spirits they knew the truth about Christ. In the presence of
Christ, they dared speak only the truth. The persons possessed with unclean spirits fell before Jesus, and again acknowledged him as the Son of God. This proves the existence
of evil spirits. If these were only diseased persons, then it is
strange that they should be endowed with knowledge so much
superior to those in health. How complete these spirits possessed the bodies of men is seen to the extent they used the
powers and organs of those possessed in seeing, falling down
before him as a sort of an act of homage, and proclaiming him
to be the Son of God. They did not fall down before him to
worship him in spirit and in truth.

saying, Thou art the Son of God. 12 And he charged them much that they should not make him known.

---

12 **And he charged them much that they should not make him known.**—Who he was. The witness of devils would not be believed even when true; and, the more of such testimony willingly received, the more it would hinder men from believing the truth, for it would be charged that Jesus was in alliance with evil spirits, and that he cast out demons through Beelzebub, the prince of the demons. [He gave a strict charge to those who were healed that they should not make him known. He hushed the mouths of the demons when they were disposed to confess him, but often when he healed the afflicted he charged they should not tell it. The chief motive seems to have been to avoid the crowds of men, curiosity mongers, that were led to follow him by these reports. There was no prospect of that class of people being benefited, yet they followed and thronged him in his ministrations. Only the sincere, honest-hearted people would believe in him.] There was nothing in common between Jesus and demons; there was no friendly relationship between him and Satan. The effects of Christ's mission proved it to be divine. And today, as in those days, the convincing proof of Christianity is found in its beneficent effects. It makes everybody better who accepts it. The drunkard becomes sober, the selfish becomes generous, the vile becomes pure. Schools, colleges, education, hospitals, missions, all forms of benevolence spring up where Christ is believed. Wherever there is the most Christianity, there is the most of all things that raise and bless men. The map of the world is a proof of the Christian religion.

7. THE TWELVE APOSTLES APPOINTED
3: 13-19
(Matt. 10: 1-4; Luke 6: 12-16)

13 And he goeth up into the mountain, and calleth unto him whom he

---

13 **And he goeth up into the mountain,**—[Luke (6: 12, 13) says: "That he went out into the mountain to pray; and he continued all night in prayer to God. And when it was day, he called his disciples; and he chose from them twelve, whom

himself would; and they went unto him. 14 And he appointed twelve, [3]that

[3]Some ancient authorities add *whom also he named apostles.* See Lk. 6. 13; comp. ch. 6. 30.

also he named apostles." The example of Jesus going aside and alone praying through the whole night to God as a preparation for choosing twelve apostles is suggestive to us. He felt the infirmity and the weakness of the flesh as we do. He felt the burdens and responsibilities of his position and his actions, on which depended the future well-being of the world. While he was divine in person, knowledge and power, it did not relieve him of the feeling of human weakness, so he carried the matter to God, and spent the whole night in humble and earnest prayer to God for wisdom to guide him in the matter. If Jesus felt the need of such prayer and was strengthened by it, how much more do we—poor, frail men and women—need constant help and strength, wisdom and guidance from God in our work? And how constant, humble, and earnest should we be in prayer to God for wisdom and strength." "Pray without ceasing." After praying through the night he called his disciples to him, and they came.]

and calleth unto him whom he himself would; and they went unto him.—"He himself" is very emphatic, and lays stress on the fact that the twelve were called and chosen by Jesus, not through the influence or at the suggestion of others. He prepared the way for a spiritual revolution by selecting and training men who should accomplish it. This included the establishment of his church. This revolution was to rest upon his own atoning death as its foundation. For the same reason, he did not develop the whole system of Christian doctrine but left both these tasks to be accomplished after his resurrection and ascension, yet preparing the way for both, by teaching and training those who should complete the church, both as to its organization and doctrine. This preparatory process was a gradual one. The first was in calling disciples to be with him as their teacher, and now selecting from these his apostles, whom he continues to school and prepare for completing the new movement after his departure. They were disciples before they were apostles. They were well trained by Christ before he allowed them to undertake such a

they might be with him, and that he might send them forth to preach, 15 and
to have authority to cast out demons: 16 [4]and Simon he surnamed Peter; 17

[4]Some ancient authorities insert *and he appointed twelve*.

public charge. Even then, he sent them the Holy Spirit to
guide them in their work. (John 6: 13.) We here reach a
turning point in the ministry of Jesus. Hitherto his work had
been personal and preparatory. This call of apostles begins a
broader work by trained workers.

14 **And he appointed twelve,**—The number twelve is significant. It expresses fullness, completeness, and strength.
There were the twelve patriarchs; the twelve tribes of Israel;
the twelve stones of the Urim and the Thummim on the
breastplate of the high priest (Ex. 28: 17-21); the twelve
loaves of showbread (Lev. 24: 5-8); the altar and twelve pillars which Moses erected by Mount Sinai (Ex. 24: 4); the
altar of twelve stones, by Elijah (1 Kings 18: 31); the New
Jerusalem with twelve foundation stones (Rev. 21: 14; "Upon
her head a crown of twelve stars" (Rev. 12: 1); a wall having
twelve gates and at the gates twelve angels (Rev. 21: 12); the
twelve gates were twelve pearls (Rev. 21: 21); and "the tree
of life, bearing twelve manner of fruits" (Rev. 22: 2). The
number occurs often in the Bible.

that they might be with him,—Apostle is one sent or commissioned. They were messengers. As constant personal attendants, and as learners, to be trained for their subsequent
work. He reveals the purpose for which he appointed them.
He appointed them at this time, but did not send them out
now. They are in the spiritual college, where they may complete their spiritual training, under Christ. Heretofore, they
were in the primary department.

and that he might send them forth to preach,—As they
were prepared to deliver the message. He "began to send
them forth by two and two." (6: 7.) After the ascension of
Christ, they were to preach everywhere (16: 15), but not until
after receiving power on Pentecost were they to be Christ's
witnesses, in Jerusalem, Judea, Samaria, and unto the utmost
parts of the earth (Acts 1: 8).

15 **and to have authority to cast out demons:**—Matthew
(10: 1) adds, "And to heal all manner of disease and all man-

and [5]James the *son* of Zebedee, and John the brother of [5]James; and them he surnamed Boanerges, which is, Sons of thunder: 18 and Andrew, and Philip,

[5]Or, *Jacob*

ner of sickness." Jesus would send the apostles to preach with authority to perform the same miracles he himself performed. [This power was given them to attest that God was with them, and that they had authority from him to act and teach for him. Their words were his words. Having given the apostles these signs, the world may rest assured that in hearing the words of the apostles they hear God himself. "He that heareth you heareth me." (Luke 10: 16.)]

16 and Simon he surnamed Peter;—The apostles are now named. Peter stands first and Judas at the end. [Andrew, Peter's brother, was one of the two disciples that came to Jesus on the testimony of John. So soon as he saw Jesus he believed he was the Christ. "He findeth first his own brother Simon, and saith unto him, We have found the Messiah (which is, being interpreted, Christ)." (John 1: 41.) To Andrew and Peter he first said: "Come ye after me, and I will make you to become fishers of men." (Mark 1: 17.) And now when he calls them to qualify for the work of apostles, Peter is the first called. In all lists of the apostles his name is first, indicating a preeminence. In enumerations in the New Testament the greatest come first.]

17 and James the son of Zebedee, and John the brother of James;—[James was the elder of the two, from the order of their names. They were called to the discipleship immediately after Peter and Andrew.]

18 and Andrew,—[Andrew was the brother of Peter, the first to find Jesus and bring Peter to him. Occasionally he is mentioned next to Peter as his brother, but when not so placed he was mentioned first after James and John. He seems to have had Peter's promptness in deciding his aggressive force in pushing work forward. We have no account of his afterlife. Tradition says he preached in Scythia, in Greece, in Asia Minor.]

and Philip,—[He was of Bethsaida, the home of Andrew, Peter, James, and John. Jesus told him, "Follow me," among

and Bartholomew, and Matthew, and Thomas, and [5]James the *son* of Alphaeus, and Thaddaeus, and Simon the [6]Cananaean, 19 and Judas Iscariot,
who also [7]betrayed him.

[6]Or, *Zealot.* See Lk. 6. 15; Acts 1. 13.
[7]Or, *delivered him up*

the first of his disciples called. He sought Nathanael and told
him: "We have found him, of whom Moses, in the law, and
the prophets, wrote." (John 1: 45.) Philip is always placed
first in the second group of three; is mentioned a few times in
the life of Jesus by John, but of his afterlife we know nothing.]

and Bartholomew,—[He is thought to be Nathanael, called
to Jesus by Philip, in connection with whose name his is always associated. He asked, "Can any good thing come out of
Nazareth?" and when he came, Jesus said of him: "Behold, an
Israelite indeed, in whom is no guile!" (John 1: 47.) He is
mentioned in John 21: 2 as of Cana, in Galilee, to whom, with
others, Jesus appeared after his resurrection. Tradition says
he preached in Judea.]

and Matthew,—[Matthew was a publican, a gatherer of
taxes, is called "Levi the son of Alphaeus." (2: 14.) He
wrote the gospel of Matthew. Of his later life nothing is
known.]

and Thomas,—[Of him we know but little. He is mentioned as one of the twelve apostles. When Jesus determined
to go into Judea against the protest of his disciples that they
had sought to kill him, Thomas said: "Let us also go, that we
may die with him." (John 11: 16.) This shows doubt and
gloomy forebodings, yet he was willing to go with him and
share his fate. Again he asks of Jesus, "Lord, we know not
whither thou goest; how know we the way?" (John 14: 5.)
Then after his resurrection he refused to believe the testimony
of the apostles that they had seen Jesus, but when Jesus
showed him his hand and side, he said: "My Lord and my
God." (John 20: 28.) Tradition says he preached in Persia.]

and James the son of Alphaeus,—[Or Cleophas, and brother
of our Lord, was the brother of Jude.]

and Thaddaeus,—[He was called Judas. (Luke 6: 15; Acts
1: 13.) He is brother of James the Less. He is mentioned in

John 14: 22: "Judas, not Iscariot, saith unto him, Lord, what is come to pass that thou wilt manifest thyself unto us, and not unto the world?" He, with James, is called the brother of the Lord; is thought to have written the epistle of Jude.]

and Simon the Cananaean,—[Luke calls him Simon Zelotes. (Luke 6: 15; Acts 1: 13.) Smith's Bible Dictionary says: "These names point him out as belonging to the faction of the Zelots who were conspicuous for their fierce advocacy of the Mosaic ritual." This refers to his position before he became a follower of Christ. We have no account of his later life. Beyond his name we really know nothing.]

19 **and Judas Iscariot, who also betrayed him.**—[He completes the list, and is always placed last as a mark of his unworthiness. We know but little of his early life. He is said to be the son of Simon, and is supposed to have been born in Judea in the village of Kerioth, hence the name Iscariot. But this is supposition without much ground. If he was of Judea, he is singular in this, since all the others were of Galilee. In John 6: 70, 71 Jesus says: "Did not I choose you the twelve, and one of you is a devil? Now he spake of Judas the son of Simon Iscariot, for he it was that should betray him, being one of the twelve." He was doubtless chosen because of his fitness in character for the work to which he was called. Jesus must be betrayed. One in character fitted for the work must do it. God could not impose such work on a good man. Peter might impulsively deny him, but could not coldly betray him. Judas was with the disciples during the ministry of Christ, seemingly earnest as his follower, and was endowed with miraculous powers as were the others. (Matt. 10: 1.) He was like many others. While without temptations and while things went favorably, he ran well. When the pathway darkened and the temptations multiplied, he failed and fell. He was weak, with sinful propensities that could not resist temptation, and when tried, fell. God tries all men, and unless they can stand temptation they are not fitted for his service.]

8. JESUS' FRIENDS ALARMED
3: 20, 21
(Matt. 12: 22 to 13)

And he cometh [8]into a house. 20 And the multitude cometh together again, so that they could not so much as eat bread. 21 And when his friends heard it, they went out to lay hold on him: for they said, He is beside him-

---

[8]Or, *home*

And he cometh into a house.—The meaning probably is found in the margin: "They came home." That is, to Capernaum (Matt. 9: 1), the headquarters of their operations.

20 **And the multitude cometh together again, so that they could not so much as eat bread.**—Jesus enters upon one of the busiest and most eventful days in all his history. He was so engaged about his Father's business there was no time for eating.

21 **And when his friends heard it, they went out to lay hold on him:**—They meant to take him away from the multitude, and to remove him to a place of safety and where he might be given medical attention (if need be) and be absent from the causes of excitement.

for they said, He is beside himself.—Probably the enemies of Jesus started the report that he was delirious, or deranged. The charge of derangement on account of attention to religious matters has not been confined to Jesus. Festus said: "Paul, thou art mad; thy much learning is turning thee mad." (Acts 26: 24.) Men may endanger themselves on the bosom of the ocean, or in the bowels of the earth, for wealth; or may plunge into the flood of fashion and folly, and vice, and break in upon the hours of repose, and neglect their duties to their family, and the demands of business, and in the view of the world it is wisdom. But, let a godly man lend his time and attention in the same way in building up the kingdom of God and saving souls, the charge comes, he is crazy or a crank—he is carried away by an unwise enthusiasm.

Jesus has been constantly teaching and healing amid enthusiastic crowds. Shortly before this he spent a whole night in prayer on a mountaintop, and now he is hindered from taking the necessary food; so his kindred determined to take charge of him, and stop all this. Solicitous of her son's welfare, his mother goes with them.

9. CHRIST'S POWER ASCRIBED TO BEELZEBUB
3: 2-27
(Matt. 12: 22-37; Luke 11: 14-22)

self. 22 And the scribes that came down from Jerusalem said, He hath
[9]Beelzebub, and, [10]By the prince of the demons casteth he out the demons. 23
And he called them unto him, and said unto them in parables, How can
Satan cast out Satan? 24 And if a kingdom be divided against itself, that

[9]Gr. *Beelzebul.*
[10]Or, *In*

---

22 And the scribes that came down from Jerusalem—
Scribes were wise men among the Jews, doubtless sent by
those in authority to watch the movements of Jesus. They
were his enemies and seeking to destroy his influence.
Matthew gives a fuller report of this matter. (Matt. 12: 22-
29.) The leaders were a delegation of men from the religious
sects at Jerusalem that finally put him to death.

said, He hath Beelzebub,—The meaning is, he is possessed
with Satan—Satan is with or in him, hence he has power over
inferior evil spirits—he is in league with the devil.

**and, By the prince of the demons casteth he out the de-
mons.—**"The prince of the demons" was the captain—that is
the chief ruler over all the devils. He was leader and com-
mander over all the host of evil spirits. Hence he is called the
devil. We can now see what use the scribes would have made
of the testimony before borne to Jesus, by evil spirits (Ch. 1:
34; 3: 12), if he had not rejected it; as well as the wisdom of
Jesus in rejecting it.

23 And he called them unto him,—Those who had made the
charge. Jesus, on this, as on other occasions, knew the
thoughts of the Pharisees (Matt. 12: 25), and now proposes to
discuss it out with them and expose their reasoning.

and said unto them in parables,—Parable means comparisons. It is commonly applied to our Lord's beautiful comparisons in the form of a narrative, but sometimes, as here, to
comparisons simply stated without the form of a story.

How can Satan cast out Satan?—Jesus begins his reply by
asking a question which was not answered except by himself.
The mere asking the question shows the absurdity and the impossibility of Satan fighting against his own agents and representatives. How can he fight against himself? To do this

kingdom cannot stand. 25 And if a house be divided against itself, that house will not be able to stand. 26 And if Satan hath risen up against him-

---

would be self-destructive. He would be fighting for God and against himself. [The scribes had said this to the people, not to him. Luke (11: 17) says: "He, knowing their thoughts"— that is, by divine wisdom he read their thoughts, perceived what they were thinking, so he called them to him, and spoke in parables. He used the effect of such a division in a kingdom or family presented in succeeding verses to show how, if their statements were true, then Satan was destroying his own kingdom. To cast a demon out was to dispossess him of his home; was to destroy his power to serve Satan. Demons did harm only as they entered into and misled men. How could Satan cast them out?]

24 And if a kingdom be divided against itself, that kingdom cannot stand.—He uses this as his first illustration to show them their folly in the charge they had made against him. If Satan casteth out Satan, he is divided against himself and hath risen up against himself; "how then shall his kingdom stand?" In this way Satan himself "cannot stand, but hath an end." [If an earthly kingdom be divided against itself, one part destroying another part, that kingdom would weaken and waste itself so as to be not able to stand, be brought to desolation, as Matthew says (12: 25.)] Their subtle and cunning device was completely overthrown, and Jesus made their own arguments recoil on their own heads. Jesus does not teach that the kingdom of Satan is at peace with itself. It is a kingdom of anarchy, conflict, hate. But in its relation to the kingdom of God it stands a unit.

25 And if a house be divided against itself, that house will not be able to stand.—This is the second illustration used by Jesus to show the folly of the scribes. Here, the word "house" is used for family. A family divided against its own interest and existence will not be able to stand, for the reason it has no solid foundation upon which to stand. It is resting upon sand which will give way. [The welfare of every family, nation, or body of any kind depends upon its unity of purpose and harmony of action. A ruling head must be recog-

self, and is divided, he cannot stand, but hath an end. 27 But no one can
enter into the house of the strong *man*, and spoil his goods, except he first

nized. If discord prevails and faction fight against faction,
ruin must come to the whole body.]

26 And if Satan hath risen up against himself, and is divided, he cannot stand, but hath an end.—Here our Lord applies what he has already said.

[If he by the power of Satan was casting out demons, the subjects and servants of Satan, dislodging them from the homes they had secured to go forth as homeless wanderers through desert places (Matt. 12: 43), then Satan in and through him was making war upon and destroying his own subjects; then he is so divided against himself that he cannot stand, but must come to an end. Matthew (12: 27, 28) tells he made his further reply: "And if I by Beelzebub cast out demons, by whom do your sons cast them out? Therefore shall they be your judges. But if I by the Spirit of God cast out demons, then is the kingdom of God come upon you." Some of their children claimed to cast out demons, and he made the thrust that "if I cast out demons by the power of Satan," they doubtless did also. The point he makes is, Satan would be foolish to so destroy his servants, and Satan has never been a fool. The weakness and ruin pictured here as produced by division in the household, the kingdoms of earth, or the kingdom of Satan, ought to warn Christians of the fearful weakness of division and strife in the church of Christ which so fearfully prevails, and ought to keep before Christians the important thought that union and harmony can be maintained in the church only by all accepting the things God has required, and rejecting every service not required by God in his holy word.]

27 But no one can enter into the house of the strong man,—The "strong man" is Satan. His house or palace is this lower world and the heart of man, the center of his work. These are his dwelling places. Satan, as well as Jesus, works and operates upon the heart. The human heart is the great battlefield. The future destiny of man depends upon which party succeeds in forcing the other out and gaining possession of the heart.

bind the strong *man;* and then he will spoil his house. 28 Verily I say

and spoil his goods, except he first bind the strong man; and then he will spoil his house.—The stronger than the "strong man" and who binds him is Christ. He first bound him when Satan endeavored to invade the heart of Jesus through his temptations and when he triumphed over the temptations. (Luke 11: 21, 22.) Here Jesus presses home one of his highest thoughts. [Jesus entered the heart of man, in which the subjects of Satan are fixed as their home, and has cast them out. Now, no man can enter a strong man's house (Satan is a strong man) and spoil his goods until he has first bound the strong man. If he binds him he shows he is stronger than the strong man. Jesus has done this with Satan, entered his house and bound him, and so shows he is stronger than he . Only God is stronger than Satan. Therefore he is God.] There is now, as there has ever been, no middle ground, between truth and error, right and wrong, true worship and vain worship. The fact that one endeavors to be noncommittal, "indifferent" or "on the fence," places him on the wrong side. If one is not actively engaged in the service of Christ, he is against Christ. One must work, climb up, and prove faithful until life ends to be saved; but he can be lost by doing nothing. He who does nothing is lost. But one of the most dangerous and despicable characters is he who identifies himself with God's true worshipers while he works subtly to undermine the truth and to advance false systems of worship.

10. SIN AGAINST THE HOLY SPIRIT
3: 28-30

unto you, All their sins shall be forgiven unto the sons of men, and their blasphemies wherewith soever they shall blaspheme: 29 but whosoever

28 Verily I say unto you, All their sins shall be forgiven unto the sons of men,—This embraces all responsible sons and daughters of men. All sins committed by the different members of the human race will be forgiven, upon proper repentance and obedience, except the one mentioned in next verse.

and their blasphemies wherewith soever they shall blaspheme:—Blasphemy is any kind of injurious speech about an-

shall blaspheme against the Holy Spirit hath never forgiveness, but is guilty

other. The scribes blasphemed when they attributed Christ's power to work miracles to the power of the devil. The statement that all manner of sin and blasphemy shall be forgiven to men is not an affirmation of universal pardon. But that all manner of sin and blasphemy, with the exception stated in the text, will be forgiven through the blood of Christ, some to one man and some to another, every conceivable sin will be forgiven except the one in question. [Sin is to violate the law or rule given by God to men. Violation of law is sin, and brings the penalty of sin. Intentional and conscious sin intensifies the guilt of sin. Paul sinned and obtained forgiveness because he did it ignorantly in unbelief (1 Tim. 1: 13), thinking he was doing God's service. To violate the law, thinking he did God's service, was a sin. To violate it, knowing it was God's law, would have been a greater sin. Blaspheme is to rail upon, to speak evil of. This verse intimates that speaking evil of all other beings, including God and Jesus Christ, should be forgiven men—on their repentance, of course, is meant. In this distinction drawn, to violate the law given by God is to sin against God, to violate a law given by Jesus is to sin against him, to violate a law given by the Holy Spirit is to sin against the Spirit.]

29 but whosoever shall blaspheme against the Holy Spirit —There seems to be three grades or degrees of blasphemy. (1) That against the Holy Spirit. This seems to be the greatest and the most dangerous. (2) That against the Son. (Matt. 12: 32.) (3) That against God, the Father.

hath never forgiveness,—I take it that Jesus did not charge the scribes had committed the unpardonable sin. He was warning them not to go this far. They had almost reached it when they accused him of casting out demons by the power of the devil, and he warns them not to take the next step of blaspheming the Holy Spirit for this would be the fatal step. [Hath never forgiveness because they cannot repent. So long as man can repent he can find forgiveness. This and corresponding passages in Matt. 12: 31 and Luke 12: 10 have been the occasion of much controversy and of much trouble and anxiety to despondent minds. Many think they have commit-

of an eternal sin: 30 because they said, He hath an unclean spirit.

ted the sin for which there is no forgiveness, and give themselves much trouble over it. Matthew says (12: 31, 32):
"Therefore I say unto you, Every sin and blasphemy shall be
forgiven unto men; but the blasphemy against the Spirit shall
not be forgiven. And whosoever shall speak a word against
the Son of man, it shall be forgiven him; but whosoever shall
speak against the Holy Spirit, it shall not be forgiven him,
neither in this world, nor in that which is to come." From
this we see that the speaking against the Son of man may be
forgiven, but speaking against the Holy Spirit cannot be forgiven. Blasphemy, speaking against, and all manner of sin,
are placed on an equality. What is the sin, then, against the
Holy Spirit? Many think these people committed that sin.
But did they speak against Christ or against the Holy Spirit?
Clearly against Christ; Jesus, as we understand it, told them,
in this you speak against me. For this there is chance for
forgiveness. But when the Holy Spirit is come, if you speak
against him, if you reject him, as you now reject me, there
will then be no forgiveness. It was a warning given on the
occasion of their speaking against him that they cannot so
treat the Holy Spirit when he shall come, and find forgiveness. The reason is, they speak against Christ during his life,
and when the Holy Spirit shall come he will give additional
evidence that Jesus is the Son of God, and opportunities to
hear God and turn. But when the Spirit shall have come and
given his testimonies and revelations, the testimony will be
complete, and he who rejects that will have nothing more to
move him to repentance.]

but is guilty of an eternal sin:—That is, a sin never to be
forgiven and will be punished eternally. Both the sin and
punishment are eternal. The penalty is eternal because the
sin is eternal. This is one of the most fearful sentences ever
spoken. With sin, penalty and punishment must ever go; and
to be cut off forever from moral remedy, to have no hope of
reformation, every one who is capable of thought knows what
that means. The terror of an evil life is its *final* choice, its
fixedness of character. There is nothing more sure than that
there is an unpardonable sin—a sin for which there is no

space for repentance. It is possible to go beyond the reach of God's mercy—bounds beyond which forgiveness never reclaims. "There is a sin unto death: not concerning this do I say that he should make request." (1 John 5: 16.) Then let us heed the wisdom of the stage driver, who, in speaking of a dangerous precipice by the roadside, said: "Instead of seeing how close to its edge I can drive without going over, I try to see how far from it I can get." So instead of trying to see how close we can get to the unpardonable sin without committing it, let us see how far away from it we can stay. This is wisdom.

30 **because they said, He hath an unclean spirit.**—[He gave them this warning because they thus spoke of him; they must not so treat the Holy Spirit.]

11. CHRIST'S MOTHER AND BRETHREN
3: 31-35
(Matt. 12: 46-50; Luke 8: 19-21)

31 And there come his mother and his brethren; and, standing without,

---

31 **And there come his mother and his brethren;**—This gives the arrival of friends at Capernaum, who probably came from Nazareth to take charge of Jesus. (Verse 21.) The names of his brethren are recorded in Mark 6: 3 and Matt. 13: 55; James, Joses, Simon, and Judas.

and, standing without, they sent unto him, calling him.—Jesus was teaching when they came seeking him. The report of his strange teaching and the dangerous antagonism he had provoked had of course reached them. Mary's heart doubtless was much troubled, and she wished he were out of the crowd, and with her again in the home at Nazareth. This is natural for a mother. The crowd was so packed that they could not reach him (Luke 8: 19) on their arrival so had to "stand without." Either outside of the house, or beyond the circle of his hearers in the open. Not being able to reach him they "sent unto him." That is, passing the message probably from one to another until it reached him that they were waiting for him. The fact that his mother would join his brethren in disturbing him while publicly engaged in teaching shows her great anxiety for her son.

they sent unto him, calling him. 32 And a multitude was sitting about him; and they say unto him, Behold, thy mother and thy brethren without seek for thee. 33 And he answereth them, and saith, Who is my mother and my brethren? 34 And looking round on them that sat round about him, he saith, Behold, my mother and my brethren! 35 For whosoever shall do the will of God, the same is my brother, and sister, and mother.

---

32 And a multitude was sitting about him; and they say unto him, Behold, thy mother and thy brethren without seek for thee.—This was the message passed from one to another until it reached him. (Matt. 12: 47.)

33 And he answereth them, and saith, Who is my mother and my brethren?—[He made this the occasion of teaching them that there is a relationship to him as strong and near as the dearest fleshly relation. He doubtless knew the object of the coming of his brethren.] Our Lord did not despise human relationship. He loved his mother. (John 19: 26, 27.) He esteemed the spiritual relationship the more. He knew better than they what, when, and how long to speak. This and other scriptures (Luke 2: 48, 49; John 2: 4) show the folly of the Roman Catholic doctrine of Mary as an object of invocation and worship. She regarded herself by nature a sinner, and in need of a Savior. (Luke 1: 47.) It was as necessary for Jesus to suffer and die to redeem his mother from sin as it was to redeem others. He used these fleshly relationships as an illustration of the divine. He taught them that his earthly relations had no control of his divine work and that the spiritual must come first. They were not competent to judge correctly as to his duty. The time had come to impress a lesson as to life's truest relationships.

34 And looking round on them that sat round about him,—These were they who were so drawn to him as to forsake all to follow him.

he saith, Behold, my mother and my brethren!—How strangely the words must have echoed to the hearts of those who stood without desiring to see him, but what a glow of joy —the joy of being tenderly loved—must have come to the little band of disciples near by! They knew he held a deep and holy love for his mother and his brethren; and it was even so to them. [His disciples were near him. He looked on them and said: "Behold, my mother and my brethren!" Those he recognized as his mother and brethren were among these. Let none think he lightly esteemed his mother, who had borne him and nursed him and followed him with anxious heart. If they should so think, go with him to the cross, see him there forget the anguish and pain of the cross in his anxiety to provide for the comfort of his mother for her few remaining days on earth. (John 19: 26, 27.) He committed her to his beloved and loving John. He loved his mother tenderly, and could forget his own anguish to provide for her. His example in this love for his mother is worthy of commendation to all children. But as dear to him as was that relation of mother, there is a spiritual relation just as near and as strong into which we may enter.]

35 **For whosoever shall do the will of God, the same is my brother, and sister, and mother.**—Here Jesus enlarges the circle, and takes in the dutiful souls of all the ages. Whoso shall do the will of God, he is a child of God. The truest relationships of life are not of flesh and blood, these are the accidental and artificial ties. The truest ties are ever of the spirit. They are his brother, sister, and mother because born of the same Father. (John 3: 3, 5.) [He defines here how the humblest and the lowest may enter into the relation as near and dear to him as that of his own fleshly mother, brother, sister. Whoso will do the will of my Father, the same is my mother, brother, sister. "Not every one that saith unto me, Lord, Lord, shall enter into the kingdom of heaven; but he that doeth the will of my Father who is in heaven." (Matt. 7: 21.) "If a man love me, he will keep my word: and my Father will love him, and we will come unto him, and make our abode with him." (John 14: 23.) "For this is the love of God, that we keep his commandments." (1 John 5: 3.) Jesus loved the human family while in sin. He so loved it that he gave up heaven with its glories to redeem man from sin and the ruin sin brings upon man.]

SECTION FOUR

A SERIES OF PARABLES
4: 1-34

1. THE PARABLE OF THE SOWER
4: 1-9
(Matt. 13: 1-9; Luke 8: 4-10)

1 And again he began to teach by the sea side. And there is gathered unto him a very great multitude, so that he entered into a boat, and sat in

---

1 **And again he began to teach**—Mark, having stated the opposition of the scribes and Pharisees to Jesus, which resulted in organized action, and in charging Jesus with being in league with the devil, now gives a change in the manner of our Savior's teaching—that of parables. This was not the beginning of his teaching, but only of one form of it.

by the sea side. And there is gathered unto him a very great multitude,—This shows the eagerness of the people to see and hear Jesus. The scribes and Pharisees slandered and tried to discredit the person and hinder the ministry of Jesus, yet the people followed in great multitudes, more than ever, to hear and be instructed by him. All the power and malice of the devil and evil men is not able to suppress the gospel, or kill the force of it. The more the gospel is opposed, the more it prevails. The more the scribes and Pharisees tried to disgrace our Savior, and vilify his doctrine, the more the people followed him to be partakers of his ministry. They were good advertisers of both him and his work. When the church at Jerusalem was persecuted through the influence of the devil and all were scattered abroad except the apostles (Acts 8: 1-4), the disciples went everywhere preaching the word, and as a result new congregations sprang up wherever they went. Instead of checking the work and the influence of the gospel, the devil aided in spreading it. He doubtless thought his plan of persecution would put an end to it, but he could not have adopted a better plan in spreading it.

so that he entered into a boat,—The multitude was so large that it was necessary for Jesus to enter into a boat, and from it speak to the people on the shore.

the sea; and all the multitude were by the sea on the land. 2 And he taught them many things in parables, and said unto them in his teaching, 3 Hearken: Behold, the sower went forth to sow: 4 and it came to pass, as he sowed, some *seed* fell by the way side, and the birds came and devoured it.

---

and sat in the sea; and all the multitude were by the sea on the land.—He sat in the sea on the boat.

2 **And he taught them many things in parables, and said unto them in his teaching,**—The parables that follow are a specimen of his teaching. All that Jesus said and did are not recorded. What is recorded was written to produce faith that Jesus is the Son of God. (John 20: 30.) Only samples of the *many things* taught by Jesus are preserved. Teaching is important in the scheme of redemption. So much so that no man can come to Jesus except he first be taught. Jesus draws men to him through teaching. (John 6: 44, 45.) Jesus taught much by parables. A parable is literally the placing of two things side by side. It is a comparison of things familiar and well known to illustrate and enforce things obscure or not well known.

3 **Hearken:**—Hear. Give attention.

Behold, —Lo, see. Introduces something unexpected and surprising.

the sower went forth to sow:—"Sower" is a general term meaning any one who sows or scatters seeds. Machinery for sowing seed was unknown at this time, hence farmers broadcast, sowing by handfuls from a bag hung over the shoulder. The sower is Jesus who went out from heaven to sow the spiritual seed in this world. Luke (8: 11) says: "The seed is the word of God." Every Christian is a sower as well as a hearer. Seed scattered from the hand of a child will grow as readily as if from a grown man; though it may not be scattered as skillfully. So the spiritual seed, the Word of God, will develop as readily when sown by a new convert as when sown by an old and well developed Christian. The sowing should not cease.

4 **and it came to pass, as he sowed, some seed fell by the way side, and the birds came and devoured it.**—"The way side" was not only where the road and fields joined, but was the many narrow footpaths trodden through the fields. The

5 And other fell on the rocky *ground,* where it had not much earth; and straightway it sprang up, because it had no deepness of earth: 6 and when the sun was risen, it was scorched; and because it had no root, it withered away. 7 And other fell among the thorns, and the thorns grew up, and

---

fields were not fenced, and many paths led across them. These paths were hard, and the seed lay naked upon them.

5 **And other fell on the rocky ground, where it had not much earth;**—Not simply rocky land, for often soil is deep and very productive in rocky places, but a rocky surface slightly covered with soil. The stones did not lay upon the surface, but where the rocks lay just under the surface with only an inch or two of soil on top.

and straightway it sprang up, because it had no deepness of earth:—The underlying rock held the heat from the sun like a hotbed, and forced the seed to sprout and immediately come through the thin soil. It would grow here more quickly than elsewhere, as long as there was any moisture, because of the heat of the rock. The rocks attracted the heat of the sun, which forced the grain up.

6 **and when the sun was risen, it was scorched; and because it had no root; it withered away.**—Matthew says: "No deepness of earth." The thin layer of soil on the rock, having nothing below it to draw moisture from, would soon dry out; the root, short because there was no deep soil into which to bury itself, was soon deprived of vitality, and the plant died. For a plant to thrive, its roots must grow downward, as the stalk grows upward.

7 **And other fell among the thorns, and the thorns grew up, and choked it, and it yielded no fruit.**—Where thorns grow deep and brambles are not rooted up by the plow we may sow the good seeds, they will germinate, spring up, make a feeble growth, but the thorns and brambles, already deeply rooted in the soil and congenial to their surroundings, will spring up and grow vigorously and rapidly. In their growth they will draw the substance and moisture from the soil, starve and choke the feeble wheat until it perishes and fails to bear fruit. This is a common state and results in badly cultivated grounds. The thorns are not bushes already developed, but an after-growth as suggested in the phrase, "The thorns grew up, and

choked it, and it yielded no fruit. 8 And others fell into the good ground, and yielded fruit, growing up and increasing; and brought forth, thirtyfold, and sixtyfold, and a hundredfold. 9 And he said, Who hath ears to hear, let him hear.

---

choked it." They are stumps with their roots penetrating deep in the ground, and which the farmer fails to dig out and extirpate, contenting himself with chopping down the year's growth. Matthew (13: 7) says they "fell upon the thorns." That is, upon thorn roots left in the ground, or seeds from last year's growth waiting their opportunity to seek the light and heat of the sun, and able to grow much more quickly and luxuriantly than the grain.

8 And others fell into the good ground,—That is, ground well prepared for receiving the seed. Deep rich soil, neither hard, nor rocky, nor infested with thorns.

and yielded fruit, growing up and increasing;—It went through all the processes of growth and development until the fruit was perfected.

and brought forth, thirtyfold, and sixtyfold, and a hundred-fold.—[Only one class of soil out of four sown brings fruit to perfection. The thirty, sixty and hundredfold may indicate the common yield of grain in Galilee in the days of Jesus. This is above what is common in our country. Special cases, with favorable surroundings, greatly surpass this. A truthful and observant man says he planted a few grains of wheat in his garden under very favorable circumstances, cultivated them well. One grain put up thirty stalks that produced an average of fifty grains to the head, or fifteen hundred grains from one. But Jesus, I take it, gave the ordinary results of what was common in the country in which he was, and that is much above the average in our land and time. But the good seed must find lodgment in good soil to bear fruit. It is not enough for the soil to be naturally strong, but it must be prepared. The rocks, the thorns, and briers are rooted out so that nothing may hinder the growth of the seed. Ground naturally rocky and full of thorns may be made good by well-directed labor.]

9 And he said, Who hath ears to hear, let him hear.—Having spoken the parable, Jesus requested all to heed the truths therein contained. Jesus said this to impress all with the importance of giving heed to what he said. (See Matt. 11: 15; Luke 8: 8; 14: 35; Rev. 2: 7, 11, 17, 29; 3: 6, 13, 22; 13: 9.)

2. WHY JESUS SPAKE IN PARABLES
4: 10-13

10 And when he was alone, they that were about him with the twelve asked of him the parables. 11 And he said unto them, Unto you is given the mystery of the kingdom of God: but unto them that are without, all things

10 **And when he was alone, they that were about him with the twelve asked of him the parables.**—Jesus spake many parables and now the disciples ask concerning the design of all his parables. Matthew (13: 10) says: "Why speakest thou unto them in parables?" Before this, the teaching of Jesus had been plain and direct, but now "without a parable spake he nothing unto them." (Verse 34.) Luke (8: 9) says they "asked him what this parable might be."

11 **And he said unto them, Unto you is given the mystery of the kingdom of God:**—[So also there were profound and sublime truths of the kingdom of God, which men could grasp and appreciate, only when they had put themselves under the tutelage of Christ. We are not to understand "mystery" in the sense of something which never could be understood, as some take it even now. This was spoken to and of his disciples.]

but unto them that are without,—Mere idle, careless hearers, who have not interest enough to put themselves under the special teaching of the Master.

all things are done in parables:—This and the next verse were also spoken to his disciples but about those not disciples. The parables are really the testing point. If they are ready for the kingdom, they will not be satisfied with the parable. The spiritual nature realizes there is a truth hidden, and desires to know that truth, and will come within and seek the special teaching of Jesus to know it. The "mysteries of the kingdom" does not mean a doctrine incomprehensible in itself but doctrine about the establishment and work of the kingdom of God which had not been fully understood. The apostles and first disciples of our Lord thought that his mission on

are done in parables: 12 that seeing they may see, and not perceive; and hearing they may hear, and not understand; lest haply they should turn again, and it should be forgiven them. 13 And he saith unto them, Know ye

---

earth was to establish a political kingdom; and the spiritual nature of this kingdom was a mystery to them until they understood it.

12 that seeing they may see, and not perceive;—They had organs of vision which could observe natural objects but their mental perceptions were so filled with gross cares as to prevent their mental perception of receiving the truths contained in the parable.

and hearing they may hear, and not understand;—They had ears that could hear the voice of the teacher, who spoke in a known tongue to them, and they doubtless knew the outward facts of the Savior's works, but the spiritual truths Jesus designed to teach by these things they did not understand for the reason they made no effort upon their part. Man must make some effort to understand the teaching of Jesus, or else, he will go through life blinded.

lest haply they should turn again, and it should be forgiven them.—The hearing, understanding, and turning is man's duty, the forgiving is God's pleasure. But he cannot and will not forgive, until man does his part. He must show interest by acting his part. He must come to Christ for complete instruction. It was so then. It is so now. The Spirit speaks to him through the Word. (John 6: 44, 45.) If he listens with such interest as induces him to seek anxiously the whole truth, there is no aid that it will not afford, and he will turn again and be forgiven. The eyes that are blinded are the eyes that do not desire to see, and the ears that are deafened are the ears that do not desire to hear—moral unwillingness resulting in moral inability. To hear, and understand what we hear, is necessary in order to conversion—at least understand enough to know what the Lord requires, in order that it may be obeyed and man saved.

The scribes and Pharisees had hardened their hearts, stuffed their ears, and closed their eyes, as the Jews had done in the days of Isaiah. They were determined not to believe the teachings of Jesus. Now he speaks in parables—not that he does not desire all to know the truth, but that those who desire the truth may be separated from those who have rejected it. God has so arranged it that people must desire the truth in order to receive it, and yet all who desire it—hunger and thirst after it—have the blessed assurance that they can understand and receive it. This is the key to the whole matter. Careless seeing and careless hearing destroy the soul. God will afford to every soul so much as it is willing and anxious to receive. Matthew (13: 13-15) says: "Therefore speak I to them in parables; because seeing they see not, and hearing they hear not, neither do they understand. And unto them is fulfilled the prophecy of Isaiah, which saith, By hearing ye shall hear, and shall in no wise understand; and seeing ye shall see, and shall in no wise perceive; For this people's heart is waxed gross, and their ears are dull of hearing, and their eyes they have closed; Lest haply they should perceive with their eyes, and hear with their ears, and understand with their heart, and should turn again, and I should heal them." This Isaiah foretold of the condition of the Jewish people. They would close their eyes, stop their ears, harden their hearts, refuse to hear God's word, lest they should be converted, and then God would heal them. Men usually fail to hear and understand God because they will not do it. When they thus show themselves unwilling to obey God he determines to destroy them, and so speaks to them as to harden their hearts and lead them down to destruction. He, too, spoke truth that they could have understood to their salvation had they been willing to be taught of God. But in their unwillingness to learn of God they perverted the truths to their own ruin. God hardened Pharaoh's heart because he was wicked, to publicly lead him to ruin as an example to others.

The means God used to harden Pharaoh's heart was the truth—the same truth he used to touch and tender the hearts of the children of Israel. The truth that softened and tendered the hearts of one class and caused them to follow Moses to freedom hardened the heart of the other and led him to ruin. So in the case before us. The truths which drew the disciples closer to Jesus drove the scribes and Pharisees further from him. The Lord said: "So shall my word be that

not this parable? and how shall ye know all the parables?

goeth forth out of my mouth : it shall not return unto me void, but it shall accomplish that which I please, and it shall prosper in the thing whereto I sent it." (Isa. 55 : 11.) God's word will have success. It will prosper and succeed in accomplishing the thing for which it was sent. It was sent into the world to either save or damn the souls of men. If man receives it and is guided by it, it will be the means of saving him. If he rejects it, it will be the means of damning him. Man's eternal destiny depends upon how he treats the word of God. It is a steppingstone to heaven, if accepted, but a stumbling stone to hell if rejected. (1 Cor. 1 : 22-24.) God did not take away their freedom. "Come unto me . . . and I will give you rest" was and is the invitation to all. Their moral inability was the result of their moral unwillingness. (John 5 : 40.) They were reaping the fruit of the seed they had sown.

13 And he saith unto them, Know ye not this parable?—This which is so plain and obvious. The disciples had asked its meaning. (Luke 8:9.) This question is preparatory to the one that follows.

and how shall ye know all the parables?—That is, if you do not understand one so plain and simple as this one, how will you comprehend those more difficult and obscure?

3. THE MEANING OF THE PARABLE
4 : 14-20
(Matt. 13 : 18-23; Luke 8 : 11-15)

14 The sower soweth the word. 15 And these are they by the way side,

14 The sower soweth the word.—The seed is the word of God. (Luke 8 : 11.) The sower is, primarily, Jesus himself, but subsequently the apostles, and as the ages roll on, all those who seek to plant in human hearts the word of God. [The first and essential point of likeness between the word of God and the seed is that the seed, the germ of the fruit to be produced, is enclosed in it. Without the seed no fruit can be produced in the material world. The fruit must correspond to the seed. "And God said, Let the earth put forth grass, herbs yielding seed, and fruit-trees bearing fruit after their

where the word is sown; and when they have heard, straightway cometh Satan, and taketh away the word which hath been sown in them. 16 And

kind, wherein is the seed thereof, upon the earth." (Gen. 1: 11.) The law of God is that seed must produce its like. So when in the field the man who had sown wheat found tares, he knew other seed had been sown. "An enemy hath done this," he said. In the word of God is enclosed the germinal principle of spiritual life. Without that word no spiritual fruit can be borne. The fruit borne from that seed must correspond to the seed. If plants grow or fruit is borne in the kingdom of God that is not in the word of God, it is because other seed has been sown there, and it is an enemy of God that sows other seed than the word of God.] Sower, learn this lesson. It is your duty to sow. Sow only the *word*. Sow not mingled seed. Give to perishing souls only the living word. It is God's power to save. (Rom. 1: 16.)

15 **And these are they by the way side,**—In the plains of Palestine you may see miles of verdure without a fence, yet with different ownership. Instead of fences are wayside paths, narrow and hard trodden. On these, with broadcast sowing, some seed will fall. The modern drill would have deprived us of this part of the parable. (It is not improbable we drill too much in our modern church work.) The seed lay hard and round upon this smooth, hard surface, and the watchful birds, as soon as the farmer's back was turned, caught at them, and they were gone.

where the word is sown; and when they have heard,— Heard *only*. Just with the ear. The word lies on the surface of their hearts. When truth is heard and not fully received and practiced, it will, sooner or later, lose its power over the heart. No matter how full the reservoir is, if not replenished, it will finally become dry from evaporation.

straightway cometh Satan,—Could Jesus have spoken these words without recognizing, and teaching his disciples to recognize, the personal existence of Satan? "Satan" means adversary. That he is quick to act is seen by his *coming immediately*.

and taketh away the word which hath been sown in them. —Luke (8: 12) says: "From their heart." How is not speci-

these in like manner are they that are sown upon the rocky *places*, who,
when they have heard the word, straightway receive it with joy; 17 and they

---

fied. He has a thousand ways of brushing away the slight
surface impression that may have been made upon the heart
of a careless hearer. The heart is the spiritual soil in which
the sower sows the word of God. God has always operated
upon the heart of man. So does the devil. The religion produced by the spiritual seed, the word of God, is in the heart,
and therefore, preeminently a heart religion. Luke (8: 12)
says: "That they may not believe and be saved." The devil
recognizes that the word of God produces faith, hence,
snatches it away as quickly as possible. The human heart is
the battleground. Here God and the devil meet for the conflict.

[Many, under the evil influences and surroundings of life,
hear the word. It is not honored or cherished, overrun by sinful influences and indulgences, given no chance to germinate,
and is plucked out of the hearts by the evil one. He uses his
servants to do this. Sometimes he uses the man's own appetites or his own wicked associates, and sometimes he finds a
child of God that he can pervert and use to pluck the good
seed out of the heart in which it is not cherished. The word
plucked out of the heart cannot save. James 1: 21: "Receive
with meekness the implanted word, which is able to save your
souls." He admonished that we must not be forgetful hearers, but "doers of the word."]

16 **And these in like manner are they that are sown upon
the rocky places,**—The rocky places were spots where the
underlying rock formation cropped up near the surface. We
have seen places where the underlying limestone formation
was sometimes many feet, and not very far off, only a few
inches below the surface, and sometimes on the surface.
Places where the soil is thus very shallow are meant by
rocky places.

who, when they have heard the word,—Please observe, all
the classes have *heard*. They stand on common ground in
this. "Take heed therefore how ye hear." (Luke 8: 18.)

straightway receive it with joy;—Hearing the gospel, and
considering the pleasures and advantages of salvation, they

have no root in themselves, but endure for a while; then, when tribulation or persecution ariseth because of the word, straightway they stumble. 18 And others are they that are sown among the thorns; these are they that have

are for the moment highly pleased without counting the cost. (Luke 14: 25-33.) Their joy is not the joy flowing out of genuine repentance and from a real changed heart. Their emotions are touched for the time being, but the gospel does not reach their moral nature, and their will and character are unchanged. They are moved by the winds of popular excitement or enthusiasm, but there is no new life. Joy is a characteristic of *shallow* as well as of *deep natures*.

17 and they have no root in themselves,—They are wanting in the true principles of true religion, such as humility, love, repentance, faith and change of heart, and therefore rootless. They are destitute of that spiritual life which "is hid with Christ in God." (Col. 3: 3.) They are not "rooted and grounded in love." (Eph. 3: 17.)

then, when tribulation or persecution ariseth—Providential dealings and chastisements. It takes these to separate the wheat from the chaff.

because of the word,—The truths of the gospel always create opposition and put the adversary to work.

straightway they stumble.—Stumble and fall away because this was not an obstruction they expected in their heavenly career.

[Matthew (13: 21) says: "Yet hath he not root in himself, but endureth for a while; and when tribulation or persecution ariseth because of the word, straightway he stumbleth"—or led into sin. [This class represents the excitable, the light-minded, those lacking in depth and strength of character, so who readily receive, but cannot persist in a begun course. They hear, are easily aroused, act quickly, show great zeal for a time, run well while things all prosper and seem to be full of promise. But when the ebb tide in religion comes, as come it must, they grow weary, become faint at heart, turn aside, and walk with God no more.]

18 And others are they that are sown among the thorns;—The thorny ground was neither hard nor shallow. It was good deep, rich ground, but the roots of thorns were lurking

heard the word, 19 and the cares of the ¹world, and the deceitfulness of
riches, and the lusts of other things entering in, choke the word, and it becometh unfruitful. 20 And those are they that were sown upon the good

¹Oh, *age*

in the ground. They were not removed. They grew rapidly
—more so than the wheat—and became so rank that they
choked and smothered it till it brought no fruit to perfection.
Practically the result was the same as before—nothing but
leaves.

these are they that have heard the word,—All these classes
are hearers. All are to be found in the public church meetings. All have heard, but says James, "Be ye doers of the
word, and not hearers only, deluding your own selves."
(James 1: 22.) In this case the heart is like the plowed
ground but poorly prepared. The soil is deep and rich, but
the thorn roots have not been grubbed out. They are convicted that they are sinners, show signs of sorrow and repentance, and pass through a form of obedience; but the heart is
divided between these and cherished sins and the soul and
body are not wholly given to the Lord.

19 and the cares of the world,—Overanxious cares about
worldly things—those that divide the heart between them
and God. (James 1: 6-8.)

and the deceitfulness of riches,—This is another altogether.
The business or the profession has been made successful, the
home is bought, the money is amassed. Such intense application is no longer necessary, but the man now possesses the
golden key that unlocks a hundred avenues of *enjoying* life
and employing time. There is no more time for Christ and religion than before. Still it is self, or that broadening of self
which we name family, which engrosses time, and thought,
and activity, instead of Christ, and no fruit is produced.

and the lusts of other things entering in,—Luke (8: 14)
says: "As they go on their way they are choked with cares
and riches and pleasures of this life." The golden key is possessed that opens these avenues. The phrase "pleasures of
this life" does not indicate that the Christian is to have no
pleasures. God never intended that his children should be deprived of the good and perfect gifts that he has bestowed

ground; such as hear the word, and accept it, and bear fruit, thirtyfold, and sixtyfold, and a hundredfold.

upon man. It is not a sin for a Christian to be happy. Such "pleasures" as destroy spirituality, and deaden religious sensibility, and wean from Christ, are, of course, forbidden.

choke the word, and it becometh unfruitful.—By the contact and pressure of the thorns—the above-mentioned evils—the word is choked and smothered so it can bear no perfect fruit. Luke (8: 14) says they "bring no fruit to perfection." The unfruitfulness of the seed represents the unfruitfulness of those receiving the word of God.

20 **And those are they that were sown upon the good ground;**—These are they who, after having received the word, develop a Godly life. The good ground is the human heart well prepared by casting out all evil motives and purposes, to receive the word honestly, and to give it full opportunity to grow—a heart that submits itself to the full power and influence of the gospel, unchecked by the cares and anxieties of worldly things—a heart fully under the showers and summer suns of the grace of God—a heart spread wide open, like a broad luxuriant field, to the rays of the morning and evening dews, ready for the reception of the truths of God. A heart thus prepared is a rich mellow spiritual soil in which the spiritual seed can take deep root and grow because it has full room for development. The good ground is of no better inherent quality than the others, but in a different condition, and the condition our own making.

such as hear the word,—They have had no advantage over others in this respect. The others all heard but paid no heed to the message.

and accept it,—Before this comes the "understandeth" or "considereth, payeth attention" of Matt. (13: 23), and after it the "hold it fast" of Luke (8: 15). The order is hear, heed, accept, hold fast. Luke adds: "In an honest and good heart." The meaning of the adjectives is to be ascertained by remembering that the phrase expresses a condition different from all the preceding states. One was hard, stubborn, unreceptive; this, then, is soft, yielding, receptive. The second was shallow and frivolous with hardness beneath; this is deep and thoughtful. The third was full of germinal weeds, this is comparatively free. This we understand from the conditions of the parable to be the significance of the "honest and good heart." The seed does the work. Understanding the word involves giving it close attention. The understanding arises from attention.

and bear fruit,—Luke adds "with patience." Where all these exist spiritual fruit must follow. Spiritual fruit is anything in the name of Christ (that is, by his authority) that conduces to God's glory or our fellow man's good. They *continue* to bring forth fruit. It is not a mere religious spasm through which they have passed.

thirtyfold, and sixtyfold, and a hundredfold.—Both Matthew and Mark add here the three grades of production. Not all are capable of producing the same amount of fruit, but it is the same kind—spiritual and good. The marked difference in the capacity of men is thus indicated by a threefold division.

The good and honest hearts which bear fruit and heed, and accept, and hold fast, are by no means equal in their ability to bear fruit, and God will hold them responsible only according to that ability. If thou canst only bear thirty, bear thirty and receive God's blessing. If thou canst bear a hundred, thank God for thy glorious capacity, and bear them, but think not to deceive God with the thirty which might have been a hundred. Every faithful Christian may find comfort and encouragement in this feature of the parable.

[The heart is the inner man. The heart thinks, fears, hopes, loves, hates, believes. The heart is the soil into which the word of God, as the seed, is sown. It embraces the perceptions, emotions, and volitions—the whole inner man. The heart must have clearness of understanding, depth of feeling, and strength of purpose to continue to the end, despite difficulties and trials, to bring forth fruit unto perfection—not brilliancy, but an earnest, thoughtful mind. Sincerity of feeling and singleness of purpose must be cultivated to make the heart good and honest. These qualities of heart can be cultivated, and are much under a man's own control. When a man cultivates the habit of honest inquiry that he may know the truth and do it, cherishes a love for what is right and true and good, and then continually follows the purpose of doing what is right, his heart will become an honest and understanding heart. To practice these things will make the heart honest and understanding. Persons that will take these characters of the heart here presented by Jesus, and in the light of them study their own hearts, may understand the things needed, and may cultivate their hearts and make them good.]

4. A LAMP IS NOT TO BE PUT UNDER A BUSHEL
4: 21-25
(Luke 8: 16-18)

21 And he said unto them, Is the lamp brought to be put under the bushel, or under the bed, *and* not to be put on the stand? 22 For there is nothing hid, save that it should be manifested; neither was *anything* made secret, but that it should come to light. 23 If any man hath ears to hear, let

21 **And he said unto them, Is the lamp brought to be put under the bushel, or under the bed, and not to be put on the stand?**—[This parable, like the parable of the sower, deals with the word of God as beneficial to man. The word, represented by the seed in the parable of the sower, is here represented by a lighted lamp. A lamp is brought into a room not to be hid under something, but is to be placed on an elevated stand so it can give light all around it. So the word of God, intended for the spiritual enlightenment of men, is not to be left in obscurity, but to be held up before the world, so it may receive the benefit of the light flowing from it. All the instructions given by Jesus were designed to give spiritual light, and all his hearers are responsible for their measure of light. (Matt. 13: 12; Luke 8: 16-18.) Compare Matt. 5: 15; 7: 2; 10: 26, where Jesus uses the same language on other occasions. The end and design of Christ in revealing his word and will to his disciples, and in communicating to men the light of spiritual knowledge, is that they may communicate it to others, and not keep it close unto themselves.]

22 **For there is nothing hid, save that it should be manifested; neither was anything made secret, but that it should come to light.**—Nothing in the wisdom and purpose of God concerning man and his redemption but that will be revealed.

23 **If any man hath ears to hear, let him hear.**—A warning to his disciples to listen to and accept the truth. [Jesus dropped the figure of the lamp, and returned to the *word*

him hear. 24 And he said unto them, Take heed what ye hear: with what measure ye mete it shall be measured unto you; and more shall be given unto you. 25 For he that hath, to him shall be given: and he that hath not, from him shall be taken away even that which he hath.

which the lamp represented. Since it was to make clear all that had been hid in types and shadows, and to bring to light all that had been kept secret in the mind of God regarding man and his redemption, it is the duty of every one to use his ears in hearing it. Nothing is more worthy of being heard than the word of God.]

24 And he said unto them, Take heed what ye hear:—That is, consider carefully what you hear before accepting it. Probably disciples then, as some are now, inclined to hear only so much as corresponded with their desires and notions and hence this admonition.

with what measure ye mete it shall be measured unto you; —The general meaning is: as you treat others so shall you be treated by them. But here it means: as you treat me as a teacher so will I treat you as learners. The measure of careful attention given me will be the measure of instruction given you. What you receive as hearers and disciples will correspond to your ability and diligence.

and more shall be given unto you.—To you who are attentive, and who improve what you hear. The specific application of the whole thing here must be determined, not by the same words on the mount (Matt. 7: 2; Luke 6: 37), where they have reference to *censorious judgments,* but by their connection here. The essential meaning in both cases is that *giving* and *receiving* are reciprocal, like *action* and *reaction* as a law of physics. The specific application here is that he who would receive instruction must give something in return, to wit, *intelligent attention,* a desire to be instructed, and a *proper use* of what he knows already.

25 For he that hath, to him shall be given:—He that has received opportunities and improved them, to the good of others as well as to himself, shall have more opportunities. He shall have greater means and facilities in attaining greater knowledge of God and his wonderful works.

and he that hath not,—Has not a teachable spirit and no desire nor inclination to know the truth—has no desire to be taught and has made no effort to learn.

from him shall be taken away even that which he hath.— Luke (8: 18) explains the clause by saying: "Even that which he seemeth to have." It is only apparent and imaginary. His speculative views and notions shall become more confused and darken in proportion to his neglecting the opportunities and means of increasing true spiritual knowledge. The means and opportunities which enlighten and carry one man to heaven will send another to hell. It all depends upon the way we treat our opportunities. Judas is an example of this class. He had the same opportunities the other apostles had, but he allowed what little grace and favor he *seemed* to have to slip away by neglecting his opportunities for increasing his knowledge and doing good.

It is a law of God often repeated by Jesus, that to him who has, more shall be given, and from him who has not, even that he has shall be taken away. In order to understand this singular phraseology, we must observe that the thing which is taken away from him who has not is necessarily something that he has. He has, and at the same time he has not. We must also observe that two sides are here represented—the human and the divine. Man has the opportunity to learn of and accept Christ in the sense of both being offered him by God. In this sense he has it. He has it so far as God is concerned. But man has neither the will nor the desire to accept either. In this sense he has it not. When man in heart reaches this state, then that which he had upon God's part, but had it not upon his part, is taken from him. Man takes it away himself by refusing to accept and use it. He loses his opportunity of learning of and accepting Christ by his own neglect. [The man who wrapped the talent in a cloth and hid it is regarded as not having it. When a man fails to use his talent, or opportunity, he is regarded as not having it. So from him is taken what he does not have, or does not use. No man practically has what he does not make use of.]

<h3 style="text-align:center">5. PARABLE OF THE SEED</h3>
4: 26-29

26 And he said, So is the kingdom of God, as if a man should cast seed

---

26 And he said, So is the kingdom of God, as if a man

upon the earth; 27 and should sleep and rise night and day, and the seed
should spring up and grow, he knoweth now how. 28 The earth *beareth

*Or, *yieldeth*

should cast seed upon the earth;—The main point is that although man must sow and reap, all that lies between these
two extremes is not only independent of his power but beyond
his observation. The growth and increase is with God. Such
is the reign of Christ in its growth and development in the
hearts of men. It is like the case of the seed planted in the
ground. The seed, its germination and growth, is the prominent thing in the parable. The seed is the word of God, the
gospel. The kingdom of God always begins in communities
by the spiritual seed, the word of God, being sown in the
hearts of individuals, as vegetable crops start by seed being
planted in the soil.

27 and should sleep and rise night and day,—[Should sleep
in the night, and rise by day. That is, live in his usual way
while giving the seed time to germinate and come forth. The
germinating and coming forth is God's part. Here man is
helpless—he has no control over the seed germinating and the
plant springing forth. The seed is left hid out of his sight, to
the life God has given it, and to the forces of nature. Man
cannot give the seed life nor make it grow. Here he must rest
in hope both day and night.]

**and the seed should spring up and grow, he knoweth not
how.**—Here the wisdom of God is too deep for the mind of
man. He cannot fathom it. Human wisdom cannot penetrate
it. Here modern science, like all human wisdom, must pause.
It has failed to find what the life in the seed is. Here science
is forced to bow to the wisdom of God. After all the re-
searches of philosophers, not one has been able to tell the way
in which seed grows. They can observe one fact after another
—they can see the changes—they can see the necessity of rain
and sunshine, of care in the sowing, but beyond this they cannot go.

28 The earth beareth fruit of herself;—It is done while man
sleeps by night and is engaged in other things by day. We are
not to suppose that Jesus meant to say that the earth had any
productive power of *itself,* but only that it yields its fruits, not

fruit of herself; first the blade, then the ear, then the full grain in the ear. 29 But when the fruit [3]is ripe, straightway he [4]putteth forth the sickle, because the harvest is come.

[3]Or, *alloweth*
[4]Or, *sendeth forth*

by the *power of man.* God gives its yielding power. It, like man, has no power of its own. So the word of God in the heart is not by the *power* of man. It grows he cannot tell how. It is by the power of God. At the same time, as without labor man would have no vegetable harvest, so without active effort he would have no fruit of the Spirit. Both are connected with and enjoyed in his efforts—both are to be measured by his efforts.

first the blade, then the ear, then the full grain in the ear.— There is an orderly development both in natural and spiritual growth. This growth is in harmony with law. We cannot hope to find the ripened Christian experience in the young convert, any more than the fully matured corn in the first appearance of the blade. He who expects the end at the beginning will be disappointed. The Christian's growth is like climbing Jacob's ladder with many steps, the face always looking up toward God. There are different stages in all life. In the animal, there is childhood, youth, and manhood. In the spiritual, there is conversion, the newborn babe in Christ, childhood, and the manhood stages. The young and tender Christian, like the tender plant, needs care, kindness and culture. A light frost, a cold wave, or a burning sun alike injures the tender blade. So tender piety in the heart of a newborn babe in Christ needs shelter from the frosts and storms of a cold unfeeling world. It needs the genial dews and mild sunshine of heaven. That is, it needs instruction, prayer, and counsel from parents, teachers and all experienced Christians, that it may grow and bring forth the full fruits of righteousness.

29 But when the fruit is ripe, straightway he putteth forth the sickle, because the harvest is come.—All the growth was toward this end for which the seed was planted. Man's agency now begins again, after having been suspended since sowing the wheat. Harvest time has come, therefore time again for man to work. One sows the word of God, he does all he can in this particular, passes on to other duties, and in due course of time the seed germinates, grows, develops, and produces a harvest. It requires time to produce a harvest. It is not neglect in the man who sows wheat or other grain and sleeps during the night and is up during the day doing other things until the harvest; neither is it neglect to preach the gospel and await the time for its development in the hearts of the hearers. As the earth must receive the seed and do its part in producing a harvest, so all hearers must receive the word of God and by all processes necessary produce a harvest. The sower must do his duty in sowing and not withhold any of the seed—that is, any part of the word of God; the hearers must do their duty in bearing fruit.

In this parable Christ was showing how the kingdom of God arose and bore fruit in this life. The word of God is received into the heart. It changes the feelings, the purposes, the thoughts, and bears fruit in the life. When the fruit is ripened, the sickle is put in and reaped for the garner of God.

6. PARABLE OF THE MUSTARD SEED
4: 30-32
(Matt. 13: 31, 32)

30 And he said, How shall we liken the kingdom of God? or in what parable shall we set it forth? 31 [5]It is like a grain of mustard seed, which, when it is sown upon the earth, though it be less than all the seeds that are upon the earth, 32 yet when it is sown, groweth up, and becometh greater than all the herbs, and putteth out great branches; so that the birds of the heaven can lodge under the shadow thereof.

[5]Gr. *As unto.*

---

30 **And he said, How shall we liken the kingdom of God? or in what parable shall we set it forth?**—That is, what other parable or illustration than the ones already used shall be used showing and enforcing some other feature of "the kingdom of God"?

31 **It is like a grain of mustard seed, which, when it is sown upon the earth, though it be less than all the seeds that are upon the earth,**—Matthew (13: 31) says: "Which a man took, and sowed in his field." Luke (13: 17-27) says: "His own garden." It is a garden plant. It is the least of all seeds which were sowed in the field or garden in that country—not really the least of all seeds known to botanists. It was proverbially used to denote any small seed.

32 yet when it is sown, groweth up, and becometh greater than all the herbs, and putteth out great branches; so that the birds of the heaven can lodge under the shadow thereof.— From this very small seed grows a very large herb, "greater than all the herbs" grown in that country, "and becometh a tree"—not like the cedar or fir or oak, but so large that birds lodge in its branches. We are told by those who have traveled through that country that "in the proper season the traveler on Gennesaret may ride by mustard bushes as high as his horse, and alive with flocks of merry bullfinches or of rock pigeons feeding upon the seeds." The points of resemblance in the parable are the smallness of seed and the greatness of the production from it. So the kingdom of God, from an insignificant beginning, has grown to a huge magnitude. From a babe in a manger has grown this mighty kingdom.

7. OTHER PARABLES NOT RECORDED
4: 33, 34
(Matt. 13: 34, 35)

33 And with many such parables spake he the word unto them, as they were able to hear it; 34 and without a parable spake he not unto them: but privately to his own disciples he expounded all things.

---

33 And with many such parables spake he the word unto them, as they were able to hear it;—As they were able to comprehend it. They were weak in spiritual knowledge, and he was obliged to lead them along cautiously, and by degrees to a full understanding of the plan of salvation. Jesus taught according to ability or capacity for receiving instruction—not according to age, but according to advancement—according to ability to receive instruction. The apostles adapted their teaching to the capacities of their hearers.

34 and without a parable spake he not unto them:—Jesus spoke all that which he taught on that occasion in parables, and "without a parable" on that occasion, "spake he not unto them."

but privately to his own disciples he expounded all things. —When Jesus and the disciples were alone, he explained in detail the parables. He showed them more at length the spiritual meaning of all his parables.

SECTION FIVE

A SERIES OF MIRACLES
4: 35 to 5: 43

1. STILLING THE TEMPEST
4: 35-41
(Matt. 8: 18-27; Luke 8: 22-25)

35 And on that day, when even was come, he saith unto them, Let us go over unto the other side. 36 And leaving the multitude, they take him with them, even as he was, in the boat. And other boats were with him. 37 And there ariseth a great storm of wind, and the waves beat into the boat, insomuch that the boat was now filling. 38 And he himself was in the stern,

---

35 **And on that day, when even was come, he saith unto them, Let us go over unto the other side.**—Matthew (8: 18) says: "When Jesus saw great multitudes about him, he gave commandment to depart unto the other side." He did this for retirement and rest.

36 **And leaving the multitude, they take him with them, even as he was, in the boat.**—After teaching through the day, at Jesus' request, the disciples without further preparation started with him to the eastern side of the sea. He was already in the boat. Peter, James, and John owned their boats, and Jesus taught from Peter's boat. (Luke 5: 1-11.) Peter's example in using his boat in the Master's cause is worthy of emulation, and should teach us a lesson. Our boats, our ships, our cars, and horses should be so used.

And other boats were with him.—Boats owned by other disciples, or at their disposal.

37 **And there ariseth a great storm of wind,**—A mighty windstorm. Luke (8: 23) says: "And there came down a storm of wind on the lake"; Matthew (8: 24) says: "There arose a great tempest in the sea." This came down suddenly. All travelers describe the storms as very sudden and violent, caused by the cold air that rushes down from the mountains into the heated depression of the lake.

and the waves beat into the boat, insomuch that the boat was now filling.—This was not a large ship such as we have now, but a small rowboat, probably open—a small boat with sails, such as were commonly used for fishing on the lake. Luke (8: 23) says they "were in jeopardy." Matthew (8: 24)

asleep on the cushion: and they awake him, and say unto him, Teacher, carest thou not that we perish?   39 And he awoke, and rebuked the wind, and
said unto the sea, Peace, be still.   And the wind ceased, and there was a
great calm.   40 And he said unto them, Why are ye fearful? have ye not yet

---

says: "The boat was covered with the waves," and "was now filling." Doubtless in a sinking condition.

38 And he himself was in the stern, asleep on the cushion: —It was night, and Jesus had retired for rest. He had labored hard all day teaching, was probably weary, and slept calmly and serenely. He needed rest and sleep like other men. Like Jonah he slept in the midst of the storm; but very differently. Jonah was fleeing from duty, Jesus calmly awaiting the hour of duty.

and they awake him, and say unto him, Teacher, carest thou not that we perish?—The storm greatly frightened the disciples. They went to him, roused him up, and said: "Save, Lord; we perish." (Matt. 8: 25.) The disciples were accustomed to the lake, the winds and the waves. This, then, was to them a terrific storm to fill them with such terror.

39 And he awoke, and rebuked the wind, and said unto the sea, Peace, be still. And the wind ceased, and there was a great calm.—The wind was still, the sea ceased to dash against the vessel, the waves stopped rolling and the living made safe. His word awed the tempest, and allayed the storm. What a power was this! What irresistible proof that he was divine! There is not to be found anywhere a sublimer description of a display of power. Nor could there be sublimer proof that he was truly the Son of God. "Jehovah hath his way in the whirlwind and in the storm, and the clouds are the dust of his feet. He rebuketh the sea, and maketh it dry, and drieth up all the rivers. . . . The mountains quake at him, and the hills melt; and the earth is upheaved at his presence, yea, the world, and all that dwell therein." (Nah. 1: 3-5.)

40 And he said unto them, Why are ye fearful? have ye not yet faith?—Matthew (8: 26) says: "Why are ye fearful, O ye of little faith?" Luke (8: 25) puts it: "Where is your faith?" The terror of the disciples would have been excusable but for the presence of Jesus. With him in the vessel it argued weak-

faith?　41 And they feared exceedingly, and said one to another, Who then is this, that even the wind and the sea obey him?

---

ness of faith, because the many miracles which he had wrought should have convinced them that he had power over the winds and the waves.

41 And they feared exceedingly, and said one to another, Who then is this, that even the wind and the sea obey him?— They believed in Jesus as the Messiah, but such an exhibition of power confounded them. Notwithstanding all the other miracles which they had seen Jesus perform, this one filled them with wonder and awe. Since God "gathereth the waters of the sea together as a heap"; "layeth up the deeps in storehouses" (Psalm 33: 7); "spake, and it was done"; and commanded, "and it stood fast" (Psalm 33: 9), why should they marvel that the Son of God stills the tempest? Jesus worked every variety of miracle to leave even the weakest in faith no room to doubt his divine power, or that he is the Christ, the Son of the living God.

2. THE FIERCE DEMONIAC
5: 1-20
(Matt. 8: 28-37; Luke 8: 26-40)

1 And they came to the other side of the sea, into the country of the Gerasenes.　2 And when he was come out of the boat, straightway there met him out of the tombs a man with an unclean spirit, 3 who had his dwelling

---

1 And they came to the other side of the sea, into the country of the Gerasenes.—The country of the Gerasenes, where this demoniac was healed, is called by Matthew (8: 28) "the country of the Gadarenes." Gadara, the city from which the latter name was derived, is situated on the southern bank of the river Yarmuk, a few miles south of the lake. Its territory extended to and included the place where this demoniac was found. Gerasa was a strongly fortified city east of the lake, and at a greater distance than Gadara.

2 And when he was come out of the boat, straightway there met him out of the tombs—There are still found in the neighborhood of the ancient Gadara (the present Ummkeis) many caves and chalk ranges which served as places of burial. The calcareous mountain on which Gadara was situated was spe-

in the tombs: and no man could any more bind him, no, not with a chain; 4 because that he had been often bound with fetters and chains, and the chains had been rent asunder by him, and the fetters broken in pieces: and no man had strength to tame him. 5 And always, night and day, in the tombs and

cially suited for such sepulchers. The sepulchers of the Jews were generally cut out of the solid rock. Caves were also used for this purpose. They are now often resorted to for shelter during the night. Sometimes the wandering Arabs take up their winter abode in them.

a man with an unclean spirit,—Matthew (8: 28) says: "There met him two possessed with demons." Luke (8: 26) says: "There met him a certain man out of the city." The reconciliation of Matthew's statement that "two met him" with that of Mark and Luke that "one met him" has originated many ingenious conjectures, and some foolish ones. There is no contradiction between the three writers for he who speaks of the two includes the one, and they who speak of the one do not deny that there were two. Mark and Luke report the more important one of the two.

3 **who had his dwelling in the tombs:**—He lived in the tombs. Although belonging to the city, he had forsaken the society of living men, which Luke (8: 27) also states. "For a long time he had worn no clothes."

and no man could any more bind him, no, not with a chain; —That is, to be of any permanent use. It had probably now been given up. He had been growing worse till he could be no longer confined, binding even with chains proving ineffectual. Here is described the most terrible case of demoniacal possession recorded in the gospels.

4 **because that he had been often bound with fetters and chains,**—More than once those who were interested in him had brought him back from the wilderness, and bound him securely, as they thought, but the demoniac possession gave him such enormous strength that the fetters snapped like the green withes on Samson.

and the chains had been rent asunder by him, and the fetters broken in pieces: and no man had strength to tame him. —Fetters and chains would not hold him, and all methods to coax, persuade or influence him had failed. The attempt to

in the mountains, he was crying out, and cutting himself with stones. 6 And
when he saw Jesus from afar, he ran and [1]worshipped him; 7 and crying out
with a loud voice, he saith, What have I to do with thee, Jesus, thou Son of
the Most High God? I adjure thee by God, torment me not. 8 For he said

[1]The Greek word denotes an act of reverence, whether paid to a creature (see Mt.
4. 9; 18. 26) or to the Creator (see Mt. 4. 10).

"tame him" seems to have been abandoned, and the poor
wretch given up to his awful fate. All literature presents no
more pitiable spectacle. Matthew (8: 28) supplies another
point not mentioned by Mark, that he was "exceeding fierce,
so that no man could pass by that way." A terror to the
whole neighborhood. The history of the world is but a mel-
ancholy reiteration that fetters and chains upon evil will ever
more be broken, which are not forged and placed by divine
aid.

5 **And always, night and day, in the tombs and in the
mountains, he was crying out, and cutting himself with
stones.**—This poor victim would rove in search of mischief,
and, finding nothing upon which to spend his rage, would
bruise and cut himself with sharp stones. These are all marks
of a madman—a man bereft of all reason—wretched and outcast, strong and dangerous. Evil never rests. It works in the
daylight and the darkness. It is ever dragging its victims
lower. So the church must never rest. The warfare must be
unending.

6 **And when he saw Jesus from afar, he ran and worshipped
him;**—Jesus' confidence was vindicated. Something in the
sweetness and majesty of Jesus' face brought him to his
knees, or perhaps the clear recognition of divinity by the demons, who not only believe, but tremble as the demons recognized in Jesus the power of God, he became overawed, thinking he had come to consign him to the bottomless pit, and his
actions were caused by fear, being incapable of worshiping
Jesus in the true sense of worship, where it is done in spirit
and in truth, with a loving and obedient disposition, demons
believe and tremble.

7 **and crying out with a loud voice, he saith, What have I to
do with thee,**—The pronoun "I" may indicate that the chief of
these unclean spirits is speaking. Why interfere with me?
(Ezra 4: 3; Ch. 1: 24.) What is there in common between us?

unto him, Come forth, thou unclean spirit, out of the man. 9 And he asked
him, What is thy name? And he saith unto him, My name is Legion; for
we are many. 10 And he besought him much that he would not send them

Jesus, thou Son of the Most High God?—His divine nature
is evidently recognized. Knowing the antagonism that existed between God and the devil, and God's power over demons, this was the language of fear and dread, as though the
demon would say: "We have met, but I desire no conflict with
you, thou mighty Son of God, and I earnestly beseech thee to
drive me not now away into the abyss into which I know I
must at some time go."

I adjure thee by God,—An insolent appeal, but not at all
surprising. A demon would hesitate at no means to accomplish his purpose. I most earnestly entreat thee in the name
of God.

torment me not.—Though their whole employment was tormenting the wretched demoniac, a premonition of coming
vengeance aroused frenzied cries for their own escape. The
request is essentially devilish. Here to be tormented meant to
be prevented from tormenting another. It is worthy of notice
how instantly the demons recognize that contact with Jesus
means torment for devils. Matthew (8: 29) puts it in a question with an additional thought, "Art thou come hither to torment us before the time?" This seems to look to that final
day of doom, when all their activities for evil among men are
to be forever at an end. (Jude 6; 2 Pet. 2: 4; Matt. 25: 41.)

8 **For he said unto him, Come forth, thou unclean spirit, out
of the man.**—The opening words of the interview, alluded to
in verse 7. Jesus had been moved with compassion at the
miserable condition of the poor man, who was bruised and
mangled by the power of the demon which possessed him, and
had either already ordered the demon to come out, or the
demon clearly anticipated that he would do so; hence all the
beseeching of the demon was that they be not driven away
into, as Luke (8: 31) says, "the abyss," doubtless meaning the
place of torment for demons. (Rev. 22: 3.)

9 **And he asked him, What is thy name?**—Jesus did not ask
this question for his own information, but to show the great
combined power of demons, which he was about to overcome.

away out of the country. 11 Now there was there on the mountain side a

---

And he saith unto him, My name is Legion; for we are many.—To whomsoever Jesus spoke, it is evident the demon answered. The name was very expressive. It was originally applied to a whole Roman army; then to a corps of, say, 6,000 men. It came to be a word commonly used, as expressive of any great multitude. Christ claims, in his last hours, that he could call for and receive twelve legions of angels. Nothing could be more expressive of the concentration of evil forces in this one man. The mixed reply is worthy of notice, *"my name,"* *"we* are many." A constant shifting of identity from the man to the demons. In the next verse it again changes to the singular. That evil spirits go often in companies is to be inferred not only from this, but also from the case of Mary Magdalene, from whom were cast out seven demons. (Luke 8: 2.) How many demons there were in this case we have no means of knowing; although the number of swine, into which the demons entered, were about two thousand (verse 13), which may be suggestive of the number of demons. If only one demon entered each swine then the man had about two thousand demons in him. No wonder he was in such a deplorable condition when Jesus found him. This may, in some way, account for the fierce and fiendish manner in which they had abused him. We are not informed how it was they obtained possession of him to this extent, but probably he had not been careful to guard himself against the return of one evil spirit, who brings, when he reenters a man, seven others more wicked than himself, and they enter in and dwell there, making the last state worse than the first. (Matt. 12: 45.)

10 **And he besought him much that he would not send them away out of the country.**—The petition in the demon's prayer. He and his colleagues preferred staying where they had dwelt so long, and had exercised so much power. It seems to be a natural consequence of awful fear and dread that it manifested itself in the form of prayer. Here we have the singular truth brought to the surface that devils *pray*. James (2: 19) says, "The demons also believe, and shudder." Faith that leads not to loving obedience is of no avail. Prayer that is wrung from terror-stricken beings lacking that true regard of an earnest

great herd of swine feeding. 12 And they besought him, saying, Send us into the swine, that we may enter into them. 13 And he gave them leave. And the unclean spirits came out, and entered into the swine: and the herd

---

worshiper, seeking the honor and glory of God, will be something like the prayers of demons. Your sins will always want to remain with you. They will put up the shutters and close the front door, and submit to some *reasonable* restrictions, but they want to stay.

11 **Now there was there on the mountain side a great herd of swine feeding.**—About two thousand. (Verse 13.) Something that by Jewish law had no business there. (Lev. 11: 7, 8.) Only a recreant Jew could meddle with swine, and, if owned by Gentiles, their presence was but a symbol of the subjugation of the country by a foreign foe. A swineherd was the extremest idea a Jew could have of degradation, and therefore the prodigal son was represented as having reached the abyss of misery in this.

12 **And they besought him, saying, Send us**—The demons recognize the power of Jesus. Luke (8: 32) puts it "leave," that is, permit us.

into the swine, that we may enter into them.—These unclean swine were congenial with the unclean natures of the demons. How they could possess inferior animals is not difficult to imagine, since they so thoroughly possessed the lower and sensual nature of men. They could exert no moral and intellectual influence, as in man; but they could operate through the organs of their bodies, and through their animal and sensual natures. Why the request? Who knows? Perhaps with a malicious presence of the mischief they would do, and the hindrance it would prove to Christ's work there. Or, it may be that they must have a living body of some kind to get into in order to any degree of comfort. Matthew (12: 43) indicates this. Is it not a strange request, to be sent into swine? But is it any stranger than that a man made in the image of God should grovel in filthy lust?

13 **And he gave them leave.**—He did not *send* them as requested, but permitted them. He left them free to make their own choice. What they dreaded came from giving them permission to do what they requested, and it is certain that de-

rushed down the steep into the sea, *in number* about two thousand; and they
were drowned in the sea. 14 And they that fed them, fled, and told it in the

---

mons had no rights which Jesus was bound to respect. Nor
was he liable for their want of foresight, if such it was. But
what about the rights of the owners of the swine? What
about the morality of interfering with and destroying the
property of others? Since the demons had their own free
choice in the matter, they, not Christ, are responsible for all
evil results flowing therefrom.

**And the unclean spirits came out, and entered into the
swine:**—The poor demoniac was once more a free man, and
we may imagine the joy of his heart as he realized that again
the sweetnesses of life were possible for him, and who knows
what hearts may have been waiting for him in Gadara. The
demons had an answer to their prayer, but it is not always the
best thing that can happen to a wicked spirit, in or out of the
body, to have its prayer or dearest wish.

and the herd rushed down the steep into the sea,—Even the
swine must do evil to themselves when possessed by an evil
spirit. Labored discussions have been held as to whether an
unclean spirit can enter into swine. It is as well to discuss
whether an unclean spirit can enter into a man. All we know
is that the Bible says both occurred. We believe it. All attempts to explain the action of the swine by natural causes
are needless. It needs no explanation or apology, only faith.

in number about two thousand;—Only Mark indicates the
number of swine.

and they were drowned in the sea.—So the unclean beasts
ceased to pollute the territory. But what became of the demons? We must not be wise above what is written. Let us
live such circumspect lives that none of them may be able to
possess us mentally or bodily! You choose your own destiny.
Jesus will not deprive you of your gift of freedom of choice,
but you must be prepared to take the consequences. (Josh.
24: 15.) This miracle and that of the withered fig tree which
Jesus cursed (11: 12-14, 20) are the only ones which resulted
in any destruction of property. But Christ as the Son of God
had a right to do as he pleased with both the hogs and the
tree, since the earth and all therein are his. (Psalm 24: 1; 50:

city, and in the country. And they came to see what it was that had come to
pass. 15 And they come to Jesus, and behold ²him that was possessed with
demons sitting, clothed and in his right mind, *even* him that had the legion:

²Or, the *demoniac*

12.) There is no more need of any special vindication here
than in the case of far more serious inflictions of the same
kind by disease or accident. Besides the permission was the
Lord's; the destruction of the hogs, the work of demons.
Christ was no more responsible for what the demons did
than he is for what wicked men do now, whom he permits
to live and to hold positions of power in the world. The
swine owners may have showed contempt for the Mosaic
law, and hence this judgment upon them.

14 **And they that fed them fled, and told it in the city, and
in the country.**—They gave the report in the villages on their
way to the city.

And they came to see what it was that had come to pass.—
The whole thing was new, so unparalleled that they could not
understand the story of the swineherds. It was evident that
something very important and startling had happened, but
what it was they came to ascertain more clearly. So "all the
city came out to meet Jesus." Luke (8: 37) says: "All the
people of the country." He includes both city and country.
When an ungodly business is injured or destroyed what a
hubbub it raises, even in our day! The salvation of men
weighs nothing against the destruction of gain.

15 **And they come to Jesus, and behold him that was possessed with demons sitting,**—Luke (8: 35) says he was "sitting . . . at the feet of Jesus." A position of humility, trust,
and security.

clothed—Luke (8: 27) says: "For a long time he had worn
no clothes, and abode not in any house." Where the clothing
came from, we are not informed, but the twelve from among
them could supply sufficient clothing to cover him in that
land, where much clothing was not needed.

and in his right mind,—All disturbing influences went with
the demons, and as no other healing words are reported from
Christ, the idea of a disease of lunacy is forbidden.

even him that had the legion:—They identified him as the

and they were afraid.   16 And they that saw it declared unto them how it befell ²him that was possessed with demons, and concerning the swine.   17 And they began to beseech him to depart from their borders.   18 And as he was entering into the boat, ²he that had been possessed with demons besought him that he might be with him.   19 And he suffered him not, but saith unto

poor wretch they had known under that designation.   There could be no doubt of the reality of this miracle.

and they were afraid.—They were filled with wonder and awe over the manifestation of such miraculous power. Doubtless their own consciousness of sin caused them to fear that Jesus had come to punish all violators of the law, and they were not ready for judgment.   What a delightful contrast to the poor demoniac the day before!   Just as great a contrast to angelic eyes does the redeemed sinner present, sitting at the feet of Jesus.

16 **And they that saw it declared unto them how it befell him that was possessed with demons, and concerning the swine.**—They gave a detailed account of the three main facts of the miracle, namely, the healing of the demoniac, the destruction of the swine, and by whose power they occurred. What had before been told in haste and excitement, and only in bold, rude outline, was now recounted in all its details.

17 **And they began to beseech him to depart from their borders.**—This is the effect the miracle had upon the multitude. The people entreated Jesus to leave their section of country. Luke (8: 37) gives the reason for this request, "For they were holden with great fear."   Other owners of swine may have thought their traffic in danger.   (Acts 19: 24-31.)   To what extremes do worldly interests excite men!   Worldly gain is valued above the blessings of Jesus.   Doubtless they considered the loss of the swine more than counterbalanced the cure of the demoniac.   Jesus answered their prayer—he left their borders and as far as the records show never returned.   A sad day when Jesus forsakes men and their country.   Amazing stupidity!   Salvation, blessing, right at their doors, and they sent it away!

18 **And as he was entering into the boat, he that had been possessed with demons besought him that he might be with him.**—It seems there is only one who was anxious for his company—the one that had been healed.   He may have been

him, Go to thy house unto thy friends, and tell them how great things the Lord hath done for thee, and *how* he had mercy on thee. 20 And he went his way, and began to publish in Decapolis how great things Jesus had done for him: and all men marvelled.

afraid that the demons might return, and so wished to be near his deliverer; or, more probably, in his gratitude and love he wished to serve Christ. Doubtless, he felt ashamed at the behavior of his countrymen. Let us never forget the lesson that Jesus forces himself upon none. In your own hands is the choice of your own destiny.

19 **And he suffered him not,**—Note how the prayers of the three parties are considered by the Lord. The prayer of the demons is granted to their own discomfiture; the prayer of the Gerasenes is also granted by being left to their own destruction; the prayer of the man who had been healed is not granted, for it was not best, and he had a work at home to do.

but saith unto him, Go to thy house unto thy friends, and tell them how great things the Lord hath done for thee, and how he had mercy on thee.—Jesus had had pity and compassion on the healed man. He enjoyed a compassion freely bestowed. Dismissed from the country himself, he would leave behind him one who must ever be a commanding witness to the truth of his supernatural power, his complete mastery of the power of the invisible evil world. Such a story told must inevitably awaken interest and draw men (who had lost no swine) sooner or later to desire to know more of such a healer. There was a wide field of usefulness for this man. His countrymen and friends, who had known him in such a deplorable condition, could now see him restored. He now becomes the means of circulating the power and goodness of Jesus. This he could do better in his own country than any other.

20 **And he went his way, and began to publish in Decapolis how great things Jesus had done for him:**—In obedience to the command of Jesus, the healed man began to publish what Jesus had done for him, not only to those of his own home but, in that whole region lying east and southeast of the Sea of Galilee, called Decapolis. Jesus modestly ascribes the cure to God, but the grateful man to him, and both were right, for God was in Christ manifesting himself unto the world.

and all men marvelled.—If any were led to believe on Christ or to glorify God, the record does not show it. His preaching excited wonder, but probably led not to faith and repentance. No doubt foundations were laid at that time for the subsequent and successful preaching of the gospel in that same region. As he went about preaching the power and mercy of Jesus, the people remembered what he had been and saw what he was then—a living monument of what he was proclaiming.

3. JAIRUS BESOUGHT JESUS TO HEAL HIS DAUGHTER
5: 21-24
(Matt. 9: 18-26; Luke 8: 41-56)

21 And when Jesus had crossed over again in the boat unto the other side, a great multitude was gathered unto him; and he was by the sea. 22 And there cometh one of the rulers of the synagogue, Jairus by name; and seeing him, he falleth at his feet, 23 and beseecheth him much, saying, My

---

21 And when Jesus had crossed over again in the boat unto the other side, a great multitude was gathered unto him; and he was by the sea.—Matthew (9: 1) says he "crossed over, and came into his own city." Luke (8: 40) says: "As Jesus returned, the multitude welcomed him; for they were all waiting for him." When his boat first started from the eastern shore, where he was not wanted, the people on the western shore could see it, and as soon as they saw which way it was headed, they could assemble at the spot where it was to land, and wait for him. He landed, then, at Capernaum in the midst of a waiting multitude; and this was the great multitude (verse 24) that followed him when he started for the house of Jairus.

22 And there cometh one of the rulers of the synagogue, Jairus by name;—"One of the rulers" shows there was a plurality of rulers of the synagogue, just as there is a plurality of elders in the church. He was one of the elders (Luke 4: 3), or presiding officers, who ruled over the affairs of the synagogue.

and seeing him, he falleth at his feet,—In the posture of reverence and earnest entreaty. Matthew (9: 18) says he "worshipped him." He bowed himself before Jesus with his face to the ground, an act of respect and reverence. Dropping upon the knees, and bringing the forehead to the ground, was the Oriental method of reverence and worship.

little daughter is at the point of death: *I pray thee,* that thou come and lay thy hands on her, that she may be [3]made whole, and live. 24 And he went with him; and a great multitude followed him, and they thronged him.

[3]Or, *saved*

---

23 **and beseecheth him much, saying, My little daughter is at the point of death:**—She was his only daughter, and was about twelve years of age. (Luke 8: 42.) He loved his child and spoke of her tenderly. In the last extremity, Matthew says: "Is even now dead." Luke (8: 49) says: "While he yet spake, there cometh one from the ruler of the synagogue's house, saying, Thy daughter is dead; trouble not the Teacher." Verse 35 states the same. There is no discrepancy. She was "at the point of death" when Jairus left home, and died while he was beseeching Jesus for help, and some one followed and told him of the sad fact. Matthew condenses all into the one statement: "Is even now dead." Frequently one historian does not relate all the facts, while others relate facts which he omits; but all are true. Matthew relates the main one, "Is even now dead," while Mark and Luke go more into detail and relate the condition of the child when Jairus left home and how the fact of her death was made known to him.

I pray thee, that thou come and lay thy hands on her, that she may be made whole, and live.—His faith in Jesus to heal is expressed in his leaving his dying daughter to seek the aid of Jesus, and by his earnest entreaty. Yet he thought personal contact was necessary. This is seen in the fact that he wanted Jesus to lay his hand on the child. It was the elder of that synagogue who had previously come to Jesus in behalf of the centurion whose servant was sick, requesting that he should go and heal the servant, and saying, "He is worthy that thou shouldest do this for him; for he loveth our nation and himself built us our synagogue." (Luke 7: 4, 5.) As Jairus had been concerned in the cure of that servant, it is not surprising that when his own little daughter was at the point of death, he resorted to the same unfailing source of deliverance.

24 **And he went with him; and a great multitude followed him, and they thronged him.**—In kindness and mercy and im-

mediately Jesus went with this ruler to his home. He was always ready to bless. He is now, although in a different way.

4. THE WOMAN WITH AN ISSUE OF BLOOD HEALED
5 : 25-34
(Matt. 9: 18-26; Luke 8: 41-56)

25 And a woman, who had an issue of blood twelve years, 26 and had suffered many things of many physicians, and had spent all that she had, and

25 And a woman, who had an issue of blood twelve years, —This woman had an incurable disease so far as human skill was concerned. She was able to walk, and was among the multitude that followed Jesus. She had a chronic disease, which according to the law rendered her unclean. (Lev. 15: 25.) It was of a long continuance, twelve years. This was a hemorrhage of some kind, which for these long years had been a source of much suffering. A remarkable case of wasting disease. She really, by rabbinical law, had no right in a Jewish crowd. How many, many reasons women have to love the Lord Jesus Christ! Even this very disease illustrates it. In Oriental nations where Christianity has not gone, the unfortunate victim has, added to her physical sufferings, social contempt and partial ostracism. Christianity has done this away under its sway.

26 and had suffered many things of many physicians,—The practice of physics in those days was in a very crude condition and no doubt most of it, as perhaps some of it is now, guesswork. The knowledge of the human body and its functions was exceedingly crude. The absurdest ideas passed current as medical knowledge. The most ridiculous experiments were made in the hope of lighting accidentally, as it were, upon efficient remedies. One with a baffling, long-continued disease, if he put himself in their hands at all, was tolerably sure to "suffer many things" of the physicians, including the pocketbook. The remedies that do not cure are likely to aggravate the disease. The many physicians, with their varied remedies, if there had been no malpractice, could scarcely avoid the result here mentioned, she "rather grew worse."

and had spent all that she had, and was nothing bettered, but rather grew worse,—Imperfect as was their knowledge and practice, they had carried one act to perfection—that of

was nothing bettered, but rather grew worse, 27 having heard the things concerning Jesus, came in the crowd behind, and touched his garment. 28

charging. But all that a man hath he will give for his life, and she had kept on, lured by one new, but equally false, hope after another till all her wealth was gone. When one recalls the kind of physicians and their methods of cure in those days, we do not wonder that she suffered, and that they failed to cure her, although she "spent all that she had" in the vain endeavor. How many things does the sin-sick soul suffer from the quack physicians of the soul! Dr. Morality, Dr. Atheism, Dr. Deism, Dr. Spiritualism, etc. But it grows no better; rather grows worse. Miserable comforters are they all.

27 **having heard the things concerning Jesus, came in the crowd behind,**—She had doubtless heard of his power over fever, and paralysis and unclean spirits, and her faith reached up to the hope that such a one might have power over even her apparently incurable malady. When Jairus came to Jesus he (Jesus) was surrounded by a great concourse of people, who followed him. Weak as she was, she pushed in among them. She saw now was her opportunity. The healer was near, and on the way to cure another person. She puts forth her supreme effort. Probably she came in the crowd behind to avoid being noticed. It was an act of faith. She was full of confidence that Jesus was able to heal; but she trembled on account of her conscious unworthiness.

and touched his garment.—[Matthew says: "She said within herself, If I do but touch his garment, I shall be made whole." This showed her faith in his power and willingness to heal. She acted on this faith when, in her weak and enfeebled condition, she pressed through the throng of people that followed and jostled one another against him, and touched the hem of his garment. In response to this touch of faith healing virtue went forth from him, and her blood ceased to flow. Others in the throng that pressed upon him touched him, but no virtue or power to bless or heal went forth from him. It was only the touch of faith that could draw the blessings. She felt the healing power through her whole system giving vigor and strength to her body.]. There is only one who

For she said, If I touch but his garments, I shall be ³made whole. 29 And straightway the fountain of her blood was dried up; and she felt in her body that she was healed of her ¹plague. 30 And straightway Jesus, perceiving in himself that the power *proceeding* from him had gone forth, turned him about in the crowd, and said, Who touched my garments? 31 And his disci-

¹Gr. *scourge.*

can heal the soul's malady, only one who can stop this ever-flowing fount of sin.

28 **For she said, If I touch but his garments, I shall be made whole.**—Healed of my disease. Matthew and Luke both say that she touched "the border of his garment." This woman's experience with "many physicians" was enough to destroy all confidence in the healing art, at least for her case; but not withstanding all these failures and discouragements, she comes to Christ in great faith, not as a physician, but as a being in whom there was virtue and power to heal aside from any remedies.

29 **And straightway the fountain of her blood was dried up; and she felt in her body that she was healed of her plague.**— The hemorrhage instantly ceased. The deep-rooted disease of twelve years standing was thoroughly cured. She perceived by the peculiar sensations she experienced in her body that health was restored and that she was healed. Thus, after twelve years of suffering, when all the skill of the physicians had failed, she finds relief in the healing power of Jesus. She felt it, she knew it. How? The fountain of blood was dried up. So we, when we have given ourselves unreservedly to Christ, when we have abandoned our sins, when through obedience to the gospel the fountain of sin, the rebellious will, is dried up, *know* we are saved. "He that believeth and is baptized shall be saved." (Mark 16: 16.)

30 **And straightway Jesus, perceiving in himself that the power proceeding from him had gone forth,**—He realized now this particular instance of transfer. Others touched him but felt no healing influence, because theirs was not in faith. Her cure was the result and answer of her touch of faith, which reached beyond the hem of his garment to his divine nature.

turned him about in the crowd, and said, Who touched my garments?—This question raises the question whether the healing was conscious or unconscious on his part—that is,

ples said unto him, Thou seest the multitude thronging thee, and sayest thou,
Who touched me?   32 And he looked round about to see her that had done

whether he was only made conscious by feeling the abstrac-
tion of healing power through the woman's touch, or whether,
knowing supernaturally her approach, he voluntarily permitted the power to go forth.   Most orthodox commentators
agree with Trent, who says: "We cannot for an instant suppose that this healing power went forth without the full consent of his will.   He did not ask the question to obtain information, for he had healed the woman, and must have known
on whom the blessing was conferred; but he did it that the
woman might herself make a confession of the whole matter,
by which the power of her faith and the greatness of the miracle might be manifested to the praise of God.   "By grace have
ye been saved through faith; and that not of yourselves, it is
the gift of God."   (Eph. 2: 8.)   The healing virtue comes from
Christ.   Everything was voluntary on the woman's part in
being healed bodily; so on ours in being healed spiritually.
But at the critical moment the power from Jesus goes forth;
so with us.   In either case this power is a gift.   It cannot be
bought.   It is not for sale.   The human and divine so overlap
that we cannot separate them.   The soul of the woman was
not healed, only her body.   She was healed physically, not
spiritually.

31 **And his disciples said unto him, Thou seest the multitude thronging thee, and sayest thou, Who touched me?**—Peter and his companions knew not yet the difference between
mere contact and the believing touch, between thronging
Christ and touching Christ.   Many had brushed against him
and were none the better; she had touched him and rejoiced.
Jesus responded, according to Luke: "Somebody did touch
me: for I perceive that power had gone forth from me."   As
the people were in a dense crowd, "thronging" the Savior at
the time, the disciples thought it a singular question to ask
under the circumstances, but he knew what had taken place
and they knew nothing of it.

32 **And he looked round about to see her that had done this
thing.**—Jesus was not in doubt as to the party who had
touched him.   He knew from the beginning the gender; "to
see her" implies his knowledge as to her identity.   Luke (8:

this thing. 33 But the woman fearing and trembling, knowing what had been done to her, came and fell down before him, and told him all the truth. 34 And he said unto her, Daughter, thy faith hath [2]made thee whole; go in peace, and be whole of thy [1]plague.

[2]Or, *saved thee*

47) also confirms this knowledge when he says: "When the woman saw that she was not hid."

33 But the woman fearing and trembling, knowing what had been done to her, came and fell down before him, and told him all the truth.—She revealed her heart. Not in a secret whisper, for Luke (8: 47) says she "declared in the presence of all the people for what cause she touched him, and how she was healed immediately." Thus this magnificent cure became public property, and was added to the flowing tide of Christ's fame, ever rolling on with fuller volume and to further shores. The woman was now in proper mental condition to receive the confirmation of her cure, to be disabused of all ideas of mere magical contact with Jesus, and to receive spiritual influence to go with her future life. It was her intention to keep the matter secret, but it was the will of the Savior that she should make it known. So she "told him all the truth" concerning the matter.

34 And he said unto her, Daughter, thy faith hath made thee whole;—Not faith of itself, for the touch which faith actuated evidently had an important part, from the question in the thirtieth verse. Midway between the *faith* and *touch* was the *purpose* which the faith caused her to form, and the touch executed.

go in peace,—All her self-reproach and self-questioning were now at an end. The Master had proclaimed peace, and what peace it was, after these twelve years of sickness, and shame, and pain, and contempt!

and be whole of thy plague.—Continue whole! It shall be to thee a permanent possession, this gracious healing. Probably this woman became a spiritual follower of Jesus Christ, and was saved at last. However, the Bible is silent on this point. Her faith was not a passive or inactive one; had it been, she never would have been made whole. It moved her and filled her with courage to press through the crowd and to touch the body of Jesus.

5. JAIRUS' DAUGHTER RAISED
5: 35-43
(Matt. 9: 18-26; Luke 8: 41-56)

35 While he yet spake, they come from the ruler of the synagogue's *house,* saying, Thy daughter is dead: why troublest thou the Teacher any further? 36 But Jesus, [8]not heeding the word spoken, saith unto the ruler of

[8]Or, *overhearing*

---

35 **While he yet spake, they come from the ruler of the synagogue's house, saying, Thy daughter is dead:**—Here was a new trial and test of Jairus' faith. While Jesus stopped to heal this woman and was talking to her, the messengers came to inform Jairus of the death of his daughter. People back home knew where he was and for what purpose he had gone. It seems that Jairus had come with the full knowledge and consent of his family. The crisis has come. They had faith in his power to *heal.* Capernaum was full of illustrations. But, to raise from the dead, ah, that was too much to expect. Why take his time for no purpose? Why interrupt his teaching for an impossibility?

why troublest thou the Teacher any further?—The last ray of hopeful light seemed gone. The blackness of despair seemed settling down over the heart of the ruler. Jesus saw the change in his countenance, and hastened to comfort him. They thought it useless to trouble Christ to come any further on the way. [They thought he might prevent the sick from dying, but did not think he could raise the dead to life. That was Martha's condition. She said: "If thou hadst been here, my brother had not died," but could not take it in that Jesus could raise him from the dead. So, when she died, they concluded that all hope was gone, and sent to the ruler to trouble not the Master.]

36 **But Jesus, not heeding the word spoken, saith unto the ruler of the synagogue, Fear not, only believe.**—Believe that I have power to raise your daughter from the dead. Jesus encouraged Jairus and told him not to fear. Luke (8: 50) adds, "And she shall be made whole." Notice, the sublime confidence of Jesus in his own power, in the face of the assurance that he will be called upon to grapple with Satan in the extreme manifestation of his malignant power. There was no limit to Christ's power; the only danger was Jairus' faith

the synagogue, Fear not, only believe. 37 And he suffered no man to follow with him, save Peter, and *James, and John the brother of *James. 38 And they come to the house of the ruler of the synagogue; and he beholdeth a tumult, and *many* weeping and wailing greatly. 39 And when he was en-

*Or, *Jacob*

should fail, and he not be worthy to receive the earthly blessing. By "only believe," Jesus does not mean passive faith. The faith of Jairus was very active. He had sought Jesus, leaving his dying daughter at home; had prostrated himself in reverence before him; had besought him to go, and was now returning with him. He could do no more, and Jesus assured him that his daughter should be made whole.

37 **And he suffered no man to follow with him, save Peter, and James, and John the brother of James.**—Luke (8: 51) says: "When he came to the house, he suffered not any man to enter' in with him," save these three. There were doubtless good reasons for Jesus to select these three brethren but we may never be able to know what they were. Jesus advanced to higher studies those who, by faithfulness in the lower, had made it possible for them to understand and use the higher. Without doubt these brethren were the most advanced in the knowledge of him and of his kingdom, so that they were best able to receive new light, new visions of truth. This may be the reason of their selection. If so, all their faithfulness, love, and consecration to their master had prepared them for these higher experiences.

38 **And they come to the house of the ruler of the synagogue; and he beholdeth a tumult,**—An uproar, a noise of loud lamentation, such as usually attended a funeral in that country. The confusion and weeping of the assembled people. There was always a horrible clamor at Eastern funerals; and the preparations had begun, for early burial was usual among the Jews.

and many weeping and wailing greatly.—Including professional mourners. The "weeping" was a dolorous rather than tearful series of ejaculations, and the "wailing" was beating of the breast, rending the outer garment, tearing out the hair, with outcries, in which the neighbors joined. The Greeks, Romans and Jews alike were in the habit of engaging bands of professional mourners, who practiced the art of making the

tered in, he saith unto them, Why make ye a tumult, and weep? the child is
not dead, but sleepeth. 40 And they laughed him to scorn. But he, having

most agonizing sounds as expressions of the grief of the real
mourners. Part of them also used instruments. Matthew (9:
23) mentions the flute players.

39 **And when he was entered in, he saith unto them, Why
make ye a tumult, and weep?**—Luke (8: 52) says: "Weep
not." His first words are words of comfort, and calculated to
arouse expectation. Matthew gives what was probably the
preface to this, "Give place," and Mark, in his vivid way, supplies, "Why make ye a tumult, and weep?" A natural introduction to Luke's words. "Weep not," this house is not what
you take it for, no funeral procession is to issue from its doors
at this time.

the child is not dead, but sleepeth.—Not finally dead. She
shall be aroused as one asleep. These words are given sub-
stantially by all the synoptics, except that Matthew substi-
tutes "damsel," and Mark "child," for the pronoun. It seems
hardly credible that these words of Jesus have been made
ground by many for the assertion that she was not dead at all,
and that this is a case of healing, not of raising from the dead.
We do not wonder at those who are possessed of a horror of
miracles and desire to get rid of all possible. Jesus used sub-
stantially the same words in regard to Lazarus, and did not
explain them until the disciples showed they had misunder-
stood them; then he said, "Lazarus is dead." Jesus and his
apostles and evangelists often speak of death as a sleep.
(John 11: 11-14; Acts 7: 60; 1 Cor. 15: 6, 51; 1 Thess. 4: 13.)
This is doubtless in view of the certainty of the resurrection
or living again, which was clearly a part of the faith once delivered to the saints. If the child was not literally dead and if
Jesus had intended to practice a fraud in pretending to raise
her from the dead, when he really did not, he would not have
said she "is not dead," but he would have done all in his
power to induce them to believe that she was dead. His declaration that she "sleepeth" emphasized the fact in the minds
of all present that she was really dead. He did not mean, either, to deny the fact that she was dead, but to emphasize the
truth that death is a sleep. The meaning of this passage,
then, is the child has not ceased to exist; but though her

put them all forth, taketh the father of the child and her mother and them that were with him, and goeth in where the child was. 41 And taking the child by the hand, he saith unto her, Talitha cumi; which is, being inter-

---

body is dead, yet her spirit lives, and she sleeps in the hope of resurrection.

40 **And they laughed him to scorn.**—The idea that she was not dead was absurd to them. They knew she was dead, and so they scorned and ridiculed his assertion. They did not understand him. While he said she was not dead, he meant she was as one asleep for a time, and he would awake her. What are we here for? Why this flute playing, why this wailing, if she is not dead? Jesus had not yet seen the damsel, and it seemed to them utterly absurd for him to pronounce judgment against theirs, who had been in contact with the body.

But he, having put them all forth, taketh the father of the child and her mother and them that were with him,—The crowd of noisy mourners and deriders are put out of the house. None were left besides the apostles, the father, the mother, Jesus, and the girl. Peter, James, and John were those with him. (Verse 37.)

and goeth in where the child was.—Jesus had entered the house (verse 39), now he enters the room where the child was. Today, after eighteen hundred years, we hear the echo of that laugh. Still do the mad votaries of the world laugh to scorn him who talks of the resurrection and the future.

41 **And taking the child by the hand,**—This was not necessary to the miracle, but for the good of those present. Their impression was thus deepened, and the faith of the parents strengthened.

he saith unto her, Talitha cumi; which is, being interpreted, Damsel, I say unto thee, Arise.—Our historian gives the interpretation of Talitha cumi. These are words from the language of the people of Palestine, and Mark tells us what they mean. This was the form of Hebrew then used by the common people. She heard and obeyed. Thus shall he with equal ease call forth myriads of his, who now seem perished in the dust: and it may be said with regard to them also, in reference to that day, they are not dead but sleep. The maiden

preted, Damsel, I say unto thee, Arise. 42 And straightway the damsel rose up, and walked; for she was twelve years old. And they were amazed straightway with a great amazement. 43 And he charged them much that no man should know this: and he commanded that *something* should be given her to eat.

of whom we here read arose only to a dying life; a life which needed the support of food, and was in no respect more noble, or more secure, than that of other mortals: but we look for a better resurrection, in which all the infirmities of the body shall be left behind in the grave; and there shall be no more death, neither sorrow nor crying.

42 **And straightway the damsel rose up, and walked;**— Points out the fact that she was alive and in perfect health. It shows the completeness of the cure, without a long period of convalescence. Luke (8: 55) says: "Her spirit returned, and she rose up immediately." The spirit that had left the body a lifeless corpse returned, warmed the body, animation was restored, and she lived again. At death, "the dust returneth to the earth as it was, and the spirit returneth unto God who gave it." (Eccles. 12: 7.) The spirit—the soul—the inner man—the better part comes from God at the beginning of life and returns to him at death. The word "returneth" shows the spirit had come from God at the beginning of her existence. She died and the spirit went back to the giver. When she was made alive, her spirit came back from God and entered into her body again.

for she was twelve years old. And they were amazed straightway with a great amazement.—Reason why, on being made alive, she immediately rose and walked. She was of suitable age. The great amazement of the witnesses shows that they regarded the child as really raised from the dead. The people were filled with astonishment now more than they were with ridicule a short while ago.

43 **And he charged them much that no man should know this:**—[Her parents were astonished at what had been done, but he commanded that they should not tell what he had done to the damsel. Why Jesus prohibited this being told on several occasions is by no means certain, but it is probable it was that the crowd might not be induced to follow him through idle curiosity to see the wonders he performed. Jesus is re-

corded as having raised this damsel, the son of the widow of
Nain, and Lazarus, who had already been four days in the
grave.]

**and he commanded that something should be given her to
eat.**—Jesus had raised her by *extraordinary* power, but he
willed that she should be sustained by *ordinary* means. He
also in this gave full evidence that she was really restored to
life and health. The changes were great, sudden, and certain.
There could be no illusion. So when our Savior had risen
from the dead, he gave evidence of his own resurrection, by
eating with his disciples. The wonder-working power of
Jesus has no limitations.

The quickening to life again in itself could not, of course, be
kept back secret (see on the contrary Matt. 9: 26), but probably the more detailed circumstances of the way of its
accomplishment might. There is nothing said of the good
spiritual results which accrued to this ruler and his family
from the death and resurrection of his daughter, but it all
would be well calculated to produce for them a rich harvest
of good. The simplest and most natural use of sorrow is to
lead us to the God of all comfort. Jairus came to Christ
because of trouble. Pleasures brighten as they vanish. The
only daughter doubly dear as her spirit was departing.
We are not conscious of the strength of our attachments until
they are about to be severed. An open chasm must yawn
before us ere we can realize our need. To Christ we should
come at all times; to him only can we go for solid comfort in
times of deep distress. Our Lord here, and in the other
restorations of the dead to life, gives us examples of the
soul's existence after the death of the body, and apart from the
body. He proves that the soul does not die with the body by
facts, not merely assertions. These miracles prepare us to
accept the fact of his resurrection, on which depends the
truth of the gospel and the proof of his messiahship. If
Jesus can raise others from the dead, there is nothing
incredible in his own resurrection, and the immortal life it
proves. Jesus is still the resurrection and the life. Our dear
ones are raised again by him to a life as much more than the
life here, as a plant in full bloom is more glorious than the
seed from which it sprang.

SECTION SIX

OPINIONS OF MEN, AND MORE MIRACLES
6: 1 to 7: 23

1. OPINION OF THE NAZARENES
6: 1-6
(Matt. 13: 54-58; Luke 4: 16-31)

1 And he went out from thence; and he cometh into his own country; and his disciples follow him. 2 And when the sabbath was come, he began to teach in the synagogue: and [5]many hearing him were astonished, say-

[5]Some ancient authorities insert *the*.

---

1 **And he went out from thence;**—From Capernaum, where he had raised from the dead the daughter of Jairus. Not only from the house of Jairus, but from the city of Capernaum. Then ended his stay in Capernaum.

and he cometh into his own country;—Nazareth and its neighborhood. His mother and Joseph lived here before his birth (Luke 1: 26, 27; 2: 4), and Jesus was reared there (Matt. 2: 23; Mark 1: 9; Luke 2: 39, 41, 51), and was called a "Nazarene" (Matt. 2: 23; Mark 1: 24). Nazareth is not mentioned in the Old Testament, but occurs first in Matthew (2: 23). It derives its celebrity from its connection with the history of Christ.

and his disciples follow him.—The twelve (verse 7) and probably many others who went with him from place to place.

2 **And when the sabbath was come, he began to teach in the synagogue:**—[Synagogues had been built in all the towns of Judea, Samaria, and Galilee, and in the towns of the heathen nations wherever Jews in any number dwelled. The synagogue was the house of meeting. With the building of the synagogue came the weekly meeting, reading the scriptures, and the abandonment of idol worship by the Jews. They met in the synagogues every Sabbath to read the scriptures. Jesus, in traveling around through the country, habitually entered the synagogues on the Sabbath to read the scriptures and teach the people. In these teaching journeys he healed the sick and relieved the suffering, and was praised and glorified of all. The early ministry of Jesus had a seeming success that the latter did not. This is often true of any cause.

ing, Whence hath this man these things? and, What is the wisdom that is given unto this man, and *what mean* such [6]mighty works wrought by his hands? 3 Is not this the carpenter, the son of Mary, and brother of [4]James,

[6]Gr. *powers.*

Truth commends itself to the hearts of the common people. Often a cause is popular until the opposition has time to organize and strengthen itself, and then difficulties arise, old prejudices are aroused. Then the fairweather friends turn back and walk no more with the truth; only the true and steadfast will stand in such trials.]

and many hearing him were astonished,—Probably the multitude is meant. There was a freshness, an originality in his teachings that compelled their attention and excited their wonder.

saying, Whence hath this man these things?—The designation is contemptuous—"this man" that we all know. The wisdom with which he spake created the inquiry into these things.

and, What is the wisdom that is given unto this man,—[Jesus manifested no miraculous power until the Holy Spirit came upon him as he came up out of the waters of baptism. After he received this Spirit and had been tempted he returned into Galilee, working miracles through the power bestowed upon him, and the fame of this power went abroad throughout Galilee and adjoining countries.]

and what mean such mighty works—There were whispers already circulating that he had learned in some way, since his residence in Nazareth, to use the powers of the Prince of Darkness, and this was the explanation of his miracles.

wrought by his hands?—Which so recently were employed in servile and mechanical work. Let the Lord's day find you at the Lord's house, and let it find you ready to teach always the clear revelation of God's will which must be an astonishment to the worldly.

3 Is not this the carpenter,—Not as indicating that that business is low or unworthy, but as putting him on a level with themselves. Among the Jews there was nothing degrading in a trade. Even the rabbis learned trades. Said they, "He who does not teach his son a trade, is much the same as

and Joses, and Judas, and Simon? and are not his sisters here with us? And they were [7]offended in him. 4 And Jesus said unto them, A prophet is not without honor, save in his own country, and among his own kin, and in his

[7]Gr. *caused to stumble.*

if he taught him to be a thief." "A boy with a trade is like a garden well fenced." Justin Martyr says that Jesus made plows and the like. Matthew has, "Is not this the carpenter's son?" indicating his reputed sonship to Joseph. Probably *both* sentences were uttered in the busy whispering which went on in the congregation.

the son of Mary,—His mother was also well known. Joseph, perhaps, now was no longer living, otherwise it would have been natural for his name to have been mentioned here. In his previous visit they spoke of him as "Joseph's son," a reference to Joseph as then living, or still remembered. (Luke 4: 22.)

and brother of James, and Joses, and Judas, and Simon?— Words should be taken in their first and ordinary meaning, unless there are some reasons for not doing so. These reasons are entirely wanting, and these "brothers" are to be considered the sons of Mary. (Matt. 12: 46; Gal. 1: 19.) The scriptures allude to Mary as the *wife* of Joseph and the mother of Jesus, her *first* born. (Matt. 1: 25; Luke 2: 7.)

and are not his sisters here with us?—After Jesus was born, Mary became the mother of at least six other children. The fair interpretation of this passage is that these were the sons and daughters of Joseph and Mary. The people in the neighborhood thought so, and spoke of them as such.

and they were offended in him.—That is, the foolish prejudice arising from familiarity, and disinclination to allow their equals to be exalted above themselves, caused them to stumble at his claims, and finally reject them.

4 And Jesus said unto them, A prophet is not without honor, save in his own country,—A proverbial saying, doubtless, and expressing a world-wide truth. It is rarely that a community realizes the greatness of its own sons till they come back with the stamp of greatness from the outer world. Cities contend to be considered the birthplace of men dead, who could scarcely find shelter therein when living. This is a fact in human experience, presenting a general truth, of which

own house. 5 And he could there do no [8]mighty work, save that he laid his hands upon a few sick folk, and healed them. 6 And he marvelled because of their unbelief.

[8]Gr. *power.*

the treatment of Jesus in the present instance was an example. A stranger sees the public and spiritual acts of a prophet, and recognizes his heavenly character; but neighbors and acquaintances fix their thoughts upon his earthly relationships, to a partial or total exclusion of his higher excellences, and thus come to a wrong conclusion. Prejudice and rejection are the result. That our Lord as a prophet should receive such treatment was highly unreasonable and wicked on the part of his former neighbors and acquaintances. His wisdom and miracles should have overcome all prejudice and unbelief.

and among his own kin, and in his own house.—Among his relatives, and in his own family, with whom he was brought up from childhood. His brothers did not believe on him. (John 7: 3-5.) This proverb was strikingly illustrated in this instance, when the Son of God himself, with power to work miracles, could prove to be no exception to the general rule as expressed by this saying. Jesus advances this as a general truth. There *might* be some exceptions to it, but *he* was not an exception. Everywhere else he had been more honored than at home.

5 And he could there do no mighty work,—A most significant sentence this, as showing even the miracles of Jesus to depend upon the receptivity of the subject. Their prejudices kept them from hearty faith in him; and this seems to have extended to almost the entire community. They did not believe, and they could not be healed. The frequent mention of faith as the medium of healing in the miracles that he wrought prepares us for this as an explanation of failure. It applies as well to the healing of the malady of the soul. It depends upon the sinner as much as upon God. The teaching that faith is a direct, special, and irresistible gift of God is untrue, because then the Savior would have been without excuse in failing to heal. The needy one exercises faith, and instantly the healing power responds. The reason for not doing mighty works was unbelief.

save that he laid his hands upon a few sick folk, and healed

And he went round about the villages teaching.

---

them.—[They had heard the report of his healing the afflicted in Capernaum, but did not believe it, so asked that he should do the same in Nazareth. Jesus had grown up quietly as a boy among them, with no display of power. They were slow to believe great and wonderful things of him, and demanded the evidence in a spirit that hindered his doing it. Their spirit was one of defiant unbelief like that which demanded, "Let him come down from the cross" if he be the Son of God. He stated the truth that we are slow to believe one reared among us, whom we have known as a common associate, as our companion and equal, can do great things. He had done many works in Capernaum—more than he had in his native city.]

6 **And he marvelled because of their unbelief.**—He is spoken of here simply in his humanity. To his serene spirit, which lived in an atmosphere of perfect faith, it was a marvel that his countrymen, the chosen people of God, should reject salvation when it came directly to their doors.

And he went round about the villages teaching.—Practically shut out from the city, he would not abandon the district, and therefore went among the little hamlets of which there were so many in Palestine, where no houses are built entirely alone. Not being received in Nazareth, his own city, he pursued the course he required of his disciples, by going to other places. Though rejected in his own city and by his own people, he did not allow this to keep him from going on with his mission. He moved on in his field of operation, from village to village. He now leaves Nazareth forever. A sad thought indeed.

2. FIRST MISSION OF THE TWELVE
6: 7-13
(Matt. 9: 35; 10: 42; Luke 9: 1-6)

7 And he calleth unto him the twelve, and began to send them forth by

---

7 **And he calleth unto him the twelve,**—[It was the purpose of Jesus to prepare witnesses to testify of him and his teaching to the world, after he had finished his mission and had ascended to God his Father. To prepare and fit them for this

two and two; and he gave them authority over the unclean spirits; 8 and he

work he called upon them to leave their calling, follow him, be with him daily, and hear his teachings as he repeated them day by day, and see the many wonderful works of love and mercy performed to relieve sufferings of men and women. Before he had finished his course, he chose twelve out of the number that followed with him, who should thus be witnesses of what he taught and did. This choosing was a matter of importance. Preparatory to his choosing, he spent the whole night in prayer to God. (Luke 6: 12.) He seems to have thus spent the night as a help to him in the work of selecting these twelve that were to be his witnesses. (Mark 3: 15, 16.) Their being with him was preliminary, and necessary to fit them to go forth to preach. He gave them power to cast out unclean spirits and to heal diseases, by endowing them with the Holy Spirit, who had power over these evil spirits. This sending forth, endowed by this Spirit, was to show to the Jews the power that he would bestow on them; for in this work they acted only in the name of the Lord Jesus. It seems to have been a preliminary trial of them during the life of Jesus to gradually school and fit them for the use of these spiritual powers when they would be fully bestowed on and committed to them after the ascension of Jesus. It was necessary that they should have been with Jesus when John baptized him, and henceforward. (Acts 1: 21, 22.) To do this, they were imbued with the Spirit of God, by which they were enabled to do these works, and so manifest to the world that God was with them. These chosen now were to be his witnesses to all the world after his death. Of the twelve chosen, Judas by transgression fell away, and Matthias was chosen in his place. We know but little of the lives of the apostles, save Peter, James, and John, before or after their call to the apostleship. This does not signify that they were not ardent workers in preaching Christ to the world.]

and began to send them forth—Jesus had been schooling and training them for the work he now sends them to do. He "began to send." It seems from this that he did not send them all at once—just as they were prepared.

by two and two;—This arrangement was that they might

charged them that they should take nothing for *their* journey, save a staff

counsel and encourage each other, and that a combination of traits might be found in two not possessed by one alone. The teacher and exhorter are not commonly combined in the same man. [Having selected these twelve from among those who closely followed him, and so had come to know his teaching well, he sent them forth to preach and turn the people to the Lord. He warned them to go neither to the Gentiles nor to the Samaritans, but to the children of Israel. They are called the lost sheep, because they belonged to the house of Jacob, which had been the chosen fold of God, but now had wandered from God, and were lost. Jesus had confined his labors chiefly to the "lost sheep of the house of Israel." (Matt. 15: 24.) The gospel was first preached to the Jews; afterward to all nations. (Matt. 10: 5, 6.)]

and he gave them authority over the unclean spirits;— [They were to go through the land of Israel, and as they went preach. (Matt. 10: 7.) To preach was to herald or proclaim a message to the people. It differed from teaching, which is instructing in the precepts and principles of the religion of Jesus that grow out of the acceptance of the gospel. These apostles were to preach or proclaim to the people the truth. The kingdom of heaven was at hand. Jesus had come to establish or set up a kingdom; he was preparing for it, and now they are to proclaim it as near at hand, ready to be set up. Therefore they should be ready to accept and enter into that kingdom. This was a proclamation of the same message that John the Baptist and Jesus had made, and afterwards was given to the seventy. They had received freely the authority over these demons and diseases, that they might heal them, and so they are commanded to use it freely in healing the sick and casting out demons.] Miraculous power was not bestowed upon the apostles and others to make them morally or spiritually better, but to confirm the truth which they preached. Their moral and spiritual condition depended upon their own faith and obedience to God.

8 and he charged them that they should take nothing for their journey,—They were to go as they were, in their ordinary dress, as common travelers, and not in peculiar garb, or

only; no bread, no wallet, no [9]money in their [10]purse; 9 but *to go* shod with

[9]Gr. *brass.*
[10]Gr. *girdle.*

---

with any kind of ostentation, but trusting God for necessary support.

save a staff only; no bread,—Bread is something that the poorer class of travelers in Palestine always carry with them when they can. McGarvey says: "The writer was much amused in Palestine, in seeing one of the servants with a number of loaves of bread (flat, thin, round flour cakes, perhaps a foot in diameter) under his pack saddle, from which he would occasionally obtain a bite. Others had two or three under their clothing like a breastplate." Staff was a stick used for walking or carrying a budget.

no wallet,—The wallet was a traveling bag, used for carrying provisions—more properly, a shepherd's bag, used by the shepherd for carrying food when tending his sheep away from home.

no money in their purse;—Without bread, and without money to buy bread, or anything else, they had been accustomed to carrying a purse, from which to buy what was needed (John 13: 29), but on this particular mission they were not allowed to do so.

9 but to go shod with sandals:—[In going forth they were not to provide for the expenses of their journey, but were to go depending upon the people among whom they labored to supply their wants. They were to take only what they needed now, and depend upon more being furnished, as needed on the journey. The reason given is that the laborer is worthy of his hire, of his food—rather of his living—both needed food and raiment will be supplied. They were to look to the people among, and for, whom they labored for this support. God in his providence would overrule this, but the people were to supply it.] Matthew says they were to carry no shoes. This harmonizes with Mark, who tells what they were to wear on their feet—sandals. "Sandals" were soles of leather, felt, or wood strapped across the foot with thongs.

and, said he, put not on two coats.—The coat was the undergarment or tunic. Travelers often wore two. They were

sandals: and *said he,* put not on two coats. 10 And he said unto them, Wheresoever ye enter into a house, there abide till ye depart thence. 11 And whatsoever place shall not receive you, and they hear you not, as ye go forth

to have but one. In other words, they were to be clothed as simply as possible. But these directions were only for that time. Subsequently we find they carried a bag, and money, and two coats, etc.

10 **And he said unto them, Wheresoever ye enter into a house, there abide till ye depart thence.**—[On coming to a town or city, they were to inquire or search out who were worthy. Broadus says: "A man of piety and hospitality, such as would make a fit associate and a willing host"—such as was willing to entertain them—and there they were to abide until they left the city. They were not to move their lodging place. This did not prohibit their laboring with the people where they might be met, or from house to house. The salutation common on entering a house was: "Peace be to this house." Luke (10: 5) gives the form of salutation. (See also Luke 24: 36; 1 Sam. 25: 26.) It was a prayer to God for all good to rest upon the household.]

11 **And whatsoever place shall not receive you, and they hear you not,**—[He now instructs his apostles how to act toward those who reject them and their message. They would be rejected by whole communities as well as by individuals. Thus a Samaritan village (Luke 9: 53) and the Gerasenes (Ch. 5: 17) rejected Jesus. We learn from Matthew that they were to inquire who was worthy in places where they went, but as one's reputation is not always his true character, they might go into houses where they were not welcome; if so, they were told how to proceed in testifying against them. "It shall be more tolerable for the land of Sodom and Gomorrah." This solemn warning is teeming with useful suggestions. It shows at a glance the certainty of a general judgment for all nations and people, and it also clearly reveals the truth that men shall be judged according to their opportunities. How the house was to show itself worthy or unworthy is not clear; probably by continuing the hospitality and lending a willing ear to the message they delivered. If they received kindly the message they came to make known, they would continue

thence, shake off the dust that is under your feet for a testimony unto them.
12 And they went out, and preached that *men* should repent. 13 And they

to treat them kindly; if they did not, they would withdraw their hospitality. If it is not worthy, withdraw your salutation or prayer of peace.]

as ye go forth thence, shake off the dust that is under your feet for a testimony unto them.—[The shaking off the dust from the feet against the people originated in the practice of the Jews, when they returned from a foreign country, shaking off the dust from their clothes and feet when they returned to their native land. The land in which idols were worshiped was polluted, unholy, while the land of Judah was holy, consecrated to God; so in returning to Israel they shook off the dust of the polluted land, that they bring it not into the land consecrated to the service of God. So when they went into a house or city, and they refused to hear the message delivered, or were guilty of any unworthiness, they were to shake off the dust from their feet as a testimony and declaration to them of their uncleanness and unworthiness before God. They were to be unto them as were the heathen who rejected God and worshiped the idols. Sodom and Gomorrah had been destroyed on account of their wickedness. God had proposed to Abraham that if ten righteous persons were found in Sodom he would spare it. (Gen. 18: 38.) They were not found. God holds men responsible according to their opportunities to know his will. Those to whom these twelve apostles would preach would have more and better opportunities to know and do the truth than had been granted to the men of Sodom. If they refused to hear these, they would show more unwillingness to do the will of God than had Sodom and Gomorrah; so when God comes to judge the world they will stand less chance of justification before him than the people of Sodom would. According to the light we have we will be accountable. Those of us now living have more light than any that have gone before. If we reject his word, we will be held to a severer accountability. (Matt. 11: 20-24.)]

12 And they went out, and preached that men should repent.—All men. (Acts 17: 20.) The term also includes women for the reason they are included in this free salvation.

cast out many demons, and anointed with oil many that were sick, and healed them.

(Acts 8: 12.) Repentance is a thing for man to do, not something he gets. It is a command, not a promise. We obey commands and enjoy promises when received. We are commanded to repent. The command can and must be obeyed. It is something man does for himself and not something God does for him. God now "commandeth men that they should all everywhere repent." (Acts 17: 30.)

13 **And they cast out many demons,**—The preaching of the apostles was attested not only by miracles, but by *many* miracles.

and anointed with oil many that were sick,—Not because of natural healing efficacy in the oil, but as a medium of communication, and to help the weak faith of the sick, just as Christ used spittle and clay for the blind man. (John 9: 6-12.)

and healed them.—[The apostles, endowed with this new power, "departed, and went throughout the villages, preaching the gospel, and healing everywhere" (Luke 9: 6); "and the apostles, when they were returned, declared unto him what things they had done (Luke 9: 10); "and the apostles gather themselves together unto Jesus; and they told him all things, whatsoever they had done, and whatsoever they had taught" (verse 30). The seventy (Luke 10: 1-10) were sent out the same way, with the same directions. "The seventy returned with joy, saying, Lord, even the demons are subject unto us in thy name. And he said . . . Nevertheless in this rejoice not, that the spirits are subject unto you; but rejoice that your names are written in heaven." (Luke 10: 17-20.)]

3. THE OPINIONS OF HEROD AND OTHERS ABOUT JESUS
6: 14-29
(Matt. 14: 1-12; Luke 9: 7-9)

14 And king Herod heard *thereof;* for his name had become known: and

---

14 **And king Herod**—Called by Matthew and Luke "Tetrarch," a Greek word, meaning "a ruler of the fourth part," and which became a common title for those who governed any part of a province, subject only to the Roman emperor. This

[1]he said, John the Baptizer is risen from the dead, and therefore do these powers work in him. 15 But others said, It is Elijah. And others said, *It is* a prophet, *even* as one of the prophets. 16 But Herod, when he heard

[1]Some ancient authorities read *they.*

was Herod Antipas, son of Herod the Great. His dominion comprised Galilee, Samaria, and Perea. He first married a daughter of Aretas, king of Arabia Retrea; but later took Herodias, his brother Philip's wife. Aretas, indignant at the insult offered his daughter, waged war against Herod and defeated him. This defeat, according to Josephus (Ant. XVIII. 5, 2), was regarded by many as a punishment for the murder of John. In A.D. 39 he was banished to France, whither Herodias followed him. Both died in exile. He was sensual, weak (Matt. 14: 9), cunning (Luke 13: 32), unscrupulous (Luke 3: 19), and superstitious (verse 20; Luke 9: 9).

heard thereof; for his name had become known: and he said, John the Baptizer is risen from the dead,—The guilty conscience of Herod suggested that Jesus was John, whom he had beheaded, now risen from the dead.

and therefore do these powers work in him.—Herod thought because he is risen from the dead, the powers, that is, superhuman or miraculous powers, *work* or are *active* in him. John did not work miracles (John 10: 41); but now, Herod reasons, the powers are active in John's person because he was come forth from the dead, having thus acquired new spiritual and miraculous power. His fears may have been excited lest Jesus might become a political rival, or lest his superhuman powers might be directed against him. According to Luke (9: 7) he "was much perplexed" because some said that John was risen.

15 But others said, It is Elijah.—The coming of Elijah had been foretold by the prophet Malachi (4: 5) and was expected by the Jews. John was indeed the Elijah that was to come. (Matt. 1: 14.)

And others said, It is a prophet, even as one of the prophets.—There was a diversity of opinions among the people as to who Jesus was. These were not ready to regard him as the prophet Elijah, but as *one* of the old prophets, though not so

thereof, said, John, whom I beheaded, he is risen. 17 For Herod himself had sent forth and laid hold upon John, and bound him in prison for the

---

great as Elijah. This is the general estimate of the people concerning Jesus. In opinion they were not agreed.

16 But Herod, when he heard thereof, said, John, whom I beheaded,—"I" is emphatic, made so by his feeling of guilt. Here he confesses his guilt.

he is risen.—His conscience would not allow him to abandon the idea that John had risen from the dead. His guilty conscience impelled him to this opinion. The memory of his crime doubtless haunted him so that he could not get away from the idea.

[We have presented in this case a diversity of character. Not the least important of the revelations of the Bible is that of human character. Man should know himself. He knows things only relatively. Without a correct standard no true judgment can be formed. God in his own character gives the true standard by which all character is to be tested. The delineations of the various characters laid open in the Bible by God, whose knowledge is perfect and judgment just and righteous, are a profitable study to man. In this is presented John, the stern, fearless, and impartial reprover of wrong in the subject and in the king, even though it brought to him imprisonment and death; King Herod, with strong convictions of right, overruled by unlawful attachment to a bad woman and false pride to appear consistent before his courtiers; a wicked and vindictive woman, relentless in cruelty, sacrificing her daughter's good and making her an accomplice in crime to gratify her resentfulness on account of the reproval of her wrongs, the daughter, with fleshly charms, using them to gratify the mother's vengeance.]

17 For Herod himself had sent forth and laid hold upon John, and bound him in prison—At Macherus seven miles northeast of the Dead Sea. (Josephus Ant., 18: 5, 12.)

for the sake of Herodias.—This states why John was cast into prison, on account of the instigation of the adulterous woman, a fact omitted by Matthew. Herodias was a granddaughter of Herod the Great, daughter of Aristobulus, and

sake of Herodias, his brother Philip's wife; for he had married her.   18 For

niece of Herod Antipas. As Jezebel was the foe of the first Elijah (1 Kings 19: 2), so was Herodias of the second.

his brother Philip's wife; for he had married her.—Not the tetrarch of Iturea (Luke 3: 1), but another brother, who lived in private life, having been disinherited by his father; and thus uncle to Herodias, whom he married. But she, preferring royalty, left him, and married Herod Antipas, who, to make way for her, divorced his own wife, daughter of Aretas, king of Arabia, supposed to be the one mentioned by Paul in 2 Cor. 11: 32. Philip was half brother of Herod Antipas. The imprisonment and murder of John had taken place previous to this time. It is here recalled and narrated in connection with the life of Jesus at this time, because Herod insisted that Jesus was John raised from the dead. John had reproved Herod for taking his brother's wife from him and marrying her. Herod claimed to be an observer of the Jewish law. As such he came under the teaching of John, who, regardless of his high position and his power, reproved him as he would his humblest subject. This is not common. Men, preachers, flatter the great and honorable ones of earth to secure their favor. A great source of corruption in the church is the temptation to preachers to palliate and overlook the sins of the great—to flatter them to secure their favor and help. They often persuade themselves that they do good in this, as the favor obtained helps forward the cause of truth. But the approved servants of God pursued a wholly different course. They reproved the rich equally with the poor, and Peter said to Simon, "Thy silver perish with thee." Every preacher ought to say the same, and make no impression that money can secure immunity from strict obedience to the law or favor of God without consecration. When he reproved them Herod seems to have resented the reproof not on his own account, but at the instigation of Herodias. For her sake—to gratify her—he imprisoned John. While he did this much, he refused for the time to go further to please her. But one step in the wrong direction prepares for another.]

John said unto Herod, It is not lawful for thee to have thy brother's wife.
19 And Herodias set herself against him, and desired to kill him; and she

18 **For John said unto Herod, It is not lawful for thee to have thy brother's wife.**—Here is John's rebuke and which led to his death. [It was contrary to the law of Moses, as it has been contrary to the law of God at all times, for a man to take the wife of another. Adultery with a married woman has always been a higher crime than lewdness with an unmarried one. To take a brother's wife or the wife of a near kinsman is worse than to take the wife of another. (Lev. 18: 16; 20: 21.) John had not only reproved Herod for this sin (Luke 3: 19), "but Herod the tetrarch, being reproved by him for Herodias his brother's wife, and for all the evil things which Herod had done." Although claiming to obey the law of Moses, he let his interest, his lusts, his ambition, his personal feelings, his wicked associates draw him into the commission of many wrongs. For these John fearlessly reproved him as a sinner.]

19 **And Herodias set herself against him, and desired to kill him;**—She would kill the physician who only could cure her disease. Doubtless she reasoned that if Herod yielded to John's advice, she was a lost and ruined woman, dethroned, abandoned, disgraced, with nowhere to go. Either John must die, or her whole life was lost, was the way she viewed the situation.

and she could not;—Could not as yet persuade Herod to give the necessary orders. The reason is given in the next verse. [The reproof for the unlawful marriage was as much against her as against Herod. They were partners in guilt, and John reproved them both. God regards sins alike in men and women. Only as man was the head and the stronger, he holds him to a stricter accountability as the more responsible of the two. Society holds woman the more responsible of the two, especially in all crimes of this character, but God holds man. Woman is by nature more gentle and kind, more sympathetic to suffering, more emotional than man; yet when aroused she is more bitter, unrelenting, and vindictive. Intensity of emotional feeling is her character. Whichever way it is directed she is more intense than man; hence when aroused and infuriated she is more cruel. Woman is not apt

could not; 20 for Herod feared John, knowing that he was a righteous and holy man, and kept him safe. And when he heard him, he [2]was much per-

to be lukewarm. She is either hot or cold. When a Christian she is more earnest than man; when wicked, more wicked. Herodias would have killed John, but could not. Herod restrained her. He imprisoned John for her, but would go no further. But one step in the wrong only makes ready for another.]

20 for Herod feared John, knowing that he was a righteous and holy man,—Here we get a glimpse of the esteem in which Herod held John. He was just, righteous, upright in his relations toward men; and holy, pious and devoted toward God.

and kept him safe.—From the designs of Herodias and her friends. Herod did not wish to slay John. He and his wife were divided on the question and working in opposite directions. The one seeking his life, the other protecting it.

And when he heard him, he was much perplexed;—Perplexed whether to obey his conscience or to continue in his sins. He wanted to please Herodias, but he dare not kill John on account of the people. Herod was afraid of everything except God. John feared God, but no human being.

and he heard him gladly.—[Herod knew he had sinned. He had enough sense of right to know John had done right in reproving him. So as a just man he feared him. Matthew says, "When he would have put him to death, he feared the multitude, because they counted him as a prophet"—which does not contradict Mark, but shows that fear of the multitude coincided with his own sense of right in restraining him from murdering John when he would have done so to please Herodias. Many diverse influences combine often to direct a man's course. His own and the people's respect for John made him hear John gladly, and do many things he commanded. Men are often willing to do many things God commands, but are unwilling to yield up some special sin. Herod could do many things, but could not give up his adulterous marriage at the teaching of John. The dear sin is the test of our love of God.]

21 And when a convenient day was come,—Convenient day for Herodias to execute her malicious designs. Wine, dissipation, licentiousness were all favorable to this.

plexed; and he heard him gladly. 21 And when a convenient day was come, that Herod on his birthday made a supper to his lords, and the [3]high captains, and the chief men of Galilee; 22 and when [4]the daughter of Herodias herself came in and danced, [5]she pleased Herod and them that sat at meat with him; and the king said unto the damsel, Ask of me whatsoever thou

[2]Many ancient authorities read *did many things.*
[3]Or, *military tribunes* Gr. *chiliarchs.*
[4]Some ancient authorities read *his daughter Herodias.*
[5]Or, *it*

that Herod on his birthday made a supper to his lords, and the high captains, and the chief men of Galilee;—The first men, *the chief* men of the land. [A favorable day for Herodias to carry out her purpose of vengeance on John. It was the birthday of Herod. A feast was given to the lords and chief estates—under rulers of the different sections and estates of Galilee—and his high military officers were present.]

22 and when the daughter of Herodias—A daughter by Philip, and her name, according to Josephus, was Salome. Later she was married to her uncle Philip, the tetrarch of Iturea. (Luke 3: 1.)

herself came in and danced,—Dancing was usually with the accompaniment of tambourines or bells attached to the fingers, and with songs. "No reputable maiden could ever have done what she did. The dancing girls in the Orient are exceedingly popular as entertainers, but their profession is one the practice of which, it is not too much to say, is ruinous alike to themselves and to the spectators." (W. Ewing.)

she pleased Herod and them that sat at meat with him; and the king said unto the damsel, Ask of me whatsoever thou wilt, and I will give it thee.—The scheme succeeded. [This was no doubt a daughter by her former husband, as she was not Herod's daughter. She was young, no doubt with bodily charms, and accomplished in the art of pleasing. Herod at the feast, as was usual, drank freely of wine and strong drink, had his animal feelings excited and exhilarated, was flattered and aroused by the honors done him, was thrown off his usual prudence, and made a promise that he afterwards regretted. He rashly told the young woman he would give whatsoever she desired, not thinking the revengeful feeling of the mother would lead her to make the request she did. This was prom-

wilt, and I will give it thee. 23 And he sware unto her, Whatsoever thou shalt ask of me, I will give it thee, unto the half of my kingdom. 24 And she went out, and said unto her mother, What shall I ask? And she said, The head of John the Baptizer. 25 And she came in straightway with haste

ising much for little. Excited by the dancing of the girl, he made that rash promise.]

23 And he sware unto her, Whatsoever thou shalt ask of me, I will give it thee, unto the half of my kingdom.—A wild and reckless promise that could have been made only by one who had lost his wits by drunkenness. A drinking man is not a safe business man. Herod was willing to give away half of his kingdom for the sight of an immoral dance. Poor fool! But how many in our day give away the whole kingdom of their souls, with health and hope, prosperity, peace, and goodness—yea, the whole kingdom of heaven—for the paltry price of a glass of wine; the pleasure of the table; the acquisition of a little money! The race of Esau still lives, who sell their birthright for a mess of pottage.

24 And she went out, and said unto her mother, What shall I ask?—Which of all the beautiful things offered her—palaces, jewels, gorgeous apparel—all that a girl's heart could desire.

And she said, The head of John the Baptizer.—By what argument could she persuade her daughter to ask such a gift instead of riches, palaces, and jewels? [Matthew (14: 8) says, "She, being put forward by her mother." This does not mean instructed before the offer was made, but before she decided what she would ask, she consulted her mother, and at her instigation she asked the head of John the Baptist. What a choice under such an offer! What a throwing away of an opportunity! Wealth, honors, goods to the half of a kingdom and the choice that of a bleeding head severed from the body! And then to think that such a choice was made at the suggestion of her mother! Most mothers, even the wicked and worldly, would have asked place, position, honor, and riches; but here the bitter revengeful feelings of the mother at John for having rebuked her wrong blinded her to the interests of her daughter, and made her ask for that which could bring no good or pleasure, present or future, to the daughter, but could

unto the king, and asked, saying, I will that thou forthwith give me on a platter the head of John the Baptist. 26 And the king was exceeding sorry; but for the sake of his oaths, and of them that sat at meat, he would not

gratify only her own wicked and spiteful feelings. Wicked, revengeful feelings, cherished and gratified, more completely destroy the happiness and peace of the heart that cherishes them than any other influence. They blind to the true interest of ourselves and families. God warns against cherishing them: "Vengeance belongeth unto me; I will recompense, saith the Lord." (Rom. 12: 19.) "Not rendering evil for evil, or reviling for reviling; but contrariwise blessing; for hereunto were ye called, that ye should inherit a blessing." (1 Pet. 3: 9.) Christians are called upon to suffer wrong, and return good for evil, that they may be fitted to inherit a blessing from God. Parents often gratify their vindictive feelings, deprive themselves of good, and lead their families to misery.]

25 **And she came in straightway with haste unto the king, and asked, saying, I will that thou forthwith give me on a platter the head of John the Baptist.**—[It was cruel to desire John's death. It was more than cruel, coarse, and brutal to desire the bleeding head brought her during the feast in a charger, or on a waiter or tray. What a dish ordered for a feast by the young woman! Woman with her strong, emotional nature and intensity of feeling in the way of right, virtue, and purity, is an angel of love and mercy. Traveling the downward road of impurity, sin, and crime, she is a demon of cruelty and crime.]

26 **And the king was exceeding sorry;**—He was sorry but not penitent. He was sorry for her that she should make such a choice. He was sorry that he should be called on to have a man beheaded that he knew was a just and holy man, who had only done his duty. Herod respected the man who was just and upright, although he himself let his lust and passion hinder him from so acting. He was sorry to see the just and upright man beheaded. His sense of justice protested; his conscience was not seared. He was not totally depraved. He was led on step by step from one degree of wrong to another. His first wrong step was to have John imprisoned to please his wicked wife.]

reject her. 27 And straightway the king sent forfh a soldier of his guard, and commanded to bring his head: and he went and beheaded him in the prison, 28 and brought his head on a platter, and gave it to the damsel; and

but for the sake of his oaths, and of them that sat at meat, he would not reject her.—He granted the request though against his conscience. [Herod imprisoned John. This was unjust and sinful. He did it at the suggestion of the wicked woman. The devil used the woman. He waited and watched his opportunity until the king was aroused with wine, surrounded by his courtieurs and the great ones of earth. He is excited by the dancing of the girl, and makes the rash promise and confirms it with an oath. The devil sees at once his opportunity—his pride, his show of regard for his oath, the humiliation there would be in drawing back from his oath in the presence of his great ones. He uses the woman again, and the king had John beheaded, and his head brought into the presence of the guests in a charger. How must Herod feel after having been so drawn into what he knew was wrong! The only time we can safely resist wrong is before the first step is taken in that direction. There is another principle involved here that ought to be studied. Herod made a foolish promise. It became a wicked promise when connected with the request made under it. For the sake of the oath he beheaded John. His pride prompted him to perform the oath when he knew it was wrong. What was his duty after the oath was made and he saw it led to sin? Many young people especially say when an oath is made or a promise given it should be fulfilled. If the making of the oath was wrong, it was a greater sin to perform it. Two wrongs do not make a right, but doubles the wrong.]

27 And straightway the king sent forth a soldier of his guard, and commanded to bring his head:—It seems the king had the authority to have John beheaded without a trial of justice.

and he went and behaded him in the prison,—[He did this out of false pride—a false principle of honor. Out of regard for a rash promise and an oath to do wrong he became a murderer of a holy and just person. The promise was a sin. The fulfillment made him a cruel murderer.]

the damsel gave it to her mother. 29 And when his disciples heard *thereof,* they came and took up his corpse, and laid it in a tomb.

---

28 and brought his head on a platter, and gave it to the damsel; and the damsel gave it to her mother.—[What a present! What a dish! The bleeding head of an upright and holy man of God to grace the birthday feast of a king! How one sinner leads another into sin! How yielding to one sin leads to a greater one! How false principles, false pride, an improper regard for the opinions of others, and of our own wrong promises lead on to deeper crime! How, when we start wrong, influences multiply to lead us on deeper and deeper into wrong!]

29 And when his disciples heard thereof, they came and took up his corpse, and laid it in a tomb.—Where, we do not know. Herodias was in possession of the head. Whether she allowed it to be buried with the body is not known. [It was done in prison. His disciples without heard of it, and "came, and took up the corpse, and buried him; and they went and told Jesus."]

4. RETURN OF THE APOSTLES, AND FEEDING OF THE FIVE THOUSAND
6: 30-44
(Matt. 14: 13-21; Luke 9: 10-17; John 6: 1-14)

30 And the apostles gather themselves together unto Jesus; and they told him all things, whatsoever they had done, and whatsoever they had taught.

---

30 And the apostles gather themselves together unto Jesus; —[The death of John the Baptist seems to have been the occasion of their coming together to Jesus. The greater portion, if not all of them, had been disciples of John. They regarded John as sent of God, and only second in importance, as a teacher sent from God, to himself.]

and they told him all things, whatsoever they had done, and whatsoever they had taught.—[The twelve had made a tour among the Jews working miracles and preaching the gospel of the coming kingdom, and now returned to where Jesus was, and told him all things. He sent them out to teach and to work in his name and by his authority. It was proper they should give account of their works to him.]

31 And he saith unto them, Come ye yourselves apart into a desert place, and rest a while. For there were many coming and going, and they had no leisure so much as to eat. 32 And they went away in the boat to a desert place apart. 33 And *the people* saw them going, and many knew *them*, and they ran together there [6]on foot from all the cities, and outwent them.

[6]Or, *by land*

31 **And he saith unto them, Come ye yourselves apart into a desert place, and rest a while.**—Our Lord had sought retirement and rest before (Matt. 12: 15; Mark 4: 35; Luke 5: 16); now he seeks it for his disciples, having returned weary from their mission. It is proper for Christians to take brief periods of rest from hard and incessant toil.

For there were many coming and going, and they had no leisure so much as to eat.—[All that was said is not reported. It would make the account too cumbersome. Jesus approved their work and teaching, and no doubt they had been necessarily engaged in travel and labor as he had been. [The death of John was a matter of sorrow to him and to them. He wished to be alone with his disciples, that he might have a season of prayerful communion with the Father and with them as a means of giving them spiritual strength and preparing them for labors and sufferings and disappointments yet before them. Jesus loved seasons of private prayer and communion with God.]

32 **And they went away in the boat to a desert place apart.** —[They were in Capernaum, and then went to Bethsaida. A boat seems to have always been at the service of Jesus. It was probably owned by Peter or some of his disciples, and they held it for his use when needed. They went across the Sea of Galilee to a point that would answer the demands. Those familiar with the country say it was twenty miles by land. They rowed across the sea; the people went around.]

33 **And the people saw them going, and many knew them, and they ran together there on foot from all the cities, and outwent them.**—They could probably watch the boat Jesus was in the whole way and knew how fast to travel to meet him when he landed. Some of them reached the place before Jesus did. They were attracted by what Jesus had already done.

34 And he came forth and saw a great multitude, and he had compassion on them, because they were as sheep not having a shepherd: and he began to teach them many things. 35 And when the day was now far spent, his disciples came unto him, and said, The place is desert, and the day is now far spent; 36 send them away, that they may go into the country and villages round about, and buy themselves somewhat to eat. 37 But he answered and said unto them, Give ye them to eat. And they say unto him, Shall we go and buy two hundred 'shillings' worth of bread, and give them to eat? 38

7The word in the Greek denotes a coin worth about eight pence half-penny, or nearly seventeen cents.

---

34 **And he came forth and saw a great multitude, and he had compassion on them, because they were as sheep not having a shepherd:**—They had no spiritual teacher to guide, warn and instruct them, and hence were exposed to all kinds of spiritual danger and destruction from false teachers.

and he began to teach them many things.—[When he came out of the boat he saw the multitude assembled to meet him. Their condition, without a teacher or guide, caused him to think of them as scattered, wandering sheep without a shepherd. Sheep, when scattered from the flock without a shepherd, seem to be the most aimless and helpless of creatures. Thus these children of Abraham now seem to be to Jesus. Because he pitied their scattered and lost condition he began to teach them many things concerning his mission and the coming kingdom of God.]

35 **And when the day was now far spent, his disciples came unto him, and said, The place is desert, and the day is now far spent;**—[This people had come hurriedly without preparation, were without food, and as the day waned they became hungry, and the disciples came to him and said, This is a desert place, no food can be obtained, the time for eating has passed. Their intense interest held them all day.]

36 **send them away, that they may go into the country and villages round about, and buy themselves somewhat to eat.**—[Their suggestion was to dismiss them—we would say that they may scatter among the people living in the country around and in the neighboring villages, and lodge for the night and buy bread, for they have none.]

37 **But he answered and said unto them, Give ye them to eat. And they say unto him, Shall we go and buy two hundred shillings' worth of bread, and give them to eat?**—[He

And he saith unto them, How many loaves have ye? go *and* see. And when they knew, they say, Five, and two fishes. 39 And he commanded them that all should [8]sit down by companies upon the green grass. 40 And they sat down in ranks, by hundreds, and by fifties. 41 And he took the five loaves and the two fishes, and looking up to heaven, he blessed, and brake the loaves; and he gave to the disciples to set before them; and the two fishes

[8]Gr. *recline.*

---

told the disciples he could not send them away without food, as they had walked twenty miles in the morning, remained till it is now late. The evening had come, and they have had no food. "Give them to eat"—that is, he told the disciples to furnish the food for them. And they say unto him, "Shall we go and buy two hundred shillings' worth of bread, and give them to eat?" They estimated it would take this amount to buy bread enough for them to eat, and, although the disciples knew the country, they did not know where to find the food. The quantity of food a given sum of money will buy varies so greatly at different periods of the world, it is needless to speculate as to the amount. It was a large amount. They thought the proposition unreasonable.]

38 **And he saith unto them, How many loaves have ye? go and see. And when they knew, they say, Five, and two fishes.** —All they could find. [He seems to have known there was some food in reach. Then they examine and report they find a lad with five barley loaves and two fishes. (John 6: 9.) We have no intimation as to the size of the loaf. They likely intended returning in the afternoon. If not, they would fast. John (6: 5, 6) says Jesus asked Philip, "Whence are we to buy bread, that these may eat? And this he said to prove him." Philip was of Bethsaida, and knew the country and its resources.]

39 **And he commanded them that all should sit down by companies upon the green grass.**—Jesus had a clear conception of what he would do, and so he tells the apostles to make the people sit upon the green grass, which seems to be abundant in this place and at this season.

40 **And thy sat down in ranks, by hundreds, and by fifties.** —[They were separated into companies of fifties and hundreds, and so seated that one could pass between the ranks and wait upon all in order.]

divided he among them all. 42 And they all ate, and were filled. 43 And
they took up broken pieces, twelve basketfuls, and also of the fishes. 44 And

---

41 **And he took the five loaves and the two fishes, and looking up to heaven, he blessed, and brake the loaves; and he
gave to the disciples to set before them; and the two fishes
divided he among them all.**—[He took these in hand, now before him, looked up to heaven, and blessed. He gave thanks
for them—bestowed such a divine blessing upon them that
they grew as he brake from them, so they did not grow less.
John (6: 9) tells us they were barley loaves—not so palatable
or nutritious as those of wheat. Revelation (6: 6) says: "A
measure of wheat for a shilling and three measures of barley
for a shilling." The barley was the food for the poor. But to
a multitude hungry as these were the coarsest food is deli-
cious. Jesus took the loaves, and as he brake they grew in his
hands. We cannot conceive of the work. Miracles are above
human conception. It was as though something was created
of nothing. He broke the loaves and gave to his disciples, and
they handed them to the multitudes. The two fishes were divided among the thousands. They also grew as they were divided. This is a miracle that excited wonder, yet there was
no more wisdom or power required to do this than was required to put in operation the provisions of nature by which
the multiplied millions of earth are year by year supplied with
the food needed. In this latter case wisdom and power are
manifested to provide for the necessary wants of all the animal creation. Because it is done through fixed laws, we are
unable to say who is the mover and giver of these things.
When Christ or an apostle did such works, we could identify
such person as speaking by the authority and in the name of
the creator and ruler of all' things.]

42 **And they all ate, and were filled.**—[All ate of the five
loaves and the two little fishes; all were filled; their hunger
was satisfied. They were strengthened, and more remained
than they had to begin with.]

43 **And they took up broken pieces, twelve basketfuls, and
also of the fishes.**—[The number of baskets were twelve; thus
each apostle filled his basket. We have no means of knowing
the size of the baskets, but much more was taken after all

they that ate the loaves were five thousand men.

were satisfied than Jesus took and blessed. John (6: 12) says,
"He [Jesus] saith unto his disciples, Gather up the broken
pieces which remain over, that nothing be lost." The economy of God is seen in the workings of the natural world. The
decay of one thing is taken up in the growth of others, and
here, although Jesus created this seemingly without labor or
loss of time, he was careful that nothing of it should be lost.
This is a lesson regarding wastefulness that he intended for
his children in the world. The difference between the conditions of the people of poverty and plenty depends more upon
their carefulness in saving or their wastefulness than upon
any other cause. Many families, although poor, waste more
than would support them if they were saving. They remain
poor because they waste. The careful, saving person, as a
rule, lives much better than the wasteful and profligate. The
wasteful never are able to give to those in need. A painstak-
ing care of the fragments ought to be taught as a Christian
virtue.]

44 And they that ate the loaves were five thousand men.—
Matthew (14: 21) adds, "Besides women and children."
Jesus not only gave here an object lesson in economy, but by
the amount left he showed that this was a miracle beyond all
doubt.

5. JESUS WALKING UPON THE SEA
6: 45-52
(Matt. 14: 22-33; John 6: 15-21)

45 And straightway he constrained his disciples to enter into the boat,
and to go before *him* unto the other side of Bethsaida, while he himself sendeth the multitude away. 46 And after he had taken leave of them, he de-

**45 And straightway he constrained his disciples to enter
into the boat, and to go before him unto the other side to
Bethsaida, while he himself sendeth the multitude away.**—
The disciples could row some distance away before the great
multitude could be dispersed, as the women and children must
needs be cared for; and the selection of places at which to
lodge that night would require more or less time; so Jesus
sent the disciples first on their way. The day was about gone
when all had left the grounds.

parted into the mountain to pray. 47 And when even was come, the boat was in the midst of the sea, and he alone on the land. 48 And seeing them distressed in rowing, for the wind was contrary unto them, about the fourth watch of the night he cometh unto them, walking on the sea; and he would have passed by them: 49 but they, when they saw him walking on the sea, supposed that it was a ghost, and cried out; 50 for they all saw him, and

46 And after he had taken leave of them, he departed into the mountain to pray.—Matthew (14: 23) says: "He went up into the mountain apart"—that is alone—where he spent most of the night in prayer.

47 And when even was come, the boat was in the midst of the sea, and he alone on the land.—He is now separated from both the disciples and the multitudes. This season of prayer alone with God lasted several hours, for it began in the evening after sunset, and he does not come to his disciples till the fourth watch, or between 3 and 6 o'clock the next morning.

48 And seeing them distressed in rowing, for the wind was contrary unto them,—They, while trying to go in one direction, were hindered by the wind going the opposite direction.

about the fourth watch of the night—The *ancient* Hebrews divided the night, probably the period from sunset to sunrise, into three watches. (Judges 7: 19; Lam. 2: 19; Ex. 14: 24; 1 Sam. 11: 11.) The Greeks appear to have had the same division. But after Pompey's conquest (B.C. 63) the Jews gradually adapted the Roman fashion of four watches. At this season of the year, soon after the vernal equinox (John 6: 4), the "fourth watch" would be from 3 to 6 o'clock.

he cometh unto them, walking on the sea;—Jesus knew his disciples were in distress in the sea. From the mountainside and through the darkness of the night he looked down upon them in their toil and trouble. No doubt his prayer embraced them. When, exhausted and helpless, they needed him, he appeared, "walking on the sea." When they have done all they could, he does the rest.

and he would have passed by them:—He did this to detract their attention and to reveal themselves to themselves. The disciples were not expecting Jesus to come in that way. This was a new miracle to them.

49 but they, when they saw him walking on the sea, supposed that it was a ghost, and cried out;—They did not recog-

were troubled. But he straightway spake with them, and saith unto them, Be of good cheer: it is I; be not afraid. 51 And he went up unto them into the boat; and the wind ceased: and they were sore amazed in themselves; 52 for they understood not concerning the loaves, but their heart was hardened.

nize it was Jesus but thought it was rather an apparition, and hence to them a sign of disaster or death.

50 **for they all saw him, and were troubled.**—Disturbed at the scene. This was natural. They had no knowledge of what the object seen was. Matthew (14: 26) says, "They cried out for fear." They were frightened.

But he straightway spake with them, and saith unto them, Be of good cheer: it is I; be not afraid.—You are in no danger, I am on the scene and will protect you from all harm. It is not uncommon for Jesus to come to our help in unexpected ways, and we are afraid of his coming though he is bringing blessings in disguise.

51 **And he went up unto them into the boat; and the wind ceased: and they were sore amazed in themselves;**—Jesus helped Peter back into the ship; and when they entered it, the wind ceased.

52 **for they understood not concerning the loaves,**—They comprehended not, so as to understand that he who had exercised such power over the loaves and fishes could exercise a similar power over the wind and sea. They did not perceive that all the elements of nature were under his control, those of wind and sea as well as those of loaves and fishes.

but their heart was hardened.—Dull, sluggish, insensible, so as not to recognize sufficiently his divine power and nature, and draw just conclusion from what they had previously seen. Jesus had bidden them cross the sea; and although it was rough and the winds were contrary, they should have considered that they were in the path of duty, and that Jesus never forsakes one so long as he does as Jesus bids him, and that he who could magnify the loaves and increase the fishes until they would feed thousands could walk upon the water and still the tempest, but they did not consider this.

6. CURES IN GENNESARET
6: 53-56
(Matt. 14: 34-36)

53 And when they had [1]crossed over, they came to the land unto Gennesaret, and moored to the shore. 54 And when they were come out of the boat, straightway *the people* knew him, 55 and ran round about that whole region, and began to carry about on their [2]beds those that were sick, where they heard he was. 56 And wheresoever he entered, into villages, or into cities, or into the country, they laid the sick in the marketplaces, and besought him that they might touch if it were but the border of his garment: and as many as touched [3]him were made whole.

[1]Or, *crossed over to the land, they came unto Gennesaret*
[2]Or, *pallets*
[3]Or, *it*

53-56 And when they had crossed over, they came to the land unto Gennesaret, and moored to the shore. And when they were come out of the boat, straightway the people knew him, and ran round about that whole region, and began to carry about on their beds those that were sick, where they heard he was. And wheresoever he entered, into villages, or into cities, or into the country, they laid the sick in the marketplaces, and besought him that they might touch if it were but the border of his garment: and as many as touched him were made whole.—This is a beautiful plain on the western shore of the sea, about four miles long and two or three miles wide. Capernaum was at the northern end of it. As soon as Jesus had landed, as he passed on toward Capernaum, the people from "all that region round about" flocked to him with their variously afflicted ones, and besought him that they might only touch the border of his garment: and as many as touched him were made whole.

7. JESUS ATTACKED BY THE PHARISEES AND SCRIBES
7: 1-13
(Matt. 15: 1-9)

1 And there are gathered together unto him the Pharisees, and certain of

1 And there are gathered together unto him the Pharisees, and certain of the scribes, who had come from Jerusalem,—Mark gives a glimpse of the organized opposition against Jesus. Between the events of this and the preceding chapter were Christ's discourse at Capernaum (John 6: 22-71), and the third Passover of his public ministry, which he did not at-

the scribes, who had come from Jerusalem, 2 and had seen that some of his disciples ate their bread with ⁴defiled, that is, unwashen, hands. 3 (For the Pharisees, and all the Jews, except they wash their hands ⁵diligently, eat not,

⁴Or, *common*
⁵Or, *up to the elbow Gr. with the fist.*

---

tend (John 6: 4; 7: 1). Disappointed in not seeing Jesus at the Passover (John 6: 4; 7: 1), they probably came to Galilee to watch his movements and to conspire against him. These Pharisees and scribes were sent, doubtless by the authorities in Jerusalem, to counteract the widespread influence of Jesus in Galilee. No doubt the shrewdest and most able were sent. Sent from the seat of learning and authority, able and shrewd, and they were considered better prepared to meet Jesus than the ones who resided in Galilee.

2 and had seen that some of his disciples ate their bread with defiled, that is, unwashen, hands.—These Pharisees and scribes, watching for an opportunity to attack Jesus, found it in the fact "that some of his disciples ate their bread with defiled hands." Mark explains that "defiled" hands are "unwashen" hands.

3 (For the Pharisees, and all the Jews, except they wash their hands diligently,—That is, frequently—often—carefully and up to the elbow.

eat not, holding the tradition—What had been handed down, not what was delivered by writing in the law of Moses, but what had been communicated from father to son, as being proper and binding.

of the elders;—The ancients, not the old men then living, but those who had lived formerly. This parenthetic clause is an explanation of the practices of "the Pharisees, and all the Jews," in regard to the customs mentioned, in this and next verse. "All the Jews" is a comparative expression, meaning not literally every one of them, but the most of them; for a few were Sadducees, who rejected the tradition. The Jews claim there are two laws—the written law of Moses written in the Bible and the oral law, tradition handed down, they claim, from Moses through Aaron and his sons, the elders of that time, Joshua, and the prophets—from generation to generation successively. They claim that when God gave Moses the

holding the tradition of the elders ; 4 and *when they come* from the market-place, except they [6]bathe themselves, they eat not; and many other things there are, which they have received to hold, [7]washings of cups, and pots, and brasen vessels[8].)　5 And the Pharisees and the scribes ask him, Why walk

[6]Gr. *baptize.* Some ancient authorities read *sprinkle themselves.*
[7]Gr. *baptizings.*
[8]Many ancient authorities add *and couches.*

---

written law, he gave him also the tradition, or oral law, as an explanation of the written law. This explanation of the written law is "the tradition of the elders" handed down. They attached more importance to the tradition than to the law itself, or, human-nature-like, to their interpretations of the scriptures than to the scriptures themselves. A digest of the tradition is called the "Mishua"; comments upon and explanations of the Mishua is the "Talmud." Thus the Mishua explains the law and the Talmud explains the Mishua.

4 **and when they come from the marketplace,**—Where provisions are sold. A broad place or square in the city of public resort, with the market on one side and colonnades on the other. To this place people resorted for different purposes. Here children met to play (Matt. 11: 16, 17) ; laborers to seek work (Matt. 20: 1-7) ; the sick, to be healed (Mark 6: 56) ; and philosophers, to discuss grave and great questions. In the marketplace in Athens, Paul discussed the resurrection with the Epicureans and Stoic philosophers. (Acts 17: 17, 18.) The Pharisees loved the "salutations in the marketplaces." (Mark 12: 38.) There at Philippi, Paul and Silas were dragged before the magistrates. (Acts 16: 19.)

except they bathe themselves, they eat not;—Except they immerse themselves. The word "bathe" is from the Greek "baptizo." Hence the idea of dipping or immersing themselves, thus taking a bath before eating. While in the marketplace, the whole body was in danger of being defiled by coming in contact with all classes, hence the necessity of immersing the whole body in water.

and many other things there are, which they have received to hold,—Many other like usages which the Pharisees had "received" by tradition "to hold," to adhere to and practice.

washings of cups,—In the original the baptisms of cups. Drinking vessels—those used at their meals.

not thy disciples according to the tradition of the elders, but eat their bread with 'defiled hands? 6 And he said unto them, Well did Isaiah prophesy of you hypocrites, as it is written,

---

and pots,—Vessels made of wood, used to hold liquids, etc., had to be washed—immersed.

and brasen vessels.)—Vessels made of brass, used in cooking or otherwise, if much polluted, were commonly passed through the fire; if only slightly polluted, they were washed. The religious practices of the Jews in question are named. The law of uncleanness is plainly stated in the law of Moses, but these practices of the Jews were not parts of that law; they were traditions, extensions of the law by human wisdom and authority, "doctrines" and "the precepts of men." (Matt. 15: 9.) Washing the hands, different vessels, and tables in order to cleanse them of dirt was not peculiar to the Jews. Others did that then and do it now. And this was not the practice Jesus condemned. He condemns all kinds of filthiness. However free from dirt their hands, vessels, tables, and they themselves ceremonially unclean, they performed these acts, nevertheless; they performed them as religious service, or ceremonies, or rites. This was the thing Jesus condemned. The law required the unclean to bathe themselves (Lev. 14: 9-15; 16: 24-28; 17: 15; Num. 19: 7, 8, 19), but the Pharisees by their theories had added to the word of God and were punctilious in performing ceremonies which the law did not require. Let us beware "of the leaven of the Pharisees, which is hypocrisy." (Luke 12: 1.) By our own theories, "logical deductions." and traditions, it is possible for us to become pharisaical.

5 And the Pharisees and the scribes ask him, Why walk not thy disciples according to the tradition of the elders,—They do not directly charge Jesus, but his disciples. They relied upon the authority of their tradition for the charge. Not to live according to it was to "transgress" it. (Matt. 15: 2.)

but eat their bread with defiled hands?—Without washing their hands before eating. The traditionary practices just mentioned, and the fact that the disciples were seen to eat with unwashed hands, gave rise to the discussion which now follows.

> ⁹This people honoreth me with their lips,
>   But their heart is far from me.
> 7 But in vain do they worship me,
>   Teaching *as their* doctrines the precepts of men.
> 8 Ye leave the commandment of God, and hold fast the tradition of men.
> 9 And he said unto them, Full well do ye reject the commandment of God,

⁹Is. xxix. 13.

6 **And he said unto them, Well did Isaiah prophesy of you hypocrites,**—Jesus selects as a proof text Isa. 29: 13. He gave the sense, not the exact language. He applies the text to them. Their false doctrine and practice were foretold by the prophet, but they did not seem to realize it. This is the first time Jesus addressed them openly as hypocrites.

as it is written, This people honoreth me with their lips, but their heart is far from me.—In motive and purpose. The motive and purpose, as well as the words, must be pure. Their hearts were not right.

7 **But in vain do they worship me,**—Emptiness is all you give me in your worship. He gives the reason in the next clause.

teaching as their doctrines the precepts of men.—The precepts of men were the doctrine they taught. "Doctrines" refer to those things taught as binding upon the conscience, as obligatory. Jesus applies it to the Pharisees and scribes as religious teachers.

8 **Ye leave the commandment of God,**—Set the pure word of God on the sidetrack—neglecting and disregarding the commandment of God.

and hold fast the tradition of men.—They neglected the commandment of God and clung to the traditions of men. In this they preferred man to God. They set God aside— they dethroned him and gave man his seat. A severe charge indeed.

9 **And he said unto them, Full well do ye reject the commandment of God, that ye may keep your tradition.**—They could not do both, so in order to keep their tradition they rejected the commandment of God. Note that Jesus did not deny the charge they brought against his disciples but virtually acknowledged its truth. He came down from heaven, not to do his own will, but the will of God who sent him (John 6:

that ye may keep your tradition. 10 For Moses said, [10]Honor thy father and thy mother; and, He that speaketh evil of father or mother, let him [11]die the death: 11 but ye say, If a man shall say to his father or his mother, That wherewith thou mightest have been profited by me is Corban, that is to say,

[10]Ex. xx. 12; Dt. v. 16; Ex. xxi. 17; Lev. xx. 9.
[11]Or, *surely die*

38), and not, therefore, "the tradition of the elders." "The precepts of men" are no part of the will of God. Jesus did not keep them, because they were not commandments of God. In reply to this accusation, Jesus attacked *tradition* itself and charged his accusers with three things: (1) hypocrisy, because they pretended to honor God with their lips when their hearts were far from him; (2) worshiping God *in vain,* because they taught "as their doctrines the precepts of men"; (3) rejecting the commandments of God in order to keep their tradition. He applied the declaration of Isaiah (29: 13) to them: "And their fear of me is a commandment of men which hath been taught them."

10 **For**—Jesus introduces an example where the scribes and Pharisees set aside God's law for their tradition to prove his charge against them.

Moses said,—In Ex. 20: 12. Jesus here gives his sanction of the decalogue as of divine origin and Moses as an inspired teacher and lawgiver. God gave the law through Moses.

Honor thy father and thy mother;—In every way—in word, deed and thought and by providing for them in old age or during distress.

and, He that speaketh evil of father or mother, let him die the death:—"Or, surely die." Let him end with death. A severe penalty indeed and shows the importance of honoring father and mother.

11 **but ye say,**—By your tradition and your practice in opposition to what Moses says. He arrays Moses against themselves.

If a man shall say to his father or his mother, That wherewith thou mightest have been profited by me is Corban, that is to say, Given to God;—A gift—something brought near, or devoted to God, as a gift, offering or sacrifice. It was applied to all offerings whether with or without blood, and especially

Given *to God;* 12 ye no longer suffer him to do aught for his father or his
mother; 13 making void the word of God by your tradition, which ye have

in fulfillment of a vow. (Lev. 1: 2, 10, 14; 2: 1, 4; 7: 13;
Num. 31: 50.) According to the Mosaic law, persons could
devote certain things to God with certain limitations. (Lev.
27: 2-33; Num. 30: 2-15; Deut. 23: 21, 22; Judges 13: 7.) To
these regulations were added those of tradition by the scribes
and Pharisees. And so far was it carried that even the pro-
nouncing of the word "Corban" over one's property absolved
him from the obligation of caring for his parents. And even
if this was done in the excitement of anger, it was held to be
binding.

12 **ye no longer suffer him to do aught for his father or his
mother;**—This was the result of setting aside the commandment of God and doing the tradition of men. God said to care
for father and mother, but tradition would not allow it. You
allow the children to do as they desire. Such an exposure as
this should have made them ashamed of so wicked a practice.

13 **making void the word of God by your tradition, which ye
have delivered:**—The tradition had been handed down and by
their practice had annulled the word of God. Jesus returns in
his argument to the charge made in verse 8, which he had sustained. Jesus shows the Pharisees and scribes by an example
that they had rejected the commandment of God for their tradition. The example does not touch the uncleanness, but is
against tradition, and is the stronger because it proves that
tradition is not only without authority, but sets aside the command and authority of God. To honor father and mother is to
give them the attention, care, and support necessary in their
old age or affliction. God teaches that children who have
widowed mothers and grandmothers should "learn first to
show piety towards their own family, and to requite their parents"; that this service is acceptable in his sight; and that all
who refuse to render it deny the faith and are worse than unbelievers. (1 Tim. 5: 4-8.) One of the most general and popular evils of the day is neglect of the old, disregard for parents, and throwing off home duties and restraints. This is not
taught at home, in school, or from the pulpit as it should be.
Another popular evil of the day, and one that is growing more

delivered: and many such like things ye do. 14 And he called to him the

prevalent, is the neglect of the aged by both church and the business part of the world. The old preachers and the aged laborers who bore the heat and burden of the day in building up the churches and business enterprises are "laid on the shelf" without any means of support and their places given to the young. No nation can hope to prosper as long as it suffers such injustice to its aged. God emphasizes the duty of learning this kind of piety *first*. To honor father and mother is "the first commandment with promise," and the promise is great—"that it may be well with thee, and thou mayest live long on the earth." (Eph. 6: 1-3.) Nothing can take the place of this, and it cannot be set aside for anything else. To pretend to be Christians while neglecting these home duties is to be pharisaical and worse than infidels. There is such a thing as being worse than an infidel, and this is it. There is too much self-denial, hard work, and homekeeping in Christianity to suit the Pharisees of the present or any other age.

and many such like things ye do.—After giving the above example, Jesus here made the application. Not only this one, but "many others" on the same order are practiced by you.

8. NOT WHAT ONE EATS THAT DEFILES HIM, BUT THE CONDITION OF HIS OWN HEART
7: 14-23
(Matt. 15: 10-20)

multitude again, and said unto them, Hear me all of you, and understand: 15

14 **And he called to him the multitude again,**—This indicates that the preceding incident was to some degree private but not fully. Some think it was an examination of Jesus in the synagogue by the scribes and Pharisees from Jerusalem, while Christ was separated from the people. This may be true but not necessarily so.

and said unto them, Hear me all of you,—He had something of much importance he wished to give to each of them. Hence, he demanded the closest attention.

and understand:—Give diligent attention to the meaning of my words so that you may understand. The Pharisees and scribes teach you about an imaginary and traditional defilement, and yet have heard of a ceremonial defilement (Lev. 11:

there is nothing from without the man, that going into him can defile him; but the things which proceed out of the man are those that defile the man.[1] 17 And when he was entered into the house from the multitude, his disciples asked of him the parable. 18 And he saith unto them, Are ye so without

[1]Many ancient authorities insert ver. 16. *If any man hath ears to hear, let him hear.* See ch. 4. 9. 23.

8, 26), but now hear and understand whence real defilement comes and in what it consists.

15 **there is nothing from without the man, that going into him can defile him;**—Nothing that goes into his mouth and stomach in the way of nourishment makes him common or unclean morally.

but the things which proceed out of the man are those that defile the man.—The things that come from the heart and out of the mouth—his words. What one eats does not render him defiled before God, but what he says. (Verses 18-23; Matt. 12: 24.) The impure words that indicate an impure heart. What one eats cannot make him morally unclean, impure. It cannot affect his character. Jesus does not say that it was unimportant to keep the Mosaic law distinguishing between clean and unclean meats. The meat cannot affect his character, but disobedience can. Nor does he refer at all to the fact that one may take disease into his system through eating and drinking; and that disobedience to the laws of health is a moral wrong, and deteriorates the character. Jesus lays down the principle that what is taken into the body does not *affect the character.* It is the *moral act,* and not what is eaten, that *defiles* the man. That which comes out of the man defiles him, because they come from the heart, and affect the character and the moral nature. They defile the soul, which is the man.

17 **And when he was entered into the house from the multitude,**—Jesus withdraws from the multitude and enters into the house. We take it that the teaching of the multitude was done out in the open air.

his disciples asked of him the parable.—The obscure and difficult remarks which he had made in verse 15. The word "parable," here, means obscure and difficult saying.

18 **And he saith unto them,**—Jesus now starts out to explain more fully his speech.

understanding also? Perceive ye not, that whatsoever from without goeth into the man, *it* cannot defile him; 19 because it goeth not into his heart, but into his belly, and goeth out into the draught? *This he said,* making all meats clean. 20 And he said, That which proceedeth out of the man, that

Are ye so without understanding also?—Are you, my disciples, who have been so highly favored with my teaching, so thus void of understanding?

Perceive ye not,—Do you not see and understand?

that whatsoever from without goeth into the man, it cannot defile him;—Cannot render his soul polluted; cannot make him a sinner, so as to need this purifying as a religious service; cannot make him morally unclean, or unholy.

19 because—He is now ready to give the reason why food cannot defile the man.

it goeth not into his heart, but into his belly,—Does not reach or affect the mind, the soul, and therefore cannot pollute it. Even if it should affect the body, yet it cannot the soul. The theories of the Pharisees, therefore, are not founded in reason, but are mere superstition. The heart is the seat of the emotions and the center of the inner man, the soul, and it cannot be reached through the stomach. Food in the digestive organs cannot affect the morals of men.

and goeth out into the draught? This he said, making all meats clean.—The process of digestion is a cleansing one. Whatever is impure is separated from the food and carried off, leaving whatever is nutritious to enter into the blood and become part of the body. What is thrown out of the body is the innutritious part of the food taken into the stomach, and leaving only that which is proper for the support of life, and cannot, therefore, defile the soul. All food is taken into the body to support life. The meaning is that the economy or process by which life is supported purifies or renders nutritious all kinds of food. The unwholesome parts are separated, and the wholesome only are taken into the system.

20 And he said, That which proceedeth out of the man,—Having stated what does not defile a man, Jesus now states what does defile him. It is that which comes out in a moral sense, from the mouth (Matt. 15: 18), and from the heart or soul (verses 19, 21), such as he mentions in the two following verses.

defileth the man. 21 For from within, out of the heart of men, [2]evil thoughts proceed, fornications, thefts, murders, adulteries, 22 covetings, wickednesses, deceit, lasciviousness, an evil eye, railing, pride, foolishness: 23 all these evil things proceed from within, and defile the man.

[2]Gr. *thoughts that are evil.*

that defileth the man.—"That" is what defiles the man, not food, which never enters into the soul. His words from an evil heart are really polluted, or offensive in the sight of God. They render the soul corrupt and abominable in the sight of God.

21 **For from within,**—The reason of the statement is given. Opposite "from without" of verse 15.

out of the heart of men,—The mind, the inner man—the seat of all moral intentions and actions.

evil thoughts proceed,—The spiritual heart, which includes the mind, thinks evil thoughts as well as good ones. It has both evil and good designs.

fornications,—Violations of chastity by unmarried people.

thefts,—Of all sorts and degrees.

murders,—Taking of human life. Cruelty and hard dealings toward others.

adulteries,—Violations of the marriage vow.

22 **covetings,**—Desiring and wishing to have more—greediness of gain which leads to fraud and extortion. Craving that possessed by others.

wickednesses,—Evil dispositions, wicked counsels, and acts.

deceit,—Fraud—concealed dishonesty.

lasciviousness,—unbridled lust, lewdness.

an evil eye,—An envious, grudging, malicious spirit, which reveals the temper and evil within, and grieves at the happiness of others.

railing,—Reviling; abusive language against God or man.

pride,—Arrogance, self-exaltation.

foolishness:—Senselessness, folly.

23 **all these evil things proceed from within,**—Originate in, and come from the heart. They are evil things.

and defile the man.—The moral, the inner, the spiritual part of man. The best way to check the process of sin in the life is to mortify it in the heart, to crucify all inordinate motions, lusts, and corruptions in their root; for the heart is the first seat and subject of sin, whence it flows forth into the life and conversation. It is out of a wicked and sinful heart that all sin and wickedness proceed. Though the occasions of sin are from without, yet the source and origin of it are from within. The heart of man is as a cage full of unclean birds; hence proceed evil thoughts, either against God or our neighbor. Our Savior instructs the disciples in a very necessary and useful doctrine, touching the true and original cause of all spiritual pollution and uncleanness; namely, the filthiness and impurity of man's heart. And that it is not the meat eaten with the mouth, but the wickedness of heart vented by the mouth, which pollutes a person in God's account, and which defileth the inward man. The heart of man is the sink and seed plot of all sin, the source and fountain of all pollution. All the impurity of the life proceeds from the impurity and filthiness of the heart.

It is not the coming out of the mouth that defiles, but the kind of things which come out. The uttering them not only shows what is in the heart, but also intensifies the evil qualities themselves. Every vile word a man speaks, every base, low story he tells for the joke he sees in it, every angry word, every oath one utters, and all the list Jesus mentions, these show the kind of soul a man has, and uttering them stirs up the dregs like the dregs in the bottom of a swamp.

The disciples had probably imbibed many of the popular notions of the Pharisees and they could not understand why a man was not defiled by external things. The saying of Jesus was dark to his disciples. They, therefore, styled it a parable, regarding it as containing or illustrating some truth which they did not fully comprehend. This question gives us a view of the spiritual dullness of the disciples and of the low attainments in spiritual knowledge. At this point, Matthew (15: 12-14) relates that the disciples inform Jesus that the Pharisees had taken offense at what he had said to them, and the reply of Jesus to his disciples. This conversation, which is omitted by Mark, may have taken place as he was entering the house, or just after. Peter acted as spokesman of the disciples. (Matt. 15: 15.)

SECTION SEVEN

TOUR TO TYRE AND SIDON
7: 24 to 8: 13

1. THE SYROPHENICIAN WOMAN'S DAUGHTER CURED
7: 24-30
(Matt. 15: 21-28)

24 And from thence he arose, and went away into the borders of Tyre [3]and Sidon. And he entered into a house, and would have no man know it; and he could not be hid. 25 But straightway a woman, whose little daughter had an unclean spirit, having heard of him, came and fell down at his feet.

[3]Some ancient authorities omit *and Sidon.*

24 **And from thence he arose, and went away into the borders of Tyre and Sidon.**—The frontier region, or according to Matthew (15: 21), into the parts of region of Tyre and Sidon. Tyre and Sidon were the two principal cities of Phoenicia, on the coast of the Mediterranean Sea. Tyre was about twenty miles south of Sidon, and about one hundred miles northwest of Jerusalem. In the days of David and Solomon, Tyre was the leading seaport of the world. It was afterwards taken by the Babylonians, the Persians, and Alexander, but up to the time of Christ it remained a great commercial city. Since then its harbor has been filled with sand, and there remains only a wretched shadow of its former greatness. Both were Gentile cities in a Gentile country. This is the only instance in the Lord's ministry when he went beyond the bounds of Palestine.

And he entered into a house, and would have no man know it;—Probably he intended to give private instruction to the apostles. He desired privacy for a short time.

and he could not be hid.—He was unable to be hidden. No doubt he used every precaution so that no one might know who or where he was.

25 **But straightway a woman, whose little daughter had an unclean spirit, having heard of him,**—Of his miracles, arrival, and where he was abiding.

came and fell down at his feet.—It seems that she knew where he was and had no trouble in finding him. This was an act denoting reverence and earnest entreaty. Her faith in his power is thus at once manifested. His concealment was the

26 Now the woman was a ⁴Greek, a Syrophoenician by race. And she besought him that he would cast forth the demon out of her daughter. 27 And

⁴Or, *Gentile*

first means in its development. Faith led her to Jesus.
Matthew (15: 22) adds, "O Lord, thou son of David." It is
remarkable that two of the brightest examples of faith seen in
the ministry of Christ were exhibited by Gentiles, that of the
centurion (Matt. 8: 8, 9) and of this woman. The fact that
she addressed Jesus as the "son of David" shows that she
knew of the prophecies concerning the Christ and that he
would be the Son of David.

26 **Now the woman was a Greek,**—Mark describes the
woman as a Gentile. The Jews called all persons Greeks who
were not of their nation. (Rom. 1: 14.) The whole world
was considered as divided into Jews and Greeks. All who
were not Jews were also considered Gentiles. The term
"Greek" is here used, as it was frequently by the Jews, in the
sense of Gentile. (1 Cor. 1: 24.) After Alexander's con-
quests, when all the world was in subjection to the Greeks,
the Jews divided the world into Jews and Greeks.

a Syrophoenician by race.—"Syrophoenician" is com-
pounded of Syrian and Phoenician, and means a Syrian of
Phoenicia, Phoenicia being at that time a part of the province
of Syria. She was also a Canaanite. (Matt. 15: 22.)

**And she besought him that he would cast forth the
demon out of her daughter.**—Matthew (15: 23) says: "He
answered her not a word." He neither repelled her nor made
favorable answer. There were reasons for hesitations. (Matt.
15: 24.) No doubt he intended to have mercy. He delayed to
bring out a great lesson. His disciples intervened for her,
but he said: "I was not sent but unto the lost sheep of the
house of Israel." (Matt. 15: 24.) That is, to the Jews. His
personal mission was to the Jews.

27 **And he said unto her, Let the children first be filled :—**
That is, suffer the children, the Jews, first to be satisfied. The
Jews were first to have the gospel and its blessings offered to
them. It was not yet time for the Gentiles. The request of
the woman was unseasonable. There was, however, hope for
her in the future.

he said unto her, Let the children first be filled: for it is not meet to take the children's [5]bread and cast it to the dogs. 28 But she answered and saith unto him, Yea, Lord; even the dogs under the table eat of the children's crumbs.

[5]Or, *loaf*

for it is not meet to take the children's bread—It is not good, proper and right. The Jews considered themselves as the peculiar children of God. To all other nations they were accustomed to apply terms of contempt, of which *"dogs"* was the most common. "Children's bread" was that which Jesus came to offer to the Jews.

and cast it to the dogs.—Throw it to the Gentiles. Gentiles were styled dogs by the Jews. The woman knew that, in comparing the Jews to the children of God's family, and the Gentiles to the dogs without, Jesus simply used customary language of a Jew. He would bring out fully the greatness of her faith. The gospel was offered first to the Jews and then to all. He was putting her faith to a severe test. Many a woman, at such a speech, would have risen in despair, and gone away in anger, but she kept calm. Jesus means to say that he was sent to the Jews. The woman was a Gentile. He meant that it did not comport with the design of his personal ministry to apply benefits intended for the Jews to others. Jesus did not intend to justify or sanction the use of such terms. He meant to try her faith.

28 But she answered and saith unto him, Yea, Lord;—Yea, I admit all you say; it is not proper and right to take away the children's bread and cast it to the dogs. I am indeed one of the dogs—a Gentile—and am willing to take my place as one. It is not fit for the dogs to be fed before the children.

even the dogs under the table eat of the children's crumbs. —I am willing to accept the crumbs—that which is left after all the children are filled. (Verse 27.) Let the children have the best food. Let the Jews have the chief benefit of thy ministry. But the dogs, beneath the table, eat the crumbs. So let me be regarded as a dog. A Gentile, as unworthy of everything. Yet grant *one* exertion of that almighty power displayed among the Jews, and heal the despised daughter of a despised heathen mother. Grant the dogs this much. The answer of the woman is a wonderful illustration of faith, turn-

29 And he said unto her, For this saying go thy way; the demon is gone out of thy daughter. 30 And she went away unto her house, and found the child laid upon the bed, and the demon gone out.

---

ing the most untoward circumstances to a good account. We know not which to admire more—the readiness of her wit, or the depth of her humility.

29 And he said unto her, For this saying go thy way;—Her speech showed a strong faith in Jesus. Matthew (15: 28) says: "O woman, great is thy faith." We can see how greatness of faith is manifested: (1) she came to Christ under difficulties, (2) she persevered when her prayer seemed to be denied, (3) she still pleaded when obstacles were presented, (4) she waited at the feet of Jesus until he had mercy. Such faith always prevails.

the demon is gone out of thy daughter.—Her request is granted. The same hour Jesus said: "Be it done unto thee even as thou wilt." (Matt. 15: 28.) The demon left the daughter.

30 And she went away unto her house,—She returned home in full confidence that her child had been or would be blessed.

and found the child laid upon the bed, and the demon gone out.—The mother found the Master's declaration verified, and her faith realized. The daughter is no longer raving, or in convulsions, but lying quietly on the bed, healed in consequence of her mother's faith and prayers. Doubtless her mother's heart was full of joy.

2. JESUS HEALS A DEAF STAMMERER
7: 31-37
(Matt. 16: 29-31)

31 And again he went out from the borders of Tyre, and came through Sidon unto the sea of Galilee, through the midst of the borders of Decapolis.

---

31 And again he went out from the borders of Tyre,—How long Jesus remained in Tyre and Sidon is not stated. Having completed his work there he now starts on his way to another field of operation.

and came through Sidon unto the sea of Galilee, through the midst of the borders of Decapolis.—He starts from Tyre and passes through Sidon. He travels northward. From Sidon he passed over into the borders of Decapolis, on the

32 And they bring unto him one that was deaf, and had an impediment in his speech; and they beseech him to lay his hand upon him. 33 And he took him aside from the multitude privately, and put his fingers into his ears, and he spat, and touched his tongue; 34 and looking up to heaven, he sighed, and

east of the Jordan, thus approaching the northeastern shore of the Sea of Galilee. Decapolis was a region of "ten cities," lying east of the Jordan. Only Mark gives an account of the following miracle.

32 And they—Friends of the deaf. Those interested in him. The demoniac of Gadara, after his healing, went through this region declaring what great things Jesus had done for him. (5: 20.) Thus his fame was spread abroad in that region.

bring unto him one that was deaf,—His friends conduct him to Jesus. He was merely diseased and not possessed of a demon.

and had an impediment in his speech;—He was "a deaf stammerer." He was not entirely without hearing, but spoke indistinctly or with difficulty.

and they beseech him to lay his hand upon him.—That is, to cure him. Blessings were commonly imparted by laying on the hands.

33 And he took him aside from the multitude privately,— From the crowd in the presence of only a few witnesses. Why? Many reasons may be given and none be correct. (1) His friends had suggested their way of healing (to put his hands upon him) (verse 32); they needed to be taught that they should leave the way to Jesus. (2) The people may have gathered to see a great miracle. But Jesus would make no display; nor satisfy mere curiosity. (Matt. 12: 15-21.) (3) He would withdraw from observation; and produce as little excitement as possible. (6: 31, 32; 8: 22, 23.) (4) While he would strengthen their faith, he would not feed their superstition. (5) For the good of the man himself; that he might have a proper view of Christ's healing power. Jesus showed that he was not limited to any one way of exercising his miraculous power.

and put his fingers into his ears, and he spat, and touched his tongue;—The diseased organ. Jesus spat on the eyes of the blind man at Bethsaida (8: 23), and "on the ground, and made clay of the spittle, and anointed" the eyes of the blind

saith unto him, Ephphatha, that is, Be opened. 35 And his ears were opened, and the bond of his tongue was loosed, and he spake plain. 36 And he charged them that they should tell no man: but the more he charged them, so much the more a great deal they published it. 37 And they were

man at Jerusalem (John 9: 6). Why Jesus used the spittle in either case can only be an opinion on our part. But surely not on account of any healing power in it. This may be one way that Jesus teaches us that we are not to enter into the reasons of all his actions; and that when he has appointed any observance, we are humbly to submit, though we may not be able to see why it might not be different.

34 and looking up to heaven,—Heaven is upward. To lift up the eyes to heaven is an act imploring aid from God, and denotes an attitude of prayer. (Psalm 121: 1, 2; Mark 6: 41; John 11: 41.) By looking up to heaven, as representing the abode of God, he gave God recognition in the miracle.

he sighed,—Groaned, pitying the suffering man who stood before him. The expression of his compassion in his sigh heavenward would naturally impress all present with the necessity of looking to God for help.

and saith unto him, Ephphatha, that is, Be opened.—A word in common language in Judea at that time.

35 And his ears were opened,—Every obstruction was removed, and a perfect action of the organs enjoyed.

and the bond of his tongue was loosed,—The difficulty in speaking was removed. There is nothing for, but rather everything against, the supposition of some, that the cure was gradual.

and he spake plain.—His stammering was all gone. A perfect cure. He spoke without difficulty—all could understand his speech. The process adopted in this case was peculiar. Jesus first put his fingers in the man's ears, then spat. He then touched the man's tongue, looked up to heaven, heaved a sigh, and exclaimed, "Be opened," and the man was healed.

36 And he charged them that they should tell no man:—Why, he does not state, but we may be assured he had good reasons. It was, however, an impressive way of showing that he did not seek the praise of men.

but the more he charged them, so much the more a great

beyond measure astonished, saying, He hath done all things well; he maketh even the deaf to hear, and the dumb to speak.

deal they published it.—Forbidding them publishing it seems to have created a great desire to spread the news. A very common freak of human nature is seen here, the more he charged them to keep the cure a secret, "the more a great deal they published it."

37 **And they were beyond measure astonished,**—Exceedingly —very much. In the Greek, "very abundantly."

saying, He hath done all things well;—All things in a remarkable manner; or he has perfectly effected the cure of the deaf and the dumb. It is an exclamation of the highest approval and satisfaction. All God's creation was very good.

he maketh even the deaf to hear, and the dumb to speak.— Mark refers to this case and probably to others. Matthew (15: 30, 31) states that many miracles were performed, among which were the dumb speaking. In this, and the parallel in Matthew, the characteristic difference between the two writers is seen. Matthew says that "there came unto him great multitudes, having with them the lame, blind, dumb, maimed, and many others, and they cast them down at his feet; and he healed them"; but he gives no particular description of any single case. Mark, on the other hand, selects a single one of these cures, and describes minutely both it and its effect on the people.

3. CHRIST FEEDING THE FOUR THOUSAND
8: 1-9
(Matt. 15: 32-38)

1 In those days, when there was again a great multitude, and they had nothing to eat, he called unto him his disciples, and saith unto them, 2 I have

1 In those days, when there was again a great multitude,— Similar to that which had often gathered about him in Galilee, and especially the one he had previously fed not far distant on the northeastern shore of the lake.

and they had nothing to eat, he called unto him his disciples, and saith unto them,—Having come unprovided, or having consumed what they had brought. He tells them of his sympathy for the multitude.

compassion on the multitude, because they continue with me now three days, and have nothing to eat: 3 and if I send them away fasting to their home, they will faint on the way; and some of them are come from far. 4 And his disciples answered him, Whence shall one be able to fill these men with [6]bread here in a desert place? 5 And he asked them, How many loaves have ye? And they said, Seven. 6 And he commandeth the multitude to sit down

[6]Gr. *loaves.*

---

2 I have compassion on the multitude, because they continue with me now three days, and have nothing to eat:—The reason for his compassion is here given. Whether they had been without food three days is not clearly expressed. If they brought any food it was all consumed, and they were in a wilderness (verse 4) where no food could be bought and were in immediate need.

3 and if I send them away fasting to their home, they will faint on the way;—Become exhausted, for want of food and by fatigue on their way home.

and some of them are come from far.—Come a long distance and they could not possibly reach their respective homes without perishing, unless they got food. Jesus by his power could as easily have preserved them from fainting without food as have created food by multiplying the loaves and fishes for their support.

4 And his disciples answered him, Whence shall one be able to fill these men with bread—Where is the food to be had to satisfy their appetite? The disciples, it seems, did not reflect on the miracle which Christ had lately wrought for the relief of the five thousand.

here in a desert place?—The location is pointed out. The disciples were still babes in faith and knowledge, as is frequently illustrated. (Mark 7: 18; 9: 10, 28, 29; Luke 24: 25-27.) We find similar examples of weak faith among God's people. The Israelites murmur immediately after their deliverance at the Red Sea (Ex. 15: 24; 17: 1-3); and Moses showed unbelief when God was about to feed Israel with flesh in the wilderness (Num. 11: 21-23).

5 And he asked them, How many loaves have ye? And they said, Seven.—"They had a few small fishes." The disciples seem now to have suspected what Jesus was about to do, for they do not ask, as on the former occasion, "What are

on the ground: and he took the seven loaves, and having given thanks, he brake, and gave to his disciples, to set before them; and they set them before the multitude. 7 And they had a few small fishes: and having blessed them, he commanded to set these also before them. 8 And they ate, and were filled: and they took up, of broken pieces that remained over, seven baskets. 9 And they were about four thousand: and he sent them away. 10 And

these among so many?" (John 6: 9.) Jesus did not reprove the disciples for their forgetfulness of what he had so lately done in feeding the five thousand, but meekly asked what food they had.

6 **And he commandeth the multitude to sit down on the ground:**—Probably under the direction of the disciples, who, on the occasion of feeding the five thousand, arranged the people in companies by hundreds and fifties. (6: 39, 40.)

and he took the seven loaves, and having given thanks, he brake, and gave to his disciples, to set before them; and they set them before the multitude.—We should follow the example of Jesus and offer thanks for our daily meals before eating them. Here, as in the former miracle, the disciples distributed the food to the people.

7 **And they had a few small fishes:**—In addition to the seven loaves. This was all the food they had on hand.

and having blessed them, he commanded to set these also before them.—Jesus gave thanks for the fishes separately, thus showing the order in which the two kinds of food were served.

8 **And they ate, and were filled:**—Matthew says: "They all ate, and were filled." All were abundantly satisfied. Not a partial but a full satisfaction.

and they took up, of broken pieces that remained over, seven baskets.—The fragments after the people were filled were more than they had at the first. Jesus ordered the gathering of the fragments that he might convince them, in the strongest manner, of the greatness of the miracle and teach them also at the same time to practice economy in the midst of plenty.

9 **And they were about four thousand:**—"About," may have been a few more or less than four thousand. This together with the feeding of the five thousand gives us some idea as to what the historians mean when they speak of great multitudes

following Jesus. At what moment was the miracle performed? Was it before or after the breaking and distribution? Did the increase take place while the bread was passing through and from the hands of Jesus similar to that of the widow's oil (2 Kings 4: 5-7), which filled vessel after vessel, and was only stayed when there were no more to fill? Was it after small pieces were placed in the hands of the multitude? We do not know. Since Jesus did not reveal this point, we will not undertake to do so. But the important point is stated that the miracle was performed; just when is comparatively of no consequence. Some think this miracle is only another account of feeding the five thousand. This, however, is absurd. The questions Jesus asked in verses 19 and 20 prove beyond a doubt that there were two instances of miraculous feeding. Besides the accounts of the two show marked differences. The journey to the former was from Galilee, probably from Capernaum; to the latter from Sidon through Decapolis. That was in the spring; this in the summer. The one was in the vicinity of Bethsaida, northeast of the Sea of Galilee; the other in Decapolis, a few miles further south. In that the people were principally Jews from the western side of Jordan who had been with Jesus one day; in this they were a mixed multitude, partly Jews and partly heathen, from the west of Jordan and had been with Jesus three days. There the number of men was five thousand, who reclined on the grass; here four thousand who reclined on the ground. In that case there were five loaves and after eating twelve baskets of fragments; in this there were seven baskets of fragments. All this shows there were two miraculous feedings.

4. THE PHARISEES SEEK A SIGN
8: 10-13
(Matt. 15: 39; 16: 4)

straightway he entered into the boat with his disciples, and came into the parts of Dalmanutha.

---

10 **And straightway he entered into the boat with his disciples, and came into the parts of Dalmanutha.**—Matthew (15: 39) says: "Came into the borders of Magadan." These were probably small towns situated close to each other. Some think there was but one town, having two names. Neither exists now. Note the evangelists do not say that he went to ei-

11 And the Pharisees came forth, and began to question with him, seeking
of him a sign from heaven, trying him. 12 And he sighed deeply in his

ther of those towns, but only to the *coasts,* or *parts,* where
they were situated. This leaves no contradiction between the
two writers.

11 **And the Pharisees came forth, and began to question
with him,**—The Pharisees were looking for a great earthly
king and conqueror, with vast wealth, and invincible armies,
breaking in pieces Rome and all its kingdoms, and making Jerusalem the capital of the world. They were questioning
whether Jesus, who could heal the wounded, feed multitudes,
calm storms, raise the dead, could be this conqueror and redeemer of the nation.

seeking of him a sign from heaven,—That would prove him
to be this kind of a king and conqueror they were expecting.
They saw no other way of the fulfillment of God's promisès,
for they had shut their eyes and were blind to a large part of
them. Probably they were seeking from him a miracle from
the sky, such as the standing still of the sun and moon during
the life of Joshua (Josh. 10: 12, 13), or as the thunder and
lightning on Sinai (Ex. 19: 16), and not a sign on the earth,
such as his miracles were. Samuel had caused it to thunder
(1 Sam. 12: 16-18) ; Isaiah had caused the shadow to go back
ten degrees on the dial of Ahaz (Isa. 38: 8) ; and Moses had
sent them manna from heaven. (Ex. 16: 4; John 6: 31.)
Probably it was something like this for which they were asking.

trying him.—They wished to test the extent of his miraculous powers. As they could not deny the miracles which he
had wrought, they wanted to be able to say that there were
some miracles which he could not work. Once before a demand like this had been made of him (Matt. 12: 38), and his
refusal then inspired them with a greater boldness in again
making the demand. Thus, with ingenuity truly devilish,
they sought an apparent advantage over him before the people. This is the first and only time that the Pharisees and
Sadducees are mentioned as acting in concert against
Jesus. Their extreme jealousy toward each other, and the different grounds on which they were opposed to Jesus, rendered
concert of action almost impossible. The chief cause for

spirit, and saith, Why doth this generation seek a sign? verily I say unto
you, There shall no sign be given unto this generation.   13 And he left them,
and again entering into *the boat* departed to the other side.

which the Pharisees opposed him was his disregard of their
tradition; and in this the Sadducees sympathized with Jesus,
because they also denied the authority of tradition.   Relative
to his miracles the Pharisees and Sadducees occupied common
ground, and hence their agreement in asking for a sign from
heaven.

**12 And he sighed deeply in his spirit, and saith, Why doth
this generation seek a sign?**—When so many signs, so many
incontrovertible proofs of my mission from the Father have
been already given, and continue to be given daily?

**verily I say unto you, There shall no sign be given unto this
generation.**—That is, no such sign as they asked, namely, a
sign from heaven.   He said one should be given, the same as
was furnished by Johah (Matt. 16: 4); but this was not what
they asked, nor would it be given because they asked for a
sign.   He wrought no sign for the sake of the sign and wonder; his miracles were wrought because they were needed and
thus became signs of his love, his character, and his authority
from God.   It was a sin for the Pharisees to ask for new signs
and miracles for a confirmation for that doctrine which has
been already confirmed by miracles; so it is a sin today for
one to ask for a new message of something independent of the
gospel of Christ to save him.   "The gospel: it is the power of
God unto salvation," and we need not look for any other
power to save.   To the gospel God has tied us, and from it we
cannot turn and expect salvation.   Matthew (16: 4) also adds:
"An evil and adulterous generation seeketh after a sign; and
there shall no sign be given unto it, but the sign of Jonah."
From the statement of Jesus it has been thought that the
Jews of the Savior's time were a very adulterous people.
They certainly were when compared with a *perfect* standard,
but not when compared with the heathen nations about them.
The denial of a sign from heaven did not preclude such a sign
as that of Jonah.   On coming from the dead Jesus gave the
only sign he promised to give them.

**13 And he left them, and again entering into the boat de-
parted to the other side.**—The one used by and for Jesus and
his disciples.

SECTION EIGHT
8: 14 to 9: 50.

1. THE LEAVEN OF THE PHARISEES AND OF HEROD
8: 14-21
(Matt. 16: 5-12.)

14 And they forgot to take bread; and they had not in the boat with them more than one loaf. 15 And he charged them, saying, Take heed, beware of the leaven of the Pharisees and the leaven of Herod. 16 And they reasoned

14 **And they forgot to take bread;**—Probably through their anxiety and interest in the attack of the Pharisees on Jesus the disciples forgot to take food on their journey.

and they had not in the boat with them more than one loaf. —Our Lord noticed their search and disappointment, and took occasion to call their attention to something of infinitely greater importance.

15 **And he charged them, saying, Take heed, beware of the leaven of the Pharisees**—"Leaven" is generally, though not always, used in scripture to represent that which is corrupt and evil. The leaven was their teaching (Matt. 16: 12), both by word and by example. Leaven is the type of an active, persuasive influence, whether for good or bad. It works out of sight; it eats its way in the dark; it never ceases till it makes a full end. A dull unlikely something was hid in a measure of meal, and it proved itself there a secret, silent force that first contaminated and then changed the whole. The disciples were dull, in comprehending the meaning of Christ's language. They thought he had spoken unto them of the leaven of bread; what he intended was the leaven of the Pharisees' doctrine.

and the leaven of Herod.—The leaven of Herod was a corrupting political influence. They had need to be guarded against this, because the disputes of political partisans are not only corrupting to those who indulge in them, but they impair the influence of men whose business it is to guide all parties in the way of holiness. The apostles adhered strictly throughout their career to the rule of action here given. Christ compares false doctrine to leaven, because as that diffuses itself into the whole mass or lump of dough with which it is mixed, so false doctrine is not only evil and corrupt in

one with another, [1]saying, [2]We have no bread. 17 And Jesus perceiving it saith unto them, Why reason ye, because ye have no bread? do ye not yet perceive, neither understand? have ye your heart hardened? 18 Having eyes, see ye not? and having ears, hear ye not? and do ye not remember?

[1]Some ancient authorities read *because they had no bread.*
[2]Or, It is *because we have no bread.*

itself, but apt to spread its contagion further and further, to the affecting of others with it. Error is as damnable as vice, and persons erroneous in judgment are to be avoided, as well as those who are wicked in conversation; and he that has a due care of his soul's salvation will be as much afraid of erroneous principles as he is of debauched practices. Jesus does not command his disciples to separate from communion with the Pharisees and oblige them not to hear their doctrine, but only to beware of their errors, which they mix with their doctrine. More truth there is mixed with error, the more dangerous it is, for the reason the error is harder to detect.

16 And they reasoned one with another, saying, We have no bread.—The disciples talked the matter over among themselves, comparing their views, and agreed that it was a reproof for their neglecting to take bread along with them.

17 And Jesus perceiving it saith unto them, Why reason ye, because ye have no bread?—How could they be so troubled about bread when they so recently saw him provide bread for thousands?

do ye not yet perceive, neither understand?—They did not understand his meaning, neither did they comprehend what he said.

have ye your heart hardened?—No abiding impression had yet been made upon their minds by the many great miracles he had performed in their presence, and the many discourses they had heard him deliver. The real need is a better life. The real danger is not from hunger for the want of physical bread, but from the forces and influences around you that are working silently in so many hearts. Put down, crush out, destroy in yourselves the first signs and workings of these leavens of evil.

18 Having eyes, see ye not? and having ears, hear ye not? and do ye not remember?—Having the powers of seeing and

19 When I brake the five loaves among the five thousand, how many
³baskets full of broken pieces took ye up? They say unto him, Twelve. 20
And when the seven among the four thousand, how many ³basketfuls of broken pieces took ye up? And they say unto him, Seven. 21 And he said unto
them, Do ye not yet understand?

³*Basket* in ver. 19 and 20 represents different Greek words.

hearing, they did not exercise them so as to remember the miraculous feeding of the large multitudes. If they had properly
exercised these powers, they would have seen and understood
that he did not refer to literal bread but to the doctrines of the
Pharisees.

**19-20 When I brake the five loaves among the five thou-
sand, how many baskets full of broken pieces took ye up?
They say unto him, Twelve. And when the seven among the
four thousand, how many basketfuls of broken pieces took ye
up? And they say unto him, Seven.**—Their anxiety about
food to nourish the body, which Jesus rebuked, showed a dullness of spiritual perception and probably a want of faith.
These questions of Jesus show beyond doubt that he fed the
multitudes on two different occasions and not one as some
suppose.

21 And he said unto them, Do ye not yet understand?—
Matthew (16: 11, 12) says: "How is it that ye do not perceive
that I spake not to you concerning bread? But beware of the
leaven of the Pharisees and Sadducees. Then understood
they that he bade them not beware of the leaven of bread, but
of the teaching of the Pharisees and Sadducees." They at the
last understood that, which they ought to have understood at
the first. But they, like we, were slow to understand.

2. A BLIND MAN CURED AT BETHSAIDA
8: 22-26

22 And they come unto Bethsaida. And they bring to him a blind man,

22 And they come unto Bethsaida.—This is not the Bethsaida in which Peter, Andrew, and Philip had formerly lived,
but another Bethsaida, afterward called Julias, which was situated on the east bank of the Jordan, just above its entrance
into the lake of Galilee. This is evident from the fact that
Jesus and the apostles had crossed from the west to the north-

and beseech him to touch him. 23 And he took hold of the blind man by the hand, and brought him out of the village; and when he had spit on his eyes, and laid his hands upon him, he asked him, Seest thou aught? 24 And he looked up, and said, I see men; for I behold *them* as trees, walking. 25 Then again he laid his hands upon his eyes; and he looked stedfastly, and

east side of the lake, to reach the place.

And they bring to him a blind man, and beseech him to touch him.—This man had become blind by disease or some other cause as seen from verse 24. His friends brought him to Jesus to be healed by him. They had faith that he could do it.

23 And he took hold of the blind man by the hand, and brought him out of the village;—So as to guide him in walking. This shows his willingness to help the helpless. Why he took him out of the village the sacred writers have not told us.

and when he had spit on his eyes, and laid his hands upon him, he asked him, Seest thou aught?—Why this was done no one knows. There was no peculiar power or medical virtue in these acts. The miracle is remarkable for its external applications similar to that of the deaf man. (7 : 33.)

24 And he looked up, and said, I see men; for I behold them as trees, walking.—He could see men walking, but indistinctly. This shows he was not born blind, or he would not have known how trees appear as distinguished from men; but having lost his sight, when it was partially restored he received distorted vision of the men about him, so that they appeared tall and rough in their outline like trees.

25 Then again he laid his hands upon his eyes; and he looked stedfastly, and was restored, and saw all things clearly. —The second touch of the hand of Jesus completed his restoration. Jesus adopted this method of cure to give variety to the manifestations of his power by showing that he could heal in part and by progressive steps, as well as by his more usual method of effecting a perfect cure at one word. This cure was not less miraculous than others, but rather more so: for it was really the working of two miracles, each effecting instantaneously all that was intended by it. His sight was completely restored. It was foretold that the Messiah should open the eyes of the blind. (Isa. 29: 18.) We have the account of several miracles of healing the blind. (10: 46-52;

was restored, and saw all things clearly. 26 And he sent him away to his home, saying, Do not even enter into the village.

Matt. 9: 27-31; 15: 29-31; John 9: 1-7.) All go to show Christ to be the true Messiah.

26 And he sent him away to his home, saying, Do not even enter into the village.—Had he gone into the town seeing, or had told persons what had occurred, the whole population might have gone out in pursuit of Jesus, and thus the privacy which he was seeking to maintain would have been broken up.

3. CONVERSATION NEAR CESAREA PHILIPPI
8: 27-30
(Matt. 16: 13-20; Luke 9: 18-21)

27 And Jesus went forth, and his disciples, into the villages of Caesarea Philippi: and on the way he asked his disciples, saying unto them, Who do men say that I am? 28 And they told him, saying, John the Baptist; and others, Elijah; but others, One of the prophets. 29 And he asked them, But

---

27 And Jesus went forth, and his disciples, into the villages of Caesarea Philippi:—Cesarea Philippi is interesting to the modern world chiefly from the fact that the conversation found in this division occurred in its vicinity. It stood at the northeast corner of the upper Jordan valley, and is about twenty-six miles north of the lake of Galilee. The famous spring, which is one of the three sources of the river Jordan, bursts forth from the base of the mountain.

and on the way he asked his disciples, saying unto them, Who do men say that I am?—Christ had not a large interest in this question, but it was a convenient introduction to the one which was soon to come.

28 And they told him, saying, John the Baptist; and others, Elijah; but others, One of the prophets.—Men believed, from Mic. 5: 5 and other passages, that they were warranted in concluding that at the time of the Messiah different prophets would again appear. It was evident from these answers that all felt that Jesus was an extraordinary man, even though they denied him his true character. The variety of opinions shows that the people were thinking and discussing the question. It is not improper to seek to ascertain what men think of us. It may help us to correct a fault, or save us from de-

who say ye that I am? Peter answereth and saith unto him, Thou art the Christ. 30 And he charged them that they should tell no man of him.

spondency. Christ was not ignorant as to what men thought and said of him, nor did he vaingloriously inquire after the opinion of the multitude concerning himself; but with an intention more firmly to settle and establish his disciples in the belief of his being the true and promised Messiah. Jesus teaching his disciples "on the way" teaches us our duty to take advantage of all occasions and opportunities for good discourse touching spiritual things, when in the house, in the field, and when traveling.

29 And he asked them, But who say ye that I am?—The emphasis is on "ye." All that had gone before simply led up to this question.

Peter answereth and saith unto him, Thou art the Christ.— Mark's answer is short but inclusive. Luke (9: 20) adds to it, "the Christ of God"; Matthew (16: 16) gives it in full, "the Christ, the Son of the living God." The most wonderful combination of words in any language. It disposes of atheism in its final word, of polytheism in its final word with the article, of pantheism in its adjective, of unitarianism in "the Son," of Gnosticism in "the Christ," and of Socinianism in its completeness. It links together the human and divine, and brings to the soul comfort that could come from no other source. This truth is the bedrock of the universe of salvation, the great underlying *petra*, upon which was laid the cornerstone, Jesus, as he planted himself upon this truth and died for it, and around whom was laid the foundation of apostles and prophets, from whom rise, course by course, the living stones, *petroi*, that from the stately temple of the Holy Spirit, the church of Christ. *The Christ*, the Messiah, or the anointed of God; *living God*. The term *living* was applied to the true God, to distinguish him from *idols* that are dead, or lifeless blocks of stone. He is also the source or life, temporal, spiritual, and eternal.

30 And he charged them that they should tell no man of him.—They were not to tell of the full revelation of himself which he had made in his indorsement of Peter, because they themselves were not yet prepared to be its intelligent proclaimers. They had yet no adequate conception of the kingdom of God. This restriction to tell no man he was the Christ lasted until after his resurrection and ascension (Matt. 17: 9; 28: 19, 20; Mark 16: 15, 16; Luke 24: 45-47), and the coming of the Holy Spirit on the day of Pentecost (Acts 2: 1-36).

4. JESUS FORETELLS HIS DEATH AND RESURRECTION
8: 31-33
(Matt. 16: 21-23; Luke 9: 22)

31 And he began to teach them, that the Son of man must suffer many things, and be rejected by the elders, and the chief priests, and the scribes, and be killed, and after three days rise again. 32 And he spake the saying

31 **And he began to teach them,**—This does not mean that he had never mentioned the matter of his sufferings before. He had *alluded* to them again and again (Matt. 9: 15; 10: 38; 12: 40; John 2: 19; 3: 14; 6: 51), but these allusions were figurative and covert, and conveyed no clear idea to their minds. A *suffering* Messiah was so utterly foreign to all their conceptions of Messiah that only the most explicit declaration could induce them to accept it.

that the Son of man must suffer many things,—The few prophets who had ever applied the prophecies to suffering, such as Isaiah (53), to the Messiah, had made no large impression either on rabbinical teaching or the views of the nation. A conquering, triumphant Messiah was what the people liked to hear of, and what the rabbis announced. How startling then this communication.

and be rejected by the elders, and the chief priests, and the scribes,—An examination of 14: 43; Matt. 27: 41, with parallel passages, will show how actively all these classes participated in making him suffer. Their authority with the people threatened to be displaced by that of Jesus, and they made common cause against him.

and be killed,—The first direct statement of this truth, the most appalling that could come to their minds. The Sanhedrin was composed of the elders, chief priests, and scribes. It was the highest civil and ecclesiastical court of the Jews, and consisted of seventy-one members. The whole Sanhedrin would join in these terrible evils against Jesus.

openly. And Peter took him, and began to rebuke him. 33 But he turning about, and seeing his disciples, rebuked Peter, and saith, Get thee behind me,

---

and after three days rise again.—A most explicit declaration of the resurrection. Yet it is not at all likely that they took in the full force of his words. They sometimes understood his figurative expressions literally (Matt. 16: 7; John 4: 33; 11: 12), and sometimes his literal expressions figuratively (Matt. 15: 15-17). In this case the attitude of their minds was so averse to the idea of death that they would scarcely receive the other, which depended on death. After his resurrection it is said: "For as yet they knew not the scripture, that he must rise again from the dead." (John 20: 9.) With their erroneous ideas, it was hard for them to learn the truth. So it is with people now. "After three days" is equivalent to "the third day" of Matthew (16: 21) and Luke (9: 22). The Jews were accustomed to reckon the odd parts of a day as a whole day. Jesus died on Friday afternoon, and rose early on the first day, or Sunday morning; the time intervening was one whole day and parts of two days, which were reckoned as three days.

32 **And he spake the saying openly.**—Jesus spoke freely, frankly, and boldly, without concealment or ambiguity.

And Peter took him, and began to rebuke him.—To chide him for the utterance of such sad forebodings. He probably considered them simply as coming from low spirits occasioned by his recent trials in Galilee. Matthew gives the chiding words, "Be it far from thee, Lord: this shall never be unto thee." The word "rebuke" here means to *admonish* or *earnestly to entreat,* as in Luke (17: 3).

33 **But he turning about, and seeing his disciples, rebuked Peter, and saith, Get thee behind me, Satan;**—The same words used by Jesus in the wilderness to Satan himself, and probably a reminiscence. At all events the temptation was the same, and put beyond doubt that the clearness of Peter's confession did by no means show clearness of conception of the surroundings of the Messiah. Christ rebuked Peter, doubtless for his good and that of the other disciples. Peter's rebuke of his Lord was presumptuous and worldly; Christ's rebuke of Peter was deserved, timely and wise. He thus

Satan; for thou mindest not the things of God, but the things of men.

checked the spirit of insubordination and of worldly ambition in his disciples. The word "Satan" means literally an *adversary,* or one that opposes us in the accomplishment of our designs. It is applied to the devil commonly, as the *opposer* or *adversary* of man. But there is no evidence that the Lord meant to apply this term to Peter, as signifying that *he* was Satan or the devil, or that he used the term in anger.

for thou mindest not the things of God, but the things of men.—His mind fell in naturally with the carnal expectations of the perverse Jewish nation, rather than those purposes of God of which Jesus and the prophets have spoken. It is hard to imagine him to whom such words were spoken as *the* foundation of the church. Matthew (16: 23) adds: "Thou art a stumblingblock unto me." Peter's advice and wishes were in the way of Jesus. If followed, they would prevent the thing for which he came. Peter thought those things should not be done, which God wishes to be done. He judged of this matter as men do, who are desirous of honor; and not as God, who sees it best that Jesus should die to promote the great interests of mankind.

5. ALL MUST BE GIVEN UP FOR CHRIST
8: 34; 9: 1
(Matt. 16: 24-28; Luke 9: 23-27)

34 And he called unto him the multitude with his disciples, and said unto them, If any man would come after me, let him deny himself, and take up his

34 And he called unto him the multitude with his disciples, and said unto them, If any man would come after me,—This was spoken to the multitude as well as to the disciples, and the principles spoken applied to both—rich or poor, high or low.

let him deny himself,—Renounce himself, abstaining from everything that stands in the way of duty. Let him surrender to God his will, affections, body and soul. Let him not seek his own happiness as the supreme object, but be willing to renounce all, and lay down his life also, if required. Our Savior commends his religion to every one's election and choice, not attempting by force and violence to compel any person to the

cross, and follow me. 35 For whosoever would save his life shall lose it;

embracing of it. *If any man will come after me.* That is, if any man chooses and resolves to be a Christian. Observe our Savior's terms propounded; namely, self-denial and gospel service. *Let him deny himself.* That is, a willingness to part with all earthly comforts and temporal enjoyments for the sake of Christ, when called thereunto. He must bring his own wishes into subjection to those of God.

and take up his cross,—He includes the inner and outer struggles pertaining to the Christian life. He had just told his disciples that he must suffer; now he teaches them and the people that discipleship also involves sufferings and self-denials. It consists simply in doing our duty, let the world think or speak of it as they may. It does not consist in *making* trouble for ourselves (unless obedience to God makes the trouble), or doing things merely *to be opposed;* it is doing just what is required of us in the scriptures, let it produce whatever shame, disgrace, or pain it may. This every follower of Jesus is required to do.

and follow me.—Follow me *thus,* in the path of self-denial and suffering. Like master, like man. He is to obey the commands of Christ, and imitate his examples. He must set the life and doctrine of Christ continually before him, and be daily correcting and reforming his life by that rule and pattern. The cross must be taken willingly. He must follow Christ, not the world. Self-denial lies at the very threshold of Christ's kingdom. He who does not deny himself cannot become a Christian. The "cross" is a synonym of suffering and shame, and means that one must suffer everything necessary for Christ's sake. He must obey God at all cost. Luke (9: 23) says he must "take up his cross daily"—not occasionally.

35 **For whosoever would save his life shall lose it;**—Whosoever would save his life by abandoning this pathway shall lose that spiritual life which carries existence into the joys beyond the grave. The truth here expressed shows the necessity and saving results of self-denial and self-sacrifice for Christ, and thus gives a reason for what Jesus had just said in the preceding verse. Whoever purposes to save his natural or temporal life, makes this his great object, and hence rejects

and whosoever shall lose his life for my sake and the 'gospel's shall save it.
36 For what doth it profit a man, to gain the whole world, and forfeit his
life? 37 For what should a man give in exchange for his life? 38 For who-

'See marginal note on ch. 1. 1.

Christ, shall lose his higher spiritual life. As Jesus was to
lose his life for man, so man must be willing to lose his life for
Christ.

and whosoever shall lose his life for my sake and the gospel's shall save it.—Whosoever dies in the path of duty
because he will not desert Christ. There is not power enough
in the world to kill a true follower of Jesus. They may
temporarily sever body and spirit, but he lives on. Why can
we not more clearly grasp this great truth today? "Whosoever liveth and believeth on me shall never die." The love
of this temporal life is a great temptation to men to deny
Christ, and to renounce his holy religion. To save one's
life means to deny Jesus in order to enjoy present ease and
comfort and to escape persecution, prison, and death. Whosoever will suffer the loss of all things earthly, and even life
itself, for Christ's and the gospel's sake will save his soul.
This is the only way to be saved. (2 Tim. 2: 11-13.)
This is self-denial. The life that is preserved or *supported*
by disobeying Christ is a lost life.

**36 For what doth it profit a man, to gain the whole world,
and forfeit his life?**—Some may feel as though they had lost
something by the change here in the American Revised Version from "soul" to "life." But the original demands it, and,
if we but realize that Christ is here speaking of life that endures, eternal life, we shall see we have lost nothing.

To gain the whole world means to possess it as our own—
all its riches, honors, and pleasures. To lose his own life
means to be cast away, to be shut out from heaven, to be sent
to hell. Two things are implied by our Lord in these questions: (1) that they who are striving to gain the world, and
are unwilling to give it up for the sake of Christ, will lose
their souls; (2) that if the soul is lost, nothing can be given in
exchange for it, or it can never afterwards be saved. There is
no redemption in hell.

37 For what should a man give in exchange for his life?—A

soever shall be ashamed of me and of my words in this adulterous and sinful generation, the Son of man also shall be ashamed of him, when he cometh in the glory of his Father with the holy angels. 1 And he said unto them,

man would give any and everything earthly in exchange even for natural life. Should he not then be willing to give everything, even natural life itself, for eternal life? The antithesis is between earthly life plus earthly comfort and pleasure and eternal life plus eternal joys. If a man forfeits his life, what shall be given *as an exchange,* ransom price or equivalent for it? How can he possibly redeem it is the thought. He cannot possibly find an equivalent; the ruin will be irretrievable, and therefore perpetual. He can never redeem it. He is lost forever.

38 For whosoever shall be ashamed of me and of my words in this adulterous and sinful generation,—A faithless and wicked people. A perverse and apostate race. This age given to wickedness, particularly to adultery.

the Son of man also shall be ashamed of him,—At a time when the friendship of no one else will avail anything. He will be rightly and justly disowned and rejected by Jesus in the judgment.

when he cometh in the glory of his Father—In the day of judgment. This can only be referred to the final manifestation of Christ when he comes in glory to judge the world. (Matt. 26: 64; Luke 21: 27; 1 Thess. 4: 16; Rev. 1: 7.) Then the confessor shall be confessed, the denier shall be denied. (Matt. 10: 32, 33; Luke 12: 8, 9.) Thus the conversation that began in the exaltation of spiritual confession has gone through the pathway of suffering down to the gates of death, and then up to the siftings and the glories of the final manifestation, and through all it is the same Holy One, Son of God, born of Mary, anointed by the Holy Spirit, suffering, crucified, dead, buried, rising again, ascending to heaven, and at length coming from heaven to judge the world before his Father and the holy angels.

with the holy angels.—"Holy" as distinguished from fallen angels, evil spirits. Jesus, in his second coming, will be accompanied by angels. Whosoever shall refuse, through pride or wickedness, to acknowledge and serve Christ here shall be excluded from his kingdom hereafter. But he will come again in awful grandeur—not as the babe of Bethlehem; not as the man of Nazareth; but as the Son of God, in majesty and glory. They that would not acknowledge him *here* must be rejected by him *there;* they that would not serve him *always,* will *never* enjoy him; they that would cast *him* out and despise him, must be cast out *by* him, and consigned to eternal, hopeless sorrows. The Father there, the angels there, the redeemed there, my dear ones there, my record there, the Bible there, and Jesus ashamed of me? Oh, how my shame then must sink me down to the depths!

1 **And he said unto them,**—When the New Testament was first written, it was not divided into chapters and verses as we now have it. Each book was one continuous article without any breaks. Later they were divided into chapters and verses, by uninspired man for his convenience in reading and studying the Bible. Sometimes in dividing a chapter, the division was made at the wrong place and cut the sentence in two. That is true with this chapter. This verse belongs to the eighth chapter.

6. THE TRANSFIGURATION
9: 2-10
(Matt. 17: 1-13; Luke 9: 28-36.)

Verily I say unto you, There are some here of them that stand *by,* who shall in no wise taste of death, till they see the kingdom of God come with power.

Verily I say unto you, There are some here of them that stand by, who shall in no wise taste of death, till they see the kingdom of God come with power.—"Some," not all, were to live to see the kingdom come. Judas hanged himself before it came. He is the only one of the twelve that did not live to see this prediction fulfilled.

The kingdom and power had not come at this time. Both were yet to come. The kingdom was to come with the power. The power was to come with the Spirit. (Acts 1: 8.) The Spirit came on the first Pentecost after the resurrection of Christ. (Acts 2: 1-4.) As the kingdom was to come with the power, and as the power was to come with the Spirit, and since the Spirit and power came on Pentecost, therefore, the **kingdom came on that day.**

2 And after six days Jesus taketh with him Peter, and [1]James, and John, and bringeth them up into a high mountain apart by themselves: and he was transfigured before them; 3 and his garments became glistering, exceeding

[1]Or, *Jacob*

We now come to one of the most sublime scenes of all sacred history—the transfiguration.

2 And after six days—[This was six days after Peter had confessed that Jesus is the Christ, the Son of the living God, in Cesarea Philippi, with the incidents following it. Luke says, "About eight days," counting both the day on which the confession was made and this on which the transfiguration took place. Matthew and Mark count the intervening days.]

Jesus taketh with him Peter, and James, and John,—[Jesus takes with him, as he did on other occasions, the three favored disciples. Jesus had these three with him when he raised the daughter of Jairus, and a few months later they were with him in the Garden of Gethsemane. Paul (Gal. 2: 9), speaking of his visit to Jerusalem, called them "pillars." This does not indicate favoritism; but they were active, prompt; and he accorded to each the position to which his fidelity and activity entitled him.]

and bringeth them up into a high mountain apart by themselves:—This mountain upon whose heights he led them was on the road from Cesarea Philippi toward Jerusalem. Some think it was Mount Hermon or some of its projections; others, Mount Tabor. The former is the more probable one.] No one knows for certain what mountain the transfiguration was on. "Apart by themselves" means apart from the other disciples.

and he was transfigured before them;—["Transfigured" means changed in form and appearance. When Jesus came to the earth, he changed his glorious appearance for one in the flesh. The inhabitants of the heavenly region wear an appearance of surpassing glory. The face of Moses when he came down from the mountain after he had been forty days with God shone with such glory that the children of Israel could not look upon it. So he put a veil over it while he talked with them. (Ex. 34: 29-34.) This was a reflected glory. When Jesus appeared to Saul on the way to Damascus, a light above

white, so as no fuller on earth can whiten them. 4 And there appeared unto them Elijah with Moses: and they were talking with Jesus. 5 And Peter

the brightness of the midday sun shone round about him; so Saul was smitten with blindness. This appearance of Jesus on the mount is supposed to represent him in his glorified, or spiritual, state. Man, in the flesh, could not take in the transcendent glory of his appearance. It was a light so brilliant that it would have blinded men. When he came to earth, he veiled his glory under the flesh of humanity, so he could sympathize with man and man could approach him; now he comes on this occasion to show to his chosen disciples his true, spiritual appearance. Jesus was the "effulgence of his [God's] glory, and the very image of his substance." (Heb. 1: 3.) In him dwelt all the fullness of the Godhead bodily. This glory shone forth in his countenance. It was as bright as the sun; so to look upon it with our fleshly eyes was to be smitten with blindness.]

3 **and his garments became glistering, exceeding white, so as no fuller on earth can whiten them.**—[His raiment was as white as the light. The brilliance from his body flowed through the raiment and it was as white as the light. "So as no fuller on earth can whiten them" means nothing on earth can surpass it or add to its whiteness. This was a picture and a promise to the true follower of Jesus of what he shall become in the future state. "Who shall fashion anew the body of our humiliation, that it may be conformed to the body of his glory, according to the working whereby he is able even to subject all things unto himself." (Phil. 3: 21.) "Beloved, now are we children of God, and it is not yet made manifest what we shall be. We know that, if he shall be manifested, we shall be like him; for we shall see him even as he is." (1 John 3: 2.) Luke (9: 29) says as he "was praying" he was transfigured into his glorious state. The blessing came in prayer.] From these and other circumstances it seems plain that in heaven in glorified bodies Christians will preserve their identity.

4 **And there appeared unto them Elijah with Moses: and they were talking with Jesus.**—[The two who appeared with him from the spirit land were Moses, the giver of the law, the

type of Christ, and Elijah, or Elias, as he was called in Greek, the greatest of all the prophets of the Old Testament times. Moses died "in the land of Moab over against Bethpeor: but no man knoweth of his sepulchre unto this day." (Deut. 34: 6.) Elijah did not die, but ascended into heaven in a chariot of fire; was translated, that he did not see death. (2 Kings 3: 11.) They were in the state of the dead; were not yet raised, since Jesus was the first-born from the dead. He had not yet died. They were in the spirit form. Many think that this occurred that Moses the lawgiver of the Old Testament, and Elijah, the greatest of the prophets in the dispensation that was ended because of transgression, and was the schoolmaster to bring the Jews to Christ, should give their testimony to Jesus. Luke says they "appeared in glory." The same halo of glory and of light that shone from Jesus glowed from the faces of Moses and Elijah. His decease, which was to occur at Jerusalem, to which he had now turned his face for the last final journey, was the subject of their conference. They likely came to encourage and strengthen him for the trials and sufferings that he must undergo. With his death the dispensation of which Moses was the lawgiver and mediator, and of which Elijah was the most prominent prophet and restorer, would end. Blotting "out the bond written in ordinances that was against us, which was contrary to us: and he hath taken it out of the way, nailing it to the cross." (Col. 2: 14.) The law of Moses was fulfilled in Christ. "It was added because of transgressions, till the seed should come to whom the promise hath been made. . . . So that the law is become our tutor to bring us unto Christ, that we might be justified by faith. But now that faith is come, we are no longer under a tutor." (Gal. 3: 19-25.) The time was nigh when this dispensation preparatory to the coming of the kingdom must be done away, and when this kingdom, which shall never be destroyed, but shall stand forever, was to be opened to man. This conference with Moses and Elias on the mount in the presence of the three apostles was concerning the death of Jesus that would usher in this kingdom that would never be destroyed. Luke says Peter and they that were with him were heavy with sleep. They had come up to the mount, had been up all night. The conference was toward day, and they

answereth and saith to Jesus, Rabbi, it is good for us to be here: and let us make three [2]tabernacles; one for thee, and one for Moses, and one for Elijah. 6 For he knew not what to answer; for they became sore afraid. 7 And there came a cloud overshadowing them: and there came a voice out of the

[2]Or, *booths*

---

were heavy with sleep; but they awakened and saw his glory and the two men that were with him. How the apostles knew who they were we are not told. Jesus probably informed them. Only the leading facts are told.]

5 **And Peter answereth and saith to Jesus, Rabbi, it is good for us to be here: and let us make three tabernacles; one for thee, and one for Moses, and one for Elijah.**—A tabernacle is a tent or something to protect people from the heat of the sun and the weather. It was a temporary fixture, not permanent. Peter was rejoiced at the vision and desirous of continuing it. He proposed, therefore, that they should prolong this interview, and dwell there.

6 **For he knew not what to answer; for they became sore afraid.**—[Luke says, as they (Moses and Elijah) were departing from them, Peter said: "Master, it is good for us to be here: and let us make three tabernacles; one for thee, and one for Moses, and one for Elijah." This seems to have been spoken as if to stay their departing visitants. Luke says he said it, "not knowing what he said." It seems from all the accounts that they reached the mountain tired and wearied, and during the prayers of Jesus, as afterwards in Gethsemane, they fell asleep; and when they awoke and saw the glory of Jesus and of the two men who stood with them, they were struck with awe and wonder. As Moses and Elijah started to leave, Peter made this proposition. He was so perturbed he hardly knew what he said, or it may mean he did not understand the things he proposed were ill suited to the wants of these persons now in the spirit state.]

7 **And there came a cloud overshadowing them:**—Matthew (17: 5) says: "A bright cloud." It is probable the cloud was similar to the one that attended the Israelites through the wilderness, a pillar of fire by night and a cloud by day. This was during the night. Luke (9: 37) says: "And it came to pass, on the next day, when they were come down from the mountain, a great multitude met him." This would indicate that

cloud, This is my beloved Son: hear ye him. 8 And suddenly looking round
about, they saw no one any more, save Jesus only with themselves.
    9 And as they were coming down from the mountain, he charged them

---

they spent the night on the mount. It was probably one of
the all-night seasons of prayer to God which Jesus was given
to holding. This cloud, the representative of the divine glory
and presence, came down upon them; so they entered into it,
and the apostles feared, as they were enveloped in the
bright cloud. He was veiled from human sight by the cloud.
No eye could behold him and live. "He made darkness havi-
lious around about him, dark waters and thick clouds of the
skies. Through the brightness before him were coals of fire
kindled."]

**and there came a voice out of the cloud, This is my beloved
Son: hear ye him.**—[Out of this cloud came the voice of God,
as it did from the cleft heavens at his baptism, and declared:
"This is my beloved Son, in whom I am well pleased." It
now adds: "Hear ye him." Then he was declared to be the
Son of the living God; now the command is added: "Hear ye
him." This is the command of God to man to hear Jesus. It
is equivalent to the declaration that whosoever hears Jesus
hears God who sent him. To hear Jesus or his apostles is to
hear God.] "Hear ye him" is the chief significance of the
whole affair. They had heard Moses (the law) and Elijah
(the prophet); now they must hear Christ. Jesus is the
prophet and the lawgiver now. He is the one who speaks
from heaven, and the mediator of the new covenant. (Heb.
12: 22-25.)

8 **And suddenly looking round about, they saw no one any
more, save Jesus only with themselves.**—[The cloud had
passed away, and carried these visitors from the spirit land
back to their abodes; and Jesus was left alone.] Moses and
Elijah were gone. They had abdicated in his favor.
Henceforth there is to be but one authoritative teacher and
lawgiver. The prescriptions of Moses and Elijah are to be no
more binding except as they may be endorsed or re-enacted by
him. Fifteen hundred years before, Moses had told of a
prophet to come, to whom they must especially hearken.
Now he has come, and his exclusive authority is proclaimed,

that they should tell no man what things they had seen, save when the Son
of man should have risen again from the dead. 10 And they kept the saying,
questioning among themselves what the rising again from the dead should

"Hear ye him," and him alone, for everything depends upon
it.

9 **And as they were coming down from the mountain, he
charged them that they should tell no man what things they
had seen, save when the Son of man should have risen again
from the dead.**—Luke (9: 36) says: "And they held their
peace, and told no man in those days any of the things which
they had seen." Peter delighted to refer to it. It made a last-
ing impression upon him, and he understood its import.
"For we did not follow cunningly devised fables, when we
made known unto you the power and coming of our Lord
Jesus Christ, but we were eyewitnesses of his majesty. For
he received from God the Father honor and glory, when there
was born such a voice to him by the Majestic Glory, This is
my beloved Son, in whom I am well pleased: and this voice we
ourselves heard borne out of heaven, when we were with him
in the holy mount. And we have the word of prophecy made
more sure; whereunto ye do well that ye take heed, as unto a
lamp shining in a dark place, until the day dawn, and the
daystar arise in your hearts." (2 Pet. 1: 16-19.) "The word
of prophecy" was always true and sure, but God's voice here
pointed Jesus out more specially and directly as the antitype
of Moses and the Son of God in fulfillment of all prophecy.

10 **And they kept the saying, questioning among themselves what the rising again from the dead should mean.**—[It
was likely morning when they came down from the mountain.
As they came down Jesus told them to tell no man of the vision, what ye have seen, until the Son of man is risen from the
dead. "They kept the saying, questioning among themselves
what the rising again from the dead should mean." It seems
to us singular that, when Jesus so frequently and so clearly
told he must be crucified and rise again, they did not understand it. He had told it six days previous to this, when Peter
reproved him, and was told to get behind him. (Matt. 16:
23.) Now he tells it again. They cannot take it in or understand what he means. They kept these matters among themselves, talking one with another, as to what he meant by this

language. This vision seems to have been to give them now a vision of the future glory. They could not now understand or take in its meaning; but after his resurrection, they remembered it, understood it, and it made the prophecies concerning Jesus more sure to them, and gave an illustration of the appearance of the Son of God in the glorified body; so that we may have a clearer idea of what we shall be when we see him as he is, and are thereby transformed into the likeness of the Son of God.]

7. JESUS ANSWERS THE QUESTION CONCERNING ELIJAH.
9: 11-13

mean. 11 And they asked him, saying, *How is it* that the scribes say that Elijah must first come? 12 And he said unto them, Elijah indeed cometh first, and restoreth all things: and how is it written of the Son of man, that he should suffer many things and be set at nought? 13 But I say unto you,

³Or, *The scribes say . . . come.*

---

11 And they asked him, saying, How is it that the scribes say that Elijah must first come?—The scribes were learned men in the scriptures and in the traditions of the elders and were teachers of the Jews. They expected a literal fulfillment of Malachi's well known prediction concerning the coming of Elijah (Mal. 4: 5, 6), and under this influence the disciples were surprised that when he appeared in the mountain he did not remain to do the work predicted of him; hence their question.

12 And he said unto them, Elijah indeed cometh first,—He did not mean by this that Elijah was yet to come for he directly tells them he had come; but he meant to tell them it was a true doctrine which the scribes taught, that Elijah would appear before the coming of the Messiah.

and restoreth all things:—That is, to put into the former situation. (Matt. 12: 13.) Here it means to heal, to correct, to put in proper order. It means that Elijah would put things in a proper state; be the agent in reforming the people, of restoring them in some measure to proper notions about the Messiah, and preparing them for his coming. It is a brief summary of the prophecy concerning Elijah.

and how is it written of the Son of man, that he should suffer many things and be set at nought?—Henceforth he keeps

that Elijah is come, and they have also done unto him whatsoever they
would, even as it is written of him.

---

the lesson of his suffering constantly before them. His suffering and death would be in the conformation of the "restoration of all things." It took these to complete it. After all, the
disciples were not prepared for it when the hour came. This
prepares the way for what is said regarding Elijah in the next
verse. This was written of Jesus particularly in the fifty-third
chapter of Isaiah. To be set at "nought" is to be esteemed as
worthless, or as nothing; to be cast out and despised. No
prophecy was ever more strikingly fulfilled. (Luke 23: 11.)

13 **But I say unto you, that Elijah is come,**—John the Baptist, who came in the spirit and power of Elijah. Jesus teaches
them a second time that Malachi used the name of Elijah figuratively to represent John the Baptist.

**and they have also done unto him whatsoever they would,
even as it is written of him.**—That is, they had done to John
as they pleased—they had put him to death. Matthew (17:
13) adds the disciples then understood that he spoke of John
the Baptist. See Luke 1: 17.

8. A DEMON CAST OUT BY JESUS THAT THE DISCIPLES
COULD NOT CAST OUT
9: 14-29
(Matt. 17: 14-21; Luke 9: 37-43)

14 And when they came to the disciples, they saw a great multitude about
them, and scribes questioning with them. 15 And straightway all the multitude, when they saw him, were greatly amazed, and running to him saluted

---

14 **And when they came to the disciples, they saw a great
multitude about them, and scribes questioning with them.**—
After the transfiguration they now came down from the
mountain and again joined the other disciples. They had
gathered around the disciples to see if they could heal this demoniac. Doubtless when the scribes and the curiosity seekers
in the midst of the multitude saw their inability to heal the
son, they used this opportunity of exulting over the failure of
the disciples, and in a caviling manner, disputed with them.

15 **And straightway all the multitude, when they saw him,
were greatly amazed,**—Why, we do not know unless it was

him. 16 And he asked them, What question ye with them? 17 And one of
the multitude answered him, Teacher, I brought unto thee my son, who hath
a dumb spirit; 18 and wheresoever it taketh him, it [4]dasheth him down: and
he foameth, and grindeth his teeth, and pineth away: and I spake to thy

[4]Or, *rendeth him* See Mt. 7. 6.

---

the sudden and unexpected appearance of Jesus just at this
time while the scribes were engaged in caviling and disputing
with his disciples.

and running to him saluted him.—Received him with the
customary marks of affection and respect.

16 And he asked them, What question ye with them?—
What is the subject of your inquiry or debate with my disciples? Before any one had time to tell Jesus what had been
going on, he surprised the scribes with his question. They
saw at once that he knew all, and their failure to answer
shows that they felt a deserved rebuke for their exultation.

**17 And one of the multitude answered him, Teacher, I
brought unto thee my son,**—Doubtless this father did not
know Jesus was absent until he arrived with his son. In the
absence of Jesus, the disciples undertook to do this work.
From this we ought to learn a lesson; namely, not to undertake to do a work for which we are not prepared.

who hath a dumb spirit;—Called a dumb spirit because it
deprived its victim of speech. It was also a "deaf spirit."
(Verse 25.) The son was not only deaf and dumb, but a luna-
tic, and subject to fits. (Matt. 17: 15.) It was a severe and
complicated case. Probably the complication rendered the
disciples unable to heal the afflicted. (Luke 9: 39, 40.)

**18 and wheresover it taketh him, it dasheth him down: and
he foameth, and grindeth his teeth, and pineth away:**—Becomes thin, haggard, and emaciated. This was the effect of
the violence of his struggles and probably for the want of
food. Matthew (17: 15) says: "For oft-times he falleth into
the fire, and oft-times into the water; and Luke (9: 39):
"Hardly departeth from him, bruising him."

and I spake to thy disciples that they should cast it out;—
He asked the disciples to cast it out.

and they were not able.—Lack of power was due to their
weak faith. (Verse 29; Matt. 17: 20.) They had been given

disciples that they should cast it out; and they were not able. 19 And he answereth them and saith, O faithless generation, how long shall I be with you? how long shall I bear with you? bring him unto me. 20 And they brought him unto him: and when he saw him, straightway the spirit [5]tare him grievously; and he fell on the ground, and wallowed foaming. 21 And he asked his father, How long time is it since this hath come unto him? And he said, From a child. 22 And oft-times it hath cast him both into the fire and into the waters, to destroy him: but if thou canst do anything, have

[5]Or, *convulsed* See ch. 1. 26.

---

power to cast out unclean spirits. (6: 7.) The three favored apostles were with Jesus. Had they been present probably they could have cast the demon out. The faith of the nine was not equal to the task. It was an extremely difficult case.

19 **And he answereth them and saith, O faithless generation,** —Unbelieving race. Matthew (17: 17) and Luke (9: 41) say: "Faithless and perverse generation." The generation and race among whom Jesus was laboring were indeed faithless.

how long shall I be with you? how long shall I bear with you? bring him unto me.—Jesus had confidence in himself. The emphasis is upon *me*.

20 **And they brought him unto him: and when he saw him, straightway the spirit tare him grievously; and he fell on the ground, and wallowed foaming.**—Other effects of demon workings are here expressed. The boy fell and wallowed on the ground, foaming at the mouth like one with epilepsy. Here the truth expressed by the father (verse 18) is demonstrated.

21 **And he asked his father, How long time is it since this hath come unto him?**—This careful inquiry of Jesus as to when the demon afflicted the boy was doubtless made, not for his own information, but for the trial and strengthening of the father's faith.

And he said, From a child.—He does not fix the exact age, but it was from childhood.

22 **And oft-times it hath cast him both into the fire and into the waters, to destroy him:**—He looked upon the demon as an enemy who would kill his only son. The demon was hard-hearted, but no more so than the devil is today. He would destroy not only the soul of the only son of one father in hell, but all the sons of every father.

compassion on us, and help us. 23 And Jesus said unto him, If thou canst!
All things are possible to him that believeth. 24 Straightway the father of
the child cried out, and said, [6]I believe; help thou mine unbelief. 25 And
when Jesus saw that a multitude came running together, he rebuked the unclean spirit, saying unto him, Thou dumb and deaf spirit, I command thee,

[6]Many ancient authorities add *with tears.*

but if thou canst do anything,—Here, the father without knowing it, shows a weak faith. Probably the failure of the disciples to cure the boy served to weaken the faith he originally had. This is true with us today. When one doctor fails to cure, it lessens our faith in the efforts of another.

have compassion on us, and help us.—Have pity on us. A cure of the son would also relieve the distressed father. Both would be benefited.

23 And Jesus said unto him, If thou canst!—The authorized version puts it, "If thou canst believe." The difficulty was not whether Jesus can, but whether the father can. That is, can he have the necessary faith in Jesus? Faith in the father was the great need.

All things are possible to him that believeth.—All things can be effected or accomplished by God in favor of him that believes; and if thou canst believe, this will be done. Some draw an argument for infant baptism from this father's faith for his child to be healed. But faith by proxy either in baptism or salvation is unscriptural. (Prov. 19: 12; Mark 16: 16.) Salvation from sin is one thing and being healed physically is a different thing. The boy was healed physically, not spiritually.

24 Straightway the father of the child cried out, and said, I believe; help thou mine unbelief.—The spark of faith has been kindled sufficiently strong to pray for an increase of faith. Supply then the defects of my faith. Give me strength and grace to put entire confidence in thee. He first asked the Savior's help for his son, but having his own unbelief pointed out, and seeing the necessity of faith in himself in order to have his request granted, he asked help for himself, and that thus his son may be cured. He desired the barrier in the way of his son's healing removed. He labored to that end.

25 And when Jesus saw that a multitude came running together, he rebuked the unclean spirit, saying unto him, Thou

come out of him, and enter no more into him. 26 And having cried out, and
[5]torn him much, he came out: and *the boy* became as one dead; insomuch
that the more part said, He is dead. 27 But Jesus took him by the hand, and
raised him up; and he arose. 28 And when he was come into the house, his
disciples asked him privately, [7]*How is it* that we could not cast it out? 29
And he said unto them, This kind can come out by nothing, save by prayer[1].

[7]Or, saying, *We could not cast it out*
[1]Many ancient authorities add and *fasting*.

dumb and deaf spirit, I command thee, come out of him, and
enter no more into him.—The demon would desire repossession without interference from Jesus; so the attempt is divinely forbidden. If he ever attempted to re-enter and take
possession of the boy we have no record of it.

26 And having cried out, and torn him much, he came out:
—The demon obeys the command of Jesus most reluctantly
and tries to destroy one whom he can no longer use.

and the boy became as one dead;—The paroxysm of departure was fearful, and left the boy exhausted and as dead. His
bodily powers were exhausted—apparently having no breath
and life in him.

insomuch that the more part said, He is dead.—This was
the decision of the greater part of those present.

27 But Jesus took him by the hand, and raised him up; and
he arose.—The touch of Jesus completed the cure. Such torture as was inflicted by the demon gives an awful conception
of the state of society which must prevail among these God-forsaken spirits. While those standing by were saying that
the son was dead, the touch of Jesus, who alone can deliver us
from the power of the devil, brought instant restoration to
him, and joy to the father's heart. Luke (9: 43) adds: "They
were all astonished at the majesty of God."

28 And when he was come into the house, his disciples
asked him privately, How is it that we could not cast it out?
—They were interested in the cause of their failure to accomplish their purpose.

29 And he said unto them, This kind can come out by nothing, save by prayer.—Here Jesus intimates that there are
grades among demons and that this one was one of the worst.
Matthew (17: 20) adds: "Because of your little faith." The
whole difficulty centered in their want of faith. No demon

could defy them if only they had faith enough. And then Jesus illustrated the power of faith by showing that even a small amount of active, living faith, like a grain of mustard seed (Matt. 17: 20), could remove "this mountain," perhaps pointing to Mount Hermon, at whose base they were, and which towered in its grandeur above them. Faith comparable to a mustard seed is very weak faith, and if this would enable them to remove "this mountain," how weak must be the faith they had exercised! This remark added a rebuke to the explanation. That "this kind" goes not out but by prayer shows that it was more difficult to cast out this kind than some other kinds. The faith which will be effective must be a faith exercised in prayer.

9. JESUS THE SECOND TIME FORETELLS HIS DEATH AND RESURRECTION
9: 30-32
(Matt. 17: 22, 23; Luke 9: 43-45)

30 And they went forth from thence, and passed through Galilee; and he would not that any man should know it. 31 For he taught his disciples, and

---

30 And they went forth from thence,—From the vicinity of Cesarea Philippi (8: 27; Matt. 16: 13), at the base of Mount Hermon, where Jesus had healed the "only son" of a father just after the descent of Jesus from the transfiguration.

and passed through Galilee;—They were returning from Cesarea Philippi (8: 27), whither they had gone by passing east of the upper garden through the district called Iturea. That they returned "through Galilee" shows that they came down on the west of the Jordan. They were on their way back to Capernaum. (Verse 33.) They traveled in a quiet and private manner.

and he would not that any man should know it.—This is the last mention made of the privacy which Jesus had maintained ever since his journey to the vicinity of Tyre. (Compare 7: 24, 33, 36; 8: 26; 9: 25.) It was this privacy which occasioned the taunting remark of his unbelieving kindred, "Depart hence, and go into Judea, that thy disciples also may behold thy works which thou doest. For no man doeth anything in secret, and himself seeketh to be known openly." (John 7: 3, 4.)

said unto them, The Son of man is ²delivered up into the hands of men, and they shall kill him; and when he is killed, after three days he shall rise again.　32 But they understood not the saying, and were afraid to ask him.

²See ch. 3. 19.

31 **For he taught his disciples,**—This seems to be the purpose of the private journey. He had before predicted his suffering and death (8: 31) to his disciples. He wished to further instruct them, hence did not want to be interfered with by the multitude.

and said unto them, The Son of man is delivered up into the hands of men,—Here Jesus uses the present tense, probably because the event was so vividly present to his mind. Some think it refers to his betrayal by Judas, a future fact being spoken of as present, as indeed it was present in the mind of Jesus. It would be better to regard this as referring to the fact that Jesus had already been given up by his Father to men, in order that he might suffer and die for the sins of the world. This was the Father's purpose in giving him to the world. (Acts 2: 23.) The divine plan of his sufferings and death was the topic of discourse on the mount (Luke 9: 31); and now it is the topic of his disciples.

and they shall kill him; and when he is killed, after three days he shall rise again.—Through his divine power he will rise from the dead. (John 10: 18.) He would be delivered up in a treacherous manner. This was done by Judas Iscariot, the traitor. (Matt. 26: 14-16, 47-50.)

32 **But they understood not the saying,**—They could not understand the prediction, probably because they did not want to receive the words in their obvious import. It is often true in our day that a plain passage of scripture is obscure to people simply because they are unwilling to accept the truth it reveals. They were slow to learn the full truth. They could not understand how he could be the Messiah, and yet be put to death in this manner. The reason was they had the wrong conception of the kingdom of God, and his death did not correspond with it. They did not understand it fully until after the resurrection.

and were afraid to ask him.—Probably they were afraid to ask what he meant for fear he would rebuke them as he had rebuked Peter when the subject was first mentioned. (8: 33.)

10. DISPUTE ABOUT WHO SHALL BE GREATEST IN THE KINGDOM
9: 33-37
(Matt. 18: 1-35; Luke 9: 46-50)

33 And they came to Capernaum: and when he was in the house he asked them, What were ye reasoning on the way? 34 But they held their peace: for they had disputed one with another on the way, who *was* the [3]greatest.

[3]Gr. *greater.*

---

33 **And they came to Capernaum:**—Capernaum was his headquarters and the center of his operations in Galilee. He has once more returned to the base of his operation. This city was highly favored of Jesus, who taught frequently there, and also did many mighty works in that place and vicinity. The citizens did not, however, improve their opportunities, and were doomed to severe judgment in consequence of it. (Matt. 11: 23.)

and when he was in the house he asked them, What were ye reasoning on the way?—Aside from Jesus the disciples discussed among themselves who would be the greatest in the kingdom of heaven. (Matt. 18: 1.) They asked the question because they wished to know who would have the principal offices and posts of favor and profit. Luke (9: 47) says that Jesus perceived the thought of their heart. This act implies omniscience, for none can search the heart but God. (Jer. 17: 10.) The disciples, conscious that the subject of their dispute was known, asked Jesus to decide it. He did so by using a little child as an object lesson. (Matt. 18: 2-4.)

34 **But they held their peace:**—For the moment they were silent, being confounded with the question, and probably ashamed to own to the truth.

for they had disputed one with another on the way, who was the greatest.—That is, the most eminent, doubtless among themselves. This dispute shows their worldly views of the kingdom of God. They expected the kingdom to be a temporal earthly kingdom, and that those who are greatest now would be greatest when it was set up. Aspirations for greatness are proper and right provided the mind has a correct estimate of what true greatness is. Self-denying service in his kingdom is true greatness.

35 And he sat down, and called the twelve; and he saith unto them, If any man would be first, he shall be last of all, and ⁴servant of all. 36 And he took a little child, and set him in the midst of them: and taking him in his

⁴Or, *minister*

---

35 **And he sat down, and called the twelve;**—Whether all the apostles were involved in the dispute over who should be the greatest in the kingdom or not, all of them had mistaken ideas about the kingdom of God and needed the instructions Jesus now purposes to give. Hence he called all of them to hear.

and he saith unto them, If any man would be first,—In rank and honor. Or as expressed by them, "the greatest." There were probably as many candidates to be "first" as there were hearers of these words.

he shall be last of all, and servant of all.—The path that leads to the highest honors in the kingdom of God is through humility. (Matt. 20: 27; 23: 12.) In God's kingdom the high is lowered, the lowly exalted, and hence all come to a spiritual level. "Servant" is not a slave but a minister. (Col. 1: 25.) A waiter—an attendant—one who renders voluntary service. The thought is, he shall be the most distinguished Christian who is the most humble, and who is willing to be esteemed *least,* and last of all. To esteem ourselves as God esteems us is humility. And it cannot be degrading to think of ourselves *as we are.* But pride, as an attempt to be thought of more importance than we are, is foolish, wicked, and degrading. To be willing to sacrifice self, and to be servant of all, even to the least disciples, was the path to true distinction and honor.

36 **And he took a little child, and set him in the midst of them:**—Here Jesus introduces an object lesson regarding humility. Children are, to a great extent, destitute of ambition, pride and haughtiness. They are characteristically humble and teachable. By requiring his disciples to become like them (Matt. 18: 3), he did not mean to express any opinion about the moral character of children, but simply that *in these respects* they should become like them. That is, they should lay aside their ambitious views, and pride, and be willing to occupy their proper station—a very lowly one as compared with their present views of greatness.

arms, he said unto them, 37 Whosoever shall receive one of such little children in my name, receiveth me: and whosoever receiveth me, receiveth not me, but him that sent me.

and taking him in his arms, he said unto them,—Christians must be childlike. (1) Both in mind and speech (1 Cor. 14: 20; 13: 11); (2) in humility and freedom from jealousy (1 Cor. 14: 20); (3) in teachableness and submission to divine authority (1 Cor. 6: 1).

37 **Whosoever shall receive**—Cordially to his heart and fellowship. It means to approve, love, or treat with kindness; to aid in time of need.

one of such little children—That is, whoso shall receive and love one with a spirit like this child—one who is humble, meek, unambitious, is a real Christian. By reference to Matthew (18), it will be seen that it has reference to the humble disciple who should be in disposition as a little child.

in my name, receiveth me:—Whoso receiveth one possessed of my spirit, and who, because he has that spirit, receives him, receives me also; because such a one is his representative and one with himself.

and whosoever receiveth me, receiveth not me, but him that sent me.—In receiving a representative of Christ, we not only receive Christ himself, but the Father also. Here he pointed out their nearness to himself and the honor and esteem in which he holds them. He traces the relation back to his Father. The Father is represented in Christ, and Christ in his true followers. He teaches that his kingdom is spiritual, and that humility and a childlike spirit are essential to true greatness. Children are not to be despised. Children and their improvement are the hope of the church, and of every worthy secular enterprise. The human hands that can hold these must soon lose their power to grasp. A child's hand must soon take their places. A child's hand is on the door of all domestic and foreign missions. If mothers wish to guide the world, they must do it at home with their children. They can never do it at the ballot box nor in civil offices—neither can they do it at card parties and club meetings while their children are running loose on the streets or trained by colored cooks and housemaids. They ought to realize that "the hand that rocks the cradle is the hand that guides the world" and learn to stay at home and out of politics, and teach and train their children in the way God intended they should.

11. JOHN'S JEALOUSY, AND REMARK ABOUT OFFENSES
9: 38-50
(Matt. 18: 6-9)

38 John said unto him, Teacher, we saw one casting out demons in thy name; and we forbade him, because he followed not us. 39 But Jesus said, Forbid him not: for there is no man who shall do a [5]mighty work in my

[5]Gr. *power.*

---

38 **John said unto him, Teacher, we saw one casting out demons in thy name;**—What Christ had said regarding his little ones caused John to speak of a recent occurrence. Having found one who did not accompany the apostles casting out demons, they forbade him. This one casting out demons did it by Christ's authority—in his name. He did not merely attempt, but actually cast out demons. He seems to have been a follower of Jesus, though he did not accompany Jesus and the twelve.

and we forbade him,—John probably took a leading part in this. The faith of the apostles was very imperfect at this time, and doubtless he of whom he spake had very crude ideas of Jesus, and yet had faith enough to work miracles in his name.

because he followed not us.—That is, he was not one of the immediate attendants of Jesus. Seeing such a man casting out demons excited John's jealousy, because he thought that no others than the chosen twelve ought to be honored with this power. Such jealousy in regard to official prerogative is a very common passion, and one against which men occupying positions of trust and authority should be constantly on their guard. Luke (9: 49) says, "He followeth not with us." I take it that he was a disciple but did not travel with Christ and the twelve.

39 **But Jesus said, Forbid him not:**—There was a degree of prejudice toward the person referred to that Christ did not approve of, and the apostles did wrong in hindering his work. Do not prevent him or anyone else in a similar position from doing good. If he can work a miracle in my name, it is sufficient proof of attachment to me, and he should not be prevented. If the man had been an enemy of truth, it would have

name, and be able quickly to speak evil of me. 40 For he that is not against us is for us. 41 For whosoever shall give you a cup of water to drink, *because ye are Christ's, verily I say unto you, he shall in no wise lose his

*Gr. *in name that ye are.*

been right to forbid him; but, according to John's own statement, he was casting out demons in the name of Jesus, and this showed he was a friend. He was working to build up the cause of Christ.

for there is no man who shall do a mighty work in my name, and be able quickly to speak evil of me.—The meaning is that he whom God gave the power of working miracles by that gave evidence that he could not soon be found among the enemies of Christ. He ought not, therefore, to be prevented from doing it. Jesus neither praises nor condemns the man for following an independent course—for working as an individual—and not working with the disciples. Christians may do acceptable work for the Lord in two ways. (1) As an individual. (2) Through the church. These are the only two ways in which a Christian can work and meet God's approval. Here we have an example of a disciple of Christ working as an individual. Christ declares that he must not be forbidden, and that those who work the same kind of work that we do should be regarded, not as enemies, but allies. Many, in every period of church history, have spent their lives in copying John's mistake. They have labored to stop every one who will not work for Jesus in their way from working for Jesus at all. Christians should rejoice in all the good done by others, whether they agree in all things or not. We ought to accept all teaching and practice by others that are authorized by Christ.

40 For he that is not against us is for us.—Here, our Lord clinches his argument. There is no neutral ground in the contest between God and sin. A man is either for or against Christ.

41 For whosoever shall give you a cup of water to drink, because ye are Christ's,—Matthew (10: 41) says, "In the name of a prophet." He who receives a prophet because he is a prophet, or a righteous man because he is a righteous man, or who gives a drink of water to a disciple because he is a disciple, distinctly recognizes the person's relation to Christ as

reward. 42 And whosoever shall cause one of these little ones that believe
[7]on me to stumble, it were better for him if [8]a great millstone were hanged

[7]Many ancient authorities omit *on me*.
[8]Gr. *a millstone turned by an ass*.

the ground of the act, and to that extent Christ is honored by
the act. Not so, however, with him who performs a similar
act in the name of humanity, or because the recipient is a
man.

verily I say unto you, he shall in no wise lose his reward.—
The great power of expelling demons should be rewarded the
faithful, unknown disciple, whom the apostles had sought to
hinder, and not only such great things as that, but any approved service, however simple and commonplace, should also
be amply rewarded. This contains a promise which reaches
to the present day. Miracles have ceased, but the time has
not passed when acts of kindness in the name of Christ are
out of date. It yet behooves every disciple to abound in every
good word and work, seeing their labor shall not be in vain in
the Lord. (1 Cor. 15: 58.) Matthew (10: 41) says he "shall
receive a prophet's reward." A prophet's reward is not syn-
onymous with final salvation; for while it is true that in
heaven we will have full reward for all the good we do on
earth, we will have infinitely more than this, and our admission into heaven is a matter of *grace,* and not of reward. So,
then, the promise of the text does not imply the salvation of
all that receive a prophet's reward, but simply that he shall be
rewarded. If he be a pardoned man, he may receive his reward in heaven; if not, he will receive it only on earth.

**42 And whosoever shall cause one of these little ones that
believe on me**—"Little ones" are not infants for the reason
they cannot believe on Christ; and the little ones here mentioned believe on him. No ground here for infant baptism.

to stumble,—While the path to honor and glory was of easy
access, by ministering to the wants of Christ's disciples, the
way to shame, condemnation, and death was possible by causing them to stumble. "Stumble" here means to offend. That
is, to put temptations before others that induce them to sin.

it were better for him if a great millstone—This was not the
common handstone which was turned by women (Matt. 24:
41), but the larger kind, which was turned by the strength of
an animal—usually the ass.

about his neck, and he were cast into the sea. 43 And if thy hand cause thee
to stumble, cut it off: it is good for thee to enter into life maimed, rather
than having thy two hands to go into [9]hell, into the unquenchable fire.[10] 45
And if thy foot cause thee to stumble, cut it off: it is good for thee to enter
into life halt, rather than having thy two feet to be cast into [9]hell. 47 And if
thine eye cause thee to stumble, cast it out: it is good for thee to enter into
the kingdom of God with one eye, rather than having two eyes to be cast
into [9]hell; 48 where their worm dieth not, and the fire is not quenched. 49

[9]Gr. *Gehenna.*
[10]Ver. 44 and 46 (which are identical with ver. 48) are omitted by the best ancient
authorities.

were hanged about his neck, and he were cast into the sea.
—Contentions as to who shall be greatest always give offense, and at the same time, by exciting evil passions, they ensnare the persons engaged in them. Jesus desired that his
disciples should see this tendency of their discussion (verse
33), and to show how fearful the final result would be to the
offender, he assures them that it were better for such to have
a millstone hung to his neck, and to be cast into the sea. It
were better, because his actual fate will be worse than that.
(Matt. 18: 8, 9.)

43-48 **And if thy hand cause thee to stumble, cut it off: it is
good for thee to enter into life maimed, rather than having
thy two hands to go into hell, into the unquenchable fire.
And if thy foot cause thee to stumble, cut if off: it is good for
thee to enter into life halt, rather than having thy two feet to
be cast into hell. And if thine eye cause thee to stumble, cast
it out: it is good for thee to enter into the kingdom of God
with one eye, rather than having two eyes to be cast into hell;
where their worm dieth not, and the fire is not quenched.**—
"Hand," "foot," and "eye" are the most valuable of the visible
members of the human body, and here used to denote anything peculiarly dear and valuable—the dearest objects of
one's desires—the honors, possessions, or enjoyments he most
prizes. If these "offend thee"—cause thee to stumble—to
sin—to fall away. That is, if the dearest object of your desire
causes thee to do this, "cut it off," "pluck it out." That is,
mortify and subdue the passions, evil desires, or inclinations
which animate the hand, the foot, or the eye, let the conflict
cost what it may. (Col. 3: 5; Gal. 5: 24.) "Into hell," Gehenna, which is here correctly translated, is hell. Jesus here
shows the sense in which he uses the word by adding the ex-
planatory clause, "into the fire that never shall be quenched."

For every one shall be salted with fire[11]. 50 Salt is good: but if the salt

[11]Many ancient authorities add *and every sacrifice shall be salted with salt*. See Lev. 2. 13.

Hell, then, is equivalent to the fire that never shall be quenched. It is also placed here in opposition to "life"; "It is good for thee to enter into life maimed, rather than having thy two hands to go into hell." The life here referred to is not the temporal life, nor the Christian life, into both of which the disciples addressed had already entered; but eternal life, into which they had not yet entered.

49 **For every one shall be salted with fire.**—Perhaps no passage in the New Testament has given more perplexity to commentators than this, and it may be impossible now to fix its precise meaning. It cannot be successfully denied but that the word "for" introduces the verse as a reason for the solemn declaration in verses 43-48. "Every one," is limited to every one who, contrary to the teaching just given in the context, refusing to cut off the offending hand, or to pluck out the offending eye. Jesus had just taught that all such would be cast into hell-fire; it is now stated that every such one shall be *salted* with fire. As salt, on account of its power to preserve meats, is the symbol of perpetuity, to be salted with fire is to be perpetually permeated by fire, or to be kept perpetually in a state of the severest pain. This passage kills the annihilation theory.

"Every one," that is, every one of them mentioned above, who refuses to cut off a right hand and pluck out a right eye; that is, to mortify their bosom lusts and beloved corruptions, which are as dear as a right hand or a right eye. All such wicked and unmortified persons shall be salted with fire. That is, thrown into hell-fire where the worm dieth not and the fire is not quenched. Their being salted with fire imports and implies that as to their beings they shall be preserved even as salt preserves things from corruption that they may be the objects of the eternal wrath of God.

50 **Salt is good:**—And useful for purifying and preserving. (2 Kings 2: 19-22.) A general statement. Salt is here used, as in the preceding verse, to symbolize that principle in Christian life which leads to perseverance amid all required self-sacrifice.

have lost it saltness, wherewith will ye season it?   Have salt in yourselves, and be at peace one with another.

Every Christian who has given himself a real sacrifice unto God shall be salted, not with fire to be destroyed, but with salt—the grace of mortification to be preserved and kept savory.   The grace of mortification is that to the soul which salt is to the body.   It preserves it from putrefaction and renders it savory.   Every Christian ought to be a spiritual sacrifice unto God.   There is a putrid and corrupt part in every Christian which must be purged out.   The grace of mortification is the salt which must clarify the soul, and with which every sacrifice must be salted.

but if the salt have lost its saltness, wherewith will ye season it?—If the salt has lost its saltness it cannot be recovered. It is good for nothing.   If a Christian lose the power of perseverance, there is no restoration for him.

Have salt in yourselves,—Have the preserving and purifying influences of divine grace and the spirit of Christ in your heart.   Maintain in yourselves the quality of perseverance by making every sacrifice necessary thereto—keep all evil desires and causes leading to sin pruned off.

and be at peace one with another.—Among yourselves.   Do not exercise an ambitious and contentious spirit, or an uncharitable zeal; but according with the spirit of Christianity, act out the principles of the grace of God and be at peace among yourselves.   Peace is one of the fruits of the spirit.   (Gal. 5: 22.)   The contention of the apostles as to who should be greatest in the kingdom of God (verses 33, 34), and their jealousy toward the brother who had been casting out demons in the name of Christ (verse 38), were calculated to impair this quality by causing alienations and discouragements among themselves.   Strife among them would destroy their salt; peace would tend to preserve it.   Let each one retain a seasoning virtue in himself that he may sweeten and season others even all with whom he converses, and thus upholding union and peace one with another will declare that you have the saving qualities of salt in yourselves.   In so doing you will avoid contention and quarreling, struggling for places, honors, and office and seek each other's welfare and thus be the means of honoring and glorifying God.

PART SECOND

FROM THE DEPARTURE OUT OF GALILEE TO THE ASCENSION
10: 1 to 16: 20

SECTION ONE

EVENTS IN PEREA
10: 1-52

1. QUESTION ABOUT DIVORCE
10: 1-12
(Matt. 19: 1-12)

1 And he arose from thence, and cometh into the borders of Judaea and beyond the Jordan: and multitudes come together unto him again; and, as he was wont, he taught them again.

2 And there came unto him Pharisees, and asked him, Is it lawful for a man to put away *his wife?* trying him. 3 And he answered and said unto

---

1 And he arose from thence, and cometh into the borders of Judaea and beyond the Jordan:—This is the final departure of Jesus from Galilee. He returned thither no more until after his resurrection from the dead, when he suddenly appeared to his disciples there on two occasions. (Matt. 28: 16, 17; John 21: 1.) He had labored in Galilee about twenty-two months.

and multitudes come together unto him again; and, as he was wont, he taught them again.—Some came for one cause and some for another—and, as usual, he taught them and healed the afflicted.

2 And there came unto him Pharisees, and asked him, Is it lawful for a man to put away his wife?—Matthew (19: 3) adds, "For every cause?" That is, every cause satisfactory to her husband. They had found fault with him for violating the law (2: 24); and transgressing the tradition of the elders (7: 5); had referred his power to Beelzebub (3: 22); and had demanded a sign from heaven (8: 11; Matt. 12: 38). But now they seek to entangle him in existing controversies, which, they thought, would be impossible to answer without displeasing one or another of the Jewish parties.

them, [12]What did Moses command you? 4 And they said, Moses suffered to write a bill of divorcement, and to put her away. 5 But Jesus said unto them, For your hardness of heart he wrote you this commandment. 6 But from the beginning of the creation, Male and female made he them. 7 For this cause shall a man leave his father and mother, [13]and shall cleave to his

[12]Dt. xxiv. 1. 3.
[13]Some ancient authorities omit *and shall cleave to his wife*.

trying him.—the Pharisees asked the question, not for information, but with wrong motives, "trying him." If he answered in the affirmative, they would accuse him with moral laxity; if in the negative, with disregarding the authority of Moses. Probably they wished to call forth a condemnation of Herod Antipas in his adulterous relationship with his brother's wife, and thus insure to Jesus an end similar to that of John the Baptist.

3 **And he answered and said unto them, What did Moses command you?**—He does not discuss their distinctions, but appeals to their own law. The wisdom of Christ is seen in his reply. In it he sanctions the law of Moses. (Luke 10: 26.)

4 **And they said, Moses suffered to write a bill of divorcement, and to put her away.**—This reply of the Pharisees is found in Deut. 24: 1-3.

5 **But Jesus said unto them, For your hardness of heart he wrote you this commandment.**—He did not command to give a writing of divorcement, and then to put her away: he only *suffered* them to do so, and suffered it on account of the hardness of their hearts, though it had not been so from the beginning. The Mosaic law was not intended as a code of perpetual obligation, but was preparatory to something better and higher, when the people were able to bear it. (Gal. 3: 19-25.)

6 **But from the beginning of the creation, Male and female made he them.**—God made Adam and Eve. They were designed one for the other. Thus God shows that man and woman should live together in the marriage state, and that polygamy be excluded. Jesus excluded polygamy in the Christian law.

7 **For this cause**—Because Eve was taken out of Adam, and was bone of his bone and flesh of his flesh. (Gen. 2: 21-24.)

shall a man leave his father and mother, and shall cleave to his wife;—Shall be joined unto and adhere. The relation be-

wife; 8 and the two shall become one flesh: so that they are no more two, but one flesh. 9 What therefore God hath joined together, let not man put

---

tween husband and wife is stronger than that between parent and child.

8 and the two shall become one flesh:—They shall be united in the flesh—one being the part of the other. Jesus quotes the language of Adam, showing the strong and close relation of husband and wife. (Gen. 2: 24.)

so that they are no more two, but one flesh.—Having a oneness in all their interests and relations pertaining to this life.

9 What therefore God hath joined together, let not man put asunder.—Man is here used in the broad sense—including all men. Let no human authority, civil or otherwise, in any way annul the ordinance of God. That relation between husband and wife authorized by God, and to which all other relations, even that of parent and child, must yield, can be severed only by God himself. The marriage relation, however, ceases at the death of either partner for the reason the unity is based on *one flesh*. (Verse 7.) The union in the flesh is for this world. (12: 25; Rom. 7: 2.) This is the law of Christ. There was never a time when there was greater need for the discussion of this subject than there is in this "evil and adulterous generation." Christ's law of marriage has been set aside by the civil authorities of many countries by granting divorces for almost any cause. By many, the marriage vow and relationship are no longer held sacred, and husband and wife separate on an impulse to cohabit with someone else. All Christians should earnestly teach against this widespreading evil. God is the author of the marriage; he joins husband and wife, and no civil court can divorce them. Man cannot put asunder what God has joined together. God-made ties cannot be broken by human laws. He who marries a woman that has been divorced for some other cause than fornication commits adultery because he is thus joined to another man's wife; she commits adultery because she is living with another than her husband. (Matt. 19: 1-8; Rom. 7: 1-3; 1 Cor. 7: 10-16, 19.) Fornicators and adulterers cannot enter the kingdom of heaven. (1 Cor. 6: 9-10.)

asunder. 10 And in the house the disciples asked him again of this matter.
11 And he saith unto them, Whosoever shall put away his wife, and marry
another, committeth adultery against her: 12 and if she herself shall put away
her husband, and marry another, she committeth adultery.

10 **And in the house the disciples asked him again of this matter.**—They did not fully understand the teaching of Jesus on marriage and divorce, so they asked him again of this matter. "Again" refers to the question asked by the Pharisees in verse 2.

11 **And he saith unto them, Whosoever shall put away his wife,**—"Saving for the cause of fornication." (Matt. 19: 9.)

and marry another, committeth adultery against her:—Should husband and wife separate for some other cause than fornication, neither is at liberty to marry another. In some cases when a separation occurs in the absence of fornication, one party waits for the other party to marry another, thinking when he or she does, that this frees the other party and that that party is at liberty to marry again. But this is not true, for the adultery occurred after the second marriage, and therefore, was not the cause of the separation. For one party to be free to marry again after a separation, the adultery must have been committed *before* the separation and be the *grounds* of the separation. In this case, the innocent party is, in my judgment, at liberty to marry again.

12 **and if she herself shall put away her husband, and marry another, she committeth adultery.**—That which is implied in other passages is here directly stated—that this law applies to both wife and husband. Christians should regard no one as really divorced except for the one cause—fornication.

2. JESUS BLESSES LITTLE CHILDREN
10: 13-16
(Matt. 19: 13-15; Luke 18: 15-17)

13 And they were bringing unto him little children, that he should touch

13 **And they were bringing unto him little children,**—Luke (18: 15) says: "Their babes." The mothers of the children were doubtless the ones who carried them to Jesus. The children no doubt were of different ages, hence they are spoken of as "little children" and "babes."

them: and the disciples rebuked them. 14 But when Jesus saw it, he was moved with indignation, and said unto them, Suffer the little children to come unto me; forbid them not: for [1]to such belongeth the kingdom of God.

[1]Or, *of such is*

---

that he should touch them:—Matthew (19: 13) is more definite, "That he should lay his hands on them, and pray." What more natural than that mothers should desire this blessing from the gentle-faced and sweet-voiced Galilean teacher? Here incidental testimony is borne to a high appreciation of him in this part of Perea. "He took them in his arms, and blessed them, laying his hands upon them." (Verse 16.) Jesus did for the children that for which they were brought. He did not baptize them, neither did he sprinkle water upon them. They were not brought to him for that purpose.

and the disciples rebuked them.—Rebuked those who brought the children. The disciples had engaged the Savior in a very interesting discussion of the law of marriage, and were listening eagerly to his sayings, therefore, it seemed to them a waste of time to turn from such discussions to the needs of little children.

14 But when Jesus saw it, he was moved with indignation, and said unto them, Suffer the little children to come unto me;—Their rebuke was to those who brought them, but Jesus regarded it as word of refusal to the little ones. He not only has no complaint to make of those who have come, but he wishes the way to be open for all others to come who so desire. Luke (18: 16) tells in addition that he called to him the little ones who had been hindered by the angry voices of the disciples.

forbid them not: for to such belongeth the kingdom of God.—The kingdom of God requires innocence, purity, docility, submission in its votaries and possessors. These were just the traits belonging to the ideal child. To have the kingdom of God is to get close to Christ, and these were just the ones who might well be close against his bosom. Jesus is always made indignant by whatever comes between a child and him. Beware how you oppose any movement of a child toward Jesus! Some children are ready to obey the Lord much earlier in life than many suppose. It depends upon the instruc-

15 Verily I say unto you, Whosoever shall not receive the kingdom of God as a little child, he shall in no wise enter therein. 16 And he took them in his arms, and blessed them, laying his hands upon them.

---

tion the child has received as to the time of its readiness of obedience.

15 Verily I say unto you, Whosoever shall not receive the kingdom of God—The principles of the gospel—the new dispensation by Christ, or the reign of Christ as a mediator—in their hearts. (Luke 7: 21.) Receiving the kingdom of God and entering into it are two separate and distinct acts. Receiving it precedes entering into it, and means no more than accepting its principles. This a little child does with an implicit faith from the time that its understanding is sufficiently developed.

as a little child,—Simple trusting faith, quick repentance, ready and implicit obedience, readiness to be led, transparent frankness. These are all qualities of the ideal child, and they are also of the true Christian.

he shall in no wise enter therein.—There is a caution here to his disciples. They were not cherishing the right spirit. They were selfish, and rudely tyrannical; needed to love the children more, that they might imbibe the childlike spirit. We can only enter the kingdom by receiving Christ and his laws in a proper spirit. This verse shows that the meek, humble, and childlike disposition implied in the preceding verse is essential to true discipleship. The kingdom, as a principle in the heart, is unfolded and developed into the fellowship of Christ's manifestation. All pride, vanity, and self-sufficiency must be laid aside. Childlike, we must do just as Jesus tells us, if we would become Christians.

16 And he took them in his arms, and blessed them, laying his hands upon them.—He goes beyond the mothers' expectations. They were expecting Jesus to do as others—put his hands upon their heads, as they stood or were carried before him. But as gently as a mother he takes them in his arms. It was a plain, simple act, but it spoke volumes to the hearts of those mothers.

3. THE RICH YOUNG RULER
10: 17-22
(Matt. 19: 16-22; Luke 18: 18-23)

17 And as he was going forth ²into the way, there ran one to him, and kneeled to him, and asked him, Good Teacher, what shall I do that I may inherit eternal life? 18 And Jesus said unto him, Why callest thou me

---

²Or, *on his way*

---

17 **And as he was going forth into the way,**—Matthew tells us that, immediately after laying his hands upon the young children, Jesus departed thence. "Into the way"—this is, the road leading toward Jerusalem whither his face was now set.

there ran one to him,—This was a "young man," and he was rich (Matt. 19: 20, 22); he was also a "ruler" (Luke 18: 18)—occupied a position of honor. The case of this young man is a remarkable one, from the fact of this youth, wealth, position, character, and the manner of his approach. He came running.

and kneeled to him, and asked him, Good Teacher,—Worshiped him. In kneeling to him he recognized Jesus as divine, and entitled to worship. Others had come to Jesus, but it was that their bodies might be healed, or it was a father pleading for his son, or a mother for a daughter. But here was one who from trouble of soul alone sought him.

what shall I do that I may inherit eternal life?—He made it a personal matter which was proper. We cannot go to heaven by proxy. The young man seemed to recognize this fact. [Since Jesus had brought it to light, he was the proper one to teach how it could be obtained; so he says, "Good Teacher, what shall I do that I may inherit eternal life?" Matthew says he asked, "What good thing shall I do?" The ruler understood enough of the dealings of God with men to understand he must do some good thing to fit him for such a blessing. What God requires is good. He calls Jesus good, and Master or Teacher. An authorized teacher was called Master among the Jews.] How to inherit eternal life should be the great concern of all.

18 **And Jesus said unto him, Why callest thou me good? none is good save one, even God.**—[This question, and the further statement that none is good save God, disavowing his own goodness, has long been a puzzle to many Bible stu-

good? none is good save one, *even* God. 19 Thou knowest the commandments, [a]Do not kill, Do not commit adultery, Do not steal, Do not bear false

[a]Ex. xx. 12-16; Dt. v. 16-20.

dents. Why should Jesus, who was sinless, disavow the claim
that he is good? Other passages convey the same idea.
Heb. 2: 10: "For it became him, for whom are all things, and
through whom are all things, in bringing many sons unto
glory, to make the author of their salvation perfect through
sufferings." Heb. 5: 8, 9: "Though he was a Son, yet learned
obedience by the things which he suffered; and having been
made perfect, he became unto all them that obey him the author of eternal salvation." The explanation of it, I think, is
that Jesus had the nature of man. He felt all the impulses
and emotions to sin that man does. So long as he felt the
emotions to sin in his members he did not call himself good,
nor did the Holy Spirit call him perfect. So long as he felt
the impulse and disposition to sin he was imperfect, and could
not become "unto all them that obey him the author of eternal
salvation." Suffering purged out this impulse to sin. So,
through suffering, he was made perfect, and hence he that
hath suffered hath ceased from sin; and only when the motions of sin in his members were purged out did he call himself good. In this sense only God is good.]

19 **Thou knowest the commandments,**—Our Lord proceeds
to the second part of his answer, and attends to the great end
which the young man wishes to attain, namely, *eternal life*.
He does not wait for a reply to his question. Matthew (19:
17) says: "If thou wouldest enter into life, keep the commandments." When Jesus said this, the young man said:
"Which?" (Matt. 19: 18.) Evidently he thought Jesus did
not mean the ones with which he was familiar. Then Jesus
referred to the ten commandments, passing over the first four,
specifying the rest, but substituting for "Thou shalt not
covet" its equivalent, as stated here, "Do not defraud," and as
stated by Matthew (19: 19), "Thou shalt love thy neighbor as
thyself." This man being under the law, he was referred to
its teachings, the leading precepts of which are here mentioned, and which indeed have been incorporated into the gospel dispensation, and therefore are as binding upon us as on
him. (Rom. 11.)

witness, Do not defraud, Honor thy father and mother. 20 And he said unto him, Teacher, all these things have I observed from my youth. 21 And Jesus looking upon him loved him, and said unto him, One thing thou lackest: go, sell whatsoever thou hast, and give to the poor, and thou shalt have

Do not kill, Do not commit adultery, Do not steal, Do not bear false witness, Do not defraud, Honor thy father and mother.—[Jesus refers him to the commandments, as preparing for eternal life. There are two classes of commandments —one defining man's duties to God, the other defining his duties to man. He quotes the latter here. These all regulate the conduct toward our fellow men. The questioner was a sincere worshiper of God—he recognized that God required something of him in order to inherit eternal life.]

20 **And he said unto him, Teacher, all these things have I observed from my youth.**—He was not a hypocrite, pretending to have done what he had not done. Jesus would not have "loved him" had he been a hypocrite, and Jesus knew his heart and difficulty. That he had "observed" these things means that he had made them the rule of his life. He was a splendid, moral young man, candid and honest, and for this reason Jesus loved him. Matthew (19: 20) states that he asked: "What lack I yet?" He was not yet satisfied or fully assured that he was an heir of eternal life, and he had confidence in Jesus to tell him.

21 **And Jesus looking upon him loved him.**—[Jesus loved him for his character, and because he loved him, he gave him the further direction that would perfect his character, and fit him for higher blessings of God in the world to come. His was a character approved by God so far as it went.]

and said unto him, One thing thou lackest:—But one thing, and yet the chief thing, which was not being done.

go, sell whatsoever thou hast, and give to the poor,—[This last requirement tested whether he loved God with all his heart. Love to God expresses itself in good to man. Nothing in the law of Moses required that spirit of self-sacrificing devotion that constitutes the chief excellency and distinguishing feature of the Christian religion. A man may have the life of morality and virtue set forth in the life of this young man, may fulfill all the requirements of the moral law, yet lack the true Christian spirit. The leading trait of Christ was self-denial and self-sacrifice for the good of others. He yielded up the honors he had with the Father before the world was to come to earth to save man. This was a new manifestation to man of the divine life. The love of God as manifested in Christ was not known to the law of Moses; so the self-sacrifice was not then required of man, as it now is, that he may be like God. "Have this mind in you, which was also in Christ Jesus: who, existing in the form of God, counted not the being on an equality with God a thing to be grasped, but emptied himself, taking the form of a servant, being made in the likeness of men; and being found in fashion as a man, he humbled himself, becoming obedient even unto death, yea, the death of the cross. Wherefore also God highly exalted him, and gave unto him the name which is above every name; that in the name of Jesus every knee should bow, of things in heaven and things on earth and things under the earth, and that every tongue should confess that Jesus Christ is Lord, to the glory of God the Father." (Phil. 2: 5-11.) This shows that Jesus was moved with pity and love so strong that he gave up the glories of the throne of God to bear man's nature, and took upon himself the death of the cross to lift up and save man. For this God exalted him with honors higher than he had before known. This was the example for man. If man is a worshiper of God, he must be like him.]

and thou shalt have treasure in heaven:—Renouncing earth, we receive heaven. It is worth the sacrifice; the exchange is a profitable one. The test of character is whether we so regard it. The heart that is fixed on earth, so that it hesitates at the exchange, is not yet fit for heaven, therefore, for eternal life.

and come, follow me.—The mere giving of his possessions was not in itself to save him. It only tested his fitness for discipleship. It was discipleship that would save him. To follow Jesus now is to have the mind of Christ and to do God's will as Jesus did. To give to the poor in Christ's name is to "have treasure in heaven." We are not required to sell all we have at once, but we are required to hold it for God and to use it in his service. Willingness to give up all for Jesus was the test then, and it is the test now. Will we do it? The cross may not be to give up wealth; it may be business, profession,

treasure in heaven: and come, follow me. 22 But his countenance fell at the saying, and he went away sorrowful: for he was one that had great posses·sions.

rank, pleasure, unworthy friends, present church relations when innovations are introduced. It is found in whatever prevents singlehearted consecration to Christ.

22 But his countenance fell at the saying,—As Jesus began his answer, "One thing thou lackest," his countenance, no doubt, lighted up with pleasant anticipation. A legalist by education, he was now to hear the "one thing" that should put the capsheaf to his righteous life, and give him eternal life. And then comes like a thunderclap the remainder of the reply, something utterly out of the question to a man of his wealth and position. Then he stood confounded. The aspect of his whole countenance was changed, indicative of great disappointment. Most persons are, to a great extent, unacquainted with themselves, until Christ, in his providence, lays bare at one stroke the poverty of their souls, and the insincerity of their lives.

and he went away sorrowful:—Sorrowful because eternal life was offered at only such a price as he was not willing to pay. Thus the secret of his heart must have been revealed even to himself. [The young man was like the masses of professed Christians to this day. He did not recognize that to give away his possessions in the name of the Lord was to increase his riches—to invest them in a bank that will never break, and yet will yield the richest dividends through life and in eternity. Christ was the happiest being that ever lived on earth. He was happy because he denied himself to help others. He taught the lesson in this world that the only pathway to true happiness is in denying self in God's name and for God's glory to help others. His example and precepts have been before the world for more than nineteen hundred years. His servants today turn sadly away, and refuse to follow his teaching, as did this rich young man, for they have great riches; or, which is the same thing, their affections are greatly set on their possessions, great or small. The willingness to give up all for Christ was the test of his acceptance with Christ, and is ours today. What God requires us to do is for our happiness and for our good. God requires service and gifts at our hand not because he needs them, but because we need the discipline and training that they give. Whatever of self-denial we make in obeying God will yield a hundredfold of good in this world and in the world to come.]

for he was one that had great possessions.—"He was very rich." (Luke 18: 23.) Hè had a hard struggle and a severe one, but he could not give up the world. Here was an act of obedience he could not perform. Here was a turning point in his history. How solemn that moment!

4. THE DANGER OF RICHES
10: 23-27
(Matt. 19: 23-26; Luke 18: 24-27)

23 And Jesus looked around about, and saith unto his disciples, How hardly shall they that have riches enter into the kingdom of God! 24 And the disciples were amazed at his words. But Jesus answereth again, and saith unto them, Children, how hard is it ⁴for them that trust in riches to

⁴Some ancient authorities omit *for them that trust in riches.*

---

23 **And Jesus looked round about, and saith unto his disciples, How hardly shall they that have riches enter into the kingdom of God!**—[When the young man went away sorrowful Jesus was sad. He and the angels in heaven rejoice when a sinner repents. They are sad and sorrowful when one—especially one so near the kingdom as this man seemed to be—turns from the way of truth. So he looked round about upon his disciples, to see the effect on their minds doubtless, and to prepare them for the truth he now wishes to enforce by this example. He said it is hard for a rich man to enter into the kingdom of heaven. This means that, under the rule or laws of God, it is difficult for a rich man to do this, because the riches gain such a hold on his affections, and make such a demand upon his time, that they leave neither disposition nor time to obey God.]

24 **And the disciples were amazed at his words. But Jesus answereth again, and saith unto them, Children, how hard is it for them that trust in riches to enter into the kingdom of God!**—[The astonishment was the greater because among the Jews riches were accounted the blessing of God bestowed for fidelity to him. They recognized that sometime a prosperity

enter into the kingdom of God! 25 It is easier for a camel to go through a needle's eye, than for a rich man to enter into the kingdom of God. 26 And

might come to a course of wickedness, but it would be short-lived, and that permanent prosperity was a sure sign of the blessing of God. They were, then, the more astonished when Jesus said: "How hardly"—with what difficulty—"shall they that have riches enter into the kingdom of God!" He means to say it is exceedingly difficult for a rich man to enter into the kingdom of God. They were not only amazed but terrified at the thought, because some of them possessed property, and they thought the statement cut them off.] But those already rich are not the only persons exposed to this danger. Those who are eager in the pursuit of wealth are equally exposed; for the apostle (1 Tim. 6: 9) said: "But they that are minded to be rich fall into a temptation and a snare and many foolish and hurtful lusts, such as drown men in destruction and perdition."

25 **It is easier for a camel to go through a needle's eye, than for a rich man to enter into the kingdom of God.**—This was used to denote that a thing was *impossible,* or exceedingly difficult. [There have been many explanations of this sentence. Some say there was a passage through the walls of Jerusalem very difficult for the camel with its load to pass through; others make the camel a cable that is difficult to pass through the eye of a needle. He had said it was impossible for a rich man—one who trusted in riches, one who refused to give up his riches at the demand of Jesus—to be saved, and this illustration was used to enforce that impossibility. This being so, we see nothing to be gained by changing the plain meaning of the language. It is impossible for a man who trusts in riches—whose affections are set on riches, who makes the gaining of riches the end of his labors, who refuses to give up his riches to subserve the cause of God and the good of man—to bring himself under the laws of God; and the figure that most forcibly expressed that impossibility most faithfully serves the master's purpose. Let us not try to weaken the force of the illustration, but urge it as a truth that will judge us at the last day. This still the more astonished them, and they asked, "Then who can be saved?" Clearly the apostles understood it to condemn all classes of

they were astonished exceedingly, saying ⁵unto him, Then who can be saved?
27 Jesus looking upon them saith, With men it is impossible, but not with
God: for all things are possible with God. 28 Peter began to say unto him,

⁵Many ancient authorities read *among themselves.*

people. We apply it to the millionaire, and think it does not apply to us; but it means all whose affections are placed on money. A man who lets the attainment of five dollars hinder his obedience to God as much falls under the condemnation of this law as he who lets the attainment of ten thousand dollars come between him and obedience to God. It is the spirit with which we view money, not the amount.] There are two classes of men whom Jesus considers rich and are here condemned. Namely, one who *loves* his riches, and makes an idol of them; the other who *supremely desires* to be rich. In other words, one who already "has it" and is making an idol of it, and one who does not have it, but is seeking it through undue means, and will make an idol of it if he gets it. Note that Christ did not condemn riches but the abuse of riches—the love of it. (1 Tim. 6: 10.) Extreme poverty may become as dangerous as extreme riches for the reason each has its own peculiar temptations. Then, let us pray the prayer of Agur, the son of Jakeh, and ask the position of mediocrity (Prov. 30: 8, 9), neither poverty nor riches. A man may have *great wealth,* and love God more than the wealth, and be a Christian; just as a poor man may have *little,* and love that *little* more than God, and never be a Christian. The principle works both ways.

26 **And they were astonished exceedingly, saying unto him, Then who can be saved?**—[Their astonishment knew no bounds. They understood it to condemn every one who possessed or labored for property and asked the question in despair.]

27 **Jesus looking upon them saith, With men it is impossible,**—It is beyond human power for any to be saved—to men influenced by the world this seems to be unwise. Worldly motives and principles cannot induce people to cease to trust in riches. Something more than the wisdom of men and the inducements of the world is necessary to accomplish this.

but not with God: for all things are possible with God.—[He looked upon them in their amazement and despondency, and said, "With men it is impossible." These things to men seem impossible—that is, it is impossible for a man to give up his love for what he has in order to honor God and help his suffering and needy fellow men. Left to their own unaided efforts and to human helps, this must fail. But "all things are possible with God." God can school and train men to give up all for Christ. To do it to the least of these his disciples is to do good to Christ. The evil of riches and the struggle for riches is presented frequently in the Bible.]

5. REWARD OF SELF-DENIAL
10: 28-31
(Matt. 19: 27-30; Luke 18: 28-30)

Lo, we have left all, and have followed thee. 29 Jesus said, Verily I say unto you, There is no man that hath left house, or brethren, or sisters, or mother, or father, or children, or lands, for my sake, and for the [6]gospel's sake, 30 but he shall receive a hundredfold now in this time, houses, and

[6]See marginal note on ch. 1. 1.

---

28 Peter began to say unto him, Lo, we have left all, and have followed thee.—Matthew (19: 27) adds that Peter asked, "What then shall we have?" This was an honest and fair question and something any one would wish to know under the circumstances. His question referred to the promise of Jesus, "Thou shalt have treasure in heaven." He desired to know what should be their portion since making the sacrifices they had, and whether they could claim the promise to themselves.

29 Jesus said, Verily I say unto you, There is no man that hath left house, or brethren, or sisters, or mother, or father, or children, or lands, for my sake, and for the gospel's sake,— From obedience to the requirements of the gospel, and love for the service of the gospel. Christ, his truth, and his cause are one. In the days of Jesus those who followed him were obliged generally to forsake houses and *home,* and to attend him. In our day it is not often required that we should *literally leave* them, except when the life is devoted to him among the heathen, but it is always required that we love them *less* than we do him; that we give up that which is inconsistent with devotion to the Lord, and be *ready* to give up all if devotion to him demands it.

30 but he shall receive a hundredfold—"A hundredfold"

brethren, and sisters, and mothers, and children, and lands, with persecutions; and in the [7]world to come eternal life. 31 But many *that are* first shall be last; and the last first.

[7]Or, *age*

means a hundred times as much. He will give what will be worth a hundred times as much in the peace, joy, and rewards of the blessings in Christ. No man's temporal interest is injured by the love of God.

now in this time, houses, and brethren, and sisters, and mothers, and children, and lands,—Here the spiritual relationship is intended. (Rom. 16: 13; 1 Cor. 4: 14-17; 2 Cor. 6: 13; Gal. 4: 19.) The promised return is realized usually in the enjoyments of the Christian life, which are equivalent for a hundredfold of all that is lost in serving Christ.

with persecutions;—These are not promised as a part of the reward; but amidst their trials and persecutions, they should find comfort and peace. A godly life is in opposition to ungodliness—they are at war with each other. The ungodly will assuredly persecute the godly, as they did our Lord. Persecution is one means used by Satan to draw Christians away from Christ, and permitted by God to test their loyalty to him.

and in the world to come eternal life.—Eternal life is in heaven. Hence, we must wait until we reach heaven to come in possession of it. For this reason we should not become weary in well-doing, for in due season, we shall reap if we faint not.

31 But many that are first shall be last; and the last first.— They will exchange positions. These changes are brought about by rejecting and accepting the gospel. Many who are first in prospect of everlasting life shall be last, and many who are last in this respect shall be first. The rich young ruler (verses 16-20) had been among the first, but now he is among the last. Judas, who was then among the first, was later among the last, and Matthias, who was among the last, being then only an obscure disciple (Acts 2: 21-23), took his place. The Jews looked upon themselves as first, and nearest to the kingdom of heaven, but for their infidelity they lost out as a nation. And the Gentiles, who were looked upon by them as dogs, and farthest from heaven, shall be first, on account of their conversion and faith in Christ. The Jews were offered the gospel first and rejected it—this put the first last; the Gentiles were offered it last, they accepted it—this put the last first. Another view is that many are first in their *own* esteem, and in the opinion of others, and forward in their claims in religion, yet at the day of judgment they will be last and least in God's estimation and account. And many that are little in their own, and less in the esteem of others, who had a less name and vogue in the world, shall be first and highest in God's favor. No doubt the day of judgment will frustrate a great many persons' expectations, both as touching others, and concerning themselves. Many will miss heaven, and be lost, who looked upon themselves to be first. And many will find others in heaven, whom they least expected there. It seems clear that the meaning of the first sentence, "many that are first shall be last," is many with splendid opportunities, failing to improve them, shall be last; and the second, "the last first," are those with poor or meager advantages, which, by improving them, shall have a great reward.

6. THE THIRD PREDICTION OF DEATH
10: 32-34
(Matt. 20: 17-19; Luke 8: 31-34)

32 And they were on the way, going up to Jerusalem; and Jesus was going before them: and they were amazed; and they that followed were

32 And they were on the way, going up to Jerusalem;—Jesus is now on his last journey to Jerusalem. He was going there to die for the sins of the world.

and Jesus was going before them: and they were amazed; —He was in advance of and leading his disciples, and they were amazed that he would go to the seat of his bitterest foes, when the Jews had sought to stone him (John 11: 8), and the priests and Pharisees were counseling to put him to death.

and they that followed were afraid.—Both for him and themselves. Mark does not give the cause of these feelings, but John incidentally does. Since leaving Galilee Jesus had already been to Jerusalem on a visit not recorded by Mark (John 7: 1-10; 10: 22), and had encountered such opposition there that he retired beyond the Jordan. From this retire-

afraid. And he took again the twelve, and began to tell them the things that were to happen unto him, 33 *saying,* Behold, we go up to Jerusalem; and the Son of man shall be delivered unto the chief priests and the scribes; and they shall condemn him to death, and shall deliver him unto the Gentiles: 34 and they shall mock him, and shall spit upon him, and shall scourge him, and shall kill him; and after three days he shall rise again.

---

ment he had been recalled by the sickness and death of Lazarus, and as he started in obedience to this call, the disciples had explained, "Rabbi, the Jews were but now seeking to stone thee; and goest thou thither again?" Thomas said: "Let us also go, that we may die with him." (John 11: 8, 16.)

And he took again the twelve, and began to tell them the things that were to happen unto him,—The time was drawing near when the great tragedy, upon which the foundation of the church depended, should occur and he sought to impress the minds of his disciples with these things. He wished to have them prepared for it when it came.

33 saying, Behold, we go up to Jerusalem; and the Son of man shall be delivered unto the chief priests and the scribes; and they shall condemn him to death, and shall deliver him unto the Gentiles:—Because they had no authority to inflict capital punishment, they would deliver him to those who have —the Roman authority.

34 and they shall mock him, and shall spit upon him, and shall scourge him, and shall kill him;—As explicit as this announcement was, "they understood none of these things; and this saying was hid from them, and they perceived not the things that were said." (Luke 18: 34.)

and after three days he shall rise again.—For the fulfillment of this see Matthew 28. Here, as on the two former announcements of his death, he foretells his resurrection. This was a gleam of light which shone up beyond the intervening darkness. Without his resurrection, his death would have been in vain. Jesus foretold for the third time (Matt. 16: 21; 17: 22; 30: 17) what was coming, so that his disciples would not be taken unawares and be overwhelmed in a sudden storm of temptations. But Jesus gives them a vision of hope and faith, by assuring them that death was not the end. He would not perish, but rise again to a new and greater life.

7. AMBITION OF JAMES AND JOHN
10: 35-45
(Matt. 20: 20-28)

35 And there come near unto him [8]James and John, the sons of Zebedee, saying unto him, Teacher, we would that thou shouldest do for us whatsoever we shall ask of thee. 36 And he said unto them, What would ye that I should do for you? 37 And they said unto him, Grant unto us that we may sit, one on thy right hand, and one on *thy* left hand, in thy glory. 38 But

[8]Or, *Jacob*

---

35 **And there come near unto him James and John, the sons of Zebedee, saying unto him, Teacher, we would that thou shouldest do for us whatsoever we shall ask of thee.**—They tried to get Jesus to pledge himself to grant their request before making it known to him. After Jesus had made the above statement for the third time, James and John, ambitious for chief places in his kingdom, made their request. Matthew (20: 20) says this request was made through Salome, their mother. (Matt. 27: 56; Mark 15: 40.) In making this request she worshiped Jesus, or prostrated herself in reverence before him. She, no doubt, encouraged her sons in this ambitious desire, misunderstanding as much the nature and mission of Christ's kingdom as they.

36 **And he said unto them, What would ye that I should do for you?**—He has them to state their request frankly and plainly. This was not for his own information, for he knew what was in their hearts (John 2: 25), but for their good. It was wisdom upon his part to force them to state their desire before making any reply.

37 **And they said unto him, Grant unto us that we may sit, one on thy right hand, and one on thy left hand, in thy glory.** —They desired the two highest places of honor, next to him, in his kingdom. It was an improper request made at an inappropriate time. The promise in Matthew (19: 28), that the twelve apostles should sit on twelve thrones judging the twelve tribes of Israel, may have suggested the idea of making this request. Perhaps light will be thrown upon their request if we remember that Salome was most probably the sister of Mary, the mother of Jesus, and thence James and John were his cousins. It is natural then that the family would make use of this relationship to gain an advantage over the

Jesus said unto them, Ye know not what ye ask. Are ye able to drink the cup that I drink? or to be baptized with the baptism that I am baptized

---

other disciples, especially so since they had such a poor conception of what his kingdom would be. Their request was not to sit in the trial and by the cross, but in his glory—with him as king. The first place of honor was the right hand of the sovereign; the second, the left hand. Jesus, in his reply, gave them to understand that friendship and kinship had nothing to do with promotions in the kingdom which he proposed to set up.

38 But Jesus said unto them, Ye know not what ye ask.— They knew not the greatness of the favor they asked—how blessed beyond their highest dreams it was to sit on the right and left hand of the Son of God, how radiant the glories of that kingdom were to be. They knew not how hard the way, nor how difficult the conditions on which alone they could attain their desire. They knew not what they were specially fitted for. No one knows enough to wisely choose his own lot. They only are wise who desire that God's wisdom and love should choose their lot for them. There are few things we need to be more thankful for than that some of our prayers are not answered in the way we desire.

Are ye able to drink the cup that I drink?—In ancient times it was common to execute criminals by forcing them to drink a cup of poison, and assassination and suicide were often effected by the same means. The cup, therefore, became a symbol of suffering and of death, and it is so used here. Can you, or will you, pay the price? Can you share the sacrifices?

or to be baptized with the baptism that I am baptized with? —This is not water baptism for Jesus had already submitted to that, but it is the baptism of suffering—the overwhelming suffering which Jesus was undergoing. This baptism began with his personal ministry and was completed at the cross. He was completely overwhelmed with suffering. Note that he uses not the past nor the future tense, but the present. He was then in the state of sufferings that would finally overwhelm him at the cross. Suffering with Christ is essential to reigning with him. (Rom. 8: 17.)

with? 39 And they said unto him, We are able. And Jesus said unto them, The cup that I drink ye shall drink; and with the baptism that I am baptized withal shall ye be baptized: 40 but to sit on my right hand or on *my* left hand is not mine to give; but *it is for them* for whom it hath been prepared.

---

39 **And they said unto him, We are able.**—This was perhaps a somewhat overweening assurance, but it was what they felt and believed in the face of what Jesus had just told them of his sufferings; and they were not wholly mistaken in their judgment of themselves, though no one can be quite sure what he will do, being ignorant of both himself and the future. They fled with the other disciples on the night of the arrest, but John, in the trial before Caiaphas, maintained his courage, while the brave Peter fell.

And Jesus said unto them, The cup that I drink ye shall drink; and with the baptism that I am baptized withal shall ye be baptized:—This prediction was fulfilled. James drank the cup by suffering martyrdom at the hands of Herod Agrippa, being the first of the apostles to suffer death. (Acts 12: 2.) He was slain with the sword, A.D. 44. John was the last survivor of the apostles, living to a ripe old age, and the only apostle that died a natural death, but he drank the cup by the sufferings through which he passed. His long life of trials and persecutions more than equalled the sufferings of actual martyrdom. He was scourged by the Jews (Acts 5: 40), was banished to the lonely isle of Patmos (Rev. 1: 9) by the Romans, which gives us a glimpse of the hatred and persecution which he must have endured (Rev. 1: 9). Besides all this, tradition tells us that he was at one time cast into a cask of boiling oil by which he was refreshed instead of destroyed, and at another, compelled to drink a cup of poison without injury.

40 **but to sit on my right hand or on my left hand is not mine to give; but it is for them for whom it hath been prepared.**—Positions both in the church and in heaven are not donations given out to friends and kinspeople as in the political field; but gained through faithful service and loyalty to Christ through all the vicissitudes of a godly life. They are prepared places for a prepared people.

41 And when the ten heard it, they began to be moved with indignation concerning ¹James and John. 42 And Jesus called them to him, and saith unto
them, Ye know that they who are accounted to rule over the Gentiles lord it
over them; and their great ones exercise authority over them. 43 But it is

¹Or, *Jacob*

**41 And when the ten heard it, they began to be moved with
indignation concerning James and John.**—They were offended
at their ambition, at their desire to be exalted above their
brethren. The same emulation which prompted the request of
the two now arouses the displeasure of the ten, and needed
correcting. Here is a splendid foundation for building up a
faction among the disciples. James and John laid the foundation for it and the ten began to build upon it. But Jesus, a
peacemaker, interfered and made peace among them.
Christians ought to be peacemakers today and follow the example of Jesus. This incident is of special value as showing
one of Jesus' ways of curing a fault of his disciples. To cure
it was essential to forming their character and thus advancing
their usefulness in building up his kingdom. He was the
teacher, they were his students. They all alike needed the instruction which Jesus proceeded to give. "The ten" being
"moved with indignation" shows that they had the same spirit
and desire that James and John had. Condemning others
sometimes reveals in us the faults we condemn in others.

42 And Jesus called them to him,—He called the apostles
close around him so they could hear all he had to say touching
the important matters that had arisen, and stated the principles on which they were to act.

**and saith unto them, Ye know that they who are accounted
to rule over the Gentiles lord it over them;**—The political rulers exercised dominion over their subjects, and they knew
that it was customary among nations to bestow such favors as
James and John desired. The kings of the earth raise their
favorites to posts of trust and power, and give them authority
over others. They seem to be chief, have the place and honor,
and appearance of leadership; but instead of leading they
"lord it over them"—ruling in an impervious and oppressive
manner. (1 Pet. 5: 3.)

and their great ones exercise authority over them.—Their

not so among you: but whosoever would become great among you, shall be your [2]minister; 44 and whosoever would be first among you, shall be

[2]Or, *servant*

great men, their nobles, chief in rank and power. Persons who are regarded as great possess the authority and office of greatness, to get all they can out of the people instead of doing all they can to make them prosperous and virtuous. It was a selfish authority, an utterly false ambition, full of dangers, crowded with temptations to sin and crime.

The Gentiles in particular are here meant; but the principles or facts here pointed out are equally true in all world governments. "The ten" manifested this indignation in some way, though not in the presence of Jesus. Hence, he "called them to him." Then he pointed out the great contrast between the spirit and nature of his kingdom and that of worldly and political kingdoms. This lesson is for us all today. The rulers of the Gentiles "lord it over" the people. This is still, and ever will be, the spirit of all earthly governments. He today who seeks preferment and position above others in the church does not yet understand the nature of Christ's kingdom or the principle of true greatness.

43 But it is not so among you:—My kingdom will not be a political kingdom, but a spiritual kingdom. Hence my subjects are not to exercise civil power and authority over their brethren; neither are they to lord it over God's heritage. (1 Pet. 5: 3.) A large per cent of the evils that have come to the churches of Christ have come through a disregard of the principles here given—a desire to be honored and to rule rather than to serve and help.

but whosoever would become great among you,—Jesus does not forbid the desire to be great, but only the desire for selfish greatness. The wish to be greater than others is always a wrong ambition, but the wish to be as great, as good, as useful as possible, to grow and improve, is right, and the desire to serve others can never be too strong.

shall be your minister;—Your waiter, attendant, one who ministers, or waits on you. Originally the word was applied to one who served or waited on another, principally at the

³servant of all. 45 For the Son of man also came not to be ministered unto, but to minister, and to give his life a ransom for many.

³Gr. *bondservant.*

table, and who was not a slave. In the New Testament it is applied to one who ministers to another or others; either at the table (Matt. 20: 26; John 2: 5, 9; Luke 22: 27); or as a distributor of alms (Acts 6: 1, 2); or as one who furthers or promotes a thing (Gal. 2: 7); or as a religious teacher (1 Cor. 3: 5); or deacons (1 Tim. 3: 8).

44 and whosoever would be first among you, shall be servant of all.—The kingdom of heaven would be established upon different principles from those of political kingdoms. There are to be no ranks; no places of dominion. All are tō be on a level, the rich, the poor, the learned, the unlearned, the bond, the free, are to be equal. He will be the most distinguished that shows most humility, the deepest sense of his unworthiness, and the most earnest desire to promote the welfare of his brethren. He is greatest who does the greatest service to his fellow men, confers the largest benefits on them at real cost to himself.

45 For the Son of man also came not to be ministered unto, but to minister,—He took the form of a servant when he came into the world to serve and redeem man. (Phil. 2: 7.) He came not to be served but to serve. (John 13: 4, 5.) He was in the form of God in heaven, but came to men in the form of a servant. (Phil. 2: 6, 7.) When he came he did not require men to minister to him. Instead he labored for and served them. He provided for their wants, fared as they did, went before them in dangers and sufferings, practiced self-denial on their account, and, for them, was now on his way to Jerusalem to sacrifice his life.

and to give his life a ransom—A ransom was the price paid to redeem one from death (Ex. 21: 30) or from slavery (Lev. 25: 51). It is a price paid for captives. In war, when prisoners are taken by an enemy, the money demanded for their release is called a ransom. Anything that releases any one from a state of punishment or suffering, or sin, is a ransom. Men are captives to sin. They are under condemnation (Eph. 3: 3; Rom. 3: 9, 23, 30; 1 John 5: 9) and exposed to eternal death (Matt. 25: 46; Rom. 2: 6-9). They must have perished unless there had been some way by which they could be released. This was done by the death of Christ; by his giving his life a ransom.

for many.—That is, in the stead, of many. He gave his life in their place. He substituted his own life in their place. In other words, his death was a substitute for their death. Jesus was a ransom in behalf of all. (1 Tim. 2: 6.) It is sufficient for all and is freely offered to all. (Rom. 5: 18.) The "many," the whole multitude of the human race. Here was the example, the proof, the ideal of Christ's teachings. There is much contention yet in one way and another over who shall be accounted greatest in the kingdom of Christ. Men are ashamed to own it and attribute it to some good motive; but, divested of all Satan's disguise, it is a strife for places of honor and positions of greatness in the church. What do religious *titles* mean except this?

8. BLIND BARTIMEUS HEALED
10: 46-52
(Matt. 20: 29-34; Luke 18: 35 to 9: 1)

46 And they come to Jericho: and as he went out from Jericho, with his disciples and a great multitude, the son of Timaeus, Bartimaeus, a blind beggar, was sitting by the way side. 47 And when he heard that it was Jesus

46 **And they come to Jericho:**—Jericho, where Bartimeus was healed, has passed through an eventful history, having been thrown down and rebuilt a number of times, and having now been a complete ruin for many centuries. The real site of ancient Jericho is about two miles northwest of this village at the foot of the mountains which there rise abruptly from the plain. This is known both by the ruins in that place and by the presence of the large spring now called "Elisha's fountain," near which the city stood when Elisha healed the waters of the spring. (2 Kings 2: 18-22.) Mounds of rubbish, made up of broken pottery, ashes and the dust of unburnt bricks, the chief building material of the ancient city, mark the site. In the days of our Lord, Jericho was an important city, having been embellished by Herod the Great.

and as he went out from Jericho, with his disciples and a great multitude, the son of Timaeus, Bartimaeus, a blind beg-

the Nazarene, he began to cry out, and say, Jesus, thou son of David, have mercy on me. 48 And many rebuked him, that he should hold his peace: but he cried out the more a great deal, Thou son of David, have mercy on me.

gar, was sitting by the way side.—Matthew (20: 30) says: "Two blind men." Both pleaded for mercy and were healed. Only one name is given, probably the most noted. There is no contradiction here since Mark selects the most prominent one for his history, and simply says nothing about the other. Luke (19: 35-43) mentions the healing of a blind man as Jesus entered Jericho which Matthew and Mark omit. Here are two separate and distinct cases of healing the blind—one as Jesus enters the city, the other as he leaves. He was "sitting by the way side." That is, the road that leads from Jericho to Jerusalem. The previous clause tells what he was doing— "begging."

47 And when he heard that it was Jesus the Nazarene, he began to cry out,—He had heard about Jesus, and his wonderful cures. Other blind men had been made to see, other men in trouble had been helped. Here in the Son of David was his only hope. A shrill cry rises on the air above the noise and bustle of the crowd.

and say, Jesus, thou son of David,—He addressed him not as Jesus the Nazarene. His faith takes hold of something higher and deeper. He recognized him as a royal descendant of David and successor to his throne, the Messiah. (Chron. 12: 35.) The angel of the Lord had once applied this title to Joseph. (Matt. 1: 20.) It was a popular designation of the Messiah, and by the use of it Bartimeus acknowledged the Messiahship of Jesus.

have mercy on me.—The poor man expressed both a confession of misery, unworthiness and helplessness, and an expression of confidence in the ability and willingness of Jesus to help him.

48 And many rebuked him, that he should hold his peace: —They tried to stop his piercing noise. They feared that the Master might be disturbed by this unseemly noise, and did not like it themselves.

but he cried out the more a great deal,—The rebuke of the multitude served only to arouse his earnestness, for he be-

49 And Jesus stood still, and said, Call ye him. And they call the blind man, saying unto him, Be of good cheer : rise, he calleth thee. 50 And he, casting away his garment, sprang up, and came to Jesus. 51 And Jesus answered

lieved in the ability and willingness of Jesus to heal him. It was a trial of faith, but his faith was not to be overcome—opposition only encouraged him to press his claims the more.

Thou son of David, have mercy on me.—In this cry he bore testimony to the widely-scattered stimulus given to the Redeemer's cause, since the beginning of the festal journey, amongst the masses. When the soul is awakened there are plenty to cry, "Hold your peace," and sometimes of those who profess to be in the triumphal procession.

49 **And Jesus stood still, and said, Call ye him.**—Luke (18: 40) says Jesus "commanded him to be brought unto him," which is the same in substance. The whole attitude and tone of the people now change. They who had tried to silence are now all anxious to help him, such a change does Jesus' interest make.

And they call the blind man,—Probably the same ones who had just tried to stop his cries for help. This was perfectly natural with such a crowd. Popular feelings often swing from one extreme to the other as in this case.

saying unto him, Be of good cheer: rise, he calleth thee.—Yes, when Jesus calls for him, he has the key that will unlock the avenue to all hopes. There is no hesitation with him.

50 **And he, casting away his garment, sprang up, and came to Jesus.**—His outer garment, a large piece of cloth which was folded around the body, covered the more tightly-fitting garments, and might impede his movements. He wanted to get to Jesus as quickly as possible. This act of Bartimeus denoted haste, and earnestness upon his part, in order to come to Jesus. Directed by his voice, or led by the hands, now willing, around him. He leaped up in haste, with the least possible delay, and came to Jesus. If you would come to Jesus you must "cast away" all your sins. They must be left behind. Hearty repentance is essential to seeing Jesus' face as a Savior. Then, having forsaken these, you must *"come to Jesus,"* in his appointments and ordinances. There is where he "stands still," and waits for you. There he will meet you with the word of salvation.

him, and said, What wilt thou that I should do unto thee? And the blind
man said unto him, ⁴Rabboni, that I may receive my sight. 52 And Jesus
said unto him, Go thy way; thy faith hath ⁵made thee whole. And straightway he received his sight, and followed him in the way.

⁴See John 20. 16.
⁵Or, *saved thee*

51 **And Jesus answered him, and said, What wilt thou that I
should do unto thee?**—This poor afflicted man had only made
a general petition for mercy. Jesus now calls forth his particular and special request. What mercy dost thou desire?

And the blind man said unto him, Rabboni,—There were
three titles used by the Jews to their teachers, *Rab, master,* as the
lowest degree of honor; *Rabbi, my master,* of higher dignity;
Rabboni, my great master, the most honorable of all.

that I may receive my sight.—Surely an object worth seeking, worth the most persistent crying to the Lord. And yet
spiritual sight is infinitely greater than this boon; but how
few, comparatively, cry out for it. The soul coming to Jesus
must know and state clearly what it wants. Remember that
spiritual sight will bring spiritual responsibility.

52 **And Jesus said unto him, Go thy way; thy faith hath
made thee whole.**—Or saved thee in respect to physical blindness. Mark intimates the dignity of the crisis in which the
Lord now stands, by the circumstances that he heals the blind
man simply by words. "Go thy way; thy faith hath made
thee whole." Mark brings out the most important point, that
so necessary was faith in the recipient to this healing that
Jesus could even say his faith had made him whole. So with
all healing physical or spiritual. His faith saved him by leading him to use the means necessary to arrest the attention of
Jesus and to secure the blessing desired. In the same way
does faith of a sinner save him. Faith alone, or faith without
action, could not have opened the blind man's eyes, nor can it
save a sinner from his sins. "Ye see that by works a man is
justified, and not only by faith." (James 2 : 24.)

And straightway he received his sight,—Mark's characteristic "straightway" comes in with large significance. Even
while the gracious words are being uttered, the optic nerve is
thrilling and the retina clearing, and the eyes that were turned
towards Jesus under guidance of the sense of hearing, light up

with rapture as they *see* the lips that are speaking their enfranchisement, and the eyes in whose liquid depths shines the soul that felt for him in his misery. He is now complete physically, having all his faculties in use.

and followed him in the way.—Luke (18: 43) says: "Glorifying God." He joins in the glad songs of the festal procession. Luke adds, "And all the people, when they saw it, gave praise unto God." Faith does not literally heal, but faith is essential to healing. Faith here was perfected (James 2: 22); he believed that Jesus was the Messiah, he confessed it, he cast away all hindrances, he came to Jesus, he told his need, he was healed. There are other cases of blindness healed recorded in the New Testament, and each was somewhat peculiar to itself. One occurred in or near Capernaum. (Matt. 9: 27.) In that case Jesus healed two instantaneously by a touch, and made their faith the condition of healing. Another was at Bethsaida. In that case (Mark 8: 22) the restoration was gradual. He anointed the man's eyes with spittle, then laid his hands upon him, and he saw men as trees, walking. Then again Jesus' hands were laid on his eyes, and he saw all things clearly. In both these instances Jesus forbade publication. The next was in Jerusalem. (John 9: 1.) The man had been blind from birth, and was well known. In this case Jesus spat on the ground at his feet, and made an ointment with which he anointed the blind man's eyes. He then told him to go to the pool of Siloam and wash, which the man obeyed and returned restored to sight.

The account of Bartimeus proves again the power of Jesus to heal. It also reflects additional credibility on the history of his previous miracles. Being blind this man could not have seen the previous miracles, hence he could have known of them only from the reports of those who saw them. This was sufficient evidence to produce his faith.

SECTION TWO

INCIDENTS AND DISCUSSIONS IN JERUSALEM
11: 1 to 12: 44

1. THE TRIUMPHAL ENTRY
11: 1-11
(Matt. 21: 1-11; Luke 19: 29-44; John 12: 12-19)

1 And when they draw nigh unto Jerusalem, unto Bethphage and Bethany, at the mount of Olives, he sendeth two of his disciples, 2 and saith

---

1 **And when they draw nigh unto Jerusalem, unto Bethphage and Bethany, at the mount of Olives,**—[Jesus and his
disciples were now on the way to Jerusalem from Jericho,
and, approaching the city, they came unto Bethphage and
Bethany. They were villages close together, near the Mount
of Olives, two miles out from Jerusalem. Of the former place
we know but little. It is not mentioned elsewhere than here,
and in corresponding places in Matt. 21: 1 and Luke 19: 29.
It must have been a small village, and tradition says it was
above Bethany, halfway between that town and the top of the
Mount of Olives. Bethany was the home of Lazarus—whom
Jesus had a few weeks before raised from the dead—and of his
sisters. John (12: 1) says that Jesus "six days before the passover came to Bethany." When he reached Bethany he
stopped with Lazarus, Martha, and Mary, as was his custom.
John (12: 2-7) says: "They made him a supper there: and
Martha served; . . . Mary therefore took a pound of ointment
of pure nard, very precious, and anointed the feet of Jesus,
and wiped his feet with her hair: and the house was filled
with the odor of the ointment. . . . Jesus therefore said, Suffer her to keep it against the day of my burying." The next
morning Jesus sent two of his disciples to procure an ass for
him to ride into Jerusalem.]

he sendeth two of his disciples,—Their names are not given,
but remembering the vividness of Mark's account, and the
probability that Peter was his eyewitness authority in these
scenes, it is very likely that Peter was one. John may have
been the other, though his history does not sound like that of
an eyewitness. They were two employed in preparing for the
Passover. (Luke 22: 8.) They were sent in advance to make

unto them, Go your way into the village that is over against you: and
straightway as ye enter into it, ye shall find a colt tied, whereon no man ever
yet sat; loose him, and bring him. 3 And if any one say unto you, Why do

arrangements for his royal entry into Jerusalem. It is not
certain who the two disciples were.

**2 and saith unto them, Go your way into the village that is
over against you:**—McGarvey, who visited the place, says:
"Not necessarily Bethphage, but a village opposite to them as
he spoke. The writer well remembers a spot on the road from
Bethany to Jerusalem which meets all the conditions of the
narrative."

and straightway as ye enter into it,—The description was
very definite. As soon as they entered the edge of the village
they would, without inquiring of any one, find that for which
they were sent.

ye shall find a colt tied,—Mark, Luke and John mention the
colt only, while Matthew (21: 2) tells of its mother also. The
colt was the more important of the two, as upon it Christ
should ride.

whereon no man ever yet sat;—Up to this time the colt had
run with its mother and had not been ridden. Animals for sacred usages were selected from those which had been unused
by man, ceremonially clean and unblemished. (Num. 19: 2;
Deut. 21: 3; 11; 1 Sam. 6: 7.) The fact that Matthew
mentions both dam and colt does not involve contradiction,
but simply added particulars. Christ should have the honor
of riding the colt the first time it was ridden. Probably the
mother was led in front to cause the untrained colt to proceed
without difficulty.

loose him, and bring him.—All was divinely arranged and in
fulfillment of prophecy. Such a colt could not be found any
time and place. Jesus knew that he was perfectly welcome to
the use of the animal. As God manifest in the flesh, the colt
was his (Psalm 50: 10), and he could claim its service (1 Sam.
8: 16). Probably its owner was a disciple or close friend of
Jesus, whose cheerful acquiescence is implied in the narrative.
[Asses were in common use in that land and time. Horses
are seldom mentioned. Some think the riding the ass an act
of humiliation, because they are not very respectable as riding

ye this? say ye, The Lord hath need of him; and straightway he ⁰will send

⁰Gr. *sendeth.*

animals with us, but kings and others of the great ones of earth rode them. It was not unworthy of a king! What the Lord absolutely needs is always waiting for him, but it may be our mission to get it. If so, duty is plain. If the king's entrance to the temple of a human heart is crippled by your neglect, you must give account. The master deserves the best, the freshest, the unused.

3 **And if any one say unto you, Why do ye this? say ye, The Lord hath need of him;**—They were apprised of the fact that some person might see them removing the animal, and ask about it; and if so, they were told what to say in reply. This occurred as indicated. [If the owner asks you why you take him, calls you to account for it. Those sent for it most likely did not know, and were unknown to the owner of the colt. Tell him "the Lord hath need of him." He doubtless knew the Lord, was his disciple, and when he heard he needed him, he would gladly lend him. Usually Jesus speaks of himself in terms of humiliation, but here he is to be referred to the owner as the Lord, the Master, the Ruler of all things. In reading these accounts, it is often thought these were strangers—did not know Jesus, and they sent the ass to a stranger. We know of no ground for such a conclusion; besides, the frequent sojourns of Jesus at Bethany would suggest that he was well known in the near village of Bethphage. That Jesus knew that the colt was there tied showed there was nothing hidden from him. The sending was nothing more than a disciple sending the colt to the Master at his request, for his use. Matthew (21: 4, 5) says: "Now this is come to pass, that it might be fulfilled which was spoken through the prophet, saying, Tell ye the daughter of Zion, Behold, thy King cometh unto thee, meek, and riding upon an ass, and upon a colt the foal of an ass." (Isa. 62: 11; Zech. 9: 9.)]

and straightway he will send him back hither.—This means that when Jesus was done with the colt he would return it to the owner. Jesus, having used it, of course, returned it. "The Lord hath need of" it is sufficient answer, brother, to all your excuses for the non-performance of duty and the non-

him [7]back hither. 4 And they went away, and found a colt tied at the door without in the open street; and they loose him. 5 And certain of them that stood there said unto them, What do ye, loosing the colt? 6 And they said unto them even as Jesus had said: and they let them go. 7 And they bring

[7]Or, *again*

bestowment of means. Shall your heart be less responsive than these colt owners?

4 **And they went away, and found a colt tied at the door without in the open street; and they loose him.**—From the object to which the colt was tied. [They went as Jesus directed them, found the colt tied without the gate at the meeting of the two roads, and they loosed him to carry him to the Master. The correspondence of the facts to what Jesus said would be when he could not have been there shows his knowledge. They seem to have proceeded to unloose him without asking permission, as Jesus told them. This was rather an unceremonious assumption, but they followed the direction given.] Whatsoever Jesus tells you in his word, you will always find true.

5 **And certain of them that stood there said unto them, What do ye, loosing the colt?**—Luke (19: 33) explains their right to ask questions by telling that they were the owners. [Some one of the family of the owner saw them taking the colt and asked, What are you doing loosing the colt? Who gave you such privilege?] They were probably the father and his sons, the members of the family who were interested in the property being carried away. There is always somebody ready to interfere with us if we implicitly obey Christ. They have sometimes reasonable, sometimes unreasonable, questions to ask.

6 **And they said unto them even as Jesus had said: and they let them go.**—We see no reason for imagining some secret arrangement between Jesus and the owners, and that the words he told the disciples to use were passwords secretly agreed on beforehand as claimed by some enemies of the Christ. [They responded in the words of Jesus as he had directed them, "The Lord hath need of him," and they let him go. Many think that God exercised his power to put it into the heart of the owner to send him to one he did not know. I think this a mistake, as explained under verse 3. He was a disciple of the

the colt unto Jesus, and cast on him their garments; and he sat upon him. 8
And many spread their garments upon the way; and others *branches, which
they had cut from the fields. 9 And they that went before, and they that
followed, cried, Hosanna; Blessed *is* he that cometh in the name of the

*Gr. *layers of leaves.*

Master, and sent the colt at his request. There is no miracle
in this, save the knowledge displayed by Jesus of the whereabouts of the colt.]

**7 And they bring the colt unto Jesus, and cast on him their
garments; and he sat upon him.**—The garments supplied the
want of a saddle, which they would not find with the unused
colt, "whereon no man ever yet sat."

8 And many spread their garments upon the way;—In the
road. These were also extra garments. In a frenzy of enthusiasm the "most part of the multitude" cast off their cloaks
and paved the way with them for Jesus to travel on.

and others branches, which they had cut from the fields.—
The branches of bushes which would not be large enough to
impede traveling, but would make a triumphal carpet of twigs
and leaves. All this was in accordance with the custom of
honoring kings and conquerors by carpeting the way before
them. General enthusiasm prevailed; those who could not
honor in one way would in another.

**9 And they that went before, and they that followed, cried,
Hosanna;**—The shouts of welcome and praise doubtless
began with the disciples around Jesus and were caught by the
multitude before and behind him.

Blessed is he that cometh in the name of the Lord:—"The
pilgrims' greeting on their entrance into Jerusalem at the time
of feasts" (greeting and response, Psalm 118: 26.) [A company went in front and one behind, as is usual with kings on a
march, to afford the greater protection. Each company kept
up a shout of "Hosanna; Blessed be he that cometh in the
name of Jehovah." "Hosanna" means "Save, we pray." It
was a quotation from Psalm 118: 25, 26: "Save now, we beseech thee, O Jehovah: O Jehovah, we beseech thee, send now
prosperity. Blessed be he that cometh in the name of Jehovah." This was sung by the Jews at the feast of tabernacles,
or ingathering. It was a triumphal journey recognizing and

Lord: 10 Blessed *is* the kingdom that cometh, *the kingdom* of our father David: Hosanna in the highest.

---

proclaiming him King of Israel. Luke (19: 37) says: "And as he was now drawing nigh, even at the descent of the mount of Olives, the whole multitude of the disciples began to rejoice and praise God with a loud voice for all the mighty works which they had seen." John (12: 12, 13) says: "On the morrow a great multitude that had come to the feast, when they heard that Jesus was coming to Jerusalem, took the branches of the palm trees, and went forth to meet him." They went out to Bethany and joined the throng that were there with him, and added to the triumphal shouts of those with Jesus.] So the prophets and apostles call to each other across the ages and sing the antiphonal song of praise to God. Shall our lips be dumb? Have we no word to speak for him who has redeemed us? And let us try to bless all those his servants who come to us in his name!

10 **Blessed is the kingdom that cometh, the kingdom of our father David:**—[He was praised as sitting upon the throne of his father David.] The people thought that Christ would set up a political kingdom and that he would be king. This cry of the people shows that they expected Jesus to immediately set up or restore the kingdom of David, and to assume the throne which had been vacant from the time of the Babylonish captivity. Luke (19: 11) states it as a fact, in connection with his departure from Jericho on his journey to Jerusalem, that the multitude who followed him "supposed that the kingdom of God was immediately to appear." It was the exulting thought of national independence and glory that inspired their acclamations; and the same feeling prepared them for the reverse of feeling toward Jesus, which occurred when they found him a prisoner in the hands of Pontius Pilate.

The Jews called David their father because Jesus was his son or descendant. They were looking for the immediate restoration of the throne of David in the Messiah. They had a poor conception of the nature of the kingdom of heaven. To acknowledge Jesus as the "son of David" was to acknowledge him as king.

11 And he entered into Jerusalem, into the temple; and when he had
looked round about upon all things, it being now eventide, he went out unto
Bethany with the twelve.

Hosanna in the highest.—That is, in the highest realms of
blessedness, where his salvation will be complete. Alas, how
fickle the city that shouted these praises today, and only five
days after cried, Crucify him!

11 **And he entered into Jerusalem,**—[He entered the city.
Matthew (21: 10, 11) says: "And when he was come into Jerusalem, all the city was stirred, saying, Who is this? And
the multitudes said, This is the prophet, Jesus, from Nazareth
of Galilee." The rulers, the priest, the scribes, and Pharisees
were jealous of his increasing influence, and watchful to arrest
him. Already they had ordered any who knew him to report
to them. Now both the priest and the Pharisees had given a
commandment, that, if any man knew where he was he should
show it, that they might take him. He also went into the
temple.]

into the temple;—The Lord whom they sought had suddenly come to his temple. It remained to be seen how the hierarchy, who taught man to look for him, would receive him
when he came. He went probably without a pause straight to
the temple. Here he spent the day in observation, preparatory to the cleansing of the temple, which occurred on the day
after the triumphal entry. (See verses 12-19.)

and when he had looked round about upon all things,—He
was making a thorough inspection of the temple and its surroundings, and of the desecration of its courts, with a view to
knowing for himself, as a foundation for the work of the next
few days. Having fully satisfied himself of the need of a thorough cleansing of the sanctuary he went out. [He looked
round about on what was going on. He was not pleased, but
seems to have said nothing then; but on the morrow he returned, saw the traffic and merchandise he had cast out a few
years before again flourishing, and cast those conducting it
out.]

it being now eventide,—After sunset or near that time.

he went out unto Bethany with the twelve.—Probably to
the home of Lazarus, where we leave him to the night's rest

which he will so much need to prepare for the exhausting events of the next day. [This triumphal entry into Jerusalem, with the plaudits and shouts of the multitude in contrast with the vociferous cry for his blood within a few days, when the voices of these friends were completely stilled, if they did not join in the cry, "Crucify! crucify him! Let his blood be on us and on our children," is a sad commentary on the instability of man. We have many exhibitions of the fickleness of human favor and of the professions of human faith and fidelity to God. We find none more discouraging than those manifested toward Jesus in his personal ministry. The multitudes followed him in his early ministry, but when his teachings appeared hard to them they forsook him in such numbers that he turned to the twelve in a seeming spirit of discouragement and said, "Will ye also go away?" And within less than a week of this triumphal entry into Jerusalem all forsook him. One of his chosen twelve betrayed him to his enemies; the leader, to whom he had given the keys of the kingdom of heaven, denied him, and the multitude cried for his blood. Alas for the instability of man! Hosanna! praise and glory to God for his forbearance, and long-suffering, and mercy to man!]

2. THE BARREN FIG TREE CURSED
11: 12-14
(Matt. 21: 17-22)

12 And on the morrow, when they were come out from Bethany, he hun-

---

12 And on the morrow,—The day after the triumphal entry into Jerusalem, Monday, April 11, A.D. 30. [He arrives at Bethany on Friday, April 8, six days before the Passover feast. The next day a feast is made for him at the house of Lazarus and his sisters. Mary anoints his feet with ointment and wipes them with her hair. Sunday, April 10, he makes his entry into Jerusalem, numbers accompanying him who had come with him from Jericho. Others had come into the city of Jerusalem before the Passover to make ready for the feast, who heard of his coming and went out to meet him. These had come from the communities in which he had done many of his works. He seems at no time to have had a large following in Jerusalem. The influence of the priests, scribes, and Pharisees was great in Jerusalem, and hindered many from following him.

[We are now within the last six days of the life of Jesus, and during the forty days after his resurrection to his ascension. This period, in one sense, is the most important period of his earthly life. It was the closing period. He was making ready to leave the world. He had come to the world to teach men the way of life, and in these last days he anxiously and impressively delivered his last teaching. He had come to the world to suffer, to die the shameful death of the cross at the hands of those he came to save. His betrayal, trial, shameful indignities, his condemnation, his crucifixion, death, and burial, with much of his most earnest teaching, were crowded into this eventful week. These, together with his resurrection, appearance to his disciples, and commission to them were among the last of his works on earth. Never were more important truths revealed, nor lessons of greater import to man learned. The space devoted by the four writers of his life to this period of time shows the importance attached to it. Matthew gives from Chapter 21 to the close of the book. Mark from Chapter 10 to close. Luke from Chapter 19 to close, and John from Chapter 12 to close to the last few weeks of his life up to his ascension. This period stands as the culminating period of his life and of the revelation of God to man. All the Old Testament scriptures were written to prepare the world for Jesus; all foretell of his coming, and of the blessings he would bring to the world. His life would have been meaningless and a failure had he not died, rose again, and ascended to his Father. His resurrection was the crowning proof of his claims to be the Son of God.]

when they were come out from Bethany,—He and his disciples had spent the night at Bethany and were now on their way to Jerusalem. Matthew tells us that it was in "the morning," the early morning between daybreak and sunrise. Luke (21 : 38) states that the people came early in the morning to hear him.

he hungered.—Hunger was a part of his humiliation. This shows the human, not the divine, nature in Jesus. Thus he became perfect through suffering, and able to sympathize

gered.　13 And seeing a fig tree afar off having leaves, he came, if haply he might find anything thereon: and when he came to it, he found nothing but leaves; for it was not the season of figs.　14 And he answered and said

with us in every trial.　His hunger was marked, and seems to have been intense.　It was real hunger.

13 **And seeing a fig tree afar off**—In the distance.　The fig tree was one of the most common and valuable trees of Palestine (Deut. 8: 8), and was a symbol of peace and plenty (1 Kings 4: 25).　Matthew (21: 19) says: "And seeing a fig tree by the way side."　That is, in the distance, in front of him, standing by the side of the public road.

having leaves,—Its fruit begins to appear before leaves come forth.　Having leaves, appearing healthy and luxuriant was a sign it had fruit on it.　So they turned aside in search for fruit.

he came, if haply he might find anything thereon:—The meaning is, judging from its appearance, probably it had some ripe fruit on it.　We are not to suppose that the Master was ignorant of, or could not have known, the true condition of the tree, but that he intended to teach the disciples and others a needed lesson from it.

and when he came to it, he found nothing but leaves; for it was not the season of figs.—McGarvey says: "The fact it was not yet fig time made it the worse for this tree.　On this kind of tree the fruit forms before the leaves, and should be full grown before the leaves appear: so this tree, by putting on its foliage before the time of figs, was proclaiming itself superior to all the other fig trees.　This made it a striking symbol of the hypocrite, who, not content with appearing to be as good as other people, usually puts on the appearance of being a great deal better."　It was barren, and therefore worthless. This was the point Jesus was emphasizing and from which he drew his lesson.　Its signs were false, its general appearance deceptive.　It was thus an emblem of the hypocrite, and particularly of the Jewish people, with their high professions, their show of ritual and formal worship, without the fruits of righteousness.　(Jer. 2: 21; Luke 13: 6-9.)　The Jews professed to be worshipers of God—they had all the outside appearance—all the signs, but they were barren of the fruits of

unto it, No man eat fruit from thee henceforward for ever. And his disciples heard it.

---

righteousness. This was the point Jesus drove home to the Jews.

14 And he answered and said unto it, No man eat fruit from thee henceforward for ever.—There was no vindictive feeling connected with this expression, nor any implied in the word "cursedst" as used by Peter in verse 21. He called this cursing the tree. The word "curse" does not imply here anger, or malice. It means only devoting to this destruction, or this withering away.

And his disciples heard it.—He intended for them to hear it. He spoke it for their benefit. This was the sentence of a judge. The disciples were impressed by it. [Jesus came to this tree and found it had no fruit, green or ripe. It was a barren tree that bore no fruit. So it was useless. He cursed it and dried it up to teach the end of the human beings that bear no fruit to God.]

3. THE TEMPLE CLEARED
11: 15-19
(Matt. 21: 12-16; Luke 19: 45-48)

15 And they come to Jerusalem: and he entered into the temple, and

---

15 And they come to Jerusalem: and he entered into the temple,—This was on Monday, April 11. This is the second time he enters the temple since reaching Jerusalem. The first was Sunday the day of his triumphal entry. (Verse 11.) On the evening of that day he returned to Bethany and spent the night there. During this entry he only looked around in the temple and saw the abuse of it. But now he enters it for the cleansing that is here recorded. He goes into the temple, not as a worshiper, but as its Lord. The temple of God, or the temple dedicated and devoted to the service of God, was built on Mount Moriah. The first temple was built by Solomon, about 1005 years before Christ. (1 Kings 6.) He was seven years in building it. (1 Kings 6: 38.) David, his father, had contemplated the design of building it, and had prepared many materials for it, but was prevented because he had been a man of war. (1 Chron. 22: 1-9; 1 Kings 5: 5.) This temple, erected with great magnificence, remained till it was de-

began to cast out them that sold and them that bought in the temple, and overthrew the tables of the moneychangers, and the seats of them that sold the doves; 16 and he would not suffer that any man should carry a vessel

---

stroyed by the Chaldeans under Nebuchadnezzar, five hundred and eighty-four years before Christ. (2 Chron. 36: 6, 7, 19.)

and began to cast out them that sold and them that bought in the temple,—In the court of the Gentiles was the temple market, where animals, oil, wine and other things necessary for sacrifices and temple worship were sold. The excuse for allowing this traffic was that it was a convenience for those who came to worship. But what was intended at first for an accommodation became a source of gain and extortion. It was turned into a general traffic and corruption. Jesus cast out both those that sold and them that bought. Those that bought were as guilty of corrupting the temple service as those who bought and sold. From John 2: 15 it has been thought that Jesus took a whip and drove those men out. We drive cattle, not men, with whips. The whip was used on the cattle, not on the men.

and overthrew the tables of the moneychangers,—Money was required in the three following ways: (1) Freewill offerings (Mark 12: 41; Luke 21: 1); (2) to purchase materials for offerings; (3) to pay the yearly temple tax of half a shekel due from every male Jew, rich or poor. All this had to be paid in native coin called the temple shekel, which was not generally current. Jews from a distance had to change their Roman, Greek or Eastern money at the stalls of the money-changers, to obtain the coin required. This trade was diverted into fraudulent practices, which were common.

and the seats of them that sold the doves;—[After coming into the city, he went into the temple, and there (not in the holy place, but in the outer court, a space surrounding the temple proper, called "the court of the Gentiles"), he found men selling cattle and sheep, doves and pigeons, and changing money.]

16 **and he would not suffer that any man should carry a vessel through the temple.**—Jesus drove all these animals out and cast all these traffickers out of the temple, overthrew the ta-

through the temple. 17 And he taught, and said unto them, Is it not written,
[1]My house shall be called a house of prayer for all the nations? [2]but ye have
made it a den of robbers. 18 And the chief priests and the scribes heard it,

[1]Is. lvi. 7.
[2]Jer. vii. 11.

bles of the money-changers and the seats of those who sold
doves, and would not allow any man to carry a vessel through
it. He put out all corruption. Thus should churches be
cleansed and so kept.

**17 And he taught, and said unto them, Is it not written, My
house shall be called a house of prayer for all the nations?**—
"My house," as used and applied here, is the temple which
Jesus cleansed. It was God's earthly dwelling place. Instead
of making it a house of prayer they had turned it into a house
of traffic and fraud.

but ye have made it a den of robbers.—This declaration was
made by Isaiah. (Isa. 56: 6-8.) In Jeremiah's time the Jews
were very corrupt and idolatrous, and, with all their stealing,
lying, murder, adultery, and idolatry, they would go to the
temple, which was called by God's name, to stand in his presence and say they would be delivered from their enemies.
Then God asked: "Is this house, which is called by my name,
become a den of robbers in your eyes?" (Jer. 7: 8-11.) They
were the same in Jesus' day, and were likewise called by him
"thieves and robbers."

The temple then, a house of prayer and worship, was a type
of the spiritual temple of God today. "Know ye not that your
body is a temple of the Holy Spirit?" (1 Cor. 6: 19.) "If any
man destroyeth the temple of God, him shall God destroy; for
the temple of God is holy, and such are ye." (1 Cor. 3: 17.)
Through "the deceitfulness of riches" (Matt. 13: 22) the spiritual temple of God has been profaned. To make appeals to
the flesh and its appetites, pride and vanity in order to "raise
money for the church" is to defile the temple of God. It was
a corrupt and fraudulent traffic, which a corrupt and fraudulent priesthood had permitted to encroach on the worship of
God. The priesthood should have kept the corruption out.
So it is today; the eldership should watch and keep all unlawful things out of the church.

and sought how they might destroy him: for they feared him, for all the multitude was astonished at his teaching.

19 And ³every evening ⁴he went forth out of the city.

³Gr. *whenever evening came.*
⁴Some ancient authorities read *they.*

18 **And the chief priests and the scribes heard it,**—The teaching of verse 17, and the shouts of the children. (Matt. 21: 16.) They did not appreciate his popularity nor his doctrine, so they sought to kill him.

and sought how they might destroy him:—They had plotted before to kill him. (John 11: 53-57.) Then, as now, how to accomplish it bothered them. This reveals the reason of their artifices to entrap him the next day. (Verses 27-33; Ch. 12.) They realized that their own influence and unlawful gains were endangered by the works, teachings, and influence of Jesus, and they planned to put him out of the way.

for they feared him, for all the multitude was astonished at his teaching.—At its matter, manner, authority, and its accompanying exhibition of divine power. "Never man so spake." (John 7: 46.) "For he taught them as one having authority, and not as their scribes." (Matt. 7: 29.) He taught with so great power and authority that the people were awed, and were constrained to obey. Cleansing the temple was a sad comment on the priests and scribes for allowing such things. The truth today will stir up the opposing party so that it will use unfair means to kill the influence of the faithful proclaimer of that truth.

19 **And every evening he went forth out of the city.**—When his teaching and work of the day was done. Probably, he spent the nights in Bethany. (Verse 11.)

4. THE FIG TREE FOUND WITHERED
11: 20-26
(Matt. 21: 20-22)

20 And as they passed by in the morning, they saw the fig tree withered

20 **And as they passed by in the morning, they saw the fig tree withered away from the roots.**—This must have been the first time they had seen it after Jesus pronounced a curse upon it.

away from the roots. 21 And Peter calling to remembrance saith unto him,
Rabbi, behold, the fig tree which thou cursedst is withered away. 22 And
Jesus answering saith unto them, Have faith in God. 23 Verily I say unto
you, Whosoever shall say unto this mountain, Be thou taken up and cast into
the sea; and shall not doubt in his heart, but shall believe that what he saith

21 **And Peter calling to remembrance**—From this we learn that it was Peter who made the remark attributed by Matthew to the disciples as a body. (Matt. 21 : 20.)

saith unto him, Rabbi, behold, the fig tree which thou cursedst is withered away.—Matthew's record is, "How did the fig tree immediately wither away?" It seems that the disciples were surprised that the tree had died and especially so soon.

22 **and Jesus answering saith unto them, Have faith in God.**—Have a strong abiding faith and confidence in God. A strong belief that he is able to accomplish things even through the weakest and most insignificant agents and means that appear most difficult with perfect ease, as the fig tree was made to wither away by a word. Here we learn that one of the designs of cursing the fig tree as related to the disciples was to strengthen their faith and prepare them for the great trials soon to come upon them.

23 **Verily I say unto you, Whosoever shall say unto this mountain, Be thou taken up and cast into the sea; and shall not doubt in his heart,**—Faith, doubts, and fears are not located in the fleshly lobe of the breast which pumps the blood through the veins, but in the mind, the intellect. Nothing can be availed when the heart is filled with unbelief and doubt.

but shall believe that what he saith cometh to pass; he shall have it.—He must believe that what he says will come to pass. He must have no doubts. No doubt this was *literally* true, that if *they* had *the miraculous faith* they could remove the mountain as easily as Jesus withered the fig tree by a word. God could move the mountain through them as readily as to heal the sick, or raise the dead.

[No faith that will enable people to remove mountains or perform any miracle exists now. The reason is that the day of miracles has passed. "Whether there be prophecies, they shall be done away; whether there be tongues, they shall cease; whether there be knowledge (miraculous), it shall be

cometh to pass; he shall have it. 24 Therefore I say unto you, All things whatsoever ye pray and ask for, believe that ye [5]receive them, and ye shall have them. 25 And whensoever ye stand praying, forgive, if ye have aught

[5]Gr. *received.*

done away. For we know in part, and we prophesy in part; but when that which is perfect is come, that which is in part shall be done away." (1 Cor. 13: 8-10.)]

24 **Therefore I say unto you, All things whatsoever ye pray and ask for,**—True prayer, either miraculous or common, is always in harmony with God's will (1 John 5: 14), and in the name of Christ (John 14: 13).

believe that ye receive them, and ye shall have them.—This no doubt was very encouraging to his apostles to whom it was spoken. The promise of this verse in connection with prayer and faith relates to *all things whatsoever ye pray and ask for.* This faith which Jesus was pointing out to his apostles, a lesson passed upon, and drawn from, the withered fig tree, was something that they would need all through their ministry, and especially under the great trials and darkness of the week before them. This promise was evidently a *special* one, and given to the apostles in regard to working miracles. To them it was true. But it is manifest that we have no right to apply this promise to ourselves. It was designed especially for the apostles; nor have we a right to turn it from its original meaning. Miraculous faith and miracle working power were gifts of the Spirit. (1 Cor. 12: 4-11.) Common or justifying and saving faith which is common to all God's people (Tit. 1: 4) comes by hearing, and hearing by the word of God (Rom. 10: 17). The miraculous or uncommon faith which worked miracles and was a gift of the Spirit was limited to inspired men. But the common or saving faith produced by the word of God, common to all God's people, never did and never will work a miracle. This is the faith that all Christians have today. There is no uncommon or miraculous faith now. This explains why we have no miracles at present.

25 **And whensoever ye stand praying,**—[I think the word "stand" in this and other passages does not refer to the erect position or mean to stand on the feet. "Stand" has different meanings; the dictionary gives a dozen different senses. One

against any one; that your Father also who is in heaven may forgive you
your trespasses.[6]

[6]Many ancient authorities add ver. 26 *But if ye do not forgive, neither will your Father who is in heaven forgive your trespasses.* Comp. Mt. 6. 15; 18. 35.

is to stand erect on the feet, as opposed to a prone or sitting
or lying posture; the other is to be fixed and permanent, as
opposed to being in motion. Standing water is opposed to
running water. Then there is standing on the knees, as distinct from standing on the feet; to stand on the knees is the
way of standing for prayer. To stand in prayer is to stand on
the knees. I doubt if there is a single example in the Bible of
a person's fixing himself for prayer that the kneeling or prostrate position was not assumed. To stand in prayer, as used
in the Bible, does not mean to stand on the feet, but on the
knees. Example: "And Solomon stood before the altar of Jehovah in the presence of all the assembly of Israel, and spread
forth his hands toward heaven." (1 Kings 8: 22.) Then followed the prayer he prayed. This standing was upon his
knees. Verse 54 says: "And it was so, that, when Solomon
had made an end of praying all this prayer and supplication
unto Jehovah, he arose from before the altar of Jehovah, from
kneeling on his knees with his hands spread forth toward
heaven." A literal translation of Acts 7: 60, "He, Stephen
knelt down," is "standing upon the knees." The hypocrites
who stood "in the corners of the streets that they may be seen
of men" must have stood on the knees. When they stood on
their knees and stretched forth their hands toward heaven,
people saw that they prayed.]

forgive, if ye have aught against any one;—Ill will or any
cause of complaint—all must be forgiven if we expect God to
forgive us.

**that your Father also who is in heaven may forgive you
your trespasses.**—Our forgiving those who trespass against us
opens the way for God to forgive us. Until we do our part
the door of forgiveness towards us is closed.

**26 But if ye do not forgive, neither will your Father who is
in heaven forgive your trespasses.**—This verse, taken from the
Authorized Version, is omitted in the American Revised
Version. [To forgive a man is to hold him as if he were
guiltless. No one can do this until he repents. Until he

repents he is guilty. God does not forgive a man until he repents. He cannot hold him guiltless while he persists in his wrong. To overlook a wrong is not to forgive it. To forgive is to hold him guiltless. While no one can forgive in the sense of holding him guiltless until he repents, yet he must hold himself in a forgiving spirit—ready to forgive when he does repent, and anxious to show him kindness that he may be brought to repentance. God is our example in this. While he could not forgive man in his sin, he loved him, did him kindness, and gave his only begotten Son to die for him, that he might be brought to repentance. When we pray we must forgive those who turn from their trespasses, and pray that those who have not repented may repent that we may forgive them. We are to forgive others as God forgives us.]

5. CHRIST'S AUTHORITY DEMANDED
11: 27-33
(Matt. 21: 23-32; Luke 20: 1-8)

27 And they come again to Jerusalem: and as he was walking in the temple, there come to him the chief priests, and the scribes, and the elders; 28 and they said unto him, By what authority doest thou these things? or who gave thee this authority to do these things? 29 And Jesus said unto

27 **And they come again to Jerusalem:**—This was Tuesday, April 12. On Sunday the Lord entered the city officially. Monday he cleansed the temple and dried up the fig tree. On Tuesday his disciples call his attention to the withered fig tree after which he and they again enter the city.

and as he was walking in the temple, there come to him the chief priests, and the scribes, and the elders;—These three classes constitute the Sanhedrin, which was the highest civil and ecclesiastical council of the Jews.

28 **And they said unto him, By what authority doest thou these things?**—Cleansing the temple, working miracles, teaching and taking charge of things in general.

or who gave thee this authority to do these things?—As he was neither a priest nor a civil ruler, and had not been commissioned either by Caesar or the Sanhedrin, they denied that he had rightful claim to the authority which he exercised.

29 **And Jesus said unto them, I will ask of you one question, and answer me, and I will tell you by what authority I do**

them, I will ask of you one [7]question, and answer me, and I will tell you by what authority I do these things. 30 The baptism of John, was it from heaven, or from men? answer me. 31 And they reasoned with themselves, saying, If we shall say, From heaven; he will say, Why then did ye not believe him? 32 [8]But should we say, From men—they feared the people: [9]for all verily held John to be a prophet. 33 And they answered Jesus and say, We know not. And Jesus saith unto them, Neither tell I you by what authority I do these things.

[7]Gr. *word*.
[8]Or, *But shall we say, From men?*
[9]Or, *for all held John to be a prophet indeed*

these things.—They had propounded to him two questions, but Jesus proposes but one to them. He does not evade them, but he brings them face to face with a fundamental fact in this discussion, the admission of which would lead them to an irresistible conclusion that God had sent him.

30 **The baptism of John, was it from heaven, or from men? answer me.**—They saw, when they considered the question, that if they answered it they would convict themselves. This is a fundamental question. Did John act by the authority of God, or by his own? Was he a true or false prophet?

31 **And they reasoned with themselves, saying, If we shall say, From heaven; he will say, Why then did ye not believe him?**—They saw immediately that if they took this road they would be in a trap so they turned aside from it.

32 **But should we say, From men—they feared the people: for all verily held John to be a prophet.**—Luke (20: 6) says: "All the people will stone us." They really preferred this answer, and doubtless would have given it, but for fear of the people. They feared to come out against popular opinion and probably a popular tumult. So Jesus had them in a dilemma either way they went. Jesus put the matter clearly before them and left them to take either horn of the dilemma they wished.

33 **And they answered Jesus and say, We know not.**—This was a falsehood. They did know.

And Jesus saith unto them, Neither tell I you by what authority I do these things.—Since they turned his question aside unanswered, he felt he was under no obligation to answer them. He exposed their hypocrisy and at the same time made it clear to the people that his authority was the same as John's.

6. THE WICKED HUSBANDMEN
12: 1-12
(Matt. 21 : 33-46; Luke 20: 9-26)

1 And he began to speak unto them in parables. A man planted a vineyard, and set a hedge about it, and digged a pit for the winepress, and built a tower, and let it out to husbandmen, and went into another country. 2 And

1 **And he began to speak unto them in parables.**—This is a continuation of his work in the temple on Tuesday, April 12.

A man planted a vineyard,—[The vineyard is a piece of land planted in vines to produce grapes and make wine.]

and set a hedge about it,—[It is fenced, or hedged, to protect the vines from destruction by beasts, or being robbed by marauders. Sometimes a vineyard was protected by both a fence and a wall. (Isa. 5: 5.) A common way of inclosing fields in Judea was either with a fence of wood or stones, or more probably with thorns, thickset and growing.]

and digged a pit for the winepress,—[The winepress—the winevat, as it is frequently written—was the pit dug in which the juice from the presses would flow.]

and built a tower, and let it out to husbandmen,—[The tower was the building in which the husbandmen dwelt, and sometimes under it the vats for grapes were placed one above the other. In the upper one they were trod out; in the lower one was the must. From this the juice descended into the winevat in the earth. The owner let out his vineyard, with all its fixtures, to husbandmen. They were to give him his rent at the proper seasons. He took rent or tithes in the product of the vineyard. "A man planted a vineyard." This is intended to represent that God planted a people in the land of Canaan. He hedged it around by the divine order and the divine protection. We do not know that every point of the vineyard represented something of the kingdom—at least we cannot certainly point out the thing represented. The winevat is sometimes said to be the sacrifices typical of the sufferings of Jesus, and the tower the temple in which God is worshiped. He intrusted its cultivation and management to the priests and Levites, of whom the scribes were the leaders. When these were appointed, Jesus left it to their management, under the general direction of his laws and precepts.

at the season he sent to the husbandmen a [10]servant, that he might receive
from the husbandmen of the fruits of the vineyard. 3 And they took him,
and beat him, and sent him away empty. 4 And again he sent unto them
another [10]servant; and him they wounded in the head, and handled shame-

[10]Gr. *bondservant.*

They were to be accountable to God for the faithful teaching
of these laws.]

and went into another country.—Literally, in our style,
"moved away." Luke adds "for a long time," indicating that
the parable goes far back in the years in its application. We
shall fail to get all the practical good from this lesson if we
confine it to the Jewish people. *Again* God has let out his
vineyard to husbandmen, to the professed followers of Jesus
Christ. The kingdom of God is now within us. Each of us
has a part of God's vineyard possessions to cultivate. He has
fenced us round with promises and precepts, and given us the
means for fruit.

**2 And at the season he sent to the husbandmen a servant,
that he might receive from the husbandmen of the fruits of
the vineyard.**—That is, to collect the owner's part of the produce; or as we often say, "collect the rent." The servant was
sent as the agent of the master. [When the proper season for
the fruit of the vineyard came, he sent to the husbandmen a
servant to receive his portion—the rentals due him for the use
of the vineyard and the winepresses. During the Jewish dispensation God sent his prophets to warn his people of their
departure from his law, and to demand of them the obedience
and the worship that were his dues. God had especially provided for the well-being of the Jewish people. Deut. 6: 10-12.]

**3 And they took him, and beat him, and sent him away
empty.**—Three steps taken—"took," "beat," and "sent away
empty." [So these husbandmen did to the messengers sent to
receive the fruits due the Lord; so the Jewish people, often
led by the priests and Levites, did to the prophet sent of
God.]

**4 And again he sent unto them another servant; and him
they wounded in the head, and handled shamefully.**—[The
Lord sent still other servants demanding his due for his own
vineyard that he had planted, hedged, and fitted up with the
winepress. They treated this one worse than the first. One

fully. 5 And he sent another; and him they killed: and many others; beating some, and killing some. 6 He had yet one, a beloved son: he sent him last unto them, saying, They will reverence my son. 7 But those husband-

step in rebellion and sin prepares for another. Evil men and seducers wax worse and worse.]

5 And he sent another; and him they killed:—Their wickedness increases under the patience of the owner. The climax was now reached, and the rest is merely the statement of repetition of outrage and continuance of refusal to render fruit.

and many others; beating some, and killing some.—[It is probable Jesus in his different descriptions had in mind particular leading prophets that had suffered, that he pointed out to them, in the history of the Jewish nation, and that they recognized them, but which we, in our ignorance of the facts, do not recognize. Some writers attempt to point out the different ones referred to in the different verses. There is too much uncertainty in this to be of profit. Jesus charges upon them the blood of all the prophets: "Therefore, behold, I send unto you prophets, and wise men, and scribes: some of them shall ye kill and crucify; and some of them shall ye scourge in your synagogues, and persecute from city to city: that upon you may come all the righteous blood shed on the earth, from the blood of Abel the righteous unto the blood of Zachariah son of Barachiah, whom ye slew between the sanctuary and the altar. Verily I say unto you, All these things shall come upon this generation." (Matt. 23: 34-36.) That is, one step after another in the path of crime has been taken that shall in this generation culminate in the sum of all crimes—the killing of the Son of God. These former servants were typical of Jesus.]

6 He had yet one, a beloved son:—The rest were servants, literally bond servants, slaves, in the Greek, but this is his own son.

he sent him last unto them, saying, They will reverence my son.—They will so respect and reverence my son so as to heed what he says and pay the rent on the vineyard. [The Lord of the vineyard having one only and beloved son, determined to send him as a final resort, saying, "They will reverence my son." The truth here represents God as the great lord of the

men said among themselves, This is the heir; come, let us kill him, and the inheritance shall be ours. 8 And they took him, and killed him, and cast him forth out of the vineyard. 9 What therefore will the lord of the vineyard do? he will come and destroy the husbandmen, and will give the vineyard unto others. 10 Have ye not read even this scripture:

vineyard who sends his only Son to warn the people of the dishonor and shame they bring upon God, and of the ruin they bring upon themselves in refusing to honor God. He here, while portraying the depth of wickedness, the extremity to which a course of wickedness brings the people, foretells his own death speedily to happen, and he holds out the thought that these religious teachers will do it.]

7 But those husbandmen said among themselves, This is the heir;—The son of the landlord and to whom the ownership of the vineyard will finally go.

come, let us kill him, and the inheritance shall be ours.— [The husbandmen to whom he had intrusted his vineyard, when they saw the son—the heir—plotted to kill him, and then the inheritance will be theirs. As Jesus put forth higher claims to be the Son of God than others, so their bitterness against him was correspondingly greater. Very generally it is supposed that the priests and scribes persecuted Jesus because they thought him an impostor, but many of them did it with a knowledge of the truth that he was a divine personage.]

8 And they took him, and killed him, and cast him forth out of the vineyard.—Here, as in verse 3, three steps are taken. Luke says: "And they cast him forth out of the vineyard, and killed him." So also Matthew and Luke give the facts and not the order in which they occurred. [The priests and scribes were responsible for the death of Jesus. They urged others to crucify him, and were as responsible for his death as if they had done it with their own hands. "Cast him forth out of the vineyard." They rejected him and his teaching as having no place in the dominion of God.]

9 What therefore will the lord of the vineyard do?—The design of this question was that they might condemn themselves, and admit the justice of the punishment that was soon coming upon them.

he will come and destroy the husbandmen, and will give the vineyard unto others.—[In view of this repeated rebellion,

¹The stone which the builders rejected,
The same was made the head of the corner ;

¹Ps. cxviii. 22 f.

these successive steps in rebellion, each increasing in heinousness against the Lord of the vineyard, what shall he do? The answer to that question reveals what God will do to those who have departed from his laws, set aside his appointments, and fought against his servants throughout the Jewish dispensation. He will come and destroy the husbandmen, and give the vineyard unto others. Matthew (21: 41) says: "He will miserably destroy those miserable men, and will let out the vineyard unto other husbandmen, who shall render him the fruits in their seasons." In its application God will destroy these husbandmen—the religious teachers of the Jewish people—who have disobeyed him and led the people to sin, and will deliver his vineyard to other husbandmen who will be more faithful and true to him. Their destruction prefigured the more terrible destruction that awaits those who reject Christ.]

10 **Have ye not read even this scripture: The stone which the builders rejected, the same was made the head of the corner;**—This and the next verse is a quotation from Psalm 118: 22. [This was first spoken of David, who was rejected of his parents, or passed over, but who was chosen of God, and became the builder of the kingdom of Judah. It is said to be based upon a fact that when the temple of Solomon was being built, there was an unshapely stone that was rejected of the builders as unfitted for service until they were about completing the building, and it was seen that this stone would so fit in the main arch as to be a key that would hold in position and give strength to the whole arch. Whether this is true or not, Jesus was rejected by the elders and the chief priests (his forerunners and types were rejected) ; yet he became the head of the corner—the central truth of the whole system of the divine government. The whole Jewish system is meaningless without Christ as the end and culmination of it. It is also the great central truth of the Christian system. The Jewish system is a type in its true development of the Christian system, and so this parable finds its more complete fulfillment in the

11 This was from the Lord,
And it is marvellous in our eyes? 12 And they sought to lay hold on him; and they feared the multitude; for they perceived that he spake the parable against them: and they left him, and went away.

Christian system than in the Jewish; and it is true that the religious teachers more than others pervert the will of God, and reject his divine authority by substituting ways of their own for the things commanded by God and sealed with his blood. His spiritual body now exists in which his laws, institutions, and commandments, sealed by his blood, are to be observed. When men turn from these laws sealed by his blood, and substitute other appointments for them, they as much reject Christ as the fountain as did the priests and elders his fleshly person. It is as true now as it ever was that men may reject Christ and turn from his laws while professing to follow him, and yet he is the only foundation of the true kingdom of God. To him every tongue shall confess and every knee bow.]

11 **This was from the Lord, And it is marvellous in our eyes?**—[The so ordering things that the stone which was rejected of the leaders and teachers became the head of the corner was of God's overruling and controlling, and the whole development is a marvel and a wonder to the world. It is yet, the strong and wise provisions of men must come to naught. God chose the foolish things of the world, that he might put to shame them that are wise; and God chose the weak things of the world, that he might put to shame things that are strong. "And the base things of the world, and the things that are despised, did God choose, yea and the things that are not, that he might bring to nought the things that are."]

12 **And they sought to lay hold on him;**—This expresses the effect the parable had upon them.

and they feared the multitude;—They saw the hour was not auspicious. There were too many of the enthusiastic Galileans present.

for they perceived that he spake the parable against them: and they left him, and went away.—[The scribes and Pharisees saw it was aimed at them as the leaders and teachers of the people, who misled them, who persecuted the servants of

God, and who were then fierce and bitter against him, anxious
to destroy him, but fearing the people who regarded him as a
prophet. The people most anxious to persecute are the most
cowardly.]

7. TRIBUTE TO CAESAR
12: 13-17
(Matt. 22: 15-22; Luke 20: 20-26)

13 And they send unto him certain of the Pharisees and of the Herodians,
that they might catch him in talk. 14 And when they were come, they say
unto him, Teacher, we know that thou art true, and carest not for any one;

13 **And they send unto him certain of the Pharisees and of
the Herodians,**—The Pharisees counseled together how they
might entangle him in his talk. Matthew (22: 15, 16) says:
"They send to him their disciples, with the Herodians." The
rulers did not go themselves, but sent with the Herodians
some of their disciples. Luke (20: 20) says: "Sent forth
spies." The work of a detective whose purpose is to entangle a bad man in his speech for the sake of exposing him is
not an enviable one; but to lay snares for a good man is diabolical. Yet this is exactly what the Pharisees deliberately
took counsel to do. Here enemies meet in their common
hatred of Jesus.

that they might catch him in talk.—This was the work the
spies were sent to do. The object was to ensnare or entrap
him in his answer to their question in the next verse which
they hoped he would answer *yes* or *no*. They thought that in
his answer he must fatally involve himself in his relations either to the government or the people. They are trying him
now in a way which they had never before attempted.
Namely, by complimenting him until they induced him to
utter sentences which they would almost suggest.

14 **And when they were come, they say unto him, Teacher,
we know that thou art true,**—They express the truth in a hypocritical compliment, not believed by them, but artfully said,
as compliments often are, to conceal their true design.

and carest not for any one;—That is, thou art an independent teacher, speaking your sentiments without regard to the
fear or favor of man. This was true, and probably they believed this.

for thou regardest not the person of men, but of a truth teachest the way of God: Is it lawful to give tribute unto Caesar, or not? 15 Shall we give, or shall we not give? But he, knowing their hypocrisy, said unto them, Why make ye trial of me? bring me a ²denarius, that I may see it. 16 And they

²See marginal note on ch. 6. 37.

for thou regardest not the person of men,—That is, you are not influenced by rank or position, not even by Caesar himself, in your decisions, but are perfectly impartial.

but of a truth teachest the way of God:—The way of God was taught and mapped out for men to walk in without fear or favor—neither adding to nor taking from.

Is it lawful to give tribute unto Caesar,—The family name of Julius Caesar, the first Roman emperor, and applied to his successors. The name "Caesar," after the time of Julius Caesar, became common to all the emperors, as Pharaoh was the common name of all the kings of Egypt. Now it is applied to the authorities of any civil government, national, state or city.

or not?—They worded the question, as they thought, so he would be forced to reply "yes" or "no." They were anxious for him to answer in the negative for then they would "deliver him up to the rule and to the authority of the governor" as a seditious person. (Luke 20: 20.)

15 **Shall we give, or shall we not give?**—This completes the question. They thought they had brought him to a point where he would be forced to answer as a rebel against Caesar, or a traitor to God, whose Son he claimed to be. But in this, as in all other attempts to ensnare him, Jesus in few words put them to flight.

But he, knowing their hypocrisy,—Being divine, Jesus had power to see and read their wicked thoughts, and therefore could not be deceived. This proves he was omniscient. No mere man has the power of discerning the motives of others.

said unto them, Why make ye trial of me?—That is, why try to lead me into a snare by an insidious question? As deeply as they had laid their wicked plot, and cunningly as they had framed and put their question, they could not keep from knowing, from Jesus' first word of his reply, that he saw through it all—that he detected their evil design and their hypocrisy.

brought it. And he saith unto them, Whose is this image and superscription? And they said unto him, Caesar's. 17 And Jesus said unto them, Render unto Caesar the things that are Caesar's, and unto God the things that are God's. And they marvelled greatly at him.

bring me a denarius,—A penny, a Roman silver coin in circulation at that time worth about fifteen cents. Matthew (22: 19) says: "Show me the tribute money." The money in which the tribute was paid. The tribute for the temple service was paid in the Jewish shekel; that for the Roman government in foreign coin.

that I may see it.—He now teaches an object lesson. He wishes them to see it with their natural eye as well as to hear it in words.

16 **And they brought it. And he saith unto them, Whose is this image and superscription?**—It is his time now to ask questions and expect replies. He is now putting them in the trap they set for him, and he does it with one simple question.

And they said unto him, Caesar's.—They give the correct answer. Both the coin and the answer show they were submitting to Caesar's government, and enjoying his protection.

17 **And Jesus said unto them, Render unto Caesar the things that are Caesar's,**—Give to Caesar (the civil government under which you live) all that is due him—what rightfully belongs to him. If you are living under his domain and receiving his protection, pay the taxes he demands—pay him fully for protecting you, so long as you do not violate any divine obligation. Caesar's image and name on the piece of money proved that it was his. It was therefore proper and right to give it back to him, when he demanded it. The answer is general, and teaches that taxes are to be paid by the subject receiving protection.

and unto God the things that are God's.—While paying tribute to Caesar do not forget that you are obligated to God also—that you must give to God what he claims. He must come first. Paul says: "Ye were bought with a price; glorify God therefore in your body." (1 Cor. 6: 20.) He does not leave us to guess what belongs to God. The coin containing the image and superscription of Caesar belonged to Caesar; man is the coinage, and bears the image of God (Gen. 1:

27; 9: 6; Acts 17: 29; James 3: 9), especially the Christian man. Therefore the body and soul of the Christian belong to God and ought to be rendered unto him.

During the World War when young Christian men asked me if it was right for them to go to war and take guns and slaughter their fellow men, I cited them to what the Lord said: "Thou shalt not kill," "do good for evil," and do to others as you would have them do to you. I said in this case, it is your duty to obey the Lord and leave the result with him. You ought to obey the powers that be, until they conflict with God's law. When they do, then "obey God rather than men." (Acts 5: 29.)

The Christian's relation to human government is plain. Wherefore ye must needs be in subjection, not only because of the wrath, but also for conscience's sake. (Rom. 13: 5.) Christians are to "pay tribute" to human government and "render to all their dues: tribute to whom tribute is due; custom to whom custom; fear to whom fear; honor to whom honor." (Rom. 13: 6, 7.) The relationship of Christians to human governments is that of respectful submission, not of aggression. They must submit to "the powers that be." In no case are Christians justifiable in disobeying these powers, except only when civil governments require them to do that which God forbids, and forbid Christians doing that which God requires them to do. In such cases where human government or authority conflicts with God's authority, then, as Peter and John declare, we must obey God rather than men, or human authority, and take the consequences. (Acts 4: 19, 20; 5: 29.) It matters not to the Christian whether a ruler is a good man or a bad man, the Christian is to respect and obey all who are in authority, with the exception or limitation which has been mentioned. Christians are to obey "for the Lord's sake." This is the best motive that can be had by any one. Loyalty to Christ calls upon us to respect human authority, which God has ordained. It matters not whether the government be a monarchy, kingdom, republic, or democracy; it is all the same to a Christian who is to submit to "the powers that be." Neither does it matter to the Christian whether the ruler is a tyrant, a wicked man, or a good man; respectful obedience is to be given to the ruler by all Christians "for the Lord's sake." We are not to obey rulers because they are good men, nor refuse to obey them because they are bad men; neither are we to obey a law because it meets with our approval or disobey it because it does not meet with our approval. Our attitude is to be that of respectful submission "for the Lord's sake."

And they marvelled greatly at him.—They had been defeated in their attempt. His reply confounded both parties, and wholly prevented the use which they intended to make of it.

8. QUESTION ABOUT THE RESURRECTION
12: 18-27
(Matt: 22: 23-33; Luke 20: 27-40)

18 And there come unto him Sadducees, who say that there is no resurrection; and they asked him, saying, 19 Teacher, Moses wrote unto us, [3]If a man's brother die, and leave a wife behind him, and leave no child, that

[3]Dt. xxv. 5.

---

18 And there come unto him—Matthew (22: 23) says: "On that day." That is, the same day that Jesus put to flight the Pharisees and Herodians. They now try another plan by a different party.

Sadducees, who say that there is no resurrection;—The Sadducees were a religious sect which originated about B.C. 260. Some suppose that Zadok was founder of the sect. They were opposed to the Pharisees, and rightly rejected tradition; but denied the resurrection and the existence of angels and spirits. (Acts 23: 8.) As a sect they disappeared from history after the first century. The Jews were divided into three principal sects, the Pharisees, the Sadducees, and the Essenes. Only once previous to this time did the Sadducees engage in active opposition to Jesus. (Matt. 16: 1.)

and they asked him, saying,—The question follows in next verses.

19 Teacher, Moses wrote unto us, If a man's brother die, and leave a wife behind him, and leave no child, that his brother should take his wife, and raise up seed unto his brother.—That is, the children would be recognized in the genealogy of the deceased brother; or to all civil purposes,

his brother should take his wife, and raise up seed unto his brother. 20 There were seven brethren: and the first took a wife, and dying left no seed; 21 and the second took her, and died, leaving no seed behind him; and the third likewise: 22 and the seven left no seed. Last of all the woman also died. 23 In the resurrection whose wife shall she be of them? for the seven had her to wife. 24 Jesus said unto them, Is it not for this cause that ye err, that ye know not the scriptures, nor the power of God? 25 For when they shall rise from the dead, they neither marry, nor are given in marriage; but are as angels in heaven. 26 But as touching the dead, that they are raised; have ye not read in the book of Moses, in *the place concerning* the Bush, how God spake unto him, saying, ⁴I *am* the God of Abraham, and the God

⁴Ex. iii. 6.

---

would be recognized as his. The custom of taking a deceased brother's wife and raising up children unto his brother was older than the law that gave it divine sanction. It was observed in the family of Jacob long before the giving of the law. (Gen. 38: 6-11.)

20-23 There were seven brethren: and the first took a wife, and dying left no seed; and the second took her, and died, leaving no seed behind him; and the third likewise: and the seven left no seed. Last of all the woman also died. In the resurrection whose wife shall she be of them? for the seven had her to wife.—Having cited the law, they now state the case and we may suppose as difficult as possible.

24 Jesus said unto them, Is it not for this cause that ye err, that ye know not the scriptures, nor the power of God?—As usual he answers them in a way they were not expecting. He strikes their argument in its weak point—its assumption that marriage would exist after the resurrection.

25 For when they shall rise from the dead, they neither marry, nor are given in marriage; but are as angels in heaven. —Had they known the scripture doctrine of the resurrection, they would have known that it did not involve the continuance of marriage; and had they known the power of God, they would have known that he could raise the saints without those carnal propensities on which marriage is based.

26 But as touching the dead, that they are raised;—Having overthrown the objection of the Sadducees, Jesus now furnishes a proof of the resurrection.

have ye not read in the book of Moses, in the place concerning the Bush, how God spake unto him, saying, I am the God of Abraham, and the God of Isaac, and the God of Jacob?—

of Isaac, and the God of Jacob? **27** He is not the God of the dead, but of the living: ye do greatly err.

The burning bush. (Ex. 3: 2.) The passage he quotes is Ex. 3: 6-15. These three had been long dead when Moses wrote this: Abraham 329 years; Isaac 224 years; and Jacob 198 years. Yet God was still their God. They must, therefore, be still somewhere living; for God is not the God of the dead, but of the living.

27 He is not the God of the dead,—In the sense of *extinct,* as the Sadducees used the word *dead.* God is not the God of the non-existent. He can bear no relation to a nonentity.

but of the living :—That is, he does not rule over those who are *extinct* or *annihilated,* but he is the God only of those who have an existence. Luke (20: 38) says: "All live unto him." That is, all the righteous dead; all of whom he can be properly called their God live unto him. This proves that Abraham, Isaac, and Jacob had an existence then, or that their souls were alive. This the Sadducees denied. (Acts 23: 8.) And this was the main point in dispute. If this was admitted —if there was a state of rewards and punishments—then it would easily follow that the bodies of the dead would be raised. In the Bible the resurrection has reference to the raising of the dead body. The soul is never referred to as being resurrected.

ye do greatly err.—Matthew (22: 33) says: "They were astonished at his teaching." Their astonishment arose from two circumstances: first, that Jesus was at all able to answer the boasted objection of the Sadducees; and second that he found the answers in the writings of Moses, where it was supposed then, and has been supposed since, that the doctrine of the future life is not taught. But Jesus says it is, and when he puts his sanction on a thing, it is final with all who have faith in him.

9. THE GREAT COMMANDMENT
12: 28-34
(Matt. 22: 34-40)

28 And one of the scribes came, and heard them questioning together, and

28 And one of the scribes came,—Matthew (22: 35) says: "A lawyer." He was both a scribe and lawyer.

knowing that he had answered them well, asked him, What commandment is
the first of all? 29 Jesus answered, The first is, [5]Hear, O Israel; [6]The Lord

[5]Dt. vi. 4 ff.
[6]Or, *The Lord is our God; the Lord is one*

and heard them questioning together,—The Sadducees and
Pharisees were consulting and planning together after the defeat of the Sadducees and the lawyer heard them.

and knowing that he had answered them well,—This was
the decision of the lawyer relative to the answer given by
Jesus to the Sadducees.

asked him, What commandment is the first of all?—This
point was often disputed by the doctors of the law, and the
scribe's question was to further test Jesus' knowledge of the
law.   The Pharisees had been trying to entrap Jesus, and he
had replied successfully to them in such a way as to silence
them.   The Pharisees, it seems, had given up the contest in
regard to the miracles of Jesus, and now they hoped to defeat
him in a trial of his knowledge.   The purpose of the lawyer,
as the nature of his question implies, was not to incite Jesus
to evil, but to *test* his knowledge of the law.   All commandments of God are, in one sense, equally binding, and the spirit
of obedience is tested by all: but some relate to matters intrin-
sically more important.   Those commandments are greatest
which are most spiritual, most opposed to selfishness, most
comprehensive.   Duty to God is in itself the highest duty, and
comprehends all other duties.

**29 Jesus answered, The first is, Hear, O Israel; The Lord
our God, the Lord is one**:—"The words in which every Israelite, each morning, confessed his faith in Jehovah." (Geikie.)
These words are found in Deuteronomy (6: 4).   They announce the great foundation truth of the whole theocratic system. The unity, the aloneness of God, and the identification
of Jehovah or Jahveh as that one God, is the basis upon which
it is all built, and this truth permeates its entire history.   Its
maintenance distinguished Israel from all the nations round in
the days of Israel's theocratic purity; its disregard brought all
Israel's wars upon it.   Christ well quotes it as the introduction of his answer, although in different words from its form
in the body of the commandments.   It is, however, an exact
quotation from Deuteronomy.

our God, the Lord is one: 30 and thou shalt love the Lord thy God [7]with all
thy heart, and [7]with all thy soul, and [7]with all thy mind, and [7]with all thy
strength. 31 The second is this, [8]Thou shalt love thy neighbor as thyself.

[7]Gr. *from*
[8]Lev. xix. 18.

30 and thou shalt love the Lord thy God—These words also
are not in either of the formal lists of the Decalogue (Ex. 20;
Deut. 5); but are a quotation from Deut. 6: 5. As the first
words present the great underlying truths with regard to
Deity, so these present what should be the attitude of the
heart, the entire man in fact, toward Jehovah. This forbids
their loving any idol. They could not bow down before an
idol.

**with all thy heart, and with all thy soul, and with all thy
mind, and with all thy strength.**—Love to God must fill the
whole heart, the entire inner sphere in which all the working
of the personal consciousness originates, the whole soul, the
whole faculty of feeling and desire, and the whole understanding, all the powers of thought and will, and must determine
their operation. It is called "the great and first," as the sequel
shows (verse 40), not because, apart from all others it is
great, but because in observing it all others are observed.

**31 The second is this, Thou shalt love thy neighbor as thy-
self.**—This is a quotation from Lev. 19: 18. Even the love of
God itself is to manifest and actualize itself by love to man—
more generally, by love to all men, more particularly by
brotherly love. There is no express command in scripture for
a man to love himself, because the light of nature directs, and
the law of nature binds and moves every man to do so. God
has put a principle of self-love and self-preservation into all
his creatures, but especially in man. Note that your neighbors and yourself are to be loved by you in the same degree,
and by the same standard, even if your neighbor is your
enemy. *You* have two parties to love and in loving your
neighbor you are to apply to him the degree and standard you
apply to yourself. You cannot apply one standard or degree
to your neighbor and a different one to yourself and meet
God's approval. It is another expression of the golden rule:
"Whatsoever ye would that men should do unto you, even so
do ye also unto them: for this is the law and the prophets."

There is none other commandment greater than these. 32 And the scribe
said unto him, Of a truth, Teacher, thou hast well said that he is one; and
there is none other but he: 33 and to love him with all the heart, and with
all the understanding, and with all the strength, and to love his neighbor as
himself, is much more than all whole burnt-offerings and sacrifices. 34 And

---

If you love your neighbor as yourself, you apply the commandments in your conduct toward him as scrupulously as
you wish him to apply them to you. You must not injure him
or lie to him, or steal from him, or covet his success; you
must treat him exactly as you in his place wish to be treated
or ought to be treatd by him. The same principle of love underlies both the first and second great commandments.

There is none other commandment greater than these.—For
the reason, these embrace and include all others. When love
is working as it should, every cog in the spiritual machine is
moving. None greater because a part cannot be greater than
the whole, for every commandment is included in these.

**32 And the scribe said unto him, Of a truth, Teacher, thou
hast well said that he is one; and there is none other but he:**
—None of the schools of thought among the Jews could deny
this proposition without laying the axe at the root of the
whole system of the law and revelation. The acknowledgment of the one true God must accompany all right views of
his law.

**33 and to love him with all the heart, and with all the un-
derstanding, and with all the strength,**—Though the order of
the departments of loving is a little different in the scribe's
answer, and there is a change in the wording, yet the idea is
essentially the same, the complete consecration of every faculty and power in his love.

**and to love his neighbor as himself, is much more than all
whole burnt-offerings and sacrifices.**—When we remember the
legalism of the whole Rabbinical fraternity, the stress they
had put upon the minutest acts in and for themselves, the
practices which had led Jesus to charge them with tithing garden herbs while neglecting judgment, mercy and truth, we
must realize the immense stride this man took in this explicit
endorsement of Jesus. The form in which he states it was
especially calculated to displease his companions, and bears

when Jesus saw that he answered discreetly, he said unto him, Thou art not far from the kingdom of God. And no man after that durst ask him any question.

testimony to the enthusiasm which must have filled his heart at the moment.

34 And when Jesus saw that he answered discreetly, he said unto him, Thou art not far from the kingdom of God.—One's proximity to the kingdom of God is not an estimate of feet or inches, but in the preparation and purpose of the heart. The scribe, by virtue of his approval of this discreet classification of God's law, gave evidence of his nearness to the kingdom of God; while some of his associates (verses 36-40) were like those Ephesians, who, while walking according to the course of the world, were "afar off."

And no man after that durst ask him any question.—The result of all their questioning had been to silence the incorrigible and convince the teachable, and it was a losing business to his enemies. Christ becomes the questioner and the accuser, and the drama rushes on to its tragic close. The scribe was *near* the kingdom, he needed another step to get into it, the unreserved committal of himself to follow Jesus in love. We know not whether he took this step, but we know that it will be madness for us to stop at the point where he leaves us. To acknowledge is to be *near,* the experience and practice is to be *in.* Where are you? This closes the wicked attacks to which Jesus was subject on Tuesday of the Passion Week in the temple. All his opposers are silenced, and the last one who represented them is almost brought into the number of disciples.

10. THE LORDSHIP OF THE CHRIST
12: 35-37
(Matt. 22: 41-46; Luke 20: 41-44)

35 And Jesus answered and said, as he taught in the temple, How say the

35 And Jesus answered and said, as he taught in the temple,—He continues teaching in the temple. The attempts of his enemies to ensnare him did not unnerve him in the least. He kept cool and levelheaded through it all. As soon as his victory was won, he immediately proceeded with his regular teaching.

scribes that the Christ is the son of David?   36 David himself said in the
Holy Spirit,

> [9]The Lord said unto my Lord,
> Sit thou on my right hand,
> Till I make thine enemies [1]the footstool of thy feet.

37 David himself calleth him Lord; and whence is he his son?   And [2]the
common people heard him gladly.

[9]Ps. cx. 1.
[1]Some ancient authorities read *underneath thy feet.*
[2]Or, *the great multitude*

How say the scribes that the Christ is the son of David?—
Up to this time Jesus had been acting on the defensive; but
now he turns to the offensive and convicts the scribes and
Pharisees with ignorance and false notions of the Messiah,
which opens the way for his warning and denunciations
against them in verses 38-40. Matthew (22: 41, 42) says:
"now while the Pharisees were gathered together, Jesus asked
them a question saying, What think ye of the Christ? whose
son is he? They say unto him, *The son* of David." Their reply
was correct.

36 David himself said in the Holy Spirit,—David was under
the influence and guidance of the Holy Spirit. Luke (20: 42)
says: "David himself saith in the book of Psalms," which, in
connection with the accounts here and in Matthew, is proof of
the inspiration of that book and that Jesus so recognized it.
The Psalm from which Jesus quotes is 110: 1.

The Lord said unto my Lord,—The Messiah, as the Jews
understood the words to refer, and as our Savior applied
them. Thus David spoke of the Messiah as his Lord, his superior and sovereign.

Sit thou on my right hand,—On the throne beside me, not
merely as a position of honor, but as a partner of my sover-
eignty and power. (Psalm 110: 2, 3; Mark 10: 37.)

Till I make thine enemies the footstool of thy feet.—A stool
for thy feet. This implies their utter defeat and their most
abject subjugation. The foot was often put on the neck of the
vanquished. (Josh. 10: 24, 25; Psalm 47: 3.)

**37 David himself calleth him Lord; and whence is he his
son?**—If David acknowledged him as his superior and sovereign, from what source—by what means is he his son, and
hence his inferior? The question could only be answered by
acknowledging both the divinity and humanity of Christ. It is

thus answered in Rom. 1: 3, 4. But the Jews, especially the scribes and Pharisees, in their worldly views of the Messiah, had lost sight of his divinity, and only held to his humanity as a royal descendant of David. If they had understood the true character of the Christ, they could have answered by saying, "As man, he is David's son; but as God, David's Lord." He was divine as well as human and had an existence at the time of David, and was his Lord and Master.

And the common people heard him gladly.—As a rule all except the elders, chief priests, lawyers and scribes heard the teaching of Jesus gladly. The success of our Lord in his teaching was chiefly among the common or the poorer class of people. The rich and the great were too proud to listen to his instructions and humble themselves to his claims. So it is now. The chief success of the gospel is there, and there it pours down its chief blessings. This is not the fact of the gospel. It would bless the rich and the great as well as the poor, if they came with like humble hearts. God makes no distinction of men in conferring his favors; and wherever there is a poor, contrite, and humble spirit—be it clothed in rags or in purple—be it on a throne or a dunghill—there he confers the blessings of salvation.

11. DENUNCIATION OF THE SCRIBES
12: 38-40
(Matt. 23; Luke 22: 45-47)

38 And in his teaching he said, Beware of the scribes, who desire to walk in long robes, and *to have* salutations in the marketplaces, 39 and chief seats

---

38 **And in his teaching he said, Beware of the scribes,**—Be on your guard against the teaching of the scribes. Be cautious about hearing and following these learned men of the Jews.

who desire—This states their uppermost passion—their love and desire of display and honor "to be seen of men."

to walk—Around displaying themselves as much as possible "to be seen of men." (Matt. 23: 5.)

in long robes,—This describes their dress.

and to have salutations—Complimentary greetings. Marks of particular respect shown them in public places.

in the synagogues, and chief places at feasts: 40 they that devour widows'

in the marketplaces,—Places where they bought and sold— places where multitudes of people were assembled together.

39 and chief seats in the synagogues,—The seats usually occupied by the elders of the synagogues, near the pulpit. They loved and desired places of distinctions. (Matt. 4 : 23.)

and chief places at feasts:—The most honorable positions at the table during public feasts. Jesus forbade his followers to seek such places or titles of distinction. (Matt. 23 : 7, 8.)

The command here is an express command to his disciples not to receive such a title of distinction. They were not to covet it; they were not to seek it; they were not to do anything that implied a wish or a willingness that it should be appended to their names. Everything which would tend to make a distinction among them, or destroy their parity; everything which would lead the world to suppose that there were ranks and grades among them as servants, they were to avoid. It is to be observed that the command is that they were not to receive the title, "Be not ye called Rabbi." The Savior did not forbid them giving the title to others, not disciples, when it was customary or not regarded as improper (Acts 26 : 25); but they were not to receive it. It was to be unknown among them. This title corresponds with the title "Doctor of Divinity," and other degrees as applied to preachers of the gospel; and so far as I can see, the spirit of the Savior's command is violated by the reception of such a title or titles as it would have been by their being called Rabbi. It is a literary distinction. It does not appropriately pertain to office. It makes a distinction among preachers. It tends to engender pride, and a sense of superiority in those who obtain it; and envy and a sense of inferiority in those who do not; and the whole spirit and tendency of it is contrary to the "simplicity and the purity that is toward Christ."

40 they that devour widows' houses,—Here our Savior points out other evil traits of character of the scribes. These scribes devoured the families of widows, or the means of supporting their families. What means they used to accomplish this evil work, we may not fully know. Probably they did it under the pretense of counseling them in the knowledge

houses, ⁸and for a pretence make long prayers; these shall receive greater condemnation.

⁸Or, *even while for a pretence they make*

of law and in the management of their estates. In some way they took advantage of these poor women and robbed them of their means of support.

and for a pretence make long prayers;—As a pretext. They used religion, making a mask of it, to gain the confidence of people so they could rob even the most helpless.

these shall receive greater condemnation.—As the prayers were made for deception and for no other purpose, and made long in order to more effectually accomplish the evil purpose, they only added to the wickedness which they were designed to conceal. For the double sin of hypocrisy and fraudulent injustice, they should meet a terrible doom. The damnation was greater because the wickedness was greater. So it must ever be with men who use the cloak of religion to serve the devil in.

12. THE WIDOW'S MITE
12: 41-44
(Luke 21: 1-4)

41 And he sat down over against the treasury, and beheld how the multitude cast ⁴money into the treasury: and many that were rich cast in much. 42 And there came ⁵a poor widow, and she cast in two mites, which make a

⁴Gr. *brass.*
⁵Gr. *one.*

41 And he sat down over against the treasury,—The treasury was the receptacle into which the people deposited the contributions which the law of Moses required all of them to bring when they came up to the annual festivals. (Deut. 16: 16, 17.)

and beheld how the multitude cast money into the treasury:—Jesus sat opposite to and in full sight of the treasury, where he could see all who contributed.

and many that were rich cast in much.—"Many," not all, of the more wealthy contributed freely.

42 And there came a poor widow,—Alone and lonely, probably poorly dressed. She attracts attention of observers—probably calling forth sympathy from some; but Jesus regards

farthing. 43 And he called unto him his disciples, and said unto them, Verily I say unto you, This poor widow cast in more than all they that are
casting into the treasury: 44 for they all did cast in of their superfluity; but
she of her want did cast in all that she had, *even* all her living.

---

her with admiration. Perhaps she was one of those widows
some hypocritical scribe had robbed.

and she cast in two mites,—A small coin made of brass, the
smallest in use among the Jews.

which make a farthing.—The two mites made a farthing.
The mite was much less than any coin we have, as the farthing was less than an English farthing. It was worth about
three mills and a half, or one-third of a cent.

**43 And he called unto him his disciples, and said unto them,
Verily I say unto you, This poor widow cast in more than all
they that are casting into the treasury:**—That is, more in proportion to her means, and therefore more than was acceptable
to God. It does not mean more in value than all which
the others had put in, but it showed more love to the
sacred cause, more self-denial, and more sincerity in what she
did. This is the rule by which the Lord will reward us. (2
Cor. 8: 12.) It was in the widow's case a freewill offering.
How it was in the case of the others cannot be so decidedly
known; for some doubtless from proper motives cast in their
gifts. Yet from the character of the leading classes, very
justly represented by the scribes (verses 38-40), it may be correctly presumed that a majority of those casting in much did
it not so much from love to God as from love of human praise.

44 for they all did cast in of their superfluity;—Of their su-
perfluous store. They have given what they did not need.
They could afford it as well as not; and in doing it they have
shown no self-denial.

but she of her want—Of her poverty—out of her deficiency;
while the others gave out of their excess, superabundance—
their overflow.

did cast in all that she had, even all her living.—All that she
had on which to live. She trusted in God to supply her
wants, and devoted her scanty property entirely to him. This
poor widow gave all the money she had at that time, and all
that she had to live upon, at least for that day. Luke (21: 4)

says: "All the living that she had," would fast in order to give. She felt what she gave, they did not; to her it was real self-denial, but not to them. In love she devoted all to God, strong faith in his providential care. There are two ways in which to estimate the value of contributions; first with reference to the benevolent object on which the money is to be expended; and second, with reference to the spiritual good resulting to the contributor. Estimated according to the former standard, the larger gifts of the rich were the more valuable, because they would accomplish more in feeding the poor and in providing for the expenses of the temple. But from the latter point of view, the gift of the widow was greater than all, because she actually gave more in proportion to her ability, and secured to herself a great blessing at the hand of God. She did voluntarily what Jesus had vainly commanded the rich young ruler to do; though poor herself, she gave her all. She did this, too, when she had only her widow's hands with which to earn more; but he had refused though he had the strength and ingenuity of young manhood to guard him against future want. Many improperly apply the term, widow's mite, to their trifling contributions. To give the widow's mite, one must give all his living.

There are none who may not in this way show their love to the cause of Christ. The time to *begin* to be benevolent and to do good is in early life—in childhood. (Eccles. 12: 1.) It is every Christian man's duty to observe, not how *much* to give, but how much compared with what he has and what is the *motive* with which it is done. But few practice self-denial. Most givers give of their abundance—that is, what they can spare without feeling it. Among the large number who give, how few deny themselves of *one* comfort, even the least, that they may advance the kingdom of God!

SECTION THREE

THE DESTRUCTION OF THE TEMPLE FORETOLD
13: 1-37

1. OCCASION OF THE PREDICTION
13: 1-4
(Matt. 24: 1-3; Luke 21: 5-7)

1 And as he went forth out of the temple, one of his disciples saith unto

We approach this chapter sensitive of the fact that it is one of the most important, and yet difficult chapters to understand in the New Testament. In it we have a remarkable prophetic discourse by our Lord which has been variously explained by intelligent and well informed men. We therefore approach it cautiously and prayerfully.

1 **And as he went forth out of the temple,**—Jesus, having closed his teaching to the people in the temple, leaves it, and continues teaching his disciples privately. Matthew (24: 1) says: "Jesus went out from the temple." It was his final departure, late in the evening of Tuesday, April 12, that day of wonderful endurance, of continued intellectual labor and conflict, of grand revelations and overwhelming denunciation, of which the evangelists have given us fuller accounts than any other day in his life, unless it be that of his crucifixion. It is not merely a local and temporary departure from the temple that is meant. As the Lord of the temple, the temple had rejected him, in the person of those who had legal authority in it. That was the fall of the temple; and it was then decided that it was no more than a den of robbers, in which all—the Messiah, and the Spirit, and the hope of the Gentiles, and the blessing of Israel—were, as it were murdered. He takes farewell of the temple; and from that time forward it became no better than a hall of desolation, a dreary and forsaken ruin. Sad the day for us when Jesus leaves *our* temple, and his voice is no longer heard pleading in our souls. He goes not until our continued rejection drives him forth. He cleansed the temple of its physical desecraters, but he could not then cleanse it of spiritual wickedness, for the reason those in authority would not repent and turn to God.

him, Teacher, behold, what manner of stones and what manner of buildings!
2 And Jesus said unto him, Seest thou these great buildings? there shall not
be left here one stone upon another, which shall not be thrown down.
3 And as he sat on the mount of Olives over against the temple, Peter and

one of his disciples saith unto him,—Matthew says generally, "his disciples." Luke is still more indefinite, "some." We know not who he was, and it is useless to conjecture.

Teacher, behold, what manner of stones and what manner of buildings!—The disciples who were probably, for the most part, from Galilee, and unaccustomed to behold such magnificent architecture as the temple, with its splendid decorations and walls of stone of such great size, began to admire them very much and to call the attention of Christ to all this magnificence. Well might he thus explain in regard to the building which Tacitus declared one of the wonders of the world. Fifty years before, Herod had begun the great work of its construction, and for forty-six years the work of rebuilding the temple of Zerubbabel, on plans of surpassing grandeur, went on.

2 And Jesus said unto him, Seest thou these great buildings?—Do your eyes gloat upon them? Do they fill you with wonder and admiration? Do they seem to be eternal?

there shall not be left here one stone upon another, which shall not be thrown down.—Utter destruction should come upon the magnificent temple. A most remarkable prophecy, uttered in a time of profound peace, when nobody dreamed of the possibility of the destruction of such a magnificent work of art and sanctuary of religion as the temple at Jerusalem; a prophecy literally fulfilled forty years after its utterance, fulfilled by Jewish fanatics and Roman soldiers in express violation of Titus, one of the most humane of the Roman emperors, who wished to save it.

3 And as he sat on the mount of Olives over against the temple,—Jesus and the disciples had either left the temple by the great gate of Shushan on the east, from which they could go directly down into the valley of the Kidron, which is most likely, or through some other gate, perhaps on the north, into the city. Then through the city and out by one of its gates, to the Kidron. Crossing the brook, they had climbed the Mount

⁸James and John and Andrew asked him privately, 4 Tell us, when shall
these things be? and what *shall be* the sign when these things are all about

⁶Or, *Jacob*

---

of Olives on one of the more direct roads across it, leading to
Bethany, and, coming to one of the many knolls, from which,
while resting, the whole splendid extent of the temple enclo-
sure, two hundred feet below, could be seen, had sat down to
rest.

Peter and James and John and Andrew asked him privately,
—Jesus had just told them that one day all this grandeur
should be destroyed. This saying made a deep impression
upon their minds, and when they had reached the brow of
Olivet, from which they had a splendid view of the city and
temple, these disciples asked him to tell them when this destruction should take place, and what should be the sign of his
coming, and of the end of the world. (Matt. 24: 5.)

4 Tell us, when shall these things be?—The great drama of
destruction of which he had spoken as they were coming out
of the temple.

**and what shall be the sign when these things are all about
to be accomplished?**—For their own personal safety, as well
as their usefulness during the interviews, the disciples wished
to know how to judge of these times. In Mark the two questions seem to refer to the same "things," although the addition of "all" in the second is a widening of thought. But Matthew (24: 3) makes the matter clear by giving the second
question more definitely, "and what *shall be* the sign of thy
coming, and of the end of the world?" They wanted to know
the evidence that he was coming, and by what token they
could know that he was coming. There has always been a
yearning of the human heart to know the answer to these
questions. We yearn now to know of the end of the world,
even as his disciples. But we must not seek to be wise above
what is written. There are three questions here according to
Matthew (1) "When shall these things be?" (2) "What shall
be the sign of thy coming" and (3) "of the end of the world"?
To these questions Jesus replies, not by noticing them distinctly, but by intermingling the descriptions of the destruction of Jerusalem and of the end of the world, so that it is

sometimes difficult to tell to what particular subject his remarks apply. In the study of prophecy, here or elsewhere in God's book, we should seek the guidance of Jesus, and be sure not to go beyond that which is written. (Luke 24: 15-27, 45; 2 Pet. 1: 19; Rev. 1: 3.)

2. FALSE CHRISTS, WARS, EARTHQUAKES, AND FAMINES
13:5-8
(Matt. 24: 4-8; Luke 21: 8-11)

to be accomplished? 5 And Jesus began to say unto them, Take heed that no man lead you astray. 6 Many shall come in my name, saying, I am *he;* and shall lead many astray. 7 And when ye shall hear of wars and rumors of wars, be not troubled: *these things* must needs come to pass; but the end

---

5 And Jesus began to say unto them, Take heed that no man lead you astray.—Watch, be careful to allow no one to lead you astray on any question but especially those about which you ask. It would be a bad error to be led away by a false Christ.

6 Many shall come in my name, saying, I am he;—DeWette says, "It cannot be shown that there were any false Christs before the destruction of Jerusalem. Bar-Cochba appeared after that event." To which Lange replies, "All those are essentially false Messiahs who would assume the place which belongs to Christ in the kingdom of God. It includes, therefore, the enthusiasts who, before the destruction of Jerusalem, appeared as seducers of the people; e.g., Theudas, Dositheus, Simon Magus, etc." DeWette also asserts, "Church history generally knows of none who gave himself out as the Christian Messiah." Lange responds, "Every one who gave himself out as the Messiah gave himself out as the Christian Messiah; for Messiah means Christ."

and shall lead many astray.—In Lange's view, given above, this was fulfilled to the letter. See Acts 5: 34-37, where Gamaliel tells of the many who were led astray by these pretenders; also Acts 21: 38. All who bring to us an improved, or emasculated, or changed gospel, yea, though an angel from heaven (Gal. 1: 8), make themselves Christs, and are to be rejected. All who give themselves liberty to change ordinances are in the same category.

7 And when ye shall hear of wars and rumors of wars,—

Wars in the neighborhood, where we hear the uproar and confusion ourselves; and wars in the distance, the rumors of which are heard. These wars were very probably insurrections and rebellions of the Jews in various places throughout the Roman empire. Roman history points out that the most violent agitations prevailed in the Roman empire previous to the destruction of Jerusalem. Four emperors, Nero, Galher, Otho, and Vitellius, suffered violent death, in the short space of eighteen months. In consequence of these changes in the government, there were commotions throughout the empire. Parties were formed, and bloody and violent wars were the consequence of attachment to the particular emperors.

Wars declared, or threatened, but not carried into execution would come under "rumors of war." Josephus says that Bardanes, and after him Volageses, declared war against the Jews, but it was not carried into execution. (Ant. 20, 30.) He also says that Vitellius, governor of Syria, declared war against Aretas, king of Arabia, and wished to lead his army through Palestine, but the death of Tiberius prevented the war. (Ant. 18, 5, 3.)

be not troubled: these things must needs come to pass;—Be not confused, agitated, filled with alarm for they are in God's plan and predicted by his Son, and come they must. God overrules the events of the world for the welfare of his children; they were not to be anxious about these things.

but the end is not yet.—It is difficult to determine what "end" refers to. Some think it has reference to the old Jewish economy; others to the end of the world. Since Jesus, in the next verse, points out other calamities, it may have referred to them. What I have told you is not "the end," or all of the calamities. Here are some more of which I now tell you. I say it might refer to this—I do not know. There were to be series of commotions; they were warned to wait with patience, for in this grace they possessed their souls. (Luke 21: 19.) We still have wars and rumors of wars and the world is still standing. The end of it has not yet come. Again and again have generations magnified the great temporal disturbances of their time, and supposed "the end" was just at hand; but the end was not yet. At times all the regular em-

is not yet. 8 For nation shall rise against nation, and kingdom against kingdom; there shall be earthquakes in divers places; there shall be famines:
these things are the beginning of travail.

---

ployments of life have been hindered or abandoned. To keep
steadily onward in the pathway of duty and leave such matters in the hands of God who doeth all things well is the wise
Christian's course. Persecutions, apostasies from the faith,
false teachers, and decrease of love amid abounding iniquity
are to be expected, and should lead us to trust more in Christ,
and persevere unto the end. (Heb. 10: 39; James 5: 7-11; 1
Pet. 4: 12, 13; Rev. 2: 10.)

8 **For nation shall rise against nation,**—"This portended the
dissensions, insurrections, and mutual slaughter of the Jews
and those of other nations who dwelt in the same cities together. At Cesarea, the Jews and Syrians engaged in deadly
conflict, 20,000 of the former of whom were slain and the rest
expelled from the city. This resulted in a series of similar
conflicts in other cities, compassing the death of 20,000 Jews
at Scythopolis, 2,500 at Ascalon, 2,000 at Ptolemais, and an
equal number of Syrians in their towns and villages. At Alexandria, Damascus, and other points, there were similar
scenes."

and kingdom against kingdom;—"In fulfillment of this we
have a war of Jews and Galileans against the Samaritans, on
account of the murder of Galileans going to the feast at Jerusalem. Also a war of the Jews against Agrippa and the Romans, beginning when Gessius Florus was procurator. Also,
the civil war in Italy between Otho and Vitellius for the empire."

there shall be earthquakes in divers places;—"Crete, Smyr-
na, Miletus, Chios, Rome, Laodicea, Hierapolis are localities in
which this prediction was fulfilled in the period preceding the
destruction of Jerusalem. Josephus also tells of a terrible one
in Judea, accompanied by terrific storms."

there shall be famines:—"There was a famine in Judea
mentioned by Suetonius, Tacitus and Eusebius, in the days of
Claudius Caesar." The above quotation from Josephus is con-
densed from Newton, Lardner, and Clarke.

these things are the beginning of travail.—*The beginning,* not the *end* of sorrows. The pains of childbirth, a favorite figure of the scriptures for expressing pain and anguish. We have only to read Josephus' overwhelming description of the misery of every kind that came upon Jerusalem, to realize how fitting is the description given by our Lord to his confidential disciples at a time when all was peace, and quiet, and prosperity throughout the land. Luke (21: 20) says: "When ye see Jerusalem compassed with armies, then know that her desolation is at hand."

3. PERSECUTION OF THE DISCIPLES
13: 9-13
(Matt. 24: 9-14; Luke 21: 12-19)

9 But take ye heed to yourselves: for they shall deliver you up to councils; and in synagogues shall ye be beaten; and before governors and kings

9 **But take ye heed to yourselves:**—What he has mentioned are the general experiences of the nations, but now he invites them to that which pertains to themselves as his followers. They are to play a special part in this great drama, and it is extremely important that they shall walk so circumspectly that all men shall be made to realize that the perils and sorrows which come upon them are not deserved by any wrongdoing of theirs. While the disciples should observe with interest the approaching symptoms of the nation's overthrow, they were charged to have an eye to themselves. They were to guard against and avoid dangers which would be close to and around them. There would be some danger of their love and zeal for Christ waxing cold (Matt. 24: 12), and they are warned to guard against this. They were to be careful not to be deceived by any one, to protect their lives by not running into unnecessary danger.

for they shall deliver you up to councils;—The higher ecclesiastical courts of the Jews, the Sanhedrin, or great council of the nation. They were themselves to be put to a strong test of their faith in Christ. Peter and John before the chief priests, scribes, and elders—the Sanhedrin (Acts 4: 5-21), the body of the apostles before the high priests on a subsequent occasion (Acts 5: 27-30), Stephen before the council (Acts 6: 12-15), James and Peter before Herod (Acts 12: 2, 3), Paul before Nero the emperor, as well as before the Roman

shall ye stand for my sake, for a testimony unto them. 10 And the [7]gospel must first be preached unto all the nations. 11 And when they lead you *to*

[7]See marginal note on ch. 1. 1.

governors, Gallio, Felix and Festus (Acts 18: 12; 24, 25, 28) are illustrations of the fulfillment of this prediction.

and in synagogues shall ye be beaten;—Paul tells, himself, how, in the days of his unbelief, he helped to fulfill this prediction. "And punishing them oftentimes in all the synagogues, I strove to make them blaspheme; and being exceedingly mad against them, I persecuted them even unto foreign cities." (Acts 26: 11.)

and before governors and kings shall ye stand for my sake, —Herod, and Felix, and Festus, and Agrippa, and Gallio, and Nero (Acts 18: 12; 24, 25, 28) may all lend their names to illustrate and confirm this feature of the prophecy. This the disciples were to suffer for Christ's sake.

for a testimony unto them.—That to all classes and before all tribunals the gift of which he is presently to speak may be exercised, and testimony be borne to the reality of his claims, while their own purity and fortitude shall bear witness to the vitality of his religion. Thus by means of persecution many in authority would hear the gospel. Paul gave his testimony to King Agrippa (Acts 26: 1) and to Caesar (2 Tim. 4: 16). (Compare Acts 4: 8; 16: 20; 21: 30.) Persecution in the early church resulted in the furtherance of the gospel. (Acts 8: 4; Phil. 1: 12.) They were to bear testimony to them, or to be witnesses before them of the truth. This was for the sake of Jesus, or because they were attached to him. God would overrule it so that at the same time they should bear witness to the rulers of the truth, as was the case with Peter and John (Acts 4), with Stephen (Acts 6: 7), and with Paul (Acts 23: 24; 24, 25). All the sorrows and trials we can suffer, all the world can do against us, will only inure to the testimony for Christ, so long as we take heed to ourselves to be true. The gospel, if received, is a witness of the power of God unto salvation; but if rejected, it is a witness of the righteousness and justice of God in final condemnation. (Mark 16: 16; Acts 10: 36; 2 Cor. 2: 16; 1 John 5: 9-12.)

10 **And the gospel must first be preached unto all the na-**

judgment, and deliver you up, be not anxious beforehand what ye shall speak: but whatsoever shall be given you in that hour, that speak ye; for it is not ye that speak, but the Holy Spirit.　12 And brother shall [8]deliver up

[8]See ch. 3. 19.

tions.—Before the end. (Verse 7; Matt. 24: 14.) Suffering and preaching will go together. The evidence that this was done is to be chiefly derived from the New Testament, and there it is clear. Paul tells us it was preached to every creature under heaven (Col. 1: 6, 23); that the faith of the Romans was spoken of throughout the whole world (Rom. 1: 8); that he preached in Arabia (Gal. 1: 17); and at Jerusalem, and round about unto Illyricum (Rom. 15: 19). We know also that he traveled through Asia Minor, Greece, and Crete; that he was in Italy, and probably in Spain and Gaul. (Rom. 16: 24-28.) At the same time, the other apostles were not idle; and there is full proof that within thirty years after this prophecy was spoken, churches were established in all these regions. But they did not all obey the gospel. Oh, no, and they do not yet. This is too true. Some think "the end" refers to the end of the Jewish dispensation and the destruction of Jerusalem. But the Jewish dispensation ended on the day of Pentecost. Some think it refers to the destruction of the temple. If so the gospel was preached to every creature 63 A.D. (Col. 1: 23), about seven years before "the end." Let all the commotions, upheavals and disasters of public and private life only impel you to do more to bring about what was evidently the great burden of Christ's thought, the preaching of the gospel to all the world!

11 **And when they lead you to judgment, and deliver you up,** —Before the civil authorities to be judged—to have judgment passed upon you by the court.

be not anxious beforehand what ye shall speak:—Do not think or prepare an answer beforehand. Do not worry over what questions the court may ask nor what your answer ought to be.

but whatsoever shall be given you in that hour,—The time when the questions are asked. The Spirit will furnish the words to be spoken.

that speak ye;—You know not in advance what the accusa-

brother to death, and the father his child; and children shall rise up against parents, and [9]cause them to be put to death. 13 And ye shall be hated of all men for my name's sake: but he that endureth to the end, the same shall be saved.

[9]Or, *put them to death*

tions will be; and God will furnish you with a reply that shall be adapted to the occasion. Speak whatever God puts in your mouth.

for it is not ye that speak, but the Holy Spirit.—The Holy Spirit speaking through them. The Spirit took possession of their tongues and used them to speak his thoughts. This is a promise that they should be inspired, and consequently their defenses recorded in the book of Acts are the words of the Holy Spirit. There could be no more explicit promise that they should be under an infallible guidance; and we are not left to doubt that they were taught of God.

12 **And brother shall deliver up brother to death, and the father his child; and children shall rise up against parents, and cause them to be put to death.**—Here our Lord enlarges upon the persecutions that would come upon Christians, which would be so severe that even the nearest and dearest relations of life would not form a barrier. This was a general persecution and not limited to the apostles. This hatred, so bitter and cruel, should be because of faith in Christ. One of a family accepting Christ would create such a religious prejudice and hatred among other members of the family that they would deliver the Christian member up before the civil authorities. Religious hatred and prejudice is the worst and meanest in the world. It has led to all sorts of persecutions and crimes. It has led to bloody wars. Tacitus assures us that, in Nero's persecution, the Christians betrayed one another, Christians, of course, who had apostatized. The history of persecutions of Christianity has always been made more horrible by their insensate zeal which induced men and women to give up their nearest and dearest to death because they would not deny Christ. It is no shame to you to be abandoned by your dearest for Christ's sake, but oh! the shame of being the betrayer of Lord Jesus. Better be abandoned by all than to abandon him.

13 **And ye shall be hated of all men for my name's sake:**—

On account of their attachment to Christ, and because they bore his name. The enemies of Christianity called its representatives a sect. "Concerning this sect, it is known to us that everywhere it is spoken against." (Acts 28: 22.) "The friendship of the world is enmity with God." (James 4: 4; 1 Pet. 2: 12; 3: 16; 4: 14.) Their preaching was a crucial test. If accepted, it saved; but those who rejected it hated the preachers. There was no compromise. Jesus was divine or not. If divine, the whole fabric of Judaism and idolatry must go. If not, these disciples were publishing the most atrocious lie the world had ever heard. The logical accompaniment of rejection was hatred. But so long as hatred was not for their own sake, because of their evil-doing, but for *his name's* sake, they need not care. "If ye are reproached for the name of Christ, blessed *are ye;* . . . but *if a man suffer* as a Christian, let him not be ashamed; but let him glorify God in this name." (1 Pet. 4: 14-16.) (See also Matt. 5: 11; 2 Cor. 12: 10; James 1: 12; 1 Pet. 2: 19; 3: 14.)

but he that endureth to the end, the same shall be saved.— This is a comforting promise and a great inducement to remain faithful through all persecutions. From Luke (21: 18) we learn they were promised that not a hair of their head should perish. This does not mean that they should not suffer, for they did, but that God was their Father and friend, and would save them eternally. If we would apply this to physical salvation from the destruction of the inhabitants of Jerusalem, we have the remarkable fact that "not a single Christian perished in the destruction of Jerusalem, though there were many there when *Cestius Gallus* infested the city; and had he persevered in the siege, he would soon have rendered himself master of it; but when he unexpectedly and unaccountably raised the siege, the Christians took that opportunity to escape." (Clarke, from Eusebius.) The words however are sufficiently fulfilled in that salvation of the soul, which is to be the glad gift of him who endured unto the end. Christ's followers may be exposed to every peril, but, enduring in faithfulness, no final disaster can come to them, for beyond all is the eternal salvation at the right hand of God in heaven. We live in the happy age *when general* hatred, at least, does not come to a man because he loves Christ.

4. THE LAST SIGN, AND THE TIME FOR FLIGHT
13: 14-20
(Matt. 24: 15-22; Luke 21: 20-24)

14 But when ye see the abomination of desolation standing where he ought not (let him that readeth understand), then let them that are in Ju-

---

14 **But when ye see the abomination of desolation**—Luke (21: 20) explains this by adding, "When ye see Jerusalem compassed with armies, then know that her desolation is at hand." The armies must have been the Roman armies which finally besieged and destroyed Jerusalem. Doubtless they are called "the abomination of desolation" because, being heathen armies, they were an abomination to the Jews, and because they brought desolation on the country. Matthew (24: 15) says: "When therefore ye see the abomination of desolation, which was spoken of through Daniel the prophet." This destruction was a matter of Old Testament prophecy.

standing where he ought not—Matthew (24: 15) says: "In the holy place." Jerusalem is "the holy place." 'The devil taketh him into the holy city." (Matt. 4: 5.) All Jerusalem was esteemed holy. It means when you see the Roman armies standing in "the holy city," or encamped around it, or the Roman ensigns or standards in the temple, you may know that the desolation is at hand.

(let him that readeth understand),—Evidently meaning the reading of the prophecy of Daniel for the New Testament was not then written. (Dan. 9: 27.)

then let them that are in Judaea flee unto the mountains:—[This was spoken of all disciples or Christians. When the armies closed in around the city, then those in Judea should flee to the mountains—the mountains of Judea, which the invading armies did not occupy, and in whose caves and recesses they could escape. Jerusalem is said to have been partially surrounded in 66, but was closely invested by Vespasian in 68. Those who were in the city departed out of it, escaped from it; and those being in the surrounding countries, who frequently came to Jerusalem to the feasts, were warned to stay away. When the destruction came, those within the city would perish with it; so the warning to escape out of it, and to keep out.] In times of imminent peril and danger, it is not

daea flee unto the mountains: 15 and let him that is on the housetop not go down, nor enter in, to take anything out of his house: 16 and let him that is in the field not return back to take his cloak. 17 But woe unto them that are with child and to them that give suck in those days! 18 And pray ye that it be not in the winter. 19 For those days shall be tribulation, such as there hath not been the like from the beginning of the creation which God

only lawful, but our duty, to seek our own preservation by all good and honest means; and if God opens a door of escape, we ought to make our escape; otherwise we do not trust God.

15 **and let him that is on the housetop not go down, nor enter in, to take anything out of his house:**—In that country the roofs of houses were flat, and often used for sleeping. The meaning is the Christian, who is on the housetop when the calamity came, should flee without taking time to go down into the house and gather up clothing for the flight.

16 **and let him that is in the field not return back to take his cloak.**—His outer garment which men usually laid aside when working.

17 **But woe unto them that are with child and to them that give suck in those days!**—An exclamation of pity, with reference to women thus burdened. Their sufferings would be greatly increased, and their flight far more difficult. [They were not in a condition to flee to avoid the vengeance. This does not indicate such would be destroyed. But they were in a pitiable condition, since they could not flee from the impending wrath. The wrath hanging over the people was terrible, and the distress was great.]

18 **And pray ye that it be not in the winter.**—Because the streams were then impassable torrents from the heavy rains and the weather cold and wet, hard on homeless people. To be driven then from home, and forced to make an abode in caverns, would be a double calamity. He taught them to depend upon and trust in God by teaching them to pray God would be with them. The destruction was coming. It could not be prevented. Yet it was proper and right to pray for a mitigation of the circumstances that it might be as mild as possible,

19 **For those days shall be tribulation, such as there hath not been the like from the beginning of the creation which God created until now, and never shall be.**—The word "tribu-

created until now, and never shall be. 20 And except the Lord had shortened the days, no flesh would have been saved; but for the elect's sake,
whom he chose, he shortened the days. 21 And then if any man shall say

lation" means calamity, or suffering. The calamity would be
far greater than any preceding, or that would ever follow it.
It would be the greatest in the history of the entire world.

20 **And except the Lord had shortened the days,**—Had God
not shortened the siege.

no flesh would have been saved;—All the Jewish nation
would have been destroyed, but for the shortening of the
siege.

but for the elect's sake, whom he chose,—His disciples—the
church. (1 Pet. 1: 1, 2; Rom. 1: 7; Eph. 1: 4; 1 Thess. 1: 4.)

he shortened the days.—God shortened the siege. It is related by Josephus that Titus at first resolved to reduce the
city by famine. He therefore built a wall around it, to keep
any provisions from being carried in, and any of the people
from going out. The Jews, however, drew up their army near
the walls, engaged in battle, and the Romans pursued them,
provoked by their attempts, and broke into the city. The affairs
of Rome also at that time demanded the presence of Titus
there; and contrary to his original intention, he pressed the
siege, and took the city by storm, thus *shortening* the time
that *would* have been occupied in reducing it by famine. This
was for the benefit of the "elect." So the designs of wicked
men, intended by them for the destruction of the temple of
God, are intended by God for the good of his chosen people.

5. OTHER WARNINGS AGAINST FALSE CHRISTS
13: 21-23
(Matt. 24: 23-28)

unto you, Lo, here is the Christ; or, Lo, there; believe [1]*it* not: 22 for there

[1]Or, him

21 **And then if any man shall say unto you, Lo, here is the
Christ; or, Lo, there;**—The Jews expected the Messiah to deliver them from Roman oppression. During these great calamities they would anxiously look for him. Many would
claim to be the Messiah. Many would follow them.

shall arise false Christs and false prophets, and shall show signs and wonders, that they may lead astray, if possible, the elect. 23 But take ye heed:
behold, I have told you all things beforehand.

---

believe it not:—Believe not the message for both it and the
messenger are false. Besides you have evidence that the Messiah has come, and you are not to be deceived by the plausible
pretensions of others.

22 **for there shall arise false Christs**—Not one, but many
persons claiming to be the Messiah.

and false prophets,—Persons claiming to be the prophets
spoken of by Moses (Deut. 18: 15); or persons pretending to
declare the way of deliverance from the Romans, and asking
the people to follow them as their Messiah.

and shall show signs and wonders,—That is, shall pretend
to work miracles.

that they may lead astray,—This was their motive. None
except Christians could be led astray. All others were already astray.

if possible, the elect.—God's chosen people.

23 **But take ye heed: behold, I have told you all things beforehand.**—As I have exercised caution to foretell you these
dangers, so do you exercise a like caution in guarding against
them. To be forewarned was to be forearmed.

6. COMING OF THE SON OF MAN
13: 24-27
(Matt. 24: 29-31; Luke 21: 25-28)

24 But in those days, ater that tribulation, the sun shall be darkened, and

---

24 **But in those days, after that tribulation,**—An uncertain
period, still in the prophetic future, defined only this far, that
the great tribulation treated in the preceding verses must first
come. After that has transpired, "those days" begin. Their
length can only be determined by the fulfillment of the prophecy now to be made. Whenever it shall be fulfilled in all
its parts, we shall have the data for accurately defining the
length of "those days," which begin after "that tribulation."
They may cover days, or years, or decades, or millenniums.
"One day is with the Lord as a thousand years, and a thousand years as one day." (2 Pet. 3: 8.) The event must de-

the moon shall not give her light, 25 and the stars shall be falling from heaven, and the powers that are in the heavens shall be shaken. 26 And then

cide the prophetic significance. The "tribulation" is that mentioned in verse 19, attending the destruction of Jerusalem. The disciples had asked two questions. (Verse 4.) The first question, when shall these things be? has now been answered. Here begins the answer to the second, concerning the coming of the Lord. For other passages on the second coming of Christ, see 1 Thess. 2: 19; 3: 13; 4: 15; 5: 23; 2 Thess. 2: 1, 8, 9; 1 Cor. 15: 23; James 5: 7; 2 Pet. 1: 16; 4: 12, 1 John 2: 28. "Immediately" after the destruction of Jerusalem (the tribulation) the series of events begins that leads to the coming of Christ.

the sun shall be darkened,—I take what follows to be symbolical, as is usual in prophecy, rather than literal. Christ is "the Sun of Righteousness." After the destruction of Jerusalem, the causes began to work that led to the great apostasy of the church and produced "the dark ages" of the church.

and the moon shall not give her light,—The moon shines by reflected light of the sun and if it is darkened so will be the moon. So, too, the church shines by the light of Christ. When Christ's light was darkened by taking the Bible from the people the church gave forth little light during the long night of the Middle Ages.

25 **and the stars shall be falling from heaven,**—Stars represent great teachers of the church, apostles and evangelists. (Rev. 1: 20.) When the apostles were dethroned by the Romish apostasy, "the stars fell from heaven," figuratively. Other stars, great church lights who apostasized, fell from heaven in another sense.

and the powers that are in the heavens shall be shaken— [The powers of heaven may be used figuratively, referring to the great nations of earth; or it may mean the forces of nature are excited to unusual activity. Times have often come in the history of the world when, after years of comparative peace and quietness, when the people have waxed gross in sin, and all the institutions and the order of men are steeped in sin and rebellion, that God stirs up a mighty commotion and war

shall they see the Son of man coming in clouds with great power and glory.
27 And then shall he send forth the angels, and shall gather together his
elect from the four winds, from the uttermost part of the earth to the uttermost part of heaven.

---

among the nations that spread from one to another that they
may be punished for their sins, the hopelessly wicked destroyed, and the institutions of wickedness be wiped out that
they may start anew. "Behold, I will stir up the Medes
against them." (Jer. 25: 31; 51: 27.) Periods have since
come up—as in the days of Bonaparte—when war as a contagion spreads from nation to nation.] This was true during
the World War. Since it seems no one knows for certain
what the passage means, could it mean that the powers of
the Roman Catholic Church would be shaken by the reform-
ers?

**26 And then shall they see the Son of man coming in clouds
with great power and glory.**—He will be visible to all and his
coming will be in splendor. [The destruction of Jerusalem
and the Jewish nation seems to have been a type of the second
coming of the Son of God and the end of the world, and he
passes from one to the other. Jesus will come in a cloud with
power and great glory. "And then shall appear the sign of
the Son of man in heaven: and then shall all the tribes of the
earth mourn, and they shall see the Son of man coming in the
clouds of heaven with power and great glory." (Matt. 24:
30, 31.)]

27 And then shall he send forth the angels,—The word
"angel" simply means messenger.

**and shall gather together his elect from the four winds,
from the uttermost part of the earth to the uttermost part of
heaven.**—Christians will be in all countries, mingled with the
population of earth. The work of the angels or messengers at
that time will be to gather together God's people from the
four quarters of the earth. [This seems to me to refer to the
future coming of Christ at the end of all things.]

7. PARABLE OF THE FIG TREE
13: 28-31
(Matt. 14: 32-35; Luke 21: 29-33)

28 Now from the fig tree learn her parable: when her branch is now become tender, and putteth forth its leaves, ye know that the summer is nigh; 29 even so ye also, when ye see these things coming to pass, know ye that [a]he is nigh, *even* at the doors. 30 Verily I say unto you, This generation shall not pass away, until all these things be accomplished. 31 Heaven

[a]Or, *it*

---

28 **Now from the fig tree learn her parable: when her branch is now become tender, and putteth forth its leaves, ye know that the summer is nigh;**—[He presents the facts that when the fig trees put forth their buds or shoots we know summer is drawing nigh, since these are the results and harbingers of the approaching summer.] It puts forth its leaves usually in April.

29 **even so ye also, when ye see these things coming to pass, know ye that he is nigh, even at the doors.**—[Just as the buds are taken as the signs and forerunners of approaching summer, even so they should understand that these signs foretold the coming destruction of Jerusalem and the dispersion of the Jewish people, and "that the kingdom of God is nigh." It is difficult to fix the definite meaning of this sentence. The destruction of the Jewish kingdom was the precedent of the introduction of the reign of Christ. The final destruction of the rebellious nations of the earth will be the harbinger of the final reign of Jesus Christ.]

30 **Verily I say unto you, This generation shall not pass away, until all these things be accomplished.**—["This generation" likely refers to those then living on the earth. Jerusalem should be destroyed, and the nation destroyed during the life of many then living. This language was spoken three days before his death, is adjudged to be A.D. 30. The destruction of Jerusalem is sure. Jerusalem was destroyed by the Romans A.D. 70. "After having been the scene of horrors without example during a memorable siege, it was in A.D. 70 captured by the Romans, who razed the city and temple to the ground, leaving only three of the towers and a part of the western wall to show how strong a place the Roman armies had overthrown." (McClintock and Strong's Encyclopedia.)]

and earth shall pass away: but my words shall not pass away. 32 But of

---

31 **Heaven and earth shall pass away: but my words shall not pass away.**—[The meaning of which is that heaven and earth shall pass away before my words shall pass away and fail. It was a strong form of affirming the certainty of the fulfillment of his predictions. He did not affirm the heavens and the earth should not pass away. They were to give place to a new heaven and a new earth, as foretold in this type. Mark 13: 24-31 seems to refer to both the destruction of Jerusalem and the final winding up of the present condition of affairs. The destruction of Jerusalem is used as a picture or type of the final end; hence what applies to one will, to a greater or less degree, apply to the others. Read the corresponding accounts of the same things (Matt. 24; Luke 21), and this seems evident.

8. UNCERTAINTY OF THE DAY
13: 32-37
(Matt. 24: 36-42; Luke 21: 34-36)

that day or that hour knoweth no one, not even the angels in heaven, neither the Son, but the Father.

---

32 **But of that day or that hour knoweth no one, not even the angels in heaven, neither the Son, but the Father.**—By certain infallible signs Christ had informed his disciples that Jerusalem should be destroyed, the period when they should make good their escape to the fastnesses of the mountains, etc., but of the day when the heaven and earth should pass away, and the coming of the Son of God, no man knew; he, the Son nor the angels, did not know. This day was then only in the knowledge of the Father. But Christ often spoke of such a day, and so did his apostles who were "charged" even to make proclamation of this very truth. (Acts 10: 42.) But they were never so presumptuous as to set a day, because on this point they were not informed. They were obedient to Christ, and thus saved themselves the disgrace and humiliation of attempting to find out what Christ himself and the angels in heaven did not know. Some have at different times set the year and day for the coming of Christ; but these days came and the Master did not come. Such people only display

33 Take ye heed, watch [3]and pray: for ye know not when the time is. 34 *It is* as *when* a man, sojourning in another country, having left his house, and given authority to his [4]servants, to each one his work, commanded also

[3]Some ancient authorities omit *and pray.*
[4]Gr. *bondservants.*

their ignorance. I know not when he is coming but feel sure it will not be at a time set by uninspired men. Should he come at such a time it would be some evidence that uninspired men knew more than Jesus and the angels. This I feel confident God will never allow.

33 **Take ye heed,**—Stay awake and be on your guard. Those who take heed to God's word, and live as that word directs, are ready for his coming when it may suit the Father to send his Son to judge the world.

watch—We have need to observe this command, as much so as the disciples who were then living. The servant of the Lord must watch his feet that they wander not into the broad road of sin, but keep the narrow way. Watchfulness, then, means not a nervous anxiety about the precise time of the end, but a steady adherence to the duties of the present hour.

and pray:—When worn and weary it is a source of strength to come to the altar of prayer.

for ye know not when the time is.—The reason for watchfulness and prayer. Ignorance of the time is a reason for both watchfulness and prayer. The same reason will apply to death and the judgment which are coming on the earth. [Watch yourselves, that ye may not neglect to be ready and prepared to meet the Lord when he shall come. Watch these signs of his coming, that you may be kept in mind that he will come speedily, and we should be ready; and that the Lord may account you worthy to escape all the evils that shall come upon the disobedient. God will not permit any worthy man to suffer by the evils. He watches over and protects them, and enables them to stand before the Son of man worthy to meet him when he comes, and to stand without condemnation and without shame in his presence.]

34 **It is as when a man, sojourning in another country,**—An object lesson is here given. The Savior was soon to leave the earth and go on a journey to heaven, and the time of his return, he had already told them, would be indefinite.

the porter to watch. 35 Watch therefore: for ye know not when the lord of
the house cometh, whether at even, or at midnight, or at cockcrowing, or in

---

having left his house, and given authority to his servants,
—Each servant has a trust given him by the Lord. Each disciple should consider any power he has or can command, that can be used for the lawful furtherance of the gospel, as a talent committed by the Master.

to each one his work,—All disciples have something to do; all are talented, and all must give account to the Master when he comes. The word "house" often means family. Jesus here represents himself as going away, leaving his household the church, in its preparatory state and assigning to the apostles and all his servants their duty, and leaving it uncertain when he would return. As his return was a matter of vast consequence, and as the affairs of his kingdom were entrusted to them, just as the affairs of a house are to servants, when the master is absent: so it was of vast importance that they should be faithful at their post, defending the house from danger, and be ready for his return.

commanded also the porter to watch.—The doorkeeper. To the janitor or doorkeeper was intrusted, particularly, the faithful care of the house, whose duty it was to attend faithfully on those who came, and those who left the house. This may be an allusion to the office of the apostles, who held the highest positions under Christ.

35 **Watch therefore:**—Be diligent, faithful in all things, waiting for the return of your master who will come at an unexpected hour.

for ye know not when the lord of the house cometh,—Denoting here the Lord Jesus Christ. The application of the illustration is brief and vivid. The disciples are at once addressed as if they were porters, left in charge of their Master's house.

whether at even, or at midnight, or at cockcrowing, or in the morning;—These were the four watches into which the night was divided by the Romans and Greeks, and the system was adopted by the Jews. This mention was intended to illustrate the fact that the disciples knew not the time of the

the morning; 36 lest coming suddenly he find you sleeping. 37 And what I say unto you I say unto all, Watch.

Master's return. The four watches of the night were divided as follows. At evening, from sunset to nine o'clock; from nine to twelve; at the cockcrowing, from twelve to three; in the morning, from three to sunrise. (6: 48.) The sure way to be found ready when Christ comes is to be ready each day and night; to leave no gaps down.

36 lest coming suddenly he find you sleeping—Inaction to your post, neglecting your duty, and unprepared for his coming. Christianity, whether it pertains to the duty of an apostle or some other Christian, must be a life of activity and industry. There is no place for an idler in the kingdom of God.

37 And what I say unto you I say unto all, Watch.—These admonitions, then, are for universal application; suited for every age of the church, and suited to every member of the church. Nevertheless men must gain their souls by patience —patient endurance, not violent resistance. Men may be worn with watching, pining for peace, and weary for rest; still the same lesson has to be repeated, the same duty—watching —practiced. Watchfulness is still the duty of the church and of all Christians. The difficulty in this whole matter is in understanding how to distribute the statements to the three queries the disciples asked Jesus. Christ makes his second coming and the end of the world the same time, or he ignores the question concerning the end of the world; the destruction of the temple and the second coming, or end of the world, constitute the two events. The destruction of the temple is the type of his coming, and Jesus glides imperceptibly from the one to the other. He portrays the fearful signs antedating the fall of Jerusalem and the destruction of the temple in such a way that his servants could not misapprehend them when they appeared, so that they might escape the destruction. He then tells them the Son of man will return at an unexpected hour to them; so they must keep ever watchful and ready. The times specified when he may return are all in the night, indicating that Jesus will come at an hour when least looked

SECTION FOUR

PREPARATIONS FOR THE DEATH OF JESUS
14: 1-52

1. COUNCIL OF THE CHIEF PRIESTS AND SCRIBES
14: 1-2
(Matt. 26: 1-5; Luke 22: 1, 2)

1 Now after two days was *the feast of* the passover and the unleavened bread: and the chief priests and the scribes sought how they might take him with subtlety, and kill him: 2 for they said, Not during the feast, lest haply there shall be a tumult of the people.

---

1 Now after two days was the feast of the passover—The yearly feast celebrated in Jerusalem, by command of God, in commemoration of the "passover" of the children of Israel by the destroying angel, the night when he slew all the first-born of the Egyptians. For the origin of this feast see Ex. 12:1-14.

and the unleavened bread:—Bread in the making of which no yeast or other ferment had been used. During the days of the festival no leaven was allowed in the houses of the Israelites, and it was therefore called, also, "The feast of unleavened bread." (Luke 22: 1.) The Passover and the feast of unleavened bread occupied eight days.

and the chief priests and the scribes sought how they might take him—Unable to make a defense of their course by fair words and arguments, they were determined to destroy him who had exposed them.

with subtlety, and kill him:—That is, by some secret plan that would secure possession of him without exciting the opposition of the people. They counseled together how this could best be done. (Matt. 26: 4.)

2 for they said, Not during the feast, lest haply there shall be a tumult of the people.—The gatherings of Israelites to the feasts seem almost incredible, as many as two millions being assembled in and around the city. All their national pride was in the highest state of excitement, and they were ripe for insurrection, according to Josephus. Many of them were from the mountain regions of Galilee and its vicinity, whence Christ came, and might make an ungovernable tumult if he were arrested in their presence or while they remained in the city.

2. THE ANOINTING AT BETHANY
14: 3-9
(Matt. 26: 6-13; John 12: 1-9)

3 And while he was in Bethany in the house of Simon the leper, as he sat at meat, there came a woman having [5]an alabaster cruse of ointment of [6]pure nard very costly; *and* she brake the cruse, and poured it over his head. 4 But there were some that had indignation among themselves, *say-*

---

[5]Or, *a flask*
[6]Or, *liquid nard*

---

3 **And while he was in Bethany in the house of Simon the leper, as he sat at meat, there came a woman having an alabaster cruse of ointment of pure nard very costly;**—Mark does not give her name, but John tells that it was Mary who was sister to Lazarus and Martha. (12: 3.) The ointment of nard was highly esteemed in antiquity as a precious aromatic and a costly luxury. The cruse and its contents were very valuable, such as any woman of refinement would appreciate. Pliny says that a *pound* of this ointment cost more than four hundred *denarii* or sixty dollars. This was a perfume, and used only to give a pleasant odor.

and she brake the cruse, and poured it over his head.—John says she "anointed the feet of Jesus, and wiped his feet with her hair." She did both. That she used her hair instead of a towel to wipe his feet also indicates she did not have bobbed hair. What a supper party! a healed leper, a risen Lazarus, an incarnation of grateful love, a plotting traitor, a marvelous healer and teacher destined to crucifixion, at least two others who would die a martyr's death.

4 **But there were some that had indignation among themselves,**—They were utterly incapable of entering into the spirit of boundless gratitude and devotion that made any gift seem small to Mary, and thought only of the economical aspects of the case. Mark says "some." Matthew indicates "the disciples" collectively. But it is John who names the ringleader in this angry meanness, and also his motive. It was Judas Iscariot, who valued money so highly that he considered fifteen dollars a fair equivalent for the betrayal of Jesus and the loss of his own soul. John says Judas expressed *indignation*.

ing, To what purpose hath this waste of the ointment been made?　5 For this ointment might have been sold for above three hundred [7]shillings, and given to the poor.　And they murmured against her.　6 But Jesus said, Let her alone; why trouble ye her? she hath wrought a good work on me.　7 For ye have the poor always with you, and whensoever ye will ye can do them good: but me ye have not always.　8 She hath done what she could; she

[7]See marginal note on ch. 6. 37.

saying, To what purpose hath this waste of the ointment been made?—The loss or destruction of this valuable property.　They could see no use in it, and they therefore supposed it was lost.　From Judas' standpoint an enormous waste, three times as much value poured upon Jesus as would shortly buy him.　Sordid men still think what is bestowed upon our Lord is wasted.

5 For this ointment might have been sold for above three hundred shillings, and given to the poor.—The ointment was worth about forty-five dollars.

And they murmured against her.—They not only murmured *about* her, but spoke sharply about what she had done.

6 But Jesus said, Let her alone; why trouble ye her?—He saw in her countenance that such words, coming from his chosen apostles, disquieted her.

she hath wrought a good work on me.—It was a good work which she had done, because of the believing, grateful love which dictated it.　From the standpoint of economy and expediency it might seem unwise, but Jesus judges it by the motive.　Then, beside, he knew of its eminent appropriateness to the events so soon to occur.　It was a good work which Jesus presently explained to mean that her affectionate sacrifice should constitute an honored part of the anointing for his burial.　It was a work distinguished for its moral beauty, fitness, and grace; literally a beautiful work.

7 For ye have the poor always with you, and whensoever ye will ye can do them good: but me ye have not always.—These words were especially significant in view of the declaration he had so repeatedly made to them that he would be put to death at Jerusalem.

8 She hath done what she could;—She wished to show her loving gratitude.　All that was possible to her she had done.

hath anointed my body beforehand for the burying. 9 And verily I say unto you, Wheresoever the [8]gospel shall be preached throughout the whole world, that also which this woman hath done shall be spoken of for a memorial of her.

[8]See marginal note on ch. 1. 1.

she hath anointed my body beforehand for the burying.— Matthew says: "For in that she poured this ointment upon my body, she did it to prepare me for burial." In John, "Suffer her to keep it against the day of my burying." Jesus accepts her offering as a preliminary anointing for his burial. She, of course, knew it not, but the oncoming rush of events gives to it this mystic quality. As there would be no time for this after his death, this anointing, as it were for the sepulchre, took place, in the divine arrangement, while he was yet alive. Mary's act of love and faith stands out in striking contrast to the avarice of Judas and the murmurings of the others.

9 And verily I say unto you, Wheresoever the gospel shall be preached throughout the whole world,—With what prophetic confidence Jesus looked forward to the universal preaching of the gospel through the world! What wonderful confidence in one who felt sure of being hurried into the grave in a few days!

that also which this woman hath done shall be spoken of for a memorial of her.—A prophecy fulfilled, for where the New Testament has been carried, there has this woman's story been told, and has been a stimulus and encouragement to all the honest, buoyant spirits who have made noble offerings to the Lord, and been censured for them.

3. THE AGREEMENT WITH JUDAS
14: 10, 11
(Matt. 26: 14-16; Luke 22: 3-6)

10 And Judas Iscariot, [9]he that was one of the twelve, went away unto

[9]Gr. *the one of the twelve.*

10 And Judas Iscariot, he that was one of the twelve, went away unto the chief priests,—The high priests. The ruling man of the Sanhedrin. Luke (22: 4) says he went also to the captains. On account of the great wealth deposited there, and

the chief priests, that he might [10]deliver him unto them.　11 And they, when they heard it, were glad, and promised to give him money.　And he sought how he might conveniently [10]deliver him *unto them.*

[10]See ch. 3. 19.

its great sacredness, it was necessary to guard the temple by night.　Accordingly men were stationed around it, whose leaders or commanders were called captains.　(Acts 4: 1.)

that he might deliver him unto them.—Treacherously, of course.　A comparison of all the accounts will show that when his avarice was thus disappointed he went at the first opportunity to the priests.　Jesus was about to be put to death, he had not been permitted to enrich himself, there was now no probability that he would become the treasurer of his Master as an earthly king.　Probably he had heard it rumored that the chief priests desired to put him to death and their purpose to "take Jesus by subtlety."　(Verse 4.)　If so, he felt he could make a profitable agreement with the enemy.

11 **And they, when they heard it, were glad,**—The chief priests and captains.　His proposition was an unexpected one, so it was received with joy.

and promised to give him money.—Matthew says: "Thirty pieces of silver."　That is, the price of a slave.　(Ex. 21: 32.) They did not pay him then probably for fear he would deceive them.　When the wicked deed was committed, and before he was sensible of its guilt, they paid him.　(Matt. 27: 3; Acts 1: 18.)　Each piece of silver amounted to about fifty cents, the whole sum being about fifteen dollars.

And he sought how he might conveniently deliver him unto them.—Matthew says: "From that time he sought opportunity to deliver him."　He sought a convenient time when he thought it would be safe both to himself and them.　"In the absence of the multitude." (Luke 22: 6.)　The popular commotion was what both parties desired to avoid.　(Verse 2.)

So far as I know, Judas had no particular malice, spite, or ill will against Jesus, but a base and unworthy spirit of covetousness possessed him, and this made him sell Jesus. Covetousness is the root sin.　An eager and insatiable thirst after the world is the parent of the most monstrous sins.

4. PREPARATION FOR THE PASSOVER
14: 12-16
(Matt. 26: 1-19; Luke 22: 7-13)

12 And on the first day of unleavened bread, when they sacrificed the passover, his disciples say unto him, Where wilt thou that we go and make ready that thou mayest eat the passover? 13 And he sendeth two of his disciples, and saith unto' them, Go into the city, and there shall meet you a

12 And on the first day of unleavened bread,—[On the fourteenth day of the first month all leaven was to be put away from their houses. The lamb for the Passover feast was slain on the fourteenth day of the first month Abib or Nisan in the evening when the sun was setting. The Passover was the most sacred of the annual feasts of the Jews. It commemorated the passing over of the firstborn of the children of Israel when the firstborn of the Egyptians were slain. This feast was observed by Jesus, save one he did not go to, at Jerusalem.]

when they sacrificed the passover,—The paschal lamb, which was slain in keeping the Passover.

his disciples say unto him,—They were talking about that which had brought them to Jerusalem, the observance of the Passover in the Holy City, and which brought many from the remotest parts of the empire.

Where wilt thou that we go and make ready—This question was asked by the disciples, who knew Jesus' custom to observe the requirements of the Jewish law; they, with others, had made a considerable journey to attend this feast, and the time was now at hand. There were some things to be purchased for the feast that would require some time to provide.

that thou mayest eat the passover?—They modestly throw themselves in the background, as mere participants, making him the great central figure of the feast. [The lamb was to be prepared—made ready—a place secured where they could do it.]

13 And he sendeth two of his disciples, and saith unto them, Go into the city,—From Bethany, where they now were, into Jerusalem, where only the paschal supper could be eaten. Peter and John were the two disciples sent. (Luke 22: 8.)

and there shall meet you a man—No name is given, some

man bearing a pitcher of water: follow him; 14 and wheresoever he shall
enter in, say to the master of the house, The Teacher saith, Where is my
guest-chamber, where I shall eat the passover with my disciples? 15 And he
will himself show you a large upper room furnished *and* ready: and there

think, perhaps, to make the concealment from Judas more
complete. We have no means of knowing whether the man
they should meet would be an acquaintance or not. He gives
the two disciples a sign similar to that which Samuel gave to
Saul. (1 Sam. 10: 2-7.)

bearing a pitcher of water:—The man should be one bearing a pitcher of water. There is no need of imagining more
here than the presence of Jesus, by which he knew that the
man would thus meet him. The fact here recorded could have
been known only by the infinite knowledge of Jesus.

follow him;—They were to follow him until he entered the
house, where they should then make known their errand.
[The making ready was to secure and kill the lamb, provide
the wine, the bitter herbs, all the vessels and arrangements,
for the unleavened bread, for roasting the lamb—they were required to roast, not boil, the lamb. They are now out at Bethany.]

14 **and wheresoever he shall enter in, say to the master of
the house,**—They were to arrange with the householder—the
head of the family, for the feast.

The Teacher saith, Where is my guest-chamber,—A cham-
ber of guests or friends—an unoccupied room, the lodging
room.

where I shall eat the passover with my disciples?—[The
householder was no doubt a disciple of the Master, and the
probability is that Jesus had let him know that he would eat
the Passover at his house, and now the disciples ask to be
shown the room where he might eat of it with his disciples.
The host most probably, with his family, ate it to themselves
in their ordinary eating place. The guestchamber was given
up to Jesus and his disciples that they, as a family, might eat
it. It was customary in Jerusalem for families to furnish
rooms for others who came from a distance to the city to observe the Passover feast. This is probably the same upper
room in which they were assembled (Acts 1: 26) when Matthias was chosen to take the place of Judas.]

make ready for us. 16 And the disciples went forth, and came into the city, and found as he had said unto them: and they made ready the passover.

15 **And he will himself show you a large upper room**—The "upper room" is supposed to be what, in modern Arabic, is called the *aliyah*. It is frequently a separate room, built on the housetop, affording an airy situation and privacy.

furnished and ready: and there make ready for us.—Bread was to be made or bought, broth *charoseth,* made of fruits, wine provided, the lamb selected, bought, carried to the temple and slain, then roasted, and bitter herbs prepared. There was abundant work for the two men.

16 **And the disciples went forth, and came into the city, and found as he had said unto them:**—Everything happened according to the prediction, as is always the case when Jesus speaks.

and they made ready the passover.—Accommodations had to be made for at least thirteen—the twelve apostles and Jesus. [They were in Bethany, in the house of Simon the leper. They went forth from this place, came to the city, found the man bearing the pitcher of water, followed him into the house in which he entered, and asked for the guestchamber. It was shown them, and they made ready the Passover.]

5. THE BETRAYAL PREDICTED
14: 17-21
(Matt. 26: 20-25; Luke 22: 21-23; John 13: 21-30)

17 And when it was evening he cometh with the twelve. 18 And as they

17 **And when it was evening**—When the sun was set, sometime after six o'clock.

he cometh with the twelve.—[It says here "with the twelve." As Peter and John already are here, he likely means the remainder of the twelve—ten disciples. Luke says, "He sat down" with the twelve, and it only means that after the others had come he, with the twelve, sat down at the table.]

18 **And as they sat and were eating,**—The Passover feast. Luke quotes Jesus as saying, "With desire I have desired to eat this passover with you before I suffer."

¹sat and were eating, Jesus said, Verily I say unto you, One of you shall ²betray me, *even* he that eateth with me. 19 They began to be sorrowful, and to say unto him one by one, Is it I? 20 And he said unto them, *It is* one of the twelve, he that dippeth with me in the dish. 21 For the Son of

¹Gr. *reclined.*
²See marginal note on ch. 3. 19.

Jesus said, Verily I say unto you, One of you shall betray me, even he that eateth with me.—An announcement that none could possibly be prepared for but Judas. [They really reclined at the table, after the manner of the Jews. John leaned on the bosom of Jesus, which shows they were so reclining. (John 13: 23.) While eating, Jesus told them, "One of you shall betray me, even he that eateth with me." This came as an astounding revelation to the great number. It is thought Judas had, the day before, covenanted to betray him. Jesus, in telling this, showed his knowledge of that transaction. John (13: 21-29) gives a circumstantial account of his telling this, and of his pointing out who should betray him.]

19 They began to be sorrowful, and to say unto him one by one, Is it I?—Never was a more fateful question asked, for its answer would point out "the son of perdition," and send him "to his own place." The question seems to have gone the round, even Judas with solemn hypocrisy said: "Is it I, Rabbi?" In reply, Jesus said: "Thou hast said." (Matt. 26: 25.) Yes, Judas, you are the man. This was a dagger thrust into his heart, though it did not change his evil course.

20 And he said unto them, It is one of the twelve,—This makes it certain that it is one of the apostles. We do not wonder at their anxiety to know which would be so corrupt as to betray the Master.

he that dippeth with me in the dish.—[Matthew (26: 23) records it: "He that dipped his hand with me in the dish."] God has in all ages selected men who are in heart and character prepared to do the work to be done. If it is a clean work, he selects a clean man to do it. If an unclean work, he selects an unclean man to accomplish it. He wills that all men do the clean work. But if they refuse and will not, then God has decreed they shall do the unclean work. Judas was selected for the clean work—he was numbered with the apostles. He was a lump of clay which marred in the Potter's hand. God

man goeth, even as it is written of him: but woe unto that man through whom the Son of man is [2]betrayed! good were it [3]for that man if he had not been born.

[3]Gr. *for him if that man.*

then took the same lump and used it as an unclean vessel to do the unclean work—betraying the Son of God. By and through him, together with the aid of the wicked hands that crucified the Savior, came the greatest of all blessings to the human family—salvation. Good clean men could not have done the work. Judas fitted and prepared himself for the dirty work when he opened his heart and let the devil in. He was then selected to do the work.

21 **For the Son of man goeth, even as it is written of him:** —[Jesus says he goes, or dies as it is written in the prophets. It is for the good of the world that he should die. He came into the world to die.]

but woe unto that man through whom the Son of man is betrayed! good were it for that man if he had not been born.— [Here is work rendered necessary to be done by the sins of the world. Nobody save a vile sinner can do it, because it is the blackest of crimes. Yet God overrules the treason of Judas' heart to lead him to do work needful for the salvation of man. God overrules the wickedness of man frequently to do work made necessary by sin for man's good. John (13: 30) says: "He then having received the sop went out straightway: and it was night."]

6. THE LORD'S SUPPER INSTITUTED
14: 22-26
(Matt. 26: 26-29; Luke 22: 19, 20; 1 Cor. 11: 23-25)

22 And as they were eating, he took [4]bread, and when he had blessed, he

[4]Or, *a loaf*

22 **And as they were eating, he took bread,**—Or "a loaf" (footnote), one of the thin flat loaves of the country—made without leaven of any kind. "A loaf" does not mean two or more loaves, but one. The loaf, which was one, points to the body of Christ. Jesus had one body he offered for the sins of the world and the one loaf represents that one body. Two loaves on the Lord's table are out of place and have no divine

brake it, and gave to them, and said, Take ye: this is my body. 23 And he

sanction. One loaf is safe, two are doubtful, to say the least. It is always safe to be on the safe side.

and when he had blessed,—The word "blessed" is used interchangeably with "gave thanks." That is, the same act is sometimes expressed by the one form and sometimes by the other. Here and in Matthew (26: 26) what is expressed by "blessed" in Luke 22: 17, 19: 1 Cor. 11: 24 is expressed by saying "had given thanks." And in the account given by Matthew and Mark, the one expression is used in reference to the bread, and the other in reference to the cup. They therefore mean the same thing, or rather express the same act, for that act was both a benediction and thanksgiving; that is, it is addressed to God, and therefore may be expressed either by the words "had blessed" or "given thanks."

he brake it,—After he had expressed thanks. The Passover bread, as used by the Israelites now, is very thin and easily broken. This represented his body broken on the cross. Breaking of the bread is essential to the true idea. Cutting it is a perversion. The ordinance is even called "the breaking of bread." (Acts 2: 42.)

and gave to them,—To the eleven disciples, probably, not certainly, first partaking of it himself. They were all baptized believers. No one is authorized to eat at the Lord's table who has not been immersed into Christ. The Lord's Supper is for those who are members of the body of Christ (1 Cor. 11: 20, 33), and those who are not members of the church ought not to partake of the bread and wine. [I do not think Judas ate the Lord's Supper with Jesus and his disciples. John (13: 21-30) shows plainly that Judas went out before the supper was observed. He went out to get his band to take Jesus and betray him to the chief priests; after he had gone, the Lord's Supper was instituted. There is a distinction between the Passover feast and the Lord's Supper appointed at the feast.]

and said, Take ye: this is my body.—[When his own living body was present before them, they could not otherwise than understand that this bread that was broken was the representative of his body—the symbol of it to them. This was an-

took a cup, and when he had given thanks, he gave to them: and they all

other of the parables he had so constantly presented to them within these last days. They could not have understood it otherwise than as a representation, or symbol, of his body to them. This bread was given in view of his coming death for their sins. His body would be broken as this loaf was broken, and he gives this as the representative, or memorial, of it. To establish a memorial of a deed before it is performed is not like man, but God frequently did it. Man never knows what will happen; God does. Jesus was before him as "the Lamb that hath been slain" from the foundation of the world. The bread used in this supper was the unleaven bread of the Passover week. As the bread and the wine constitute the staff of life—that on which our bodies are sustained—even so this body broken and this blood shed for the remission of sins constitute the food upon which our spirits must feed, that they may grow into the likeness of Christ.]

23 **And he took a cup,**—"A cup" is one, not two nor a dozen. Luke says: "The cup," so also Paul (1 Cor. 11: 25), and both insert "after supper." Paul also calls it (1 Cor. 10: 16) "the cup of blessing." "Cup" here is used figuratively for what it contains. The cup contained wine, the juice of the crushed grape—a striking emblem of his own blood, which would be shed for the sins of the whole world.

and when he had given thanks,—This is what made it "the cup of blessing." He did not give thanks for the bread and cup at the same time, as some do now. To do so is a perversion of the truth—it is unscriptural. All mentions of it show thanks for the bread first, then the cup.

he gave to them: and they all drank of it.—[The cup contained the fruit of the vine. It was the cup, or wine, used in the Passover feast. For this he gave thanks. Blessing and giving thanks seem to be used interchangeably, and therefore refer to the same thing. Luke reports him as saying: "This is my body which is given for you: this do in remembrance of me." The truth, when they as yet understood so little of his death and resurrection, was not apparent to the disciples; but like so many other things which they did not understand, after he died and was raised from the dead they remembered it, and they understood it; so they believed. In Acts 2: 42 we find: "And they continued stedfastly in the apostles' teaching and fellowship, in the breaking of bread and the prayers." This refers to the breaking of bread in memory of the Lord. Many think the breaking of bread daily in verse 46 also refers to the supper; but it seems to refer to the daily meals, inasmuch as it is said: "And breaking bread at home, they took their food with gladness and singleness of heart." Eating their food for sustenance. Acts 20: 7: "And upon the first day of the week, when we were gathered together to break bread, Paul discoursed with them." Paul says: "For I received of the Lord that which also I delivered unto you, that the Lord Jesus in the night in which he was betrayed took bread; and when he had given thanks, he brake it, and said, This is my body, which is for you: this do in remembrance of me. In like manner also the cup, after supper, saying, This cup is the new covenant in my blood: this do, as often as ye drink *it,* in remembrance of me. For as often as ye eat this bread, and drink the cup, ye proclaim the Lord's death till he come. Wherefore whosoever shall eat the bread or drink the cup of the Lord in an unworthy manner, shall be guilty of the body and the blood of the Lord. But let a man prove himself, and so let him eat of the bread, and drink of the cup. For he that eateth and drinketh, eateth and drinketh judgment unto himself, if he discern not the body." (1 Cor. 11: 23-29.) From this we learn that it was a memorial institution to keep in memory the heroic deeds of Jesus in dying to redeem man. It was to be observed by their coming together on the first day of the week to break bread. It was the will of God set forth in the shedding of his blood for the sins of the world. Monuments are designed to commemorate the worthy deeds of those to whose memory they are built, with the hope that future generations, when they learn of the deeds commemorated by the monument, will be inspired with the same spirit, and be led to emulate these worthy deeds. Just so this monumental institution was ordained to perpetuate the memory of the self-denying spirit and heroic deeds of Jesus Christ for the good of man. It is done with the view that those who see these memorials of the deeds and death of Jesus will drink

drank of it. 24 And he said unto them, This is my blood of the ⁵covenant,

⁵Some ancient authorities insert *new*.

---

into the same spirit, and be led to emulate his life and deeds of self-sacrifice for the good of others.

Man builds monúments of marble and granite, of iron and brass. He seeks the imperishable. Despite all his precaution, they molder and crumble. God through Jesus selected the perishable loaf and volatile fruit of the vine as the materials out of which he would build a monument that would endure with perennial freshness through time till Jesus should come again. No mortal would ever seek to build an imperishable monument out of material so perishable as the bread and wine. God only could breathe into it a spirit that would render it immortal—that could cause it to continue in its freshness and vigor till he come.]

24 And he said unto them, This is my blood of the covenant, which is poured out for many.—He shed his blood "unto remission of sins" and so baptism is "unto the remission of your sins." (Acts 2: 38.) Both came from the same Greek word and mean the same in both passages. If baptism is not "unto remission of sins" as some contend, then Jesus did not shed his blood "unto remission of sins." They both stand or fall together.

[Just as he gave the bread as the representative of the body so he gave the fruit of the vine as the cup—as his blood. A testament is a will. God through Jesus makes a new will, or testament, as that through Moses is called the old will, or testament. This is the memorial of that blood that was shed to seal and confirm this new testament. The old testament was sealed with the blood of animals; this is sealed with the blood of Jesus Christ shed for the remission of sins. He is called "the Lamb of God," in John 1: 29, and "the Lamb that hath been slain," in Rev. 13: 8. He offered himself for man's redemption when man sinned. God accepted him as the Redeemer; but "he was manifested to take away sins." (1 John 3: 5.) "Ye were redeemed, not with corruptible things, with silver or gold, from your vain manner of life handed down from your fathers; but with precious blood, as of a lamb with-

which is poured out for many. 25 Verily I say unto you, I shall no more drink of the fruit of the vine, until that day when I drink it new in the kingdom of God.

26 And when they had sung a hymn, they went out unto the mount of Olives.

out blemish and without spot, *even the blood* of Christ: who was foreknown indeed before the foundation of the world, but was manifested at the end of the times for your sake, who through him are believers in God, that raised him from the dead, and gave him glory; so that your faith and hope might be in God." (1 Pet. 1: 18-21.) This blood of the New Testament was shed for many. "He is the propitiation for our sins; and not for ours only, but also for the whole world." (1 John 2: 2.) Jesus shed his blood for all, but only for those who appropriate its cleansing efficacy, who enter into the temple of the living God, and walk in its blood-sealed appointments and laws. Matthew (26: 28) says his blood "is poured out for many unto remission of sins"—that their sins might be remitted; that they might be freed from sins; that God "might himself be just, and the justifier of him that hath faith in Jesus." (Rom. 3: 26.)]

25 **Verily I say unto you, I shall no more drink of the fruit of the vine, until that day when I drink it new in the kingdom of God.**—[It has been a question of doubt as to what is meant by the expression: "I shall drink no more of the fruit of the vine, until that day when I drink it new in the kingdom of God." The general interpretation is that it referred to the new spiritual communion with him in the eternal kingdom of God that is typified by the partaking of the bread and wine. Others think that it means he would not partake of it again until the church of God was fully set up on Pentecost; and then, in their observance of it and through time, he would be with them in spirit when they met to remember his death in these memorials he gives. Others still think he means when he comes again to earth he will, with his disciples, partake of the bread and wine.]

26 **And when they had sung a hymn, they went out unto the mount of Olives.**—[Christ and the apostles sang at the first institution and observance of the supper. They sang—not one of them. Paul and Silas, in the Philippian jail, sang at

midnight. This might not be called a "public song service," but it was a part of the worship engaged in by these two disciples in the prison. Acts 16: 25 reads: "But about midnight Paul and Silas were praying and singing hymns unto God, and the prisoners were listening to them." They both sang, and the prayer and singing are associated as equally acceptable to God, each constituting an act of acceptable worship to God. Paul, in Ephesians 5: 19, says: "Speaking one to another in psalms and hymns and spiritual songs, singing and making melody with your heart to the Lord." They were to speak to each other in the singing. It must have been when they were called together. Again, Col. 3: 16, 17 says: "Let the word of Christ dwell in you richly; in all wisdom teaching and admonishing one another with psalms and hymns and spiritual songs, singing with grace in your hearts unto God. And whatsoever ye do, in word or in deed, do all in the name of the Lord Jesus, giving thanks to God the Father through him." This singing must be done when they were together, that each might be admonished by the singing done. This is clear and distinct authority for the song service. That it should be called in question is an indication as to what extremes people will go in trying to justify practices not required by God.] I can see no excuse for brethren, in some instances, omitting the song after the supper, when we have an example of singing set by Jesus and the apostles when the supper was instituted. There is as much authority to omit all the song service when we meet for worship as there is to omit it after the supper. There is none for either. Neither is there any authority for singing while making the contribution or partaking of the supper.

7. DESERTION AND DENIAL FORETOLD
14: 27-31
(Matt. 26: 30-35; Luke 22: 31-38; John 13: 36-38)

27 And Jesus saith unto them, All ye shall be [6]offended: for it is written,

[6]Gr. *caused to stumble.*

27 **And Jesus saith unto them, All ye shall be offended:**— You will all stumble at my being taken, abused, and set at naught; you will be ashamed to own me as a teacher, and to acknowledge yourselves as my disciples.

⁷I will smite the shepherd, and the sheep shall be scattered abroad. 28 Howbeit, after I am raised up, I will go before you into Galilee. 29 But Peter
said unto him, Although all shall be ⁶offended, yet will not I. 30 And Jesus
saith unto him, Verily I say unto thee, that thou to-day *even* this night, before the cock crow twice, shalt deny me thrice. 31 But he spake exceeding

⁷Zech. xiii. 7.

for it is written.—In Zech. 13: 7. The scripture quoted shows Jesus was familiar with the scriptures. It shows that a suffering Messiah was in accordance with the purposes of God.

I will smite the shepherd,—This is the language of God the Father, Jesus is the Shepherd. It means that God will either smite Jesus himself, or give him up to be smitten. (Compare Ex. 4: 2, Matt. 8: 15, etc.) Both were done. God gave him up to the Jews and Romans, to be smitten for the sins of the world (Rom. 8: 32); and he himself left him to deep and awful sorrows, to bear the burden of the world's atonement alone.

and the sheep—Here "sheep" means the apostles. It also refers sometimes to all the followers of Jesus, the friends of God. (John 10: 16; Psalm 100: 3.)

shall be scattered abroad.—This refers to the apostles fleeing, and was fulfilled in that.

28 Howbeit, after I am raised up, I will go before you into Galilee.—Another future event foretold, thereby establishing his divinity. This promise was given the apostles to encourage and support them, and also to give them an indication where he could be found after his resurrection.

29 But Peter said unto him, Although all shall be offended, yet will not I.—This confidence of Peter was entirely characteristic of him. He was ardent, sincere, and really attached to Jesus. Yet this declaration was made evidently: 1. From true love of Jesus. 2. From too much reliance on his own strength. 3. From ignorance of himself and of the trials through which he was soon to pass.

30 And Jesus saith unto him, Verily I say unto thee, that thou to-day, even this night,—This more definitely specifies the time.

before the cock crow twice, shalt deny me thrice,—The cock

vehemently, If I must die with thee, I will not deny thee. And in like manner also said they all.

---

is accustomed to crow twice, once at midnight, and once in the morning, at break of day—about three o'clock. The latter was commonly called cockcrowing. (Mark 13: 35.) Mark and Luke speak of the second crowing. The denial would take place before the second crowing, or three o'clock in the morning.

31 **But he spake exceeding vehemently, If I must die with thee, I will not deny thee.**—He means that he would die with Jesus before he would deny him. Here Peter shows his strong self-will and self-confidence. But this together with his denial shows how little man understands himself. Self-confidence and a presumptuous opinion of one's own strength is a sin very incident to the holiest and best of men. This good man resolved honestly, no doubt, too much in his own strength. Little did he think what a feather he should be in the wind of temptation if once left to the power and prevalence of his own fears.

And in like manner also said they all.—All the apostles. The other ten caught the spirit of Peter and took the position he did. Judas had left them and hence did not join in the conversation. [As Jesus neared his end, he pressed more and more of his teachings into the days as they passed. This fourteenth day of April—the night on which he was betrayed—was replete with service and instruction. This night the supper was instituted and eaten. At this supper, in the guest-chamber, he spoke the sermon telling of the mansions in the father's house (John 1: 14); the comforter that he would send (John 14: 31); the vine and the branches (John 15: 1-12); Christ's love for his friends, and the hatred of the world (John 15: 13-27); persecution they would endure for his sake, and the comfort of the Holy Spirit (John 16: 1-33); his intercessory prayer for the oneness of his apostles, and for all who should believe on him through their word (John 17). "When Jesus had spoken these words, he went forth with his disciples over the brook Kidron, where was a garden, into the which he entered, himself and his disciples." It is probable the greater part of his teaching was done while they were at the table in the guestchamber. Some think it was at the foot of the Mount of Olives.]

8. THE AGONY IN GETHSEMANE
14: 32-42
(Matt. 26: 36-46; Luke 22: 39-46; John 18: 1)

32 And they come unto [8]a place which was named Gethsemane: and he saith unto his disciples, Sit ye here, while I pray. 33 And he taketh with him Peter and [9]James and John, and began to be greatly amazed, and sore

[8]Gr. *an enclosed piece of ground.*
[9]Or, *Jacob*

32 **And they come unto a place which was named Gethsemane: and he saith unto his disciples,**—"Gethsemane" means a place of oil presses, and doubtless this place had once been used for pressing out olive oil, but it was at this time a garden. (John 18: 1.)

Sit ye here, while I pray.—[He was approaching the last fearful trial—his betrayal and crucifixion. As it came nearer and nearer, he felt it the more keenly and sensitively. He dreaded the trial and the pangs of the crucifixion with more than human sensitiveness. He felt all the weakness of humanity in the temptation. He knew Judas was then gone to bring the band to arrest him. He dreaded the conflict, and besought help from his Father in prayer. All through his ministry, when questions of importance pressed upon him, he went to his Father in prayer. So he said to the disciples, "Sit ye here, while I pray." Matthew (26: 36) says: "While I go yonder and pray," showing he would go away from them to pray alone.]

33 **And he taketh with him Peter and James and John.**— [He left the eight, we may suppose, near the entrance to the garden, and took these three apostles that seem to have been favorites with him—at least, he several times chose them to be with him on special occasions, while the others were not. He carried these only a short distance, and left them to watch for the coming of the soldiers while he went alone to pray.]

and began to be greatly amazed, and sore troubled.— [Struck or overcome with horror and dread at the fate that was awaiting him. He wrestled with this dread, and was oppressed with a great sorrow. His feelings as a human being

troubled. 34 And he saith unto them, My soul is exceeding sorrowful even unto death: abide ye here, and watch. 35 And he went forward a little, and fell on the ground, and prayed that, if it were possible, the hour might pass

---

prevailed and in the anguish of his soul he was "sore troubled"—depressed in soul and heart.]

34 **And he saith unto them, My soul is exceeding sorrowful even unto death:**—[He told the disciples that went with him that the sorrows that were oppressing him were such as to produce death, or that he would prefer to die rather than bear them, they were so heavy. Mental dread of impending evil is often more excruciating than the suffering of physical pain when it comes. When the resolution is once formed that we will submit to or go through the ordeal of trial, a composure of mind and heart comes that strips the ordeal of more than half its terrors. Jesus was human, with our fleshly weaknesses and temptations, with its dread of suffering intensified by the recoil of the divine element within him from sin and its consequences. We may imagine the divine element, with its hatred and horror of sin, drew back from the public manifestation before the world as a sin offering, as though God had sinned.]

abide ye here, and watch.—[He told them to tarry there and watch while he went still forward in prayer. He did not wish to be surprised in his devotions by the coming of his enemies, so he asked them to watch while he prayed. Matthew (26: 38) says: "Abide ye here, and watch *with* me." In this hour of agony Jesus desired human sympathy. He had encouraged and comforted his disciples in every hour of trouble and weakness, but now he desired them to watch with him that he might not be disturbed by the traitor and the mob in his hour of communion with God.]

35 **And he went forward a little,**—[Luke (22: 41) says: "He was parted from them about a stone's cast." He went a little distance from them, so that they could not hear or see his wrestling with God. The fact that they slept while he was undergoing these sorrows shows he was not in hearing or sight of them. When beyond their reach, in agony of soul he threw himself prostrate on the ground.]

and fell on the ground, and prayed—[Kneeling is the ordi-

away from him. 36 And he said, Abba, Father, all things are possible unto
thee; remove this cup from me: howbeit not what I will, but what thou wilt.

nary attitude of prayer to God, but in deep distress, and in his
helplessness, man throws himself prostrate before his maker
as a bodily expression of the complete helplessness of soul he
feels, and of his throwing himself upon God as his only help.]

**that, if it were possible, the hour might pass away from
him.**—[In the above attitude he prayed this prayer. Matthew
records it: "He went forward a little, and fell on his face, and
prayed, saying, My Father, if it be possible, let this cup pass
away from me: nevertheless, not as I will, but as thou wilt."
The human dread of death was drawing back with terror from
the suffering he was to endure, intensified by the divine horror of being held up before the universe as a sinner. Jesus
died as a sinner. He died for sins not his own. His prayer
was that the cup of suffering—the horror of woe that was rapidly coming upon him—might pass from him. This was the
fleshly element of his nature pleading for exemption from the
suffering that is coming upon him. While God heard him, he
did not grant the prayer as Jesus asked it should be granted.
God hears prayer that he does not grant. It is not sinful to
make prayers God cannot grant. The prayer of Jesus was answered by his being strengthened to bear the suffering.]

36 **And he said, Abba, Father, all things are possible unto
thee;**—["Abba" means "father." It is the Hebrew word preserved here, with its translation, "Father," given. He calls
him Father, and tells him all things are possible to him. All
power is in his hands; therefore he asks him to so use that
power that he may escape the sufferings that would come
upon him in that hour, or to pass this cup of suffering from
him.]

remove this cup from me:—[He means the cup of suffering
he was then to drink. The flesh seemed to get the upper hand
of him for a moment. He shrank back from the suffering and
he prayed that God would take it away. But he recovered his
faith and added: "Nevertheless not my will, but thine, be
done."]

howbeit not what I will, but what thou wilt.—He dreaded
the sufferings, and would like to escape them, he yet had

37 And he cometh, and findeth them sleeping, and saith unto Peter, Simon, sleepest thou? couldest thou not watch one hour? 38 [10]Watch and pray, that ye enter not into temptation: the spirit indeed is willing, but the flesh is

[10]Or, *Watch ye, and pray that ye enter not*

rather endure them than that God's will should not be performed, or that his purposes should not be carried out. On the day previous, looking forward to this hour, he said: "Now is my soul troubled; and what shall I say? Father, save me from this hour. But for this cause came I unto this hour." (John 12: 27.) This shows the dread of the hour—the drawing back of the flesh from the hour—yet he adds: "For this cause (to suffer) came I unto this hour." Luke (22: 44) says: "Being in an agony he prayed more earnestly; and his sweat became as it were great drops of blood falling down upon the ground." The anguish was so deep and excruciating that it wrung from his face great drops of bloody sweat that in their abundance fell to the ground. This suffering of the soul was greater than bodily suffering.]

37 **And he cometh, and findeth them sleeping,**—[They were poor watchers; yet they understood but little of the wonderful occurrences passing before them, or of the fearful struggles going on in the soul of Jesus. They had undergone the excitement and labors of the eventful day. It is now far into the night. Luke says he "found them sleeping for sorrow." (22: 45.) While they did not understand the full meaning of what was going forward, they saw Jesus was oppressed—that things were not going well. They were disappointed and downcast in spirit. That, added to their bodily weariness, caused them to sink into a heavy sleep.]

and saith unto Peter, Simon, sleepest thou?—[Jesus addressed Peter. He was more forward than the others in asserting he would die with him before he would deny him.]

couldest thou not watch one hour—Wast thou unable—not strong enough to watch as short a period as sixty minutes?

38 **Watch and pray, that ye enter not into temptation:**—That ye be not overcome and oppressed with these trials of your faith, so as to deny me. The word "temptation" here properly means what would try their faith in the approaching calamities, his rejection and death.

the spirit indeed is willing, but the flesh is weak.—[He fol-

weak. 39 And again he went away, and prayed, saying the same words. 40 And again he came, and found them sleeping, for their eyes were very heavy; and they knew not what to answer him. 41 And he cometh the third

lowed up the reproof of their failing to watch with and for him with the admonition that they should both watch and pray for themselves, lest they enter into temptation, while this conveys a general lesson to all to watch themselves, to watch their surroundings, to watch the influences that control them, to watch lest they have too much self-confidence (this was Peter's weakness and the occasion of his downfall), lest they run into temptations that they cannot bear, it had a special reference to the temptations that would soon be upon them by virtue of his trial and crucifixion. The reason he gives is, "The spirit indeed is willing, but the flesh is weak." He recognizes the two elements in man—the spirit and the flesh.]

39 **And again he went away, and prayed, saying the same words.**—[He left and went again, and made the same earnest prayer. He repeated the prayer to God earnestly and fervently in the same words. He was not afraid of worrying his Father with his petitions and repetitions.]

40 **And again he came, and found them sleeping, for their eyes were very heavy; and they knew not what to answer him.** —[They had lost much sleep; they were worn and wearied. They understood enough to know dark clouds hung around the pathway of their Master. The earthly prospects failed, their eyes were heavy, and after Jesus left them they quickly fell asleep again: and they did not know what response to make him or excuse to give him for sleep. But clearly Jesus, as he returns each time, is growing in composure and resignation. His prayer is not answered by releasing him from the hour, but he is becoming resigned and submissive to it as the will of his Father. To become resigned and submissive to any fate is to take away its bitterness—is to prepare to meet it. The angels watched over him, and when he was tired they readily gave the help needed to enable him to bear the burdens laid upon him by God. God answered him not by taking the trial from him, but by strengthening him to bear it. God so treats every child that humbly, trustingly, and faithfully seeks to do his will. He will not always take from us our burdens, but he will give us strength to bear them.]

time, and saith unto them, "Sleep on now, and take your rest: it is enough;
the hour is come; behold, the Son of man is ²betrayed into the hands of sinners. 42 Arise, let us be going: behold, he that ²betrayeth me is at hand.

¹¹Or, *Do ye sleep on, then, and take your rest?*

41 **And he cometh the third time, and saith unto them,
Sleep on now, and take your rest: it is enough; the hour is
come; behold, the Son of man is betrayed into the hands of
sinners.**—[When he returns from his prayer the third time he
finds them asleep again. But the struggle is over with him.
The spirit has overcome the flesh. He can without a struggle
now submit to the will of his Father, even by going to the
cross and the grave. So he says to them, "Sleep on now, and
take your rest." He knew their bodies needed rest.]

42 **Arise, let us be going: behold, he that betrayeth me is at
hand.**—["While he yet spake, Judas, one of the twelve, came,
and with him a great multitude with swords, and staves, from
the chief priests and elders of the people." (Matt. 26: 47.)
He is betrayed into their hands, and willingly now gives himself a ransom for the sins of the world.]

9. THE ARREST OF JESUS
14: 43-52
(Matt. 26: 47-56; Luke 22: 47-53; John 18: 2-14)

43 And straightway, while he yet spake, cometh Judas, one of the twelve,
and with him a multitude with swords and staves, from the chief priests and

43 **And straightway, while he yet spake, cometh Judas, one
of the twelve,**—Judas Iscariot, named in the lists of the apostles in Matt. 10, Mark 3, and Luke 6.

and with him a multitude with swords and staves,—And
"lanterns and torches." (John 18: 3.) A motley multitude of
soldiers of the Roman cohort, the temple guard (Luke 22:
52), chief priests, soldiers and servants. All this throng had
come to arrest one man who had no thought of resistance. It
strongly exhibits the conviction of the chief priests in the con-
sequent danger attending his arrest.

from the chief priests and the scribes and the elders.—They
sent the ruffians along with some of their number and the
"captains of the temple." (Luke 22: 52.) Just after self-sur-
render comes betrayal. So, Christian, you may have your

the scribes and the elders. 44 Now he that [1]betrayed him had given them a
token, saying, Whomsoever I shall kiss, that is he; take him, and lead him
away safely. 45 And when he was come, straightway he came to him, and
saith, Rabbi; and [2]kissed him. 46 And they laid hands on him, and took him.
47 But a certain one of them that stood by drew his sword, and smote the
[3]servant of the high priest, and struck off his ear. 48 And Jesus answered

[1]See marginal note on ch. 3. 19.
[2]Gr. *kissed him much.*
[3]Gr. *bondservant.*

---

greatest trial when you are in most perfect harmony with
God's will. Do not, therefore, lose faith! Beyond Calvary
were the resurrection and ascension.

44 Now he that betrayed him had given them a token,—For
the accomplishment of their schemes it was of the utmost importance that no mistake should be made, because if Jesus escaped all the Galileans might be put on the lookout, and it
would be impossible to arrest him subsequently.

**saying, Whomsoever I shall kiss, that is he; take him, and
lead him away safely.**—There were certainly enough to do it,
since Jesus offered no resistance.

**45 And when he was come, straightway he came to him,
and saith, Rabbi; and kissed him.**—The vilest, the most abominable piece of hypocrisy known in history, which the infernal
inspirer of treason alone could invent.

46 And they laid hands on him, and took him.—Arrested
him.

47 But a certain one of them that stood by—Matthew is
more explicit, "one of them that were with Jesus," but John
reveals the name, "Simon Peter," who had said a short time
before that he would die with Jesus rather than forsake him.

**drew his sword, and smote the servant of the high priest,
and struck off his ear.**—John tells that it was his "right ear."
Luke reports that Jesus touched the ear and healed it. Some
think these swords were provided to show the use of carnal
weapons; that those who rely on them should perish with
them. It is certain they did not use them for common. It is
also clear that the church was taught not to use the carnal,
but spiritual weapons. "For though we walk in the flesh, we
do not war according to the flesh (for the weapons of our warfare are not of the flesh, but mighty before God to the casting
down of strongholds.)" (2 Cor. 10: 3, 4.) David was not al-

and said unto them, Are ye come out, as against a robber, with swords and staves to seize me? 49 I was daily with you in the temple teaching, and ye took me not: but *this is done* that the scriptures might be fulfilled. 50 And they all left him, and fled.

lowed to build the temple because he was a man of war and blood. (2 Chron. 22:7, 8; 28:2, 3; Psalm 2:4.)

48 And Jesus answered and said unto them, Are ye come out, as against a robber, with swords and staves to seize me? —The contrast between a thief and the character of Jesus was so great that his enemies who were conversant with his inoffensive and gentle nature must have felt the force of the comparison. He who denies Christ's divinity makes him a robber.

It is in connection with these words that we learn from Luke that so thoroughly in earnest were the chief priests and elders in this matter, and so anxious that it should be successful and no mistake made, that they had come with or followed their adherents to the spot. Luke represents the words as specially addressed to them and the captains of the temple. These latter were probably subaltern officers of the guard of priests and Levites who kept watch by night in the temple. "As against a robber," one who hides himself away, and only emerges to do violence.

49 I was daily with you in the temple teaching, and ye took me not:—This is a distinct taunt of their cowardice in making all this array to take by night one whom they had feared to take by day.

but this is done that the scriptures might be fulfilled.—Luke (22: 53) has: "But this is your hour, and the power of darkness." The words in Mark, however, explain why it is their hour; simply because the Messianic prophecies, such as Isa. 50; Psalm 22; Dan. 9: 26; Zech. 13: 7, must be fulfilled, and thus proclaim him the more clearly and forever what they deny. In order to do this Jesus was willing to walk weltering in his own blood. There are scriptures for you to fulfill. At what cost are you willing to do it?

50 And they all left him, and fled.—Matthew explains, "All the disciples left him." Why? His last words indicated that he had no intention of resisting or delivering himself, either by natural or supernatural means. It was evident that his en-

51 And a certain young man followed with him, having a linen cloth cast about him, over *his* naked *body*: and they lay hold on him; 52 but he left the linen cloth, and fled naked.

emies were to have their will of him, and his disciples had not yet arrived at the point at which they were willing to follow him to death. James and John had no desire now for the place of honor on his right hand and his left, though it would have been as truly such as that for which they had longed. So they scattered in different directions in the obscurity of the grove. These disciples had protested their love for him a few hours before. Peter among the rest, but he followed afar off. (Verse 54.) These disciples were doubtless as honest as their limited knowledge of themselves would admit. The pressure of trials shows us our true character, our strength, or rather our weakness.

51 **And a certain young man followed with him,**—Only Mark relates this incident, and gives us no clue to the identity of the young man. It has been conjectured, from the fact that he alone relates the incident, and from a supposed similarity in the character of the young man, as indicated by his conduct, to that of Mark, as shown in what we know of his history (Acts 13: 13; 15: 37, 38), that it was Mark himself. But it is pure conjecture. No one knows.

having a linen cloth cast about him, over his naked body: and they lay hold on him;—Arrested him.

52 **but he left the linen cloth, and fled naked.**—He could easily slip out of their hands thus. And Jesus is left alone with the enemies who thirst for his life. The young man referred to was probably aroused from his bed by the noise of the crowd who had Christ under arrest, and may have followed him for a short distance in his nightdress, till when also arrested by the men who had charge of Christ, he fled away in great consternation, leaving the garment which was loose around the body in their hands.

SECTION FIVE
14: 53 to 15: 15

10. TRIAL BY THE SANHEDRIN
14: 53-65
(Matt. 26: 57-68; Luke 22: 66-71; John 18: 19-24)

53 And they led Jesus away to the high priest: and there come together with him all the chief priests and the elders and the scribes. 54 And Peter had followed him afar off, even within, into the court of the high priest; and he was sitting with the officers, and warming himself in the light *of the fire*.

---

53 **And they led Jesus away to the high priest: and there come together with him all the chief priests and the elders and the scribes.**—[Caiaphas was the high priest. Those assembled with him were the chief priests. These, with the elders of Israel and scribes, constituted the Sanhedrin—the Jewish high court. After the destruction of the national independence it remained as the highest tribunal of justice among the Jews. They tried all cases of heresy of religious teaching and decided cases of differences among the Jews. The Romans permitted them to decide cases, but they could not inflict punishment of death without the sanction of the Roman governor, and there was right of appeal then to Caesar at Rome. They sought grounds to put him to death; then they would bring the case before the governor for his approval. They (his avowed enemies) determined to kill him—were his judges; and they sought testimony to convict him. Such a trial is a farce.]

54 **And Peter had followed him afar off,**—John tells us that another disciple followed (18: 15), who was probably John himself, though, with his accustomed modesty, he does not name him.

even within, into the court of the high priest; and he was sitting with the officers,—Some of the force which had assisted in the arrest of Jesus.

and warming himself in the light of the fire.—The night and early morning are cool in Palestine even when the day is very warm. It was still night. Luke 22: 55 says the fire was kindled in "the midst of the court." The palace was a quadrangle around an open court, and here the fire was kindled on the ground or marble floor. Here took place "the denial." [Peter

55 Now the chief priests and the whole council sought witness against Jesus to put him to death; and found it not. 56 For many bare false witness against him, and their witness agreed not together. 57 And there stood up cer-

had courage to come back to see the end, but did not venture near.]

55 **Now the chief priests**—These were the heads of the twenty-four temple courses, and ex-high priests, members of the Sanhedrin.

and the whole council—The great Sanhedrin, variously represented as consisting of seventy, seventy-one, and seventy-two members. It was composed of chief priests, elders, originally heads of families or tribes representing the people; and scribes (or lawyers), the interpreters of the law; probably twenty-four of the first, the same of the second, and a number of the third, bringing up the full number of the council.

sought witness against Jesus to put him to death;—Why are they seeking witnesses now? Why did they not have them ready, such as they intended to accept? The explanation is found in the suddenness with which they had decided upon the arrest. They had intended to postpone it until after the feast (Mark 14: 1, 2), but when Judas came rushing to them the evening before, they yielded to his urgency and resolved to avail themselves of the opportunity of Gethesemane. They must now hunt their witnesses. Matthew (26: 59) says they "sought false witness."

and found it not.—These parties [constituted the court to try Jesus. They had predetermined the case, and became the prosecutors. In all civilized nations a man who has formed or expressed an opinion in a case involving the life or liberty of a prisoner is incompetent to try it. A judge in any way connected with a case is incompetent to try it. Yet these men, especially interested in, and seeking testimony to convict him, are the judges who decide the case. They were determined to put him to death. This was a religious body. The charge on which they sought to convict him was blasphemy against God. When they brought him before Pilate, the charge was treason against Caesar. This shows they suited the charge to excite the prejudice or interest of the judge.]

56 **For many bare false witness against him,**—These are not

tain, and bare false witness against him, saying, 58 We heard him say,
I will destroy this 'temple that is made with hands, and in three days I
will build another made without hands. 59 And not even so did their wit-

⁴Or, *sanctuary*

lacking as they are always to be found where there are in-
fluential men with means and money at their command to furnish them.

and their witness agreed not together.—The law of Moses
required that an accusation should be sustained by two witnesses at least. (Num. 35: 30; Deut. 17: 6; 19: 15.) No two
could be found, for a while, to testify to the same statement.
[Matthew (26: 59, 60) says: "Now the chief priests and the
whole council sought false witness against Jesus, that they
might put him to death; and they found it not, though many
false witnesses came." They sought witnesses that would
swear falsely in order to convict him. They found none—that
is, although many witnessed falsely, they so convicted themselves of falsehood as to destroy their testimony. It is very
difficult for a man to tell a falsehood and not expose his guilt
in it. All surroundings tend to expose it. A falsehood requires ten other falsehoods to cover it, and each of these ten
more to cover it up, and the workings of time uncover them.
A man can always afford to tell the truth. Others telling
falsehoods may contradict him for the time, but all the devel-
opments of the future will tend to confirm and vindicate truth.
So the false witness of these men contradicted and destroyed
itself.]

57 **And there stood up certain,**—Matthew (26: 60) says:
"Afterward came two," the legal number, "and bare false witness."

and bare false witness against him, saying,—Mark calls it
false witness because, although Jesus said something similar,
the words were not correctly reported. John (2: 19) tells us
that he said: "Destroy this temple, and in three days I will
raise it up," speaking of his body. In every age new witnesses arise. Satan changes the front of attack, but in every
age the witnesses fail,

58 **We heard him say, I will destroy this temple that is
made with hands, and in three days I will build another made**

ness agree together. 60 And the high priest stood up in the midst, and asked
Jesus, saying, Answerest thou nothing? what is it which these witness
against thee? 61 But he held his peace, and answered nothing. Again the

without hands.—[The Jews (John 2: 18, 19) asked: "What sign showest thou unto us, seeing that thou doest these things? Jesus answered and said unto them, Destroy this temple, and in three days I will raise it up." Jesus meant this of his body, which, if destroyed or killed, should be revived; but when spoken in those days, the Jews applied it to the temple, and replied: "Forty and six years was this temple in building, and wilt thou raise it up in three days?" But he spake of the temple of his body. They misrepresented his statement. He said this temple—his body—not made with hands. They say he said this temple—made with hands.]

59 **And not even so did their witness agree together.**—[While each gave his misrepresentation of the statement of Jesus, the testimony of these two witnesses was contradictory. The old Jewish law, as given by Moses, required that no one should be convicted save on the testimony of two or three witnesses. So there was great failure when two witnesses were brought to establish a fact, and they destroyed instead of strengthened each other's testimony. But persons who seek false testimony to destroy a man would convict him without testimony at all. Why, then, the great anxiety to find the false testimony? The reason is the case must go before the Roman governor. It must be according to the forms of law, and the testimony must justify the judgment. If not, the effort to secure testimony was to meet the demands of the Roman governor.

60 **And the high priest stood up in the midst, and asked Jesus, saying, Answerest thou nothing? what is it which these witness against thee?**—[Jesus was silent amid the false charges made against him. He replied not a word. They involved in no way his true character, and he left them to testify as they desired. The high priest seemed anxious to involve him in a controversy, and wrangle with these witnesses, hoping he might commit himself in some way so as to excite the multitude or give ground for sustaining the charges before the governor. The priests and rulers seem to have been willing to excite the multitude so they would murder Jesus in a

high priest asked him, and saith unto him, Art thou the Christ, the Son of the Blessed? 62 And Jesus said, I am: and ye shall see the Son of man sitting at the right hand of Power, and coming with the clouds of heaven. 63 And the high priest rent his clothes, and saith, What further need have

mob, so they would have been excused; or, failing in this, they desired to excite him into some act that they might condemn him before the governor.]

61 **But he held his peace, and answered nothing. Again the high priest asked him, and saith unto him, Art thou the Christ,**—[He held his peace—made no answer to the charges. The priest said, as Matthew (26: 63) records it: "I adjure thee by the living God, that thou tell us whether thou art the Christ, the Son of God." This question involved the vital point of his mission to the world, and of his relation to God. The belief that he is the Son of God, and so divine, is the turning point in man's destiny.]

the Son of the Blessed?—Matthew (26: 63) says: "The Son of God." The two phrases mean the same. The lips so resolutely shut were now opened. The witness testifies unequivocally. Jesus will answer to no side issue. We must come to the point. The greater includes the lesser.

62 **And Jesus said, I am:**—No need of summoning further witnesses. All their former trouble might have been saved. The divine Son will not deny his Sonship. But he does not stop with their question, but goes on to utter one of the most sublime declarations ever made by any one. He answered in the affirmative that he was the Messiah, and not only the Messiah but the *Judge,* who was yet to come in great power.

and ye shall see the Son of man sitting at the right hand of Power,—This expression would remind these rulers of the expression of Daniel, where "there came with the clouds of heaven one like unto a son of man." But their intentions were so determined on putting the accused to death that meekness, innocence, and scripture all pass for nothing.

and coming with the clouds of heaven.—Jesus had now said all and more than all that his enemies could desire. He had proclaimed himself the Messiah of the prophets, the Son of man of Daniel, and the actual Son of God and sharer of his authority.

we of witnesses? 64 Ye have heard the blasphemy: what think ye? And they all condemned him to be [5]worthy of death. 65 And some began to spit on him, and to cover his face, and to buffet him, and to say unto him, Prophesy: and the officers received him with [6]blows of their hands.

[5]Gr. *liable to.*
[6]Or, *strokes of rods*

---

63 **And the high priest rent his clothes,**—[To rend the clothes was to express, in such a case, violent grief that one should so blaspheme against God. He regarded this confession as blasphemy deserving death. This confession was witness enough. For a man to claim to be the Son of God in the sense here meant would be blasphemy—would be claiming for self the prerogatives of God. This is blasphemy in any one not divine. The sin of these men was to refuse to see or accept the proofs of his divine character, and so they rejected all the true testimony, and condemned him on what they knew to be false testimony.]

and saith, What further need have we of witnesses?—There *was* a great scarcity, but *now* no need. O, how the world rends its garments over the sins of the church. One peccadillo in a Christian is of more importance than a cycle of sin in those outside. But let our purpose be to walk circumspectly!

64 **Ye have heard the blasphemy: what think ye?**—The high priest now seeks to obtain the united judgment of the court to the same thing. He knows well this eagerness to find him guilty, he has but to act the part of a leader to obtain their judgment to the same effect. He has given his own decision. He now asks theirs.

And they all condemned him to be worthy of death.—[They were all anxious to condemn him, so they readily agreed it was blasphemy; and that he ought by their law to die.]

65 **And some began to spit on him,**—Matthew says: "In his face." The Jews knew of nothing more expressive of contempt.

and to cover his face, and to buffet him,—They blindfolded him with a view to mock his pretensions as a prophet. They struck him with their fists.

and to say unto him, Prophesy:—As Jesus was a prophet, they would ask him to tell who it was that struck him when he was blindfolded. "Prophesy unto us, thou Christ: who is he that struck thee?" (Matt. 26: 68.) Supernatural knowledge belonged to Messiah, the prophet. They demanded that he should show this, by telling who struck him while he was blindfolded. But he made no response. (See Isa. 53: 7.)

and the officers received him with blows of their hands.— The margin has "or strokes of rods." The members of the council having gratified their malicious hatred for the time being, they delivered him to the officers' custody till they should be ready to lead him to Pilate. In this great and marvelous combat, one strove against all, and yet for all. He suffered as a lamb yet conquered as a lion. He is overcome and yet he is the victor.

11. PETER'S DENIAL
14: 66-72
(Matt. 26: 69-75; Luke 22: 55-62; John 18: 15-18, 25-27)

66 And as Peter was beneath in the court, there cometh one of the maids of the high priest; 67 and seeing Peter warming himself, she looked upon him, and saith, Thou also wast with the Nazarene, *even* Jesus. 68 But he denied, saying, [7]I neither know, nor understand what thou sayest: and he

[7]Or, *I neither know, nor understand: thou, what sayest thou?*

---

66 And as Peter was beneath in the court, there cometh one of the maids of the high priest;—Matthew says: "A maid." It appears from John's record that she was the maid who kept the door. (John 18: 16, 17.)

67 and seeing Peter warming himself, she looked upon him, and saith, Thou also wast with the Nazarene, even Jesus.— Literally, *the Nazarene*. This was a contemptuous epithet among the Jews of Judea. (Mark 1: 24.) She may have feared being blamed for admitting him. He seems to have been in no great danger, except as he might be recognized as the one who smote Malchus. Some see in the words "thou also" a reference to John.

68 But he denied,—Matthew says: "He denied before them all."

saying, I neither know, nor understand what thou sayest: —That is, he did not see any reason why this question was asked. All this was falsehood; and Peter must have known that it was such. This is remarkable, because Peter had just before been so confident.

went out into the ⁸porch; ⁹and the cock crew. 69 And the maid saw him, and began again to say to them that stood by, This is *one* of them. 70 But he again denied it. And after a little while again they that stood by said to Peter, Of a truth thou art *one* of them; for thou art a Galilaean. 71 But he began to curse, and to swear, I know not this man of whom ye speak. 72

⁸Gr. *forecourt.*
⁹Many ancient authorities omit *and the cock crew*

and he went out into the porch;—Peter was embarrassed and confused by the question; and to save his confusion from attracting further notice, he went away from the fire into the porch, where he expected to be unobserved. Yet in vain. By the very movement to avoid detection, he came into contact with another who knew him, and repeated the charge.

and the cock crew.—True to Mark's own report of the prediction (verse 30), he here mentions the fact that a cock crowed immediately after the first denial. It was now probably between twelve and one o'clock.

69 **And the maid saw him,**—Matthew says: "Another maid." By comparing the parallel passages the reader will see that after the charge was first made by the porteress, it was repeated by quite a number of others, both male and female, and that Peter made various answers, though all amounted to but three denials.

and began again to say to them that stood by, This is one of them.—That is, one of his disciples. "Art thou also one of his disciples?" (John 18: 25.)

70 **But he again denied it. And after a little while again they that stood by said to Peter, Of a truth thou art one of them; for thou art a Galilaean.**—Matthew says: "Thy speech maketh thee known." Peter and the other Galileans spoke the same language as the Jews of Jerusalem, but they had some peculiar pronunciations like the provincialisms of our own country, by which they were distinguished. From his being a Galilean, they inferred that he was a follower of Jesus—an illogical conclusion, and yet a correct one.

71 **But he began to curse, and to swear, I know not this man of whom ye speak.**—This is Peter's third denial. This was an advance upon his second. He not only, with an oath, repeats what he had said in the second, that he knew not of whom they spake, but he affirms it with imprecations of di-

And straightway the second time the cock crew. And Peter called to mind the word, how that Jesus said unto him, Before the cock crow twice, thou shalt deny me thrice. [10]And when he thought thereon, he wept.

[10]Or, *And he began to weep*

---

vine wrath on himself if he spake not the truth.

72 And straightway the second time the cock crew.—The second crowing of the cock is around three o'clock. This is a fulfillment of the prediction of the Master, which shows his divinity.

And Peter called to mind the word, how that Jesus said unto him, Before the cock crow twice, thou shalt deny me thrice.—Luke tells us that when the cock crew Jesus turned and looked upon Peter, and that then he remembered his words. They were in the same room—Jesus at the upper end of the hall, elevated for a tribunal, and Peter below with the servants; so that Jesus could look down upon Peter standing near the fire.

And when he thought thereon, he wept.—Matthew says: "He went out, and wept bitterly." Overwhelmed and forced to tears over his fall, he went out to hide his bitter weeping and himself from his Master's eyes. He went alone into the darkness of the night and wept bitterly. It is worthy of note that the fact that the fall of Peter is recorded by all the evangelists is high proof of the honesty and candor of our sacred historians. They were willing to mention their own faults without attemping to appear to be better than they were. An uninspired historian would have omitted the fall of Peter and mentioned only his good qualities This shows the difference between an inspired and an uninspired historian and is strong evidence that the Bible is from God.

12. JESUS ACCUSED BEFORE PILATE
15: 1-5
(Matt. 27: 1, 2; 11-14; Luke 23: 1-5; John 18: 28-38)

1 And straightway in the morning the chief priests with the elders and

---

1 And straightway in the morning—The trial of Jesus before the Sanhedrin had begun in the night preceding *this* "morning."

scribes, and the whole council, held a consultation, and bound Jesus, and carried him away, and delivered him up to Pilate. 2 And Pilate asked him, Art thou the King of the Jews? And he answering saith unto him, Thou sayest.

the chief priests with the elders and scribes, and the whole council, held a consultation,—Matthew (27: 1) says: "Took counsel against Jesus to put him to death." Luke (23: 1) says: "The whole company of them rose up" together, and he was led away with their council. They desired now to make formally legal in daylight what they had hastily consummated in the illegal night and place.

and bound Jesus,—Rebound him. He had probably been relieved of his fetters while shut up with the officers. They might have simply bound him more securely.

and carried him away,—And delivered him up to Pilate. (John 18: 12-24.)

and delivered him up to Pilate.—Pilate was the sixth Roman procurator of Judea. He was the supreme authority in the province, but responsible to the governor of Syria. What a beginning for a feast day which celebrated an act of deliverance by God from death! They observe it by an act of deliverance of God's Son to death. The state has no business to meddle in religion. The church which invites it is apostate. The state has as much business to meddle in religion as the church or an individual Christian has to meddle in politics. There is no Bible authority for either.

2 And Pilate asked him, Art thou the King of the Jews?— This question indicates that something had been said to Pilate by the Jews touching this point, or he would not have asked this question. This is clearly brought out by John who reports Jesus as saying to Pilate in answer to this question: "Sayest thou this of thyself, or did others tell it thee concerning me?" Jesus answered that he was king of the Jews, but explained to Pilate that his kingdom was not of this world, and for this reason was not a rival of any earthly kingdom in the sense of which the Jews would accuse him. It was this statement of Jesus in all probability which enabled Herod and Pilate to decide there was no fault in him. (Luke 23: 14, 15.)

And he answering saith unto him, Thou sayest.—This was

3 And the chief priests accused him of many things. 4 And Pilate again asked him, saying, Answerest thou nothing? behold how many things they

---

equivalent to "Thou sayest what is true." It was answering in the affirmative.

3 **And the chief priests accused him of many things.**—[They were not present in the hall of trial, but laid the accusations against him before Pilate. To none of the accusations did he reply. To none of the questions did he answer save, "Art thou the Son of God?" "Art thou the King of the Jews?" To these he always responded, because they involved the great claims he came to establish; and the belief of these truths is the starting point to eternal life.]

4 **And Pilate again asked him, saying, Answerest thou nothing? behold how many things they accuse thee of.**—[Then Pilate entered into the judgment hall again, and called Jesus, and said unto him (John 18: 33); showing he went out to hear again or confer with the priests and the members of the Sanhedrin concerning the charges they made against him. When he returned he plied Jesus with the same question, showing this was the point on which they relied to extract the sentence of death from Pilate—that he was a rival of Caesar, and disloyal to the Roman government. Jesus, knowing he was prompted by these persons, asked: "Sayest thou this thing of thyself, or did others tell it thee concerning me? Pilate answered, Am I a Jew? Thine own nation and the chief priests delivered thee unto me: What hast thou done?" (John 18: 34, 35.) Pilate questioned him as prompted by the Jews, and asked him to state his case. Jesus then answered: "My kingdom is not of this world; if my kingdom were of this world, then would my servants fight, that I should not be delivered to the Jews: but now is my kingdom not from hence. Pilate therefore said unto him, Art thou a king, then? Jesus answered, Thou sayest that I am a king. To this end have I been born, and to this end am I come into the world, that I should bear witness unto the truth." Pilate is jealous of any one claiming to be a king, as he is the representative of Caesar the king. Jesus explains that his kingdom is not an earthly kingdom, else his servants would fight. He gave Pilate to understand he was in no sense a rival of Caesar, and that his ser-

accuse thee of. 5 But Jesus no more answered anything; insomuch that Pilate marvelled.

vants would not engage in carnal war in his behalf. While he explained this to Pilate, against the many accusations of the Jews he answered nothing. It is thought "my servants" refer to the legions of angels at his command to deliver him if he should say the word. (Matt. 26: 33.)] If Jesus would not suffer his servants to enter into carnal warfare to establish and sustain his spiritual kingdom, then he certainly does not expect them to establish and sustain human governments by and through carnal warfare. If they could not fight to establish his own kingdom, surely they cannot to establish one for some one else.

5 **But Jesus no more answered anything; insomuch that Pilate marvelled.**—[He persisted in silence to all accusations of the Jews, so that Pilate wondered at his persistent silence. The charges were chiefly false, and he could have refuted them, but he resisted not evil. Only when his claims to be the Son of God and the king of the Jews in the high unworldly sense were questioned, did he speak. Luke (23: 4, 5) says Pilate at this time said: "I find no fault in this man. But they were the more urgent, saying, He stirreth up the people, teaching throughout all Judaea, beginning from Galilee even unto this place." Galilee was in Herod's jurisdiction. When Pilate heard this, he sent him to Herod, who was at Jerusalem at the time. Pilate believed him innocent; he did not wish to offend the Jews; so he thought to shift the responsibility to Herod. (Luke 23: 8.) Herod was glad to see him—had long hoped to see him work a miracle. He questioned him in many words, but he answered him nothing. Chief priests and scribes vehemently accused him of many things. Herod, with his men of war, set him at naught, mocked him, dressed him in a gorgeous robe, and sent him to Pilate. The same day Pilate and Herod are made friends together; they had been at enmity; but Herod found nothing worthy of death in Jesus. (Luke 23: 15.) Jesus courted the favor of none of his judges.]

13. BARABBAS PREFERRED AND JESUS REJECTED
15: 6-15
(Matt. 27: 15-26; Luke 23: 13-25; John 18: 39, 40)

6 Now at [1]the feast he used to release unto them one prisoner, whom they asked of him. 7 And there was one called Barabbas, *lying* bound with them that had made insurrection, men who in the insurrection had committed murder. 8 And the multitude went up and began to ask him *to do* as he was wont to do unto them. 9 And Pilate answered them, saying, Will ye that I

[1]Or, *a feast*

---

6 **Now at the feast he used to release unto them one prisoner, whom they asked of him.**—This was a humane and beneficent usage, but it was terribly abused on this occasion when wicked men made it tributary to their diabolical hatred, killing the Prince of life and desiring a murderer to be granted unto them. (Acts 3: 14.) [The Passover feast was the most sacred of the Jewish feasts. Pilate was the Roman ruler of the Jews. They were restive under the rule of foreigners, and he was disposed to show personal kindness and favor to them as a people, that he might as far as possible reconcile them to their condition. On their great feast day he was accustomed to let them select one of their prisoners, whom he would release to them.]

7 **And there was one called Barabbas, lying bound with them**—He, together with other notorious characters, was bound in some way, in addition to being in prison. This, of course, was to keep them from escaping prison.

that had made insurrection, men who in the insurrection had committed murder.—He was "a robber" (John 8: 40), and had excited insurrection in the city (John 8: 40), and as we here learn a murderer. So he was a robber, an insurgent, and a murderer. These facts account for Matthew's statement that he was a "notable prisoner."

8 **And the multitude went up and began to ask him to do as he was wont to do unto them.**—This suggested to Pilate another way out of the difficulty, for he plainly saw the motives of the Sanhedrin, and that Jesus had committed no crime. When, therefore, they came marching back with Jesus, he addressed them with the people, declaring that he found no political fault in Jesus worthy of death, and neither had Herod.

9 **And Pilate answered them, saying, Will ye that I release**

release unto you the King of the Jews?   10 For he perceived that for envy
the chief priests had delivered him up.   11 But the chief priests stirred up

---

unto you the King of the Jews?—This was to the people.
[Pilate seized the request to again press on them that they
should agree to the release of Jesus. He thought this was an
opportunity to be just to Jesus.]

10 **For he perceived that for envy the chief priests had delivered him up.**—[Yes, the chief priests had through envy
made him a prisoner, but as the release of one prisoner was to
be left to the voice of the people and not alone to the priests,
it was hoped on the part of Pilate that the people who had
been so greatly benefited by Christ and whose safety had been
imperiled by Barabbas would certainly give Jesus the advantage, but these people like many others could be influenced by
designing politicians. It was apparent from the many false
charges made, and from the bitter feeling shown, that there
were no good grounds for his arrest; that he was guilty of no
treason against Caesar, and that he was not a disturber of the
peace of the country. They knew the charges they made were
groundless. They knew he exercised divine power, and that
he was a man of goodness and mercy to the afflicted; but he
condemned them in their course, so that his success would be
the overturning of the order of things of which they were the
head, and would strip them of their power and authority. It
so infuriated them that nothing short of his death would satisfy them. Pilate was disposed to let him go free. His judgment was that way, and he wanted to be just if it did not cost
him too much. "While he was sitting on the judgment-seat,
his wife sent unto him, saying, Have thou nothing to do with
that righteous man; for I have suffered many things this day
in a dream because of him." (Matt. 27: 19.) She knew something of Jesus doubtless, and had learned to respect him.
Then supernatural influences were exerted. She had a dream
that troubled her, and she sent and asked her husband not to
have anything to do with punishing that righteous man.
"And Pilate called together the chief priests and the rulers
and the people, and said unto them, Ye brought unto me this
man as one that perverteth the people and: behold, I, having
examined him before you, found no fault in this man touching

the multitude, that he should rather release Barabbas unto them.   12 And
Pilate again answered and said unto them, What then shall I do unto him
whom ye call the King of the Jews?   13 And they cried out again, Crucify

---

those things whereof ye accuse him : no, nor yet Herod ; for he
sent him back unto us; and behold, nothing worthy of death
hath been done by him.   I will therefore chastise him, and release him."   (Luke 23: 13-16.)   This was the formal, official
decision of the case by Pilate on the charges and the testimony presented by his accusers.   It is a strange and inconsistent sentence: I find no fault in him, yet will chastise him.
Why chastise a man without fault?   It was a proposition to
wrongly inflict degrading punishment on Jesus to please the
Jews.   It was an effort to compromise with sin and wickedness.   It was one step in the path of conscious wrong on the
part of Pilate as judge, and one step taken opens the way for
and necessitates another and another.   This does not mean a
man must not be kind and forbearing with those who do not
fully see the truth, and encourage and lead them kindly in the
right way ; but he must be firm for that truth, and uncompro-
mising in holding to the right.]

11 **But the chief priests stirred up the multitude, that he
should rather release Barabbas unto them.**—As the people
were to choose which one should be released, these malicious
priests in ceaseless efforts plead with them to choose Barabbas instead of Jesus.   [The people seem to have been willing
to listen to Pilate in his proposition.   They were more just
than the leaders.   But the chief priests and scribes stirred
them up, and encouraged and excited them to demand of Pilate that he release Barabbas (the robber) and leave Jesus in
prison, trusting yet to induce Pilate to sign his death warrant.
To compromise with wrong is to betray God—is to serve the
evil one.]   Rather the devil than Christ.   Bad enough to thus
choose, but how frightful the character of him who influences
others to choose thus.

12 **And Pilate again answered and said unto them, What
then shall I do unto him whom ye call the King of the Jews?**
—[Knowing Jesus was innocent, he asked this question.   This
was half yielding to their cries.   He showed it was against his
will, in that he taunted them, "Ye call [him] the King of the
Jews."   But he surrendered his prerogative to decide, gave up

him. 14 And Pilate said unto them, Why, what evil hath he done? But they cried out exceedingly, Crucify him. 15 And Pilate, wishing to content the multitude, released unto them Barabbas, and delivered Jesus, when he had scourged him, to be crucified.

what was his duty, and pandered to what he knew to be unjust demands to follow them.]

13 **And they cried out again, Crucify him.**—They were fully determined to put him to death; to call their attention to Jesus was but an occasion to cry again, "Crucify him." They had by this time influenced the people to join them in their request.

14 **And Pilate said unto them, Why, what evil hath he done?**—This was a hard question. The most effective answer they could give is one reported in John's account: "If thou release this man, thou art not Caesar's friend." These Jews knew exactly how to reach the governor. It was to intimate that he would lose his governorship if he did not condemn Jesus. The hour for argument or reasoning was gone by. They were determined to achieve their deadly purpose by clamor.

But they cried out exceedingly, Crucify him.—When the evil spirit takes possession of a human heart, the tendency is to wax worse and worse. As the matter was again and again referred to them, they grew more vehement and boisterous each time. There is nothing more terrible than the fierce cry of an infuriated mob. Pilate now performed a symbolic action. This was a Jewish custom, which he adopted, the better to impress them that they must take the whole responsibility. He had water brought and washed his hands, saying, "I am innocent of the blood of this righteous man; see ye to it. And all the people answered and said, His blood be on us, and on our children," the awful self-imprecation that has been so terribly filled in the history of the Jewish nation.

15 **And Pilate, wishing to content the multitude,**—It was no love of the people but a desire to have the support of the people to his office that caused Pilate to please them in this instance. What was one poor lowly man by the side of the rage and clamor of a whole populace, which might reach the ears of the Roman authorities?

released unto them Barabbas,—The bloodstained robber, who *had* opposed the Roman government, who *was* an enemy to Caesar. These hypocritical chief priests, who had "no king but Caesar," were demanding the release of Caesar's enemy.

and delivered Jesus,—By delivering Jesus to the Sanhedrin, Pilate sacrificed his lofty and independent position, as a secular judge and representative of Roman law, to the religious fanaticism of the Jewish hierarchy. The state became a tool in the hands of an apostate and bloodthirsty religious institution. How often has this fact been repeated in the history of religious persecution! By this act Pilate condemned himself and gave additional force to his previous testimony to the innocence of Christ, showing that this was dictated neither by fear nor favor, but was the involuntary expression of his remaining sense of justice from the judgment seat.

when he had scourged him, to be crucified.—The scourging was preparatory to the crucifixion, but was not an essential part of it. Washing his hands in water in the presence of the accusers, indicating that he was innocent of Jesus' death, did not exonerate Pilate from blame, but his act and deed had clothed his name with infamy and shame that will endure to eternity. A timeserver, a cowardly spirit that would deliver to death the innocent Lamb of God rather than run the risk of losing his office. His name should in itself be an everlasting warning to office seekers and panderers to public favor who will sacrifice truth and justice for self-aggrandizement. Politicians today are just as ready to please the people by releasing wrong and scourging right as in the days of Jesus. Religious politicians are no better. The Roman scourging was much more severe than the Jewish. The Jews numbered the lashes, the Romans laid them on without number or mercy.

[When a man for the sake of popularity, worldly honor, and ease turns from the truth of God and leaves it to be abused by its enemies, what differs his course and character from that of Pontius Pilate? If his course and character are the same, his destiny must be the same. Often now are the same scenes re-enacted with reference to the spiritual, more sacred body that were enacted with reference to the fleshly body by Judas and Pilate. It is often done unconsciously, because we do not see the elements of character that are condemned in them.]

SECTION SIX

THE DEATH, BURIAL, AND RESURRECTION OF JESUS
15: 16 to 16: 20

14. JESUS MOCKED AND LED AWAY BY THE SOLDIERS
15: 16-21
(Matt. 27: 27-32; Luke 23: 26-32; John 19: 1-3, 16, 17)

16 And the soldiers led him away within the court, which is the [2]Praetorium; and they call together the whole [3]band. 17 And they clothe him with purple, and platting a crown of thorns, they put it on him; 18 and they began to salute him, Hail, King of the Jews! 19 And they smote his head with a

[2]Or, *palace*
[3]Or, *cohort*

16 **And the soldiers led him away within the court,**—The scourging seems to have taken place in the open space in front of the Praetorium, and in sight of the people. It was done on the naked back.

which is the Praetorium;—This was doubtless built, like most large eastern houses, in a quadrangular form around a court. The judgment seat of Pilate had been outside, to satisfy the scruples of the chief priests. Now the soldiers take him inside to have their own amusement at his expense.

and they call together the whole band.—That is, "the cohort," from four to six hundred men, who were the garrison.

17 **And they clothe him with purple,**—The imperial color which some of the emperors had forbidden to be worn by subjects; therefore the mocking emblem of his kingly authority. Matthew says a "scarlet robe."

and platting a crown of thorns, they put it on him;—The Syrian Acacia had thorns as long as a finger. They were the buckthorn and others. Some think that the thorn used was Arabian *mulik.* "It was very suitable for their purpose, as it has many sharp thorns, which inflict painful wounds, its flexible, pliant and round branches might easily be plaited in the form of a crown." It is just so that the hypocrite decks Christ.

18 **and they began to salute him, Hail, King of the Jews!**—Matthew adds that they put "a reed in his right hand." He also says "they kneeled down before him." These things

reed, and spat upon him, and bowing their knees ⁴worshipped him. 20 And when they had mocked him, they took off from him the purple, and put on him his garments. And they lead him out to crucify him.

21 And they ⁵compel one passing by, Simon of Cyrene, coming from the country, the father of Alexander and Rufus, to go *with* them, that he might bear his cross.

⁴See marginal note on ch. 5. 6.
⁵Gr. *impress.*

---

were done to mock Jesus. They saluted him after the manner of paying obeisance to royal persons.

19 **And they smote his head with a reed,**—Driving down upon it the crown of thorns. This reed they probably placed in his hand as a scepter, and then tiring of that, they took it and whipped him over the head with it.

and spat upon him,—Expression of utmost contempt.

and bowing their knees worshipped him.—Thus they mingled mocking and abuse.

20 **And when they had mocked him, they took off from him the purple, and put on him his garments.**—His own garments which had been removed when he was scourged.

and they lead him out to crucify him.—That is, out of the city limits. (Heb. 13: 12.) Jesus goes to death with glory beyond; Pilate rests secure in his office, with shame beyond; the chief priests gloat over success which will destroy their polity; the people follow with exultation, not knowing it is the beginning of sorrows. How different do things appear in the perspective of the future! But Jesus goes onward to the cross. A world needs salvation, which only he can give.

21 **And they compel one passing by, Simon of Cyrene, coming from the country, the father of Alexander and Rufus,**—This familiar mention indicates that all these were persons known to the evangelist. But to undertake to identify them with some certain ones who bore the same name, simply because of that fact, is absurd in view of the endless repetition of names in those days, and even in the New Testament.

to go with them, that he might bear his cross.—[And "they took Jesus therefore: and he went out, bearing the cross for himself, unto the place called The place of a skull." (John 19: 17.) Matthew, Mark, and Luke all state that as "they led him away, they laid hold upon one Simon of Cyrene, coming from the country, and laid on him the cross, to bear it after Jesus." Jesus, exhausted and weakened by the long and sleepless period in which he had been on trial, was unable to bear it; so they pressed this foreigner into the service. Luke says: "And there followed him a great multitude of the people, and of women, who bewailed and lamented him." This is the only indication we have during the progress of the trial that any of the multitude that sang Hosanna on his triumphal entry remained faithful to him during his trial. "Jesus turning unto them said, Daughters of Jerusalem, weep not for me, but weep for yourselves, and for your children. For, behold, the days are coming, in which they shall say, Blessed are the barren, and the wombs that never bare, and the breasts that never gave suck." In the Sanhedrin there were some who had not consented to this condemnation. Joseph of Arimathea and Nicodemus, who first came to Jesus by night, were of this number. (Luke 23: 28, 29.) But their voices were not heard in the cry for his crucifixion.]

15. THE CRUCIFIXION
15: 22-28
(Matt. 27: 33-38; Luke 23: 33, 34, 38; John 19: 17-24)

22 And they bring him unto the place Golgotha, which is, being interpreted, The place of a skull. 23 And they offered him wine mingled with

---

22 **And they bring him unto the place Golgotha, which is, being interpreted, The place of a skull.**—"Golgotha" is Hebrew for skull. "The place of a skull" was the place of execution of criminals. "The place of a skull" has about the same significance as "bone yard," as sometimes a place of execution of criminals is called in a slangy way. "Calvary" means a bare skull, and is applied to the same place. Golgotha is Hebrew; Calvary is Greek for skull. There is nothing in the Bible that justifies it being called "Mount Calvary." They who bring him on are the soldiers, to whom he has been delivered to be crucified. The band is under the command of a centurion.]

23 **And they offered him wine mingled with myrrh:**—[Matthew says "wine to drink mingled with gall." Myrrh was bitter, hence called gall by Matthew. Vinegar was soured wine.

myrrh; but he received it not. 24 And they crucify him, and part his garments among them, casting lots upon them, what each should take. 25 And

This was given to persons about to be executed on the cross to stupefy the senses and deaden pain.] To give it was a custom of the Jews.

but he received it not.—[Matthew says, "When he had tasted it, he would not drink." He tasted, learned what it was, and refused to be stupefied by the potion. This was given before he was nailed to the cross.] He would not do his work stupefied or intoxicated. In the full possession of all his mental faculties he would "tread the winepress." He was determined not to ward off the sufferings that had been appointed for him.

24 And they crucify him,—[The crucifixion consisted in nailing the outstretched hands to the cross and leaving him to die by the suffering and exposure. The victim, with outstretched arms, was nailed to the cross, his feet nailed or tied to the upright post, and a peg was fixed in the post between the legs to support his weight. He lingered in this way until relieved by death. Sometimes he lingered in this torture two or three days. Who can imagine torture greater than this? The body was watched by soldiers until death came, otherwise the friends might take it down and the person be restored to freedom.] Crucifixion was unanimously considered the most horrible form of death.

and part his garments among them,—The garments of which he had just been stripped.

casting lots upon them, what each should take.—[They parted his garments. They divided them into four parts, corresponding to the number of soldiers engaged in his crucifixion. John says: "When they had crucified Jesus, took his garments and made four parts, to every soldier a part; and also the coat: now the coat was without seam, woven from the top throughout. They said therefore one to another, Let us not rend it, but cast lots for it, whose it shall be: that the scripture might be fulfilled, which said, They parted my garments among them, and upon my vesture did they cast lots." (Psalm 22: 18.) The soldiers, knowing nothing of this prophecy, in their course fulfilled it. When they crucified him,

it was the third hour, and they crucified him. 26 And the superscription of his accusation was written over, THE KING OF THE JEWS. 27 And

---

Luke reports that he said: "Father, forgive them; for they know not what they do." This prayer for forgiveness, I take it, was more especially for the soldiers, who ignorantly did what others planned.]

25 And it was the third hour, and they crucified him.—[The third hour, by the usual computation of time, would be nine o'clock a. m. He was betrayed during the early part of the night, Thursday, 14th. He was carried to Annas, then to Caiaphas, and tried. Then when it was day they again assembled and confirmed what had been done during the night. They brought him to Pilate; he tried him, and sent him to Herod, who heard the accusations, and questioned him, and returned him to Pilate. He parleyed with the Jews, finally yielded, signed the death warrant, and again and again pleaded with the Jews for him. He is delivered to the soldiers, carried to Calvary, and is crucified, nailed to the cross. It seems impossible that this could be done by nine o'clock a.m., but John (19: 14) says: "It was the Preparation of the passover: it was about the sixth hour" when he delivered him "unto them to be crucified." (Verse 16.) This places the crucifixion after twelve o'clock. The explanation usually accepted is that the day was divided into four parts of three hours each—the first from six to nine; second from nine to twelve; third from twelve to three; fourth from three to six. Mark called the third division, beginning at twelve noon, the third hour.]

26 And the superscription of his accusation was written over, The King of the Jews.—[Over the head of the criminal was usually a board with a label telling who the criminal was, and the crime for which he was convicted. Mark says Pilate wrote, "The King of the Jews"; Matthew, "This is Jesus the King of the Jews"; Luke, "This is the King of the Jews"; John, "Jesus of Nazareth, the King of the Jews." Three of these could be easily explained by their having been written in terms a little different in the different languages—Hebrew, Greek, and Latin. This would leave the fourth unexplained, so we must conclude the writers presented the sense without

with him they crucify two robbers; one on his right hand, and one on his

being exact as to the words. John (19: 21) says: "The chief priests of the Jews therefore said to Pilate, Write not, The King of the Jews; but, that he said, I am King of the Jews." This inscription and the reply to the request show Pilate was chagrined—that he was petulant toward them. He had trampled on right to please them, and would do no more. But when the great deed was done, the smaller matters were nothing.]

27 **And with him they crucify two robbers;**—Meyer says that this is spoken with reference to another band of soldiers, the others, according to Matthew, having sat down to watch Jesus. The two may have been those companions of Barabbas mentioned in verse 7.

one on his right hand, and one on his left.—They might well be considered as representatives of the two classes who had secured his death, the priests and the scribes. John was standing somewhere near the cross, and how vividly must have come to his mind the request which he and James had once made, to be on his right and left, and the answer that Jesus made. [This was the work of the Romans, not of the Jews. The thieves were likely already condemned and they concluded to crucify all at once. They placed one on his right hand, the other on his left. This was done to heap ignominy on Jesus. The Roman soldiers entered fully into the spirit of the Jews in heaping shame upon him, so they place him between the two thieves, utterly unconscious in so doing that they are fulfilling prophecy concerning him.]

28 **And the scripture was fulfilled, which saith, And he was reckoned with transgressors.**—This verse is omitted in the American Revised Version, but retained in the footnotes. [In that wonderful prophecy of the Savior (Isa. 53: 12) it was foretold, he "was numbered with the transgressors"; and now, under the providence of God, wicked men, who know nothing of God or these scriptures, carry out the predictions in the most striking manner. What they do to degrade him proves him beyond doubt to be the sent of God, and secures to him everlasting honor and glory. God turns ignominy, suffered by his children for his sake, into everlasting honor and glory. If we suffer with him we will reign with him.]

16. REVILINGS BY THE PEOPLE
15: 29-32
(Matt. 27: 39-44; Luke 23: 35-37)

left.[6] 29 And they that passed by railed on him, wagging their heads, and saying, Ha! thou that destroyest the [7]temple, and buildest it in three days, 30

[6]Many ancient authorities insert ver. 28 *And the scripture was fulfilled, which saith, And he was reckoned with transgressors.* See Lk. 22. 37.
[7]Or, *sanctuary*

29 **And they that passed by**—This indicates that the place of crucifixion adjoined some public thoroughfare.

railed on him, wagging their heads,—Called to him in a loud, jeering voice. Indicating by the motion of the head, according to Psalm 22: 7, 8, *a malicious jeering* at the helplessness of one who had made such lofty pretensions.

and saying, Ha! thou that destroyest the temple, and buildest it in three days,—The charge made against him before the Sanhedrin at their first meeting in the night. [They ridiculed him, hooted at him. They fulfilled the prophecy in Psalm 22: 7, 8: "All they that see me laugh me to scorn; they shoot out the lip, they shake the head, saying, Commit thyself unto Jehovah; let him deliver him: let him rescue him, seeing he delighteth in him." God so overruled the wickedness of both the Jews and Gentiles as to fulfill all the prophecies and prophetic types concerning Jesus that had gone forth in the Old Testament. The very things they did to degrade him, and show he was not divine, proved he was a child of prophecy, the Son of God. He had early in his ministry—referring to his body, and foretelling his resurrection from the dead—said, "Destroy this temple, and in three days I will raise it up." (John 2: 19.) They had this one of the chief charges to prove his blasphemy before the Sanhedrin, and now, as he is nailed to the cross, suffering its excruciating torments, they taunt him with the claim. They think his helpless and suffering condition an expressive comment upon the pretentious claim. Yet God is preparing through this course for the wonderful explanation and fulfillment of the prophecy by his resurrection from the dead. His own disciples did not understand it when spoken. "When therefore he was raised from the dead, his disciples remembered that he spake this; and they believed the scripture, and the word which Jesus had said." (John 2:

save thyself, and come down from the cross. 31 In like manner also the chief priests mocking *him* among themselves with the scribes said, He saved others; [8]himself he cannot save. 32 Let the Christ, the King of Israel, now

[8]Or, *can he not save himself?*

22.) They then understood what he meant, and saw its wonderful fulfillment in his resurrection from the dead.]

30 **save thyself, and come down from the cross.**—Matthew adds, "If thou art the Son of God." It was a challenge which, though it came from malignant hearts, Jesus must meet. It was absolutely necessary to the authenticity of his claims that he should show his power to come down from the cross, but he chose his own time to do it. Little did they know that Jesus was in the act of providing their own salvation. He did, however, more than come down from the cross—he came up again from the dead. [This reasoning was, if he could rebuild the temple in three days, he could save himself from the cross. They looked at the outward appearance, and thought his suffering and helpless condition a sad commentary upon his claims to be able to save the world, so they ridiculed him as a Savior. If he could not save himself, how could he save others? Their heartless cruelty was shown in the manner in which they could rejoice and make merry over his sufferings.]

31 **In like manner also the chief priests mocking him among themselves with the scribes**—With the same indications of malicious and derisive joy. It is easy to imagine the scene. These haughty priests and teachers would not mingle with the common people. They had gotten off in a group by themselves, to rejoice over the result of their night and day's work. They would now retain, they thought, their lease of power over the people.

said, He saved others;—The rescuing of Lazarus from death had caused them to mature and hasten their plans for his destruction. They may have heard, also, of Jairus' daughter and the son of a widow of Nain, since Jerusalem was full of Galileans.

himself he cannot save.—Or, as in the margin, "Can he not save himself?" A just question from wicked hearts. But nothing would have angered them more than its affirmative answer. [From the chief priests and scribes—the religious

come down from the cross, that we may see and believe. And they that
were crucified with him reproached him.

---

teachers—a high show of the feelings of humanity ought to
have been expected. They were teachers of the scriptures.
Solomon (Prov. 24: 17, 18) said: "Rejoice not when thine
enemy falleth, and let not thy heart be glad when he is overthrown: lest Jehovah see it, and it displease him, and he turn
away his wrath from him." But they joined in the taunts cast
upon Jesus, and said, "He saved others"—referring doubtless
to his healing their infirmities and sicknesses, and raising
them from the dead—"let him save himself." They cannot
understand but that his first and supreme desire was to be
saved from the suffering he was undergoing. While the flesh
drew back from the torture, his soul sincerely desired to do
his Father's will, and to suffer that men might be saved. So
Jesus could call twelve legions of angels to his deliverance,
but chose to suffer to redeem men. To do his Father's will
was the leading desire of his soul. He did not act as men
would act under similar circumstances.]

32 Let the Christ, the King of Israel,—Savage and exultant
irony, but, if the resurrection be not a fact, most thoroughly
deserved. But, thank God, the resurrection is a fact.

**now come down from the cross, that we may see and be-
lieve.**—Luke uses the general term "the rulers" at this point,
which would include the elders, so we have all his enemies
joining in the chorus of derision. It needs not to say that the
last words were ironical, that they had no thought of accepting him, if they had "seen" what they asked.

And they that were crucified with him reproached him.—
"The robbers also that were crucified with him cast upon him
the same reproach." (Matt. 27: 44.) They reviled him.
Luke tells us what they said: "And one of the malefactors
that were hanged railed on him, saying, Art not thou the
Christ? save thyself and us. But the other answered, and re-
buking him said, Dost thou not even fear God, seeing thou art
in the same condemnation? And we indeed justly; for we receive the due reward of our deeds: but this man hath done
nothing amiss. And he said, Jesus, remember me when thou
comest in thy kingdom. And he said unto him, Verily I say

unto thee, To-day shalt thou be with me in Paradise." (23: 39-43.)

17. THE DARKNESS AND THE END
15: 33-41
(Matt. 27: 45-56; Luke 23: 44-49; John 19: 28-30)

33 And when the sixth hour was come, there was darkness over the whole [9]land until the ninth hour. 34 And at the ninth hour Jesus cried with a loud voice, Eloi, Eloi, lama sabachthani? which is, being interpreted, [10]My God, my God, [11]why hast thou forsaken me? 35 And some of them that

[9]Or, *earth*
[10]Ps. xxii. 1.
[11]Or, *why didst thou forsake me?*

---

33 And when the sixth hour was come, there was darkness over the whole land until the ninth hour.—The sixth Roman hour, the hour of noon. Luke says, "About the sixth hour." Three o'clock in the afternoon. From one prayer hour to the other, not to be specified to the minute; about three hours. The darkness was certainly over all the land of Judea. All the attempts made to explain and identify this darkness with some event in *secular* history are so much wasted time. [At 12 o'clock, at its meridian splendor, the sun was darkened. This was doubtless an expression of horror on the part of God at the enormity of the crime that was committed in crucifying Jesus. He, too, was the light of the world, the Son of righteousness, to give light to the world. This was a significant declaration that the light of the world was put out in the death of Jesus. It began at twelve and continued until the ninth hour, or three o'clock. "Over the whole land" refers to the land of Judea, as such an expression is never applied to the whole world. The light went out in his death to appear in greater splendor and glory by his resurrection.] Out of Golgotha's darkness came the world's light.

34 And at the ninth hour—Matthew says: "Until the ninth hour." Only Matthew and Mark relate the following incident.

Jesus cried with a loud voice, Eloi, Eloi, lama sabachthani? which is, being interpreted, My God, my God, why hast thou forsaken me?—Pronounced by some a mere exclamation of agony; a human sense of abandonment to death. [As the darkness is about to pass away, Jesus utters a loud cry, "Eloi, Eloi, lama sabachthani?" This is Hebrew, and means, "My

stood by, when they heard it, said, Behold, he calleth Elijah. 36 And one ran, and filling a sponge full of vinegar, put it on a reed, and gave him to drink, saying, Let be; let us see whether Elijah cometh to take him down. 37 And Jesus uttered a loud voice, and gave up the ghost. 38 And the veil

---

God, my God, why hast thou forsaken me?" As the weakness of death comes on he feels God has forsaken him, and in distress he makes the cry. It seems to indicate a feeling of this kind. He was forsaken and betrayed by man. This he could bear, as man is weak, frail, and blind. But now he feels the support of God is withdrawn, and he asks, Why, what have I done that thou hast forsaken me? He could bear the treason, the denial, the forsaking of his chosen apostles—they were ignorant, weak, frail—but O, my God, what have I done that thou hast forsaken me?]

35 **And some of them that stood by, when they heard it, said, Behold, he calleth Elijah.**—[Some, not understanding the Hebrew, now greatly fallen into disuse, misled by the similarity of sounds, said, "He calleth Elijah." They imagined he was seeking help from Elijah. It would have been an indication of divine favor if God had sent some one from the spiritland to aid him, they thought.]

36 **And one ran, and filling a sponge full of vinegar, put it on a reed, and gave him to drink, saying, Let be; let us see whether Elijah cometh to take him down.**—[John (19: 28) says: Jesus "saith, I thirst." This was done in kindness to quench a thirst that rages under such suffering. He had refused the vinegar and myrrh in the beginning. He now receives this. Others said, "Let be; let us see whether Elijah cometh to take him down." The miraculous powers that Jesus had shown through life, the wonders of nature that now transpired, seem to have brought them to half expect and apprehend some supernatural display to deliver Jesus and bring ruin to them. Yet it did not lead them to believe in him.]

37 **And Jesus uttered a loud voice, and gave up the ghost.** —[Jesus commended the keeping of his spirit to God, then yielded it up to him. Jesus was dead. He died to save men. The next verse says the veil of the temple, that separated the outer court from the holy of holies, was rent asunder—torn from the top to bottom. Matthew (27: 51-53) adds: "The earth

of the [1]temple was rent in two from the top to the bottom. 39 And when the centurion, who stood by over against him, saw that he [2]so gave up the ghost,

[1]Or, *sanctuary*
[2]Many ancient authorities read *so cried out, and gave up the ghost.*

did quake; and the rocks were rent; and the tombs were opened; and many bodies of the saints that had fallen asleep were raised; and coming forth out of the tombs after his resurrection they entered into the holy city and appeared unto many." John (19: 26, 27) relates one occurrence while he was on the cross that has been passed over: "When Jesus therefore saw his mother, and the disciple standing by whom he loved, he saith unto his mother, Woman, behold, thy son! Then saith he to the disciple, Behold, thy mother! And from that hour the disciple took her unto his own home." This shows the deep and strong love he bore to his mother that could make him forget the sufferings of the cross to provide a home of love and comfort for her in her declining years. Let it be remembered that all these sufferings and indignities were borne by Jesus with the knowledge that he could speak the word and twelve legions of angels would come to his deliverance. He failed to seek the deliverance because his deliverance from death would leave man a helpless and lost sinner without a way of escape from ruin. He bore it all out of love to man. His love for man was so deep and strong that he found more joy in the crown of thorns and the cross with the way open for man's redemption than he found on the throne of God with the way for man's redemption closed.]

38 And the veil of the temple was rent in two from the top to the bottom.—This veil between the holy and most holy places was torn, and exposed to view the most holy place. This was done by supernatural agency.

39 And when the centurion, who stood by over against him, saw that he so gave up the ghost,—Captain of a hundred, commanding the quaternions of soldiers who had crucified Jesus and the robbers. Matthew makes this clearer and includes the other soldiers: "When they saw the earthquake and the things that were done, feared exceedingly." When they saw that he died so speedily, and amid such surroundings of sublimity.

he said, Truly this man was ⁸the Son of God. 40 And there were also
women beholding from afar : among whom *were* both Mary Magdalene, and
Mary the mother of ⁴James the less and of Joses, and Salome; 41 who, when

³Or, *a son of God*
⁴Or, *Jacob*
⁵Gr. *little.*

he said, Truly this man was the Son of God.—The centurion beholding the wonderful occurrences, the sudden darkness and light, the earthquakes, the rending of the rocks and
tombs was impressed with the truth of Jesus' claims to be the
Son of God.

40 And there were also women beholding from afar;—Matthew says: "Many women were there beholding from afar,
who had followed Jesus from Galilee, ministering unto him."
(27 : 55.) They witnessed the scene from some place as near
as they could approach. In their devotion these women
watched him to the last, and two of them (verse 47) continued
after he died and saw where they buried him.

among whom were both Mary Magdalene,—Mary of Mag-
dala. She had a real cause, peculiar to that of others, of attachment to Jesus, having been relieved by him of a most
dreadful calamity, and restored to her right mind, after being
possessed by seven devils. (Mark 16 : 9.)

and Mary the mother of James the less and of Joses,—
Probably the wife of Cleopas, or Alpheus. (John 19 : 25.)
She witnessed with Mary Magdalene, the burial of Jesus.
(Verse 47.) "James the less," literally, *the little,* but used in
a comparative sense, meaning *the younger,* to distinguish him
from James the son of Zebedee.

and Salome;—"The mother of the sons of Zebedee," mentioned by Matt. 27 : 56. She is also regarded by some as "his
mother's sister" of John 19; 25. Mary, the mother of Jesus,
is not mentioned, as she had probably gone away with John,
overwhelmed with sorrow (Luke 2 : 35), soon after she was
committed to his care. (John 19 : 25-27.)

**41 who, when he was in Galilee, followed him, and minis-
tered unto him;**—To his wants from their own substance.
(Luke 8 : 3.) While multitudes of men joined in the cry, Crucify him, and forsook him in his trying moments, it does not
appear that any of his female followers were thus unfaithful.

he was in Galilee, followed him, and ministered unto him; and many other women that came up with him unto Jerusalem.

In the midst of all his trials, and all the contempt poured upon him, they adhered to the Savior.

and many other women that came up with him unto Jerusalem.—Their names are not given. They also witnessed the scene.

18. THE BURIAL OF JESUS
15: 42-47
(Matt. 27: 57-66; Luke 23: 50-56; John 19: 31-42)

42 And when even was now come, because it was the Preparation, that is, the day before the sabbath, 43 there came Joseph of Arimathaea, a councillor of honorable estate, who also himself was looking for the kingdom of

42 And when even was now come,—The time after three o'clock in the afternoon.

because it was the Preparation, that is, the day before the sabbath,—The following day was to be a day of peculiar solemnity with the Jews, called "the great day of the feast." More than ordinary preparation was therefore made for the Sabbath on the day before. Hence the day was known as a day of preparation. This preparation consisted in food, etc., to be used on the Sabbath. It had become a preparation day by custom, and not by force of law; for there is nothing in the law on the subject. The fact that it was the preparation is given by Mark as the reason why Joseph went to Pilate and asked for the body; John states it as the reason why "the Jews" besought Pilate to have the legs of the crucified broken and their bodies taken away. (John 19: 31.) The same cause operated on both the friends and the foes of Jesus, each party having, in other particulars, a different object in view. It was not the preparation for the Passover, which had already been celebrated the evening before, but for the Sabbath of the Passover week, which was a "high day." (John 19: 31.) Mark explains it thus by adding, "That is, the day before the sabbath."

43 There came Joseph of Arimathaea, a councillor of honorable estate,—It is thought by some that Arimathaea, the home of Joseph, was the ancient Ramah, the birthplace and home of the prophet Samuel, about five miles north of Jerusalem. He

God; and he boldly went in unto Pilate, and asked for the body of Jesus. 44

was a distinguished man who probably held a high office among the Jews, as one of their great council or a Jewish senator. The word "honorable" here is not a mere title of office, but is given in reference to his personal character, as being a man of integrity, and blameless life. Matthew says of Joseph personally no more than that he was a rich man and a disciple of Jesus. Mark adds that he was an honorable councilor—that is, a member of the Sanhedrin; Luke, that he was "a good and righteous man" who "had not consented to their counsel and deed"; and John, that though a disciple of Jesus he was secretly so for fear of the Jews.

who also himself was looking for the kingdom of God;—He was waiting and expecting the kingdom of God to come. It had not come—established at this time, for surely Joseph would have known it. Then to find the time the kingdom of God did come, one must come on this side of the cross.

and he boldly went in unto Pilate,—God used this rich distinguished and secret disciple for a special and most important purpose. The outspoken male disciples of Jesus had fled, and if they had not, they had no influence with Pilate.

and asked for the body of Jesus.—Jesus was poor and left no finances for his burial expenses. Joseph was "a rich man" (Matt. 27: 57) and though he had not heretofore the courage to express his friendship and discipleship, he now steps forward with his finances desiring to bury Jesus at his own expense. Men who are ordinarily timid sometimes exhibit great boldness in a trying crisis. The boldness of Joseph in identifying himself at this crisis as a friend of Jesus is the more apparent when we contrast his actions with those of the other male disciples, not one of whom seems, so far as the record shows, to have taken any steps for the proper care and burial of the body of Jesus. It required much moral as well as physical courage to act as his friend when his cause appeared hopeless and when most all men seemed to be his enemies. If there had been no special appeal to Pilate in behalf of Jesus, his body would have been buried that night in the common grave with the two thieves: for it was a law of the Jews that

And Pilate marvelled if he were already dead: and calling unto him the centurion, he asked him whether he [6]had been any while dead. 45 And when he learned it of the centurion, he granted the corpse to Joseph. 46 And he bought a linen cloth, and taking him down, wound him in the linen cloth, and laid him in a tomb which had been hewn out of a rock; and he rolled a stone

[6]Many ancient authorities read *were already dead.*

the body of an executed man should not remain on the cross on the Sabbath.

44 And Pilate marvelled if he were already dead: and calling unto him the centurion, he asked him whether he had been any while dead.—Wondered if he was so soon dead. It was not common for persons crucified to expire under two or three days, sometimes not until the sixth or seventh. Joseph had asked Pilate for the body, which implied that he was dead. That he was had been ascertained by the soldiers. (John 19: 33.) Joseph had learned this but it seems Pilate had not. So before granting the request of Joseph, he called the centurion unto him to ascertain whether he was dead. He proceeded cautiously.

45 And when he learned it of the centurion, he granted the corpse to Joseph.—Being informed by the centurion of the fact that Jesus was really dead, Pilate gave the body, freely, as a present to Joseph, without demanding money for it.

46 And he bought a linen cloth,—A winding sheet in which the body was wrapped.

and taking him down,—The body from the cross. Jesus' enemies nailed him to the cross, but Joseph, his friend, took his body down.

wound him in the linen cloth,—The cloth he had just purchased for this purpose. John (19: 39) states that Nicodemus now joined Joseph, bringing a mixture of myrrh and aloes, about a hundred pounds weight. The cloth was wrapped about the body in such a way as to enclose the spices next to the body.

and laid him in a tomb which had been hewn out of a rock;—Matthew and John tell us it was a new tomb. It was God's wisdom that the body of Jesus be buried in a tomb where no one had before been buried. It would also prevent a false statement, after his resurrection, that some one else had been

against the door of the tomb. 47 And Mary Magdalene and Mary the
mother of Joses beheld where he was laid.

---

raised. Matthew tells us that it was Joseph's tomb. John
(19: 41) locates the tomb in a garden, and in the place where
Jesus was crucified. The tomb of Joseph was doubtless a
family vault. Thus was fulfilled the prophecy of Isaiah (53:
9): "And they made his grave with the wicked, and with a
rich man in his death; although he had done no violence, neither was any deceit in his mouth."

and he rolled a stone against the door of the tomb.—It was
a large stone and so heavy that the women, on going to the
tomb after the Sabbath had passed, were perplexed to know
how to move it. (16: 1-4.)

**47 And Mary Magdalene and Mary the mother of Joses be-
held where he was laid.**—[Jesus was nailed to the cross at
twelve noon, and died at three o'clock Friday afternoon.
(This is the generally accepted time; others dissent from the
chronology, making all the events of the week a day earlier
than we have given; but we know of no good ground to dissent, and give the commonly accepted count.) Saturday was
the Sabbath. It was a desecration of the Sabbath for dead
bodies to remain on the cross during the day. So the Jews,
anxious to get them down that day, besought Pilate that their
legs might be broken to hasten death, that they might be buried.

Touching the question, "On what day was Jesus crucified?"
I do not have the least ambition to write on that subject. I
do not think that salvation of any soul depends upon the decision of the question. The scholarship of the world for nearly
two thousand years decided that Jesus was crucified on Friday. I think they decided rightly. The Bible says seventeen
times that he was raised on "the third day." I never could
count so as to make Sunday the third day from Thursday,
counting both days, as we must. The scriptures say that he
was buried three days or raised within three days five times.
I had as soon contradict five statements of the Bible as seventeen. But when I examine the Bible and its habit of speech, I
find that "after eight days" means on the eighth day; "after
three days," on the third day. So when I adopt this method

of interpretation I contradict none of the Bible statements save it say "three days and three nights." But a part of a day sometimes passes for a day and night in their count. So I do not think my writing or my brethren's will have any weight in settling a question that has been settled for nearly two thousand years. Let us study something practical. How can we convert a sinner?]

19. THE VISIT OF THE WOMEN TO THE SEPULCHER
16: 1-8
(Matt. 28: 1-8; Luke 24: 1-11; John 20: 1, 2)

1 And when the sabbath was past, Mary Magdalene, and Mary the *mother* of 'James, and Salome, bought spices, that they might come and anoint him. 2 And very early on the first day of the week, they come to the tomb when the sun was risen. 3 And they were saying among themselves,

---

1 And when the sabbath was past, Mary Magdalene, and Mary the mother of James, and Salome, bought spices,—Mark specifies the time of purchase as after the Sabbath. Luke mentions a purchase of spices in these terms: "They returned, and prepared spices and ointments. And on the sabbath they rested according to the commandment." Some think they have found here a discrepancy. We do not. Luke does not specify the time; he is only careful to let us know that they did not break the Sabbath. Mark specifies the time.

that they might come and anoint him.—A hasty but lavish embalming of our Lord's sacred body had been begun on Friday evening by Joseph and Nicodemus, and now these women come to the tomb early Sunday morning prepared to complete the embalming.

2 And very early on the first day of the week, they come to the tomb when the sun was risen.—Matthew says: "As it began to dawn toward the first day of the week." Luke says: "At early dawn." John says: "Early, while it was yet dark." Lange translates Mark, "When the sun had begun to rise." This harmonizes all the passages, as the beginning of sunrising marks dawn and precedes his appearance. [The Sabbath, as they kept it, ended with the setting of the sun, or six o'clock, Saturday afternoon. The stone at the sepulcher was heavy, and in the night they did not attempt to go, but waited impatiently for the coming of the dawn; and while it was yet dark they started to the sepulcher, but reached it as

Who shall roll us away the stone from the door of the tomb?   4 and looking
up, they see that the stone is rolled back: for it was exceeding great.   5 And
entering into the tomb, they saw a young man sitting on the right side, ar-

the sun was rising. Luke (24: 10) says it was "Mary Magdalene, and Joanna, and Mary the mother of James: and the
other women with them."]

3 **And they were saying among themselves, Who shall roll
us away the stone from the door of the tomb?**—[These women
had followed the body, and had seen Joseph place it in his
own new tomb, which he had hewn out of a rock, and roll a
large stone to the door of the sepulcher. The stone was too
large for them to remove, and as they went to the tomb they
were troubled as to how they would remove the stone from
the sepulcher that they might get at the body of Jesus to
anoint it. They had not heard of the sealing of the stone and
the guard, else they would have been troubled much more.]
We often trouble ourselves in advance over difficulties which
God is already removing.

4 **and looking up, they see that the stone is rolled back: for
it was exceeding great.**—This is a reflective mention, indicating that the evangelist's mind was busy with the thought of
the relief and joy the women experienced in seeing that the
difficulty, so great, was removed. From John (20: 1, 2), we
learn that Mary Magdalene, as soon as she saw in the distance
that the stone was not in its place, ran to Peter and John with
her understanding of the matter, namely, that his enemies had
removed the body. The angel had sat on the stone immediately after rolling it away, and paralyzed the guards by the
splendor of his appearance, but now had gone within the
tomb. Matthew does not state that the women saw him sitting on the stone, but only at some point he spoke to them.
The other two women kept on toward the tomb. When they
came near enough to see, they found the stone already rolled
away. "There was a great earthquake; for an angel of the
Lord descended from heaven, and came and rolled away the
stone, and sat upon it. His appearance was as lightning, and
his raiment white as snow: and for fear of him the watchers
did quake, and became as dead men." (Matt. 28: 2-4.)

5 **And entering into the tomb,**—The tomb was doubtless a

rayed in a white robe; and they were amazed. 6 And he saith unto them, Be not amazed: ye seek Jesus, the Nazarene, who hath been crucified: he is risen; he is not here: behold, the place where they laid him! 7 But go, tell his disciples and Peter, He goeth before you into Galilee: there shall ye see him, as he said unto you. 8 And they went out, and fled from the tomb; for

---

large one. The stone had been removed, and they thought they would now have no difficulty in reaching the body.

they saw a young man sitting on the right side, arrayed in a white robe;—The same angel; though the overwhelming splendor of his appearance was probably abated for their sakes.

and they were amazed.—They had come to find a dead body, not a living being, man or angel.

6 **And he saith unto them, Be not amazed:**—Reassuring words, necessary at the opening of such a train of wonders as they were soon to witness. Matthew says: "Fear not ye."

ye seek Jesus, the Nazarene, who hath been crucified:— "Fear not ye; for I know that ye seek Jesus, who hath been crucified." (Matt. 28: 5.)

he is risen; he is not here:—These are the most amazing words that had fallen on human ears up to that time. Matthew adds the words, "as he said."

behold, the place where they laid him!—Matthew says: "Come, see the place where the Lord lay." The angel saw their fright, spoke gently and reassuringly, and "said unto them, Why seek ye the living among the dead? He is not here, but is risen: remember how he spake unto you when he was yet in Galilee, saying that the Son of man must be delivered up into the hands of sinful men, and be crucified, and the third day rise again. And they remembered his words" (Luke 24: 5-8), reminding them that he had told them that he would rise from the dead, which none of his disciples had as yet understood or were expecting.

7 **But go, tell his disciples and Peter,**—There is a wondrous touch of sympathy and forgiving love in this special mention of the penitent Peter, still smarting, doubtless, under the remembrance of his denial. To the women was first announced the news of Jesus' resurrection; they, like the rest of his disciples, were not expecting such an event.

trembling and astonishment had come upon them: and they said nothing to any one; for they were afraid.

He goeth before you into Galilee:—Where the great manifestation of himself to above five hundred brethren (1 Cor. 15: 6) probably took place.

there shall ye see him, as he said unto you.—Mark now brings in the significant reminder that they ought to have been prepared for all this by Christ's own prophetic statements. This suggests the deep interest that angels have ever taken in the progress of man's redemption.

8 And they went out, and fled from the tomb; for trembling and astonishment had come upon them:—The news of the resurrection was entirely unexpected to these women. Their plans were wholly frustrated and they were filled with fear and wonder that is hard to describe as they sped quickly away on an entirely new errand.

and they said nothing to any one;—On their way to "his disciples and Peter," as the angel directed. We are not to conclude, because the angel said, "Tell his disciples and Peter," that Peter was not still a disciple.

for they were afraid.—[They feared to disclose what they had heard to any but the persons to whom they had been directed by the angel. No wonder they quickly fled to their companions to tell the new and wonderful truths! They fled from the sepulcher, where the truths were revealed, that in their newness, their greatness, their far-reaching consequences, they were unable to grasp, and that oppressed their astonished and bewildered minds. They trembled with excitement and amazement, and dared not utter a word to any one, "for they were afraid."]

20. JESUS APPEARS TO MARY MAGDALENE
16: 19-11
(John 20: 1-18)

9 [7]Now when he was risen early on the first day of the week, he ap-

---

[7]The two oldest Greek manuscripts, and some other authorities, omit from ver. 9 to the end. Some other authorities have a different ending to the Gospel.

---

9 Now when he was risen early—Mark now records the fact of the resurrection. Heretofore, he had only recorded the message of the angel. "He is risen." (Verse 6.)

peared first to Mary Magdalene, from whom he had cast out seven demons.
10 She went and told them that had been with him, as they mourned and
wept. 11 And they, when they heard that he was alive, and had been seen of
her, disbelieved.

on the first day of the week,—The mention of the day a second time (verse 2) is significant, as if to emphasize that which ever after was to be the day of days. It is of the first importance that Christians maintain the sacredness of the day by assembling themselves around the Lord's table in commemoration of our Lord's suffering and death in eating the bread and drinking the cup. (1 Cor. 11 : 26.)

he appeared first to Mary Magdalene, from whom he had cast out seven demons.—Luke (8: 2) mentions that "seven demons had gone out" of her and Mark repeats it here to show the power of love and penitence. "Mary was standing without at the tomb weeping: so, as she wept, she stooped and looked into the tomb; and she beholdeth two angels in white sitting, one at the head, and one at the feet, where the body of Jesus had lain. And they say unto her, Woman, why weepest thou? She saith unto them, Because they have taken away my Lord, and I know not where they have laid him. When she had thus said, she turned herself back, and beholdeth Jesus standing, and knew not that it was Jesus. Jesus saith unto her, Woman, why weepest thou? whom seekest thou? She, supposing him to be the gardener, saith unto him, Sir, if thou hast borne him hence, tell me where thou hast laid him, and I will take him away. Jesus saith unto her, Mary. She turneth herself, and saith unto him in Hebrew, Rabboni; which is to say, Teacher. Jesus saith to her, Touch me not; for I am not yet ascended unto the Father: but go unto my brethren, and say to them, I ascend unto my Father and your Father, and my God and your God." (John 20: 11-17.) She who had been filled with Satan becomes the honored messenger of Christ.

10 She went and told them that had been with him,—"Mary Magdalene cometh and telleth the disciples, I have seen the Lord; and that he had said these things unto her." (John 20: 18.)

as they mourned and wept.—They, Peter and John, had seen the empty tomb; that was all they personally knew.

11 **And they,**—The disciples to whom Mary went after she had seen Jesus and to whom she delivered the message of Jesus: "Go unto my brethren, and say to them, I ascend unto my Father and your Father, and my God and your God." (John 20: 17.)

when they heard that he was alive, and had been seen of her, disbelieved.—That the disciples disbelieved the message of Jesus delivered by Mary reveals how completely they had given away to despair; and notwithstanding the fact that Jesus had foretold his resurrection, they did not expect it.

21. JESUS APPEARS TO TWO IN THE COUNTRY
16: 12, 13
(Luke 24: 13-35)

12 And after these things he was manifested in another form unto two of them, as they walked, on their way into the country. 13 And they went away and told it unto the rest: neither believed they them.

12 **And after these things he was manifested in another form**—Different from what they had before seen him. In some way, we know not how, his appearance was changed.

unto two of them, as they walked, on their way into the country.—The name of one of them was Cleopas. (Luke 24: 18.) They were going, that day, "to a village named Emmaus." This is a brief reference by Mark to an incident told with great minuteness of detail by Luke. (24: 13-35.)

13 **And they went away and told it unto the rest:**—To those disciples who remained in Jerusalem, especially the eleven. "And they rose up that very hour, and returned to Jerusalem, and found the eleven gathered together, and them that were with them." (Luke 24: 33.)

neither believed they them.—Not only did they disbelieve Mary Magdalene, but also these two witnesses.

22. JESUS APPEARS TO THE ELEVEN AND GIVES THE GREAT COMMISSION
16: 14-18
(Matt. 28: 18-20; Luke 24: 36-49; John 20: 19-23)

14 And afterward he was manifested unto the eleven themselves as they

14 **And afterward he was manifested unto the eleven themselves as they sat at meat;**—Mark in his narrative traces the

sat at meat; and he upbraided them with their unbelief and hardness of heart, because they believed not them that had seen him after he was risen. 15 And he said unto them, Go ye into all the world, and preach the [8]gospel

[8]See marginal note on ch. 1. 1.

way by which our Lord brought evidence of his resurrection to the apostles. First by Mary Magdalene. Matthew notices also by the other women. After this by two disciples, possibly of the seventy. Afterward he appeared to the eleven apostles. Judas had hanged himself, leaving only eleven apostles. The women who showed such devotion at the cross and grave are honored with his first appearances. But the apostles who had failed to show such devotion are favored last. Doubtless Jesus, too, intended to show them the importance of believing upon evidence.

and he upbraided them with their unbelief—Chided—probably rebuked them sharply for their lack of faith regarding his resurrection in the face of so much evidence.

and hardness of heart,—That perversity of heart attending unbelief.

because they believed not them that had seen him after he was risen.—Mark has thus far mentioned only such testimony to the resurrection as had been discredited by his disciples, and it is true that to the extent of this testimony "they believed not them that had seen him after he was risen."

15 **And he said unto them, Go ye**—Here Jesus begins giving the Apostolic Commission, or, Great Commission, as it is often called. This was given on the day Jesus ascended to heaven. It is called a commission, and properly so, because it committed to the apostles what they had not before received, the authority to preach the gospel, and to publish the conditions of salvation. Up to this time Jesus had forbidden them even to tell any man that Jesus was the Christ. (Matt. 16: 20; 17: 9.) But now their lips are unsealed with only one limitation, namely, that they are to wait in Jerusalem until they are "clothed with power from on high." (Luke 24: 47-49; Acts 1: 7, 8.) They were to go; not to wait for an invitation.

into all the world,—Not only the land of Israel, but every part of the inhabited earth. A world-wide commission.

and preach—Proclaim—make known—offer pardon and

to the whole creation. 16 He that believeth and is baptized shall be saved;

eternal life to the race on the terms of salvation offered by Christ.

the gospel—The good news. The glad tidings of joy. The assurance that Christ has come, and that sin may be forgiven, and the soul saved. The gospel is the death, burial and resurrection of Christ. By it we are saved. (1 Cor. 16: 1-6.) It is God's power to salvation. (Rom. 1 : 16.)

to the whole creation.—To every creature. That is, to every responsible human being. Christ commands his disciples to offer salvation to all men. If they reject it, it is at their peril. God is not to be blamed if they do not choose to be saved. His mercy is manifest; his love boundless; grace is free to all. The gospel message is limited to man. As man receives the gospel he is raised and elevated by it, and in turn he improves and elevates the lower animal. We find better horses, cattle and stock of all kinds in Christian lands than we do in heathen lands. This is the result of the influence of the gospel on man. As the gospel elevates him, he elevates the lower animal. This commission is backed up by all authority in heaven and on earth. (Matt. 28: 18, 19.)

16 **He that believeth**—That is, he that believeth the gospel. (Verse 15.) It was to be preached in order that it might be believed. He that credits it to be true, and acts accordingly.

and is baptized—The preaching of the gospel imposes duties and responsibilities upon those who hear it. Here it imposes faith and baptism. Water baptism is a command, not a promise. Holy Spirit baptism is a promise, not a command. We obey commands and enjoy promises. Baptism in the commission is an act of obedience performed by the believer, and therefore it is a command. This being true, and since baptism of the Holy Spirit is always a promise and never a command, therefore the baptism of the commission is not Spirit baptism. Water baptism is a burial. "We were buried therefore with him through baptism into death." (Rom. 6: 4). "Having been buried with him in baptism." (Col. 2: 12.)

shall be saved;—From past sins and their consequences. Salvation has both its negative and its positive side, freedom

but he that disbelieveth shall be condemned. 17 And these signs shall ac-

from sin and conformity to Christ. "Shall be saved" is equal to "unto the remission of your sins" in Acts 2: 38, and "wash away thy sins," Acts 22: 16. It is the new birth of John 3: 5: "Except one be born of water and the Spirit, he cannot enter into the kingdom of God." If baptism and the new birth is not one and the same, then one can be saved without the new birth for Jesus said: "He that believeth and is baptized shall be saved."

but he that disbelieveth shall be condemned.—The term "condemned" has no more reference to the eternal state than the term "saved" in the preceding clause. They both have primary reference to the present state, and the former is the exact counterpart of the latter. Condemnation already rests on those who believe not (John 3: 18), but the apostles are here told that it shall especially rest on those who *hear* the gospel and believe it not. It rests on them now, and it must, of course, rest on them forever unless, at some subsequent period of life, they shall become believers. In this way the state of condemnation which now exists will reach forward into eternity, unless its cause be removed, in like manner as the state of salvation enjoyed by the baptized believer will reach into eternity, unless it be forfeited by subsequent apostasy. It has frequently been observed that though Jesus says: "He that believeth and is baptized shall be saved," he does not, in stating the ground of condemnation, mention the failure to be baptized as part of it, but simply says: "He that disbelieveth shall be condemned." From this it is again inferred that baptism is not one of the conditions of pardon. But the conclusion does not follow for the fact that baptism is not mentioned in stating who shall be condemned can never remove it from the place it occupies in stating who shall be saved. Suppose a governor of a state should say to the convicted thieves in the penitentiary, "He that pledges himself to be honest and will restore what he has stolen shall be pardoned, but he that will not make this pledge shall serve out his time in prison," none but a crazy thief could think that because restitution is not mentioned in the latter instance he would be pardoned without making restitution. Equally unreasonable is the conclu-

company them that believe: in my name shall they cast out demons; they shall speak with ¹new tongues; 18 they shall take up serpents, and if they drink any deadly thing, it shall in no wise hurt them; they shall lay hands on the sick, and they shall recover.

¹Some ancient authorities omit *new*.

sion in question. Equally true that there is not a man in the penitentiary who would expect pardon without the restitution required. The leading thought in the commission is to state the ground on which men would be saved, and not that on which they would be condemned. The apostles were to be concerned with saving men, not with condemning them; consequently, Jesus tells them in detail on what ground they are promised salvation; but as condemnation is his own work, not theirs, he speaks of that comprehensively by naming the one sin of unbelief which renders all acceptable obedience impossible, and is the chief cause of all condemnation. He that believeth not is already judged or condemned. (John 3: 18.) One does not have to refuse to be baptized to be condemned —unbelief damns him before his refusal to be baptized. Unbelief will damn the world. A man should come to the commission, then, not to learn how he may be damned, but how he may be saved; and this it teaches him right plainly.

The assertion, "He that disbelieveth shall be condemned," implies that all who hear can believe—that no innate or acquired incredulity can justify unbelief of the gospel. This is asserting the highest possible claim in behalf of the evidences of Christianity, and he who makes the claim is he who will judge the world at the last day. If, in the face of this declaration, any man will venture to the judgment in unbelief, alleging that the evidence is not sufficient for him, he must settle the issue with Jesus himself. A responsible baptized unbeliever is under the same condemnation with the unbeliever. Hence, the unbeliever is condemned baptized or unbaptized. Baptism without faith will profit no one. "Jesus, when he was baptized, went up straightway from the water." (Matt. 3: 16.) "Jesus came from Nazareth of Galilee, and was baptized of John in the Jordan. And straightway coming up out of the water." (Mark 1: 9.) Jesus is our model, and we ought to follow him in all things.

17-18 For a full discussion of these verses see appendix.

23. THE ASCENSION OF CHRIST
16: 19

19 So then the Lord Jesus, after he had spoken unto them, was received

---

19 **So then the Lord Jesus, after he had spoken unto them,**
—The Great Commission and the instructions connected therewith.

was received—By the Father and all the heavenly host.

up into heaven,—This must have been a happy meeting since it had been about thirty-three and a half years since Jesus left heaven. He was blessing his disciples when he parted from them. (Luke 24: 51.) He was borne up from Mount Olivet and a cloud received him out of sight. (Acts 1: 9-12.) He also ascended from Bethany. (Luke 24: 50, 51.) No contradiction here as skeptics claim from the fact that Bethany is situated on the east side of Mount Olivet. He ascended from both Bethany and Mount Olivet. Jesus will return to earth again in like manner as he ascended. (Acts 1: 10, 11.) After his resurrection Jesus associated with his disciples on earth forty days. (Acts 1: 3.)

and sat down at the right hand of God.—It means that Jesus was exalted to honor and power in the heavens. It was esteemed the place of the highest honor to be seated at the right hand of a prince. So, to be seated at the right hand of God means that Jesus is exalted to the highest honor of the universe. (Eph. 1: 20-23.) The language of the verse establishes a close connection in time between the close of the speech Jesus made and his ascension. The same connection is indicated by Luke both in his gospel and in Acts, where, although he quoted none of the words reported by Mark, he reports a conversation quite similar to it which occurred on the same occasion and was immediately followed by the ascension. (Luke 24: 49-51; Acts 1: 4-9.)

24. THE APOSTLES WENT FORTH WITH SIGNS FOLLOWING
16: 20

up into heaven, and sat down at the right hand of God. 20 And they went

---

20 **And they went forth,**—The apostles, whose unbelief is related in the first part of this chapter, and who witnessed the ascension of Jesus (Acts 1: 2-4), now believing and obedient.

forth, and preached everywhere, the Lord working with·them, and confirming the word by the signs that followed. Amen.

and preached—The gospel (verse 15). They are carrying
out the Great Commission.

everywhere,—In the parts of the then inhabited world.
(Rom. 10: 18; Col. 1: 6, 23.) The apostles preached the gospel to the whole world, in harmony with the Great Commission, inside of thirty-three years, and that too, free and independent of all organized missionary societies save the church
of Christ. The church is the only missionary society authorized by the Lord, and it is all ever used by the apostles and
inspired men. This is all that ought to be used today. It was
successful then, and will be now. All human institutions attached to the church or used as aids are only parasites sucking
the life's blood from the church. Every new human institution added is only a new financial burden for the church
to bear. They are expensive besides being unauthorized by
the Lord. Then why not leave them off and use nothing in
the form of an organization except the church as the apostles
did? This is God's wisdom.

The Lord—Risen, ascended and exalted—King of kings,
and Lord of lords.

working with them,—By miracles—by removing of obstacles—by supporting them—by giving the gospel success, and
making it effectual to save men; thus fulfilling his promise,
"Lo, I am with you always, even unto the end of the world."
(Matt. 28: 20.) The Lord cooperated with the apostles. He
brought his divine power into cooperation with their human
agency. (1 Cor. 3: 9; 2 Cor. 6: 1; Eph. 1: 19.) He gave
them unparalleled success.

and confirming the word—Preached by the apostles, showing it to be the word of God—a revelation from heaven.

by the signs that followed.—The signs of verses 17, 18.
These proved the message delivered was from God. They
were signs that God was with them and had sent them forth
to preach. [Here was the fulfillment of the promise of verse
17. These powers were not given to all the believers in the
age of the apostles, nor was the power given to any for gen-

eral use—that is, this power was given not to heal generally, but to confirm the truth. Paul did not heal all the sick. Some of his own friends came near to death that he did not heal. The truth was confirmed, no one exercised this power for his own benefit. Our sanctification friends will not prove their faith by their works in drinking deadly poison or taking up venomous serpents.]

Amen.—Truly, verily. So be it.

APPENDIX
SIGNS FOLLOWING BELIEVERS
16: 17, 18

17-18 **And these signs shall accompany**—The signs or miracles mentioned below will follow as proof that those performing them, and the message delivered by them, are from God.

them that believe:—The apostles and those members of the church during the apostolic days who were endowed with like power.

in my name—By my authority, and using the power that I would in such cases, if bodily present. This was done, and in this they differed essentially from the manner in which Jesus himself wrought miracles. He did it in his own name and by his own power.

WHAT IS A BIBLE SIGN?

It is "a remarkable event, anything out of the ordinary; an event manifesting divine power for some special end; a miracle; a wonder." It is something worked. "Truly the signs of an apostle were wrought among you in all patience, by signs and wonders and mighty works." (2 Cor. 12: 12.) It is "a supernatural operation performed by the power of God." "No one can do these signs that thou doest, except God be with him." (John 3: 2.) Who worked Bible signs? God. "And they went forth, and preached everywhere, the Lord working with them, and confirming the word by the signs that followed." (Mark 16: 20.) The apostles obeyed the command, "Go ye into all the world, and preach the gospel to the whole creation." (Verse 15.) The Lord kept his promise, "Lo, I am with you always, even unto the end of the world." (Matt. 28: 20.) The Lord was not only with them, but worked with them. What did the Lord do? Confirmed the word preached by the apostles. How did he do it? "By the signs that followed." Then the promise, "These signs shall accompany them that believe" (verse 17), was fulfilled. The Lord confirmed the word preached by the apostles by working the signs. The signs were proofs that the apostles were God's messengers, and that the message delivered by them was

God's message. How did God work signs? 1. Through Christ. "Jesus of Nazareth, a man approved of God unto you by mighty works and wonders and signs which God did by him in the midst of you, even as ye yourselves know." (Acts 2: 22.) 2. Through inspired men. "All the multitude kept silence; and they hearkened unto Barnabas and Paul, rehearsing what signs and wonders God had wrought among the Gentiles through them." (Acts 15: 12.) God worked miracles (signs) through Christ and inspired men as his agents or representatives. How did God work through agents? By his spirit. "In the power of signs and wonders, in the power of the Holy Spirit; so that from Jerusalem, and round about even unto Illyricum, I have fully preached the gospel of Christ." (Rom. 15: 19.) God did not leave heaven and come to the earth to work signs, but he sent the Holy Spirit to his earthly representatives and through them worked the signs. Working signs is one thing and signs following is a different thing. Signs must be worked before it is possible for them to follow. Thunder follows lightning. But it is impossible for thunder to follow before the lightning flashes. It is as much impossible for signs to follow before they are worked as it is for thunder to follow before the lightning flashes. When the lightning flashes you may expect the thunder to follow but not before. So when the signs are worked we may expect them to follow. God worked them (verse 30) so we may expect them to follow as he promised (verse 17).

What were the signs to follow? 1. They shall "cast out demons." This was done. (Acts 8: 7; 5: 16.) 2. "They shall speak with new tongues." This was done on the day of Pentecost as well as at other times. (Acts 2: 4-11; 10: 46; 19: 6; 1 Cor. 12: 10.) A new tongue is a language not studied or known. On Pentecost the apostles preached the gospel in thirteen different languages. Languages they had never studied and knew nothing about. It was, of course, the Spirit speaking through them. 3. "They shall take up serpents." Paul did this (Acts 28: 5) and was unhurt. 4. "If they drink any deadly thing it shall in no wise hurt them." We have no record of this being done. Jesus did not say they shall drink it; but "if they drink" it. He knew he had enemies who betrayed and crucified him. He also knew that the apostles would have enemies who would seek their lives and probably would put poison in their food or drink. If they did and the apostles drank it, the promise is, "It shall in no wise hurt them." 5. "They shall lay hands on the sick, and they shall recover." This was done on several occasions. (Acts 3: 6-8; 5: 12-16; 9: 40; 20: 10-12.) Can believers work these miracles today? We have space for discussing one only—the last one. Suppose we could work this one, what would be the result? We would have no need for cemeteries for the reason we would not suffer anyone to die. As they got sick we would heal them by laying our hands on them. There would be no more deaths. We would also overthrow and dethrone one of God's decrees, which is, "It is appointed unto men once to die." (Heb. 9: 27.) Surely God would not, in one breath, make a decree and in the next one make a law by which man could and would overthrow it, by allowing him to heal all taken sick. This is evidence that signs do not follow by us reworking them. The signs are now worked and therefore ready to follow.

When will they follow? "Blessed are the dead who die in the Lord from henceforth: yea, saith the Spirit that they may rest from their labors; for their works follow with them." (Rev. 14: 13.) A man's works follow him not only while living but even after he dies and his body is sleeping in the grave. The inspired men, through whom God worked signs, died in the Lord, and therefore their works will follow them. Working signs was a part of their works hence we may expect the signs worked by them to follow. How long will our works follow? To the judgment. "For we must all be made manifest before the judgment-seat of Christ; that each one may receive the things done in the body, according to what he hath done, whether it be good or bad." (2 Cor. 5: 10.) "And they were judged every man according to their works." (Rev. 20: 13.) The works of both the good and the bad will follow man to the judgment. All will be judged according to their works. How do signs follow? By reworking them? No. At this point is where many make their fatal error. They reach the conclusion that for signs to follow we must work miracles—that signs following is the working of miracles. But as stated above working signs is one thing and signs following is a different thing. Here are two things instead of one. Mary anointed the feet of Jesus. Jesus said: "Wheresoever this gospel shall be preached throughout the whole world, that also which this woman hath done shall be spoken of for a memorial of her." (Mark 14: 9.) The works of Mary are recorded in the gospel and wherever the gospel goes the works óf Mary go. Her body has been in the grave nearly two thousand years, yet her works follow her wherever the gospel goes. This is one way the works of Bible characters follow. The signs worked by Christ and the inspired men are recorded in the New Testament and wherever the New Testament goes the signs of Christ and the inspired men go, for the reason they are in the New Testament. The works of men follow them and their children either as an honor or disgrace. It depends on the character of work done as to the nature of the report that follows. Mother Eve, in the garden of Eden, ate the forbidden fruit and turned the world into a hospital. Her works are recorded in the Old Testament, and wherever it goes the works of mother Eve go for the reason they are in the Bible. Her works have followed her six thousand years and if the world stands for six thousand more years at the end of that period her works will be there. Judas, for about fifteen dollars, betrayed his Lord and the soldiers crucified him. Their evil work is recorded in the New Testament, and wherever the New Testament goes their works go. Abraham, the father of the faithful, in obedience to God, offered Isaac, his son, upon the altar. His works are recorded in the Bible, and where the Bible goes the works of Abraham go, for they are in the Bible. Daniel, in disobedience to the king's command, kneeled and prayed to his God three times a day. His praying is recorded in the Bible, and wherever the Bible goes Daniel's prayer goes. Christ and the inspired men, while on earth, worked signs. These signs are recorded in the New Testament, and wherever the New Testament goes the signs of Christ and the inspired men go. They have followed nearly two thousand years and they will thus continue as long as the world stands.

Why do signs follow? To produce faith. "Many other signs therefore did Jesus in the presence of the disciples, which are not written in this book: but these are written, that ye may believe that Jesus is the Christ, the Son of God; and that believing ye may have life in his name." (John 20: 30, 31.) Spiritual or eternal life in the name of Christ comes through faith that believes he is the Christ, the Son of God, but that faith comes by the written signs worked by Jesus. Let these signs cease to follow and we have nothing to produce this faith, and therefore there is no salvation without these signs. This is why the Lord said signs shall follow. The greatest sign worked by Jesus was when he raised himself from the dead. Our faith and hope of eternal life beyond the grave are grounded on this sign. Do away with or let this sign cease to follow, then the race is without God and hope in the world.

We plant shrubbery and water it until we see it has taken root sufficient to draw its living from the earth, then we wean it. The mother hen shields and protects her chickens under her wings and scratches for them; but after a while weaning time comes and she weans them and the chickens scratch for themselves. The mother shields and protects her baby in her arms and on her knees and feeds it upon the food prepared by the hand of nature. But after a while weaning time comes and she weans it, and the baby goes on into a higher state of living. During the formative period of Christianity, God shielded and protected the baby church by granting to it miraculous power and fed it spiritual food flowing through direct revelations; but when the last revelation was made and it together with all other revelations were recorded in the New Testament, the perfect law of liberty (James 1: 25) was completed, the baby church reached its manhood state (Eph. 4: 13); weaning time came and God weaned it by withdrawing all miraculous power, and the perfect or new man (Eph. 2: 15) went on into a higher and better state of living by feeding himself on the milk of the word (1 Pet. 2: 2) and the strong meat of the gospel (Heb. 5: 12, 14).

Apostles set in the church. "God hath set some in the church, first apostles." (1 Cor. 12: 28.) God put the apostles in the church and he has never taken them out. They are in the church today. True their bodies are dead and in the grave, but they, through their writings, are in the church with as much power and authority as they had while here on earth.

Abraham, in speaking to the rich man in Hades, of his five brethren in this world, said: "They have Moses and the prophets; let them hear them. . . . If they hear not Moses and the prophets, neither will they be persuaded, if one rise from the dead." (Luke 16: 29-31.) At this time, Moses and the prophets were dead and had been hundreds of years, yet the five brethren still had them and in order to escape the place of torment their brother was in, it was necessary, Abraham said, for them to hear them. How did they have Moses and the prophets? They had the teachings—the writings of Moses and the prophets. Though dead in body they were still in authority on earth. To them God had tied the people and from them they could not go and reach heaven. In the same sense we have Christ and the apostles. We have them in authority. We have their teaching—writings. To these God has tied us and from them we cannot depart, either by adding to or diminishing from (Deut. 4: 2; 12: 32; 11: 26-28), and reach heaven. He who would become tired and dissatisfied with God's laws, and institutions ordained of God and sealed by the blood of his Son and recorded by the apostles change and modify them, would not be satisfied in heaven; he would tear up heaven, change and modify it to suit himself. But God has decreed that no such character can go to heaven.

[It means exactly what it says. It says those signs would accompany those that believed. They did. Many who believed did the things here foretold. All believers in the early age did not do these things, but many did enough to convince the honest-hearted that God was the author of it all. It does not say those miraculous gifts should continue always. He plainly intimated that all shall sicken and die. They would not do this if these gifts were universal or perpetual.]

[Miracles were wrought to confirm the words spoken were from God. The object of miracles has always been to confirm revelations made by God. When God has revelations to make, he works miracles. When revelations closed, no miracle has been wrought and will not be unless God has new revelations to make. It does not mean, then, that all who believe will be endowed with this miraculous power. Not all who believed in apostolic days were enabled to work miracles—only those bringing a new message. They were endowed that they might confirm the message they delivered. It means, then, only that those miracles were wrought to prove what was spoken to be from God. Then these miracles were performed to testify the truth of the revelation, and would go wherever the truths revealed went. In this sense they would follow all that believed. This agrees with the facts. Since the last revelation through the inspired men was made, no miraculous power has been possessed by mortal men.]

To claim to have these powers and never show them to the people is to act the hypocrite. In the days of Jesus and the apostles they healed all who came to them seeking help. Multitudes and multitudes were healed of their sicknesses, had demons cast out, the blind received their sight, the deaf heard. (Matt. 14: 35, 36; 9: 35; 19: 2; 15: 30; Luke 7: 21.) These, besides the individual cases and many others, show that Jesus healed all who came to him, and he left none willing to learn the truth in doubt as to his power. He refused to give more signs only when they refused to believe when they saw miracles. Then he referred them to the sign of Jonah (Matt. 12: 39) and to his resurrection from the dead. When a Mormon quotes this language, tell him Jesus only said it after working many miracles, and pointed them forward, then, to the last of all signs, his resurrection from the dead. Ask them to do as Jesus did—show signs and point forward to their resurrection on the third day, as Jesus did. Also ask them to give the one sign—the sign of the prophet Jonah. Then, the apostles left none in doubt. (Acts 2: 43; Acts 5: 12-16; Acts 19: 12; 1 Cor. 13: 8-13.) If any one has spiritual gifts or powers and fails to use them so people can see, he betrays the trust God has intrusted to him and is unworthy to be believed. All who professed gifts or powers used them to heal the afflicted and produce faith. They never left their power in doubt, nor would any one now, if he had spiritual gifts or was able to work miracles. Not a soul since the days of the apostles has been able to work miracles. The claim is a false one. If those who believe since the days of the apostles are able to do these things, there has not been a single believer, since no one has been able to work miracles. This is a point so easily tested that no one need to be deceived unless he is willing to be. Men who claim apostolic power are bound to give apostolic evidence. Rom. 10: 15 is a statement that none could originally preach the gospel unless sent of God. It does not apply to those who repeat what the original preachers taught. The Mormons are as shy of handling serpents or drinking deadly poison as any one else. God proved himself to be the true and living God by foretelling future events hundreds of years before they came to pass, and he demands the same proof from false gods. "Declare ye the former things, what they are, that we may consider them, and know the latter end of them; or show us things to come. Declare the things that are to come hereafter, that we may know that ye are gods." (Isa. 41: 22, 23.) Who but a divine being could have told the birth and death of the Son of God hundreds of years before they came to pass? Similar proofs are what God demands of all who might claim to be God. Jesus, by entering through the door into the fold of the sheep, proved himself to be the true shepherd of the sheep and the Son of God. (John 10: 1, 2.) The door through which Jesus passed is the door of prophecy found in the Old Testament scriptures. He fulfilled to a letter all the prophecies concerning his coming. Thus he proved himself to be the Christ that was to come. Now, if any one claims to be Christ without fulfilling all prophecies concerning the coming of Christ, he is a false Christ and Jesus says: "The same is a thief and a robber." On entering the fold of the sheep, Jesus became the door by which we enter the sheepfold. (John 10: 9.) The apostles proved to the world that they were sent of God and that the message they delivered was God's message by working the *signs* of an apostle. (2 Cor. 12: 12.) Now, since God, Christ and the apostles proved to the world that they were not impostors, ought not our latter day apostles and those claiming wonder-working powers prove they are not impostors by doing the signs of an apostle? They ought to go before *unbelievers* to do these things as the apostles did. (1 Cor. 14: 22.) If they would do this, it would produce faith and confidence in the unbeliever that then they are men sent of God, and would also attract attention to the message preached and cause them to believe it. This is what the apostles of Christ did. Miraculous power was granted to men, not to benefit themselves, but to help others. Inspired men never used the power given them to benefit themselves but always used it in behalf of their fellow men.

INDEX TO SUBJECTS

Women, the, remained loyal to Jesus, 365, 375, 379; many, follow him, 375, 376; the, come to anoint him, 380-383.

Word, choked the, 104; accepted the, 104; confirming the, 391.

Words, heaven and earth shall pass away, but my, shall not pass away, 315.

Work, Jesus could do no mighty, save to heal a few sick people, 141; Christians may do acceptable, in two ways, 221; she hath wrought a good, on me, 321.

Workers, do not hinder independent, 220-222.

Worship, in vain do they, me, 170.